From Orchard to Market

An account of the development
of the
fruit and vegetable trade in the UK

Peter N. Davies and David Hope-Mason

By the same author:

BOOKS

The Trade Makers: Elder Dempster in West Africa (1973)
Editor. Trading in West Africa (1976)
Henry Tyrer: A Liverpool Shipping Agent and his Enterprise (1978)
Sir Alfred Lewis Jones: Shipping Entrepeneur Par Excellence (1978)
The Sutcliffes of Grimsby. The Family and the Firm (1987)
Fyffes and the Banana: Musa Sapientum (1990)
The Japanese Shipping and Shipbuilding Industries (1990)
(with Tomohei Chida)
The Man behind the Bridge: Colonel Toosey and the River Kwai (1991)
Editor. The Diary of John Holt (1993)

REPORT

Study of Trends in the Wholesale Fruit and Vegetable Market
(Produced for the National Federation of Fruit and Potato Trades) 1985

First published 2005 by Lockwood Press Ltd
Market Towers, 1 Nine Elms Lane, London SW8 5NN

© Peter N Davies

ISBN 0-9539851-7-2

All rights reserved. No part of this publication may be reproduced, stored in a retrieval system, or transmitted in any form or by any means, electronic, mechanical, photocopying or otherwise, without prior permission in writing from the publisher.

Printed by Antony Rowe Ltd, Bumpers Farm, Chippenham, Wiltshire SN14 6LH

Contents

Chapter		Page
	Acknowledgements	IV
	List of illustrations	V
	List of tables	VII
	Introduction	X
1	The Historical Background	1
2	The Effect of the Industrial Economy	17
3	Developing International Trade	31
4	Dawn of a New Era	47
5	The Impact of War	69
6	Problems of the "Twenties"	91
7	Depression & Recovery	111
8	The Shadow of War	137
9	Peace & Recovery	159
10	Fruits of Freedom	185
11	Europe - Opportunities & Threats	213
12	Changing Patterns of Supply	223
13	Developing Efficiency in Distribution	239
14	New Challenges Facing the Trade	255
15	A Century of Publishing	275
16	Postscript by David Shapley	285
	Notes	293
	Index	303

Acknowledgements

The authors are grateful to the Worshipful Company of Fruiterers for permission to quote from the History of the Fruiterers Company by Gould.

Most pictures and illustrations are from the *Fruit Trades Journal,* though those on the following pages are from Getty Images: Front cover, 34, 53, 114, 129, 130, 133, 149, 169.

We are grateful to The Fyffes Group for the pictures on pages 57 and 61.

List of Illustrations

Covent Garden Market in the early 19th Century	Front Cover
The Arms of the Worshipful Company of Fruiterers in 1634	7
Three Cranes Wharf in London where Fruiterers first imported their fruit	8
Covent Garden Market in 1750	13
The auction of fruit was popular for imported produce from early days	14
Covent Garden Market in 1812	20
Landing Spanish Oranges and Onions by London Bridge 1874	28
Queen's Dock, Liverpool in the 1890's	34
Advertisement for J.W Draper & Son	39
Letter confirming purchase of the 'Journal' in 1907	48
Covent Garden Market in 1910	53
Advertisement for 'The "Ideal" Market Lorry	55
s.s. Port Morant, carrying the first commercial cargo of bananas from Jamaica	57
Jamaican bananas in Fyffes cellar at Neal Street in Covent Garden in 1905	61
Newly arrived Nova Scotian apples awaiting distribution in 1923	97
Advertisement for "Singer" Delivery van	101
Advertisement for 'Ideal Boxes'	104
The Chamber of Horticulture gets a royal send-off in 1921	105
Poster exhorting the public to Eat More Fruit	107
Fruit Flower & Vegetable Trades Journal stand at Imperial Fruit Show 1922	108
Advertisement for Imperial Fruit Show 1923	109
Campaign Poster extolling support for the National Government in the 1930's	114
Bananas being off-loaded at a regional depot in the 1930's	129
Early example of containerisation improving efficiency in transport around 1930	130
"Richmond Castle" one of the 'Castle' boats engaged in the South African trade	131
Auctioning imported fruits in the Spitalfields Fruit Exchange in 1930	133
The Womens Land Army at work during World War II	149
Victoria street, Liverpool in 1951, a hub of the imported fruit trade	166
Pear harvesting in Kent in the 1950's	169
Flowers from Guernsey by air are unloaded at Eastleigh, Southampton in 1956	178

The first palletized oranges from Spain in 1965	187
Westland Imports' new containers being off-loaded at Whitstable in 1967	188
Israeli exporters were quick to utilize regular charter flights to the UK and Europe	193
Repacking and sorting fruit into retail prepacks in the 1970's	203
An "igloo" refrigerated container specially designed for air transport	248
Channel Tunnel rail freight services were officially launched on June 27, 1994	254
New Covent Garden under construction in the early '70's	257
East Kent Packers's state of the art automated packhouse in 1969	269
Front page of the Centenary issue of the Journal in October 1995	283

List of Tables

Imports of Fruits and Vegetables into Great Britain and Ireland in 1840	27
Growth of UK Food Imports 1850-1896	33
Twelve Largest Counties Containing Orchards in 1901	41
Extent of Orchards in Great Britain 1887 - 1901	41
Areas of Berries & Currants in Great Britain, 1890 to 1901	41
Imports of Fruit & Vegetables into the UK 1896, 1900	50
Sources of Fresh Fruit Imports (1902-1914)	51
Annual Value of Fresh Fruit Imports into the UK 1902-1913	58
Fresh Orange Imports into the UK, £m. 1902-1913	59
Destinations of Oranges Exported from Spain 1895-1913	60
Fresh Apple Imports into the UK, £m. 1902-1913	60
Banana Imports into the UK, £m. 1902-1913	62
Lemon, Lime and Citron Imports into the UK (£ ,000) 1902-1913	64
Fresh Vegetable Imports into the UK, £m. 1902-1913	65
Fresh Flowers Imports into the UK (not liable to duty) 1902-1913	66
Shipping Losses During World War I (gross tonnage)	70
Agricultural Production of Selected Items 1909-1918	71
Annual Imports of Fresh Vegetables into the UK 1914-1918	73
Total Imports of Fresh Fruit into the UK (m.cwt) 1914-1918	74
Summary of Fruit and Vegetable Imports 1918-19	91
Summary of Fruit and Vegetable Imports for 1920 - 1928	95
Total Acreage of Principal Crops in England and Wales 1922, 1928	96
Summary of Fruit and Vegetable Imports: 1928 - 1931	111
Percentage Increase in Prices as Compared with 1911-13	112
The Effect of the Ottawa Agreement on Import Tariffs	116
Proportions of British Trade with Empire and Foreign Countries	116
Annual Imports of Fresh Fruits (1930 - 1939)	117
Trends in UK Food Consumption (lb per head per year) 1909-1960	121
Annual Imports of Fresh Fruit and Nuts 1939-45	145
Annual Imports of Fresh Vegetables 1939-45	147

Increase in Production of Field Crops: 1939 to 1944	148
Output of Fruit and Vegetables in the UK 1939-45	150
Fruit Production in England and Wales 1934-44	150
Agricultural Returns : 1939-1945	151
Origins of Fresh Fruit and Nut Imports (1945 - 1951)	161
Annual Imports of Fresh Fruits and Nuts 1945-1951	161
Annual Imports of Fresh Vegetables 1945-1951	165
Crops Harvested in Great Britain 1938-50	167
Fruit Production of the UK 1945-51	168
Vegetable Production in the UK 1944-50	168
Ministry imported fruits: Prices per cwt 1938, 1948	181
Privately imported fruits: Prices per cwt 1938,1948	181
Changes in the distribution of freight traffic 1952-80	195
Annual Imports of Fresh Fruits and Nuts (1951-1971)	198
Annual Imports of Fresh Vegetables (1951-1971)	200
Workers Employed in Agriculture 1951,1971	202
Fruit Production in the UK 1952-3 to 1970-1	203
Vegetable Production in the UK : 1950-2 to 1970-1	204
UK Food Consumption per head 1944, 1965	206
Consumers' Expenditure at Constant Prices 1951-71	206
Britain's Wholesale Markets in 1952	208
Number of Firms and Persons Engaged in the Fruit Trade in Great Britain (1950)	210
Community Imports from Greece, Spain and Portugal in 1976	219
Percentage Self Sufficiency within the EEC	219
Exports of Spanish Strawberries (tons) 1984-91	220
The falling costs of transport and communications 1920-1990	223
Annual Imports of Fresh and Dried Fruits, 1976 - 1994	224
European Community Shares in UK Fruit Imports	225
EC Imports of Southern Hemisphere Apples 1988-1992	226
European Community Share in UK Vegetable Imports	227

Annual Imports of Fresh, Frozen and Dried Vegetables, 1976-94	228
Home Grown Fruit Marketed in the UK 1971-96	229
Vegetable Output Marketed in the UK 1971-96	230
Supplies of Fruit and Vegetables in the UK 1971-96	231
Non-Edible Horticultural Crops 1971-1996	232
Organic Production In Europe 1991	233
Organic Farming in the UK	234
Average Annual Per Capita Consumption of Fresh Vegetables	234
Household Consumption Trends for Vegetables 1960-86	235
Consumption swing of selected fruits 1969-94	236
Total Volume of UK Fresh Fruit and Vegetable Market 1989-93	236
Total Value of UK Fresh Fruit and Vegetable Market 1989-93	236
Major seabourne reefer commodities	241
Demand for seaborne refrigerated transport	243
Goods Transport in Great Britain 1974-94	252
Types of Company in New Covent Garden	258
Structure of the Catering Market in 1988	258
Share of fresh vegetable sales by type of outlet 1978-90	259
Percentage Share of Produce by Retail Outlet	260
Percentage Share of Produce by Retail Outlet	261
Numbers of Supermarket Stores Operated by the Principal Groups	265
Market Share of Grocers Sales 1986-1991	266
The UK-Ireland Market	267
Total Volume of UK Fresh Fruit & Vegetables 1995	276
Total Value of UK Fresh Fruit & Vegetables 1995	276
Volume and Value of Fresh Fruit Imports 1995	277
Volume and Value of Fresh Vegetable Imports 1995	277
Volume and Value of Fresh Salad Imports 1995	278
Shares by Home-Grown and Imported Produce 1995 by volume	279

Introduction

When this study was originally envisaged it was planned to provide a detailed account of the British fruit trade in the period from 1895 to 1995. These dates had the advantage of marking the centenary of the Fresh Produce Journal (and its predecessors) while it was anticipated that the publications themselves would supply much of the necessary information.

In practice it quickly became obvious that it would not be advisable to confine the text solely to this limited time as the trade was clearly rooted in earlier years. Thus the first three chapters are consequently now devoted to its historical antecedents. It was also rapidly confirmed that the fruit business could not be examined in isolation so the study now includes vegetables and flowers as well as the general agricultural and horticultural background. In turn as the trade could not operate in a vacuum, it was thought necessary to place its activities against the relevant economic, political and social events which over the past hundred years have included two world wars, a massive depression, the growth of state intervention and entry into the European Economic Community.

The resulting account then aims to show how what is best called the fresh produce industry responded to these new developments. Although change has always been a feature of the trade with, for example, potatoes and tomatoes being introduced following the discovery of America its pace accelerated sharply after the development of steam shipping and railways. This reduction in transport costs, together with the growing industrialization of Britain, led to neglect of domestic production in favour of imports. These consisted of many tropical items of which the banana became the most important but also many products were brought in which could have been grown at home. These shipments were to place much pressure on domestic suppliers who found it difficult to compete during a period of free trade for no government protection was forthcoming until Empire Preference was adopted in 1932.

In the post-war era the industry has also had to adjust to many variations to the sources of supply and to the many technological innovations which have been introduced. The most significant of these has been the evolution of the container and the development of cool-chain systems. These have led to many types and sizes of multi-temperature bulk carriers: container ships and roll on/roll off vessels which together with the rising scale of air transport now provide extremely cost-effective links with producers throughout the world. Over the same period carriage by rail has lost some of its former importance. This has been in spite of the additional throughput contributed by the Channel Tunnel for the flexibility of road vehicles, allied to the completion of the motorway network, has provided irresistible competition on many routes.

In addition to adapting to this transport revolution the trade has been obliged to cope with numerous alterations to government and European Union policy and regulations. It has also needed to adjust to the dramatic transformation of the wholesale and retail sectors which followed the emergence of the supermarket chains and the pressure of change from a supply driven business to one led by demand. These enormous challenges have been met with some success by attempts by all involved parties to improve their efficiency. This has been aided to a degree by the consolidation of the various trade organizations and co-operative associations. It has also been assisted by efforts to spread the employment of the best practices - no doubt helped by the formation and debate provided by the Fresh Produce Journal and the activities of the Fruiterers Company.

Over recent decades this complicated series of events has resulted in enormous changes to what was always a diverse and fractured industry and these, as outlined in the Postscript, have continued to the present day. While I have been largely responsible for the text I must acknowledge the vast contribution made by my co-author, David Hope-Mason. His long association with the industry and his unique knowledge of the trade enabled the study to assume a much more practical character than would otherwise have been the case and it is far richer for his input.

It is hoped that this close co-operation has resulted in an accurate and readable account of how a dynamic and sophisticated industry has adapted to change....... the reader should now judge to what extent we have succeeded.

Emeritus Professor Peter N. Davies
University Of Liverpool   October 2005

1
The Historical Background

Once the land that was to become the British Isles was separated from the continent of Europe the existing flora and fauna began to develop its own individual characteristics. The palaeolithic men who were the original inhabitants were then subsumed by two successive invasions of celts and these gradually imposed their own forms of society and language. At first the celts followed a pattern of hunting and shifting agriculture but over time an increasing proportion adopted systems of fixed cultivation and husbandry. Thus by the time of Julius Caesar virtually all of Britain was occupied by tribes which shared a common culture and although this was a period of intermittent warfare those who lived in the southern part of the country had already begun to establish market centres and were using a currency based on gold and iron.

Throughout this early period a limited amount of trade was undertaken with fellow celts in Western Europe. This undoubtedly expanded to some extent after the Roman occupation of Gaul but substantial growth was not to take place until after the conquest initiated by the Emperor Claudius in AD 43. Thereafter Britain was increasingly integrated into the economy of the Roman Empire and for the next four centuries its inhabitants were able to benefit from many aspects of its advanced society, organization and stability.

Life in Romano-Britain revolved around a few large towns of which London and York were the most important. However most of the population lived in the country areas and, particularly in the more "romanized parts", were part of large estates or "villas" which were very nearly self-sufficient entities. Surplus from these rural communities would be traded at the nearest market or fair at convenient times. The major items were wheat and wool but, no doubt, small quantities of fruit and vegetables were offered when available. In return commodities which could not be produced locally such as salt, metalwork and millstones would be acquired and luxury goods including silks and wine would be purchased for the ruling elite. However the need for imported wine was steadily reduced by the development of local vineries which followed the Roman introduction of the vine.

The withdrawal of the last of the Roman legions in c 409 left different areas of the country in various degrees of confusion. This was because the Anglo-Saxons who moved in to fill the vacuum involved many diverse and separate groups who were to establish their own individual kingdoms. For several centuries there was intermittent conflict between both the "natives" and the "invaders" and between

From Orchard to Market

separate sections of the latter. This instability eventually led to the creation of a number of small and medium sized states. These continued to jockey for position so that although a modus vivendi was gradually achieved the country was left permanently fragmented.

These new circumstances tended to reduce the role and power of the towns and the majority of the population continued to live in small rural communities. The break-down of national law and order and the consequent difficulties of communication led to even greater degrees of isolation and insularity and thus placed a further premium on self-sufficiency. The rearing of domestic animals including oxen, sheep, cattle, pigs and fowls was supplemented by the stocking of fishponds and the keeping of bees. The principal crops which were cultivated naturally depended upon the specific conditions in each area but would include wheat and rye (for bread making) barley (for beer brewing) flax (for clothing) and hemp (for rope). Each community would also grow vegetables and have an orchard.

Although the Romans had widened the range of varieties which were available these were still commonly limited to beans, cabbages, leeks, lettuce, marrows, onions, peas and pumpkins. A wide range of herbs were cultivated as these were thought to have a special value as medicines but fruit was generally confined to apples, cherries, gooseberries and pears although some figs and grapes were produced in especially favourably circumstances. There was also considerable reliance on items which could be obtained from the "waste" where wild bilberries and blackberries, as well as nuts, could be collected each autumn.

Some milk was available but little appears to have been drunk as most was made into butter and cheese. These items, together with eggs, helped to widen the diet but the need to kill much of the stock each autumn (due to the lack of winter feed) meant that only salted meat was available for long periods of the year. While diet was to a large extent a matter of an individual's status and wealth the continuing prevalence of scurvy indicates a shortage of vitamin 'C' and so suggests that the lack of fresh meat was compounded by a failure to consume sufficient fruit and vegetables.

The Anglo-Saxon control of Britain began to be challenged by the Vikings in the late eighth century and by 871 only the Kingdom of Wessex remained unconquered. A compromise was then agreed which gave the Vikings all the land to the north of Watling Street while what became "Greater Wessex" retained the area to the south of this road which had originally been constructed by the Romans to connect London with Chester. In the course of time the two groups tended to coalesce and a unitary kingdom began to emerge. However its strength was greatly dependent

The Historical Background

upon the character of the particular king in situ and for much of the period until the Norman invasion in 1066 most individuals, both Saxon and Viking, continued to live virtually unchanged lives in small rural communities.

The new settlements introduced by the Vikings into Britain were characterized by their traditions of individual freedom but while the structure of their society differed from that of the Anglo-Saxons their methods of farming and range of animals and crops were little different. The impact of the Normans was to be much more fundamental for within a few years of their invasion nearly four-fifths of the ownership of the soil had passed to new, foreign, incumbents. This then gave a fresh impetus to the feudalism which had existed prior to their arrival so that it was made quite explicit that land was a gift from the crown and that it was held in return for homage and military service. In turn those tenants-in-chief holding land directly from the King could sub-let on similar terms to their followers and they, in their turn, could further sub-let through a series of stages down to quite small holdings which rewarded their most humble retainers. With the imposition of a much more efficient and centralized government this meant in practice that the number of freemen rapidly decreased and that henceforth society consisted of a small privileged elite and their followers and a much larger class of villeins.

While a few large towns, especially London, began to develop under the influence of the Normans and their successors the vast majority of the population continued to live in relatively small villages in the countryside. At first the method of farming followed the open-field system utilized by their predecessors. Over time, however, the division of the land into two parts - one of which lay fallow each year - was replaced by a three field rotation which reduced the area of fallow to only a third of the total. Other even more gradual and significant changes began in the 14th century. These were the consolidation of holdings so that enclosed fields could be created and the rise in the number of free tenants who carved out additional areas from the waste and then paid rent to the local lord of the manor. The onset of the "Black Death" in 1343 accelerated both of these processes by increasing the level of wages: this, in turn, also encouraged the transition from customary duties to cash payments for rent and other obligations. Yet another impact of the higher wages was to promote the expansion of sheep rearing where little labour was required but this movement was also stimulated by the increasing prices which could be obtained for wool.

The Norman conquest undoubtedly had the effect of integrating Britain into the outside world and thus helped to strengthen her trade links particularly with the Continent. Thus the export of cattle and later wool - either in its raw form or as cloth - began to grow on a quite substantial basis. In return a whole range of new

From Orchard to Market

imports, some from fresh sources, began to develop. Given the primitive state of both internal and external transport these items tended to be of the high value - low bulk types and inevitably these were usually aimed at the top end of the market. However it seems certain that at times of glut or scarcity some items of fruit and vegetables would have been imported - possibly even exported - and it is also clear that in this event any cargoes would have been dealt with in the growing London market.

Statistics indicating the growth in the population are very imprecise but it has been estimated that Saxon London reached a peak of approximately 20,000 inhabitants. A letter written by the Archdeacon of London, Peter of Blois, to Pope Innocent III in 1119 suggested that the City contained 40,000 people. It is then thought that the number fluctuated around 50,000 until c 1500, increasing to 62,000 by 1535, then rising steadily but ever more steeply until the first census for 1801 - the first really accurate statistic - gives 1,114,644 for Greater London. [1]

When these figures are set against those for the whole of the country the outstanding importance of London will be clearly seen. The Doomsday Survey, which only covered England, indicates that the population c 1100 was about one and a half million and Poll Tax returns suggest that this had risen to between two and two and a half million by 1377. Registers of births and deaths for England and Wales then estimate five and a half million in 1700 and six and a half million in 1750. A firm figure of 8,892,536 for England and Wales is then provided by the first census in 1801. [2]

As London expanded it became increasingly difficult for its inhabitants to provide for their own food so all kinds of commodities were brought in from outlying districts and the surrounding area. The use of the Thames as a transport highway enabled the bulkier items to be brought from further and further afield - especially in the case of longer-lasting cargoes such as grain. Fruit and vegetables in their respective seasons were amongst the more important daily necessities for the capital and the strength of demand became so great that it resulted in the establishment of what would now be regarded as market gardens. The handling of this produce, together with any imports, was to see the creation of firms of agents or principals who were prepared to offer the necessary services as middlemen. While these merchants would at first handle a wide range of goods a degree of specialization emerged and in 1292 reference is made to Gesin le Fruter, Richard le Frutter and William le Freuter who are all described as "Free Fruiterers".

Voluntary associations which aimed to regulate the professions and trades of the City can be traced back to the merchant guilds which had been established in Anglo-Saxon times. These began to exert a stronger influence after 1066 when

The Historical Background

the centralizing tendencies of Norman government gave London a vital and expanding role in the affairs of the nation. A survey of guilds carried out in 1180 showed that there were then nineteen of them in existence covering the major activities of the day.

At this time the Crown was extremely suspicious of any potential rivals to its power and authority and the growing wealth of the guilds was under constant scrutiny. In these circumstances it is quite feasible to conclude that many trades, including the fruiterers, chose to keep their relationships as informal as possible. Evidence of a major change in the Crown's attitude can first be seen in an ordinance granted to the citizens of London on the 8th of June 1319. This stated:-

> *".......that unless they belonged to some certain recognised craft, they should not be admitted to the freedom (of the City); it was, therefore, imperative at this period that everyone carrying on a trade should join that society or craft which represented the calling with which he was associated."* [3]

The advent of Edward III in 1327 was to witness a further relaxation in the official view and from his reign onwards the guilds were accepted as responsible bodies who, for a suitable fee, could be granted an appropriate charter. In effect this would then give a trade or profession the right to regulate its own affairs in its own interests. By confirming that the guild would be the sole arbitrator of its particular activity and by permitting it to limit its membership as it wished the charter placed the body in a powerful monopolistic position.

The approval of the Crown then encouraged the guilds to take a more prominent role in the organisation of life in the City. The more wealthy bodies adopted the practice of wearing special gowns and hoods for formal occasions and were then more appropriately referred to as "Livery Companies." The twelve most important, headed by the Mercers - the "Great Companies" - then sought to have a say in the governing of London and ultimately won:-

> *".....the right to elect Mayors and Sheriffs, and to choose from their own ranks the members of the Court of Common Council, a deliberative body which worked with the Aldermen in the running of the City"* [4]

Documentary evidence from the Calender of Wills which refers to Henry de Mekelnham as a "fruter" in 1339 and from the will of William de Elsingg which mentions Robert le Fruyter in 1348 clearly indicates that the fruit trade was fully active during this period. Unfortunately there are no records to indicate when what was undoubtedly a long-standing association adopted some form of corporate organisation. In fact the first reference to the "Mistery of Fruiterers" does not occur until 1416 when it was stated:-

> "Friturer (?) Masters of Misteries sworn 12 May, 4, Henry V, John Graunt, Geoffry Whyt, similarly sworn: to rule the mistery well and truely, sparing none for love, nor molesting any from hate, and to present to the Mayor and Aldermen and the Chamberlain any defects they may find."[5]

Details of the rights, privileges, obligations and constrains of the fruiters were provided in the first official grant of Ordinances made in 1463. This made it clear that its remit was to include other commodities as well as fruit and that it covered both domestic and foreign items in the City and its surrounding suburbs. While it was laid down that the business was for the exclusive employment of its members foreigners were to be permitted to trade but only in a restricted way. Thus they were to be confined to certain days of the week and to particular markets ie "Westchep" and "Fryers Meynours" and they were specifically prohibited from hawking. In addition foreigners were to be obliged to offer all of their wares in the open market and were not allowed to keep the best for, later, private trading.

While the Ordinance included regulations governing the size of baskets, numbers of apprentices and the use of abusive language it was the provision for their overall enforcement that was really critical. These provided for the employment of four Fruit Meters whose task - no doubt with the aid of assistants - was to measure all the:-

> "nuts, apples, pears, potatoes, carrots, etc imported into the Port of London, and whose duty it was to prevent the captain of any vessel laden with any of these commodities from breaking bulk without a permit from the Lord Mayor"[6]

The object of establishing the quantities being imported was, of course, to provide a basis for the assessing of revenue. The original charge for cherries, which was probably typical, appears to have been 4s 2d for every hundred pots or baskets (or 1/2d per basket) and this, like similar charges on other commodities, was paid to the Lord Mayor as a contribution towards the expenses of the City. The Fruit Meters were also required to calculate the amount of produce brought into the city's markets at Cheape, Newgate, Leadenhall, Gracious Street and Southworke by individual members of the Fruiterers. This was in order to levy a charge of 2d on every twenty bushels so that this could be used by the Wardens to pay for common expenses including the twenty pounds paid each year for the rent of their hall.

The Historical Background

The Arms of the Worshipful Company of Fruiterers in 1634

Over a long period the work of the Fruit Meters became more onerous with the growth of trade. Consequently their function was widened by the inclusion of Onion Meters and many inspectors subsequently dealt with both commodities and, later, also with garlic and oranges. This change, together with the nature of the work proved to be very controversial, and led to many problems. These appear to have come to a head in 1577 when a deputation from the Fruiterers successfully argued that they should pay a reduced duty on imported cherries. From that date they paid only 3s 4d instead of the 4s 2d still required of foreigners and they were also able to negotiate an end to the Fruit Meters removing unspecified quantities from every cargo. Instead the custom of presenting the Lord Mayor with one pot or basket from a single boat was initiated [7] and similar arrangements then appear to have been made for all other commodities.

The tolls, of course, still had to be paid and it was not until between 1748 and 1753 that these were finally abolished. At that time, following much controversy it was agreed that in lieu of the toll the Company should make an annual present of fruit to the Lord Mayor, a tradition which continues to this day.

An early confirmation that the Fruiterers had the status to be regarded as a separate trade was provided by its inclusion in a "list of crafts" which was written in 1422 and is in the possession of the Brewers' Company. Further lists which were produced to indicate the precedence claimed by the City Companies place the Fruiterers 48th in 1515 and thereafter they are usually to be found in the 45th position. [8] In 1606 the Fruiterers was granted its charter by James I which incorporated the Company under the title of "The Master Wardens and Commonality of the Mystery of Fruiters of London".

From Orchard to Market

This first charter, in effect, gave official sanction to virtually everything that the Fruiterers had been undertaking for at least two hundred years. It provided a written constitution which outlined the procedure for the election of officers and laid down their subsequent duties. It also provided powers to make laws and fine offenders but these were only enabling factors which then permitted the Company to regulate the fruit trade within the City and a radius of three miles which included all the then suburbs. Thus while the crown insisted that any person, either foreign or local, would continue to have the right to supply London with overseas or domestically produced commodities, the terms on which this could be done was to be left entirely to the Fruiterers' Company. The only real constraint on its authority was that the crown reserved to itself the right of metage (measurement) even though the payment of these officials was to remain the responsibility of the Wardens.

During the 16C and early 17C the Fruiterers in London imported much of their fruit and vegetables through Three Cranes Wharf where they had their wharehouses.

While the importance of London and its environments cannot be overstated it was still only a part of the national economy. As late as 1698 the only provincial towns of any real size outside the capital were Bristol and Norwich. Thus three quarters of the population were still living in villages or other small rural communities and at least half of the entire workforce earned its living from some aspect of agriculture.[9]

The Historical Background

As noted earlier the impact of the "Black Death" and the subsequent "Peasants Revolt" in 1381 marked a turning point in agricultural systems although substantial change did not take place until the 15th and 16th Centuries. These gradually ended the practice of providing labour on the Lords' domain in return for a portion of land and, instead, landowners let out part of their estates to farmers. These paid their rent in cash and those Lords who wished to remain as producers then used this money to hire free labour. This emancipation of the villein saw many aspire to become yeoman farmers on the best terms they could secure. Others, with small resources, became day labourers and worked as required for their neighbours. Most still retained some rights in the remaining open fields and in the waste but the steady advance of the enclosure movement eroded these over time. Consequently a growing number began to look for other forms of employment and a small but rising proportion moved to find work in other industries and this frequently meant that younger sons and daughters found it necessary to live in more urban areas.

For the majority who remained on the land many other innovations were to transform their lives over the longer term. The open field system was very inflexible and improvements and changes could only be made if almost everyone agreed. With the evolution of enclosed fields their owners or tenants could act in their own self-interest without the need to consult others. Thus for the first time the growing of winter wheat on a large scale became practical - this had previously been prevented by the wishes of those who wanted to use the land to graze their animals during off-season. Equally it was now possible to change the rotation of crops, install drainage, use fertilizers and breed animals in whatever ways were felt to be necessary and profitable. And although the goal of self-sufficiency was still an important factor for many families the breakdown of isolation and the move to a monetary economy encouraged the growing of at least some proportion of cash crops.

The 16th and 17th centuries saw considerable experimentation in both the methods of cultivation and in the crops themselves. In 1525 the hop was introduced from Flanders and quickly became important in the southern counties for the production of beer. It is likely that many other crops were brought over from Holland. Most of these like carrots, rape and turnips were at first grown only in kitchen gardens but following the Dutch example they were increasingly planted as field crops. Thus the turnip expanded rapidly as it proved particularly valuable in the winter feeding of cattle and sheep and a useful addition to the diet of pigs. Apart from this important contribution which ended the practice of killing much of the livestock in the Autumn, the turnip and another import from Holland, the great clover, were also significant in grain production. The general move towards the growing of more wheat and less rye and oats in England was strengthened by

From Orchard to Market

the interposing of these crops in the rotation from c 1650 which then led to the system known as alternative husbandry which was to produce much higher yields and quality.

The need to supply London with fruit and vegetables had meant that elementary forms of market gardens and orchards had emerged at an early date. The growth in the population of the capital ensured that progressively more sophisticated arrangements became profitable. One such development was pioneered by Richard Harris in the first half of the sixteenth century. He was Fruiterer to Henry VIII and a Liveryman of the Fruiterers Company when he laid out cherry, pear and apple (including the first Pippins) orchards on land near Faversham in Kent. It is interesting to note that these were situated close by Brogdale, the current home of the National Fruit Collection, and that some of Harris' varieties are still grown on this site. However commercial cultivation of this type was not typical outside the conurbation and most fruit was still produced in small quantities in an ad hoc manner for local consumption. While the quality of traditional varieties was steadily improved - especially by the commercial growers - real progress in the widening of the range of fruit and vegetables was to come via the importation of new crops from overseas.

The most significant of the new items was the potato. Its introduction from South America was originally credited to Francis Drake and John Hawkins but the tubers they brought back in 1563 have since been identified as Ipomoea Batatas or the sweet potato. As few of these were to be grown in Britain they could not be said to have made a major contribution to the popular diet. This was only to come about when Solanum Tuberosum arrived in 1585 and came about as a result of an expedition sent to North Carolina by Sir Walter Raleigh. When the party returned they brought a selection of the tubers and these were subsequently grown on Raleigh's estates near Cork. Although it spread quickly throughout Ireland and then Great Britain it took some time for it to be fully accepted. This was because "many small farmers suffered from eating the poisonous berries and leaves of the new plant instead of the tubers". [10] For a while it was then largely thought of as a food for animals. However by the eighteenth century it was well established throughout the country and formed an essential ingredient in the nation's food supply.

Another new import was the tomato. It is thought to have originated in Peru and arrived in Europe somewhere around 1650. At first it was treated purely as an ornamental plant and:-

> "....only in the mid-eighteenth century do we find reports of tomatoes being used in soups, and later at the beginning of the nineteenth century,

The Historical Background

the first tomatoes were grown in Sicily for the markets of Naples and Rome. Serious cultivation in northern Europe goes back only to the beginning of this (present) century". [11]

In spite of these additions vegetable-eating, with the exception of the potato was not popular until the nineteenth century:-

"The few vegetables that were eaten in great quantities were dried beans and peas, onions, garlick, turnips, carrots, parsnips and some kinds of cabbage. There was little demand for leaf vegetables: it was not until the eighteenth century that the first lettuces appeared on the menue". [12]

From the foregoing it will be appreciated that it was not until the 17th and 18th centuries that there had been any real broadening in the range of fruits and vegetables that were produced in Britain. Even then choice remained very restricted for the vast majority of the population. There were, of course, some imports from the Continent. These were primarily of soft fruits, apples and pears, with onions brought in from Flanders as the only vegetable of any significance. These items, however, merely supplemented domestic production and were almost entirely for the London market. In addition a small number of long-distance food trades began to evolve. These were naturally constrained by the speed and efficiency of the available shipping but two separate developments were possible even with the slowest types of transport. One of these concerned dried fruits and as these possessed very good keeping qualities quite substantial quantities of currants, dates and figs could be brought in without too much difficulty. However the cost of carrying these items from Southern Europe and Turkey meant that the market was limited to the better off and as late as 1750 the shipping required for this trade amounted to less than 10,000 tons per year. [13]

The other, parallel, development was that of the citrus trade. The orange appears to have originated in Burma and Southern China and was introduced to Spain and Sicily as a consequence of Arab expansion. The fruit also became known in Europe as a result of the crusades and by the 16th Century it was being cultivated on some scale in Italy. [14] According to one source oranges were available in London from about this time [15] and they were certainly well known by the reign of Charles II (1660-1685) as is demonstrated by his exploits with the orange-seller cum actress named Nell Gwyn. Although by then the fruit was grown in many parts of the Mediterranean the principal source of supply for Britain was probably Spain but smaller shipments from elsewhere were also recorded.

The other important citrus fruit was the lemon. This is thought to have originated in the North-West of India and was later, like the orange, spread by the Arabs

From Orchard to Market

as they occupied many parts of the Mediterranean seaboard. Although it was readily cultivated in numerous places the lemon proved to be most successful in Sicily and the Azores - production in the latter island beginning in 1494 and Britain evolving as its major market. The long shelf-life of the varieties of orange and lemon then available meant that they could easily be carried to Britain and remain in a saleable condition. However, as with dried fruits, the cost of this transport ensured that oranges and lemons were expensive and could only be enjoyed by the man in the street on special occasions.

Throughout the 17th Century the Fruiterer's Company continued to control the fruit and vegetables trade of London. However this was not without some difficulty for in 1632 the City authorities (which included the Livery Companies) refused to extend their jurisdiction to include all the new suburbs which were rapidly expanding in the surrounding area. This meant that many new trades and activities could develop unhindered by City regulations and, in retrospect The Great Refusal is regarded as a watershed which marked the beginning of the decline of the City and its institutions. This period also saw the development of the first major markets in London, Covent Garden being granted its charter in 1670 and Spitalfields in the City following in 1682. These followed the Great Fire which in 1666 devastated the heart of London and which, incidently, destroyed the halls of forty-four Companies including the Fruiterer's rented accommodation at the Parish Clerks' Hall. A serious consequence of the Fire was that many firms and individuals were forced to move into temporary premises outside the City. This meant that it was necessary to tempt these former tenants back with long leases at low rents and although this was successful it meant that the Livery Companies had little income for many years just when they were facing the heavy costs of reconstruction.

As if these problems were not enough the subsequent weakness of the Livery Companies then encouraged the King, Charles II, to cancel all their privileges. Thus the Fruiterers were obliged to surrender the charter granted by James I and although this was replaced by a new one this was felt to be unsatisfactory. However the Fruiterers, like all other Companies, found relief when an act of William and Mary in 1688 revived and restored the original charter. When it is noted that the Fruiterers were able to return to the Parish Clerk's New Hall in Cheapside during 1671 and that they maintained this tenancy until 1751 it might be thought that everything was now back to its previous position. This, however, was not to be the case for changing circumstances were increasingly making its economic role redundant.

> *Covent Garden had by now become a proper market, and the names of stall holders and suppliers began to appear. One early stall holder seems to have*

The Historical Background

been Sarah Sewell who is mentioned by Sir Richard Steele in the Tatler of August 11, 1712. Steele came down the Thames from Richmond "among a fleet of gardeners' boats, bound for the several market-ports of London". He landed "with ten sail of apricot boats at Strand Bridge, after having put in at Nine Elms and taken in melons consigned by Mr Cuffe of that place to Sarah Sewell at their stall in Covent Garden". Produce coming to Covent Garden by way of the river was usually landed at Strand wharves, but much of the fruit coming from Kent and abroad was landed between the Three Cranes Stairs and Queenhythe. At the end of the eighteenth century the whole riverside between these points was given over to the fruit trade. A colony of dealers congregated in the lanes around and a building, which was merely a roof on poles, was used as an auction room.

While most of the heavy produce came by water, packhorses and waggons were extensively employed for road work. The waggons could take as much as twenty times the load of a packhorse, but they were very slow, though they speeded up when the huge four wheeled waggons drawn by six horses began to take over.

The containers in use at this period were mostly made of whicker, willow being freely available.[16]

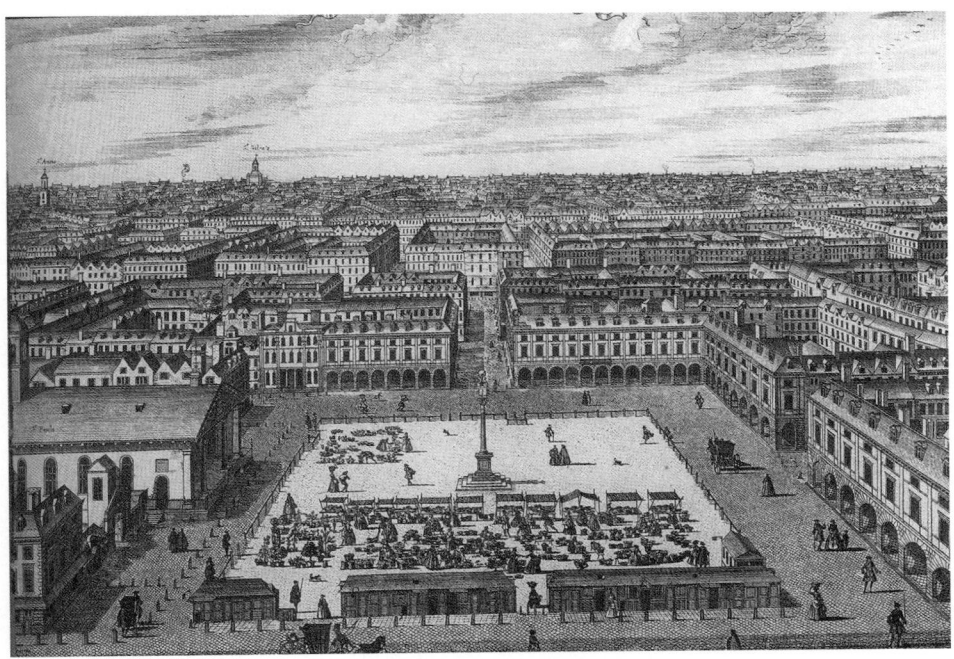

Covent Garden Market in 1750

From Orchard to Market

> **FOR SALE BY THE CANDLE,**
>
> AT
>
> GARRAWAY's Coffee-House, Exchange-Alley, Cornhill,
>
> On *Monday* the 25th of *March*, 1776, at Five o'Clock in the Afternoon,
>
> A choice Parcel of Seville four Oranges, some China, and Lemons, just landed.
>
> CONDITIONS of SALE.
>
> THE highest Bidder, in due Time, to be deemed the Buyer, who is to pay down a Deposit of 25 per Cent. on the Amount of each Lot, and Six-pence per Lot to the Broker to bind the Bargain.
>
> The Lots to be taken away, with all Faults, at the Buyer's Expence, in three Days from the Day of Sale, and the Remainder of the Purchase Money to be paid at the Delivery of the Lots.
>
> If any Lots remain uncleared after the Time limited, the Deposit Money to be forfeited to the present Proprietors, who shall not be liable to be sued for the same either in Law or Equity; the Lots shall be resold, and all Charges made good by the first Purchaser.
>
> Lastly, If any Difference arise at the Sale, the Lot in Dispute shall be put up again.
>
> N. B. To be taken as they rise from the Pile.
>
> | Lot | |
> |---|---|
> | 1 | 5 Chests four Oranges |
> | 2 | 10 ditto |
> | 3 | 5 ditto |
> | 4 | 10 ditto |
> | 5 | 5 ditto |
> | 6 | 10 ditto |
>
> Turn over

The auction of fruit was long regarded as the most efficient means of selling large shipments particularly that originating from overseas.

The Historical Background

By 1700 the strength of the British economy lay in four areas. The production of woollen goods provided a major export which had the advantages of being totally based on domestic resources. The nation had by then already secured a substantial, though undeveloped, overseas empire and had also laid down the foundations for the supremacy at sea which was to be so vital for the future expansion of foreign trade. Lastly, but most significantly, the establishment of the Bank of England in 1694 was already having important consequences. This was because it was able to attract much of the previously hoarded bullion so was able to widen the credit base, re-organise the coinage and begin the process of progressively reducing the rate of interest. This then had the effect of stimulating all forms of industrial and commercial activity - a process which was given further encouragement by the state's gradual adoption of a policy on non-intervention or laissez-faire. Thus the stage was set for the emergence of Britain as the world's first industrial power and the pace at which this occurred then led to these events being referred to as the Industrial Revolution.

The process of industrialisation and the resulting urbanisation was accompanied by an acceleration in the growth of the population. Thus, as noted earlier, London grew from approximately 550,000 in 1700 to over 1,100,000 in 1801. During the same period the population of England and Wales rose from about five and a half million to nearly nine million and while 50% of these were dependent on agriculture in 1700 the number engaged in "Agriculture, Forestry and Fishing" was down to 36% by 1801. This trend continued so that by 1901, when the total population had risen to over thirty two million the proportion reliant on this sector had been reduced to only 9%. At the same time the population living in communities of over 5,000 rose from perhaps 25% in 1800 to 50% in 1850 and to approximately 75% in 1900.[17]

The combination of industrialisation and urbanisation and the reduced emphasis on agriculture then meant that the growing population could not easily be supplied from domestic sources. This, of course, was not a new problem for throughout the 18th Century export and import of wheat and flour had fluctuated violently. However Britain's position as a net exporter of these items in the first half of the century had been reversed by 1770 and thereafter the country was a substantial net importer of what had become its staple food.[18] At first most of these grain products originated in France, the Baltic Region and Russia but later improvements in transport meant that they could increasingly be obtained most cheaply from non-European sources including North America, Argentina and Australia. The combination of industrialization, urbanization and a rapidly growing population meant that the trends evident in the 18th century were to

From Orchard to Market

accelerate in the period after 1800. Thus the 19th century was to witness a steady growth in the demands for imported foodstuffs, including fruit and vegetables but the pace at which this could be satisfied was to depend upon two important factors : the ability of the potential consumer to pay and the development of the appropriate transport networks.

2
The Effect of the Industrial Economy

The transformation of Britain from an essentially agricultural country to what was to become the world's first industrial state had made significant progress by 1800. The previous century had seen pressure for agricultural output to increase in order to cope with the demands of a rapidly rising population and this needed to be achieved at a time when the attractions of industry were drawing away many of the more dynamic members of the rural workforce. Thus a rise in production could only be secured by a growth in productivity and this had been obtained by the more widespread application of scientific principles to farming. The further spread of the enclosure movement not only allowed these new practices to be adopted without too much difficulty but also helped to bring into cultivation much of the previous "waste" ground.

These improvements included changes to the system of rotation so that the turnip could be planted as a field crop and this, transformed the whole livestock sector by providing winter fodder for both cattle and sheep for the first time. In turn this development encouraged selective breeding and the size and quality of many animals was greatly improved. The gradual extension in the employment of iron, horse-drawn ploughs and other implements together with the use of better drainage and fertilizers and aided by better yielding crops all played important roles in promoting a rise in arable output. However when the cost of production was not competitive with foreign imports - as in the case of grain - there was an inevitable move away from the domestic producer.

By 1800, however, the country was still largely dependent upon home-grown food but this was because purely economic factors were being modified by other considerations. The Governments of the day were continuing to follow policies which protected national industries, especially agriculture, while the wars in France also imposed their own restrictions. In addition foreign competition remained inhibited by the limited ability of the ships then available for these could only really cater for cargoes which could survive the rigours of slow ocean voyages. In these circumstances it is not surprising that in 1800 agriculture still employed over a third of the working population and this activity still provided over 33% of national income.[1]

Thus apart from grain, the import of which was greatly influenced by the size of the annual British harvest, only a few items were brought from overseas to supplement the basic diet. The most important of these were tea and sugar and

From Orchard to Market

by the beginning of the 19th Century these were being consumed by virtually every family in England. Coffee and, to a lesser extent, chocolate were becoming increasingly popular but at this time were still restricted to the more affluent sections of the community particularly those who lived in the growing towns and cities.

The provision of vegetables and fruit was also largely dependent upon domestic production. While in the country regions most families would attempt to provide for their needs by growing whatever was possible this was clearly not an option in many of the expanding urban areas. Thus almost every large town was gradually surrounded by a "belt" of gardens which provided the local markets with their produce. As the biggest centre of population London required the heaviest supplies and from early in the 18th Century a quite sophisticated system had been evolved. Thus growers in Lewisham and Blackheath provided the markets with ever larger quantities of asparagus, beans, cabbages, carrots, cauliflowers, celery and radish. These areas also supplied some potatoes but Wanstead and Ilford were more important in this respect. Other districts and regions tended to concentrate upon field-crops which included onions, endive and cos-lettuce while turnips, leeks, parsnips, rape and, later rhubarb were cultivated very widely throughout the country.[2]

While most vegetables for London were grown quite close to their markets and could be transported by horse-drawn wagons this was not so convenient for fruit. This came principally from Kent and consisted mainly of apples and pears, cherries, gooseberries, plums and strawberries. Thus most of these items, plus some vegetables, were brought into London by barges which then returned with cargoes of excrement and "night soil" from the City for use as fertilizer.

This system was also employed for imported cargoes. Vegetables, mainly onions, came almost entirely from the continent while fruit was already being shipped in from a wider range of producers. Soft-fruit was, of course, limited to areas adjacent to the English Channel by the speed of the available vessels and these regions were also the major source of apples - by far the biggest single item. Dried and citrus fruits with their longer shelf-life could be brought from as far afield as the Eastern Mediterranean, Portugal, Sicily, Spain and the Azores. However, as noted earlier, although oranges. lemons and limes were readily available their relatively high cost meant that they would normally only be consumed by the more affluent members of the community. In many cases these imported fruits might well be auctioned on the quay and never get as far as a market.

Until this period the Fruiterers' Company was still attempting to continue to supervise and regulate its traditional business. This had, of course, always

The Effect of the Industrial Economy

been limited to a three mile radius around the City of London and by the second half of the eighteenth century the expansion of London gave enormous scope to those who wished to stay outside its control. Thus it was possible for many local producers to supply their customers on the outskirts without reference to the Company. In addition, as the authority of the "Fruiterers'" was gradually undermined, many of its members were prepared to work with these outsiders and in the spirit of the time the Company was either unable or unwilling to exercise its previous authority. One indication of this changing status came in 1751 when the Fruiterers' gave up the tenancy of their accommodation at the Parish Clerks' Hall and moved to temporary less expensive, premises.[3] Thereafter it would seem that the Fruiterers' Company steadily moved from being a working organization to an institution which maintained its tradional support for the Lord Mayor and Corporation but whose connection with the fruit industry inclined more towards charity and education.

From the foregoing it should be understood that at the beginning of the nineteenth century Britain was still largely dependent upon domestic supplies of food. However the forces of supply and demand were ensuring that many alternatives were being actively considered on an ad hoc basis. Nevertheless in 1800 fruit and vegetables still formed only a small part of the national diet. The existing level of transport technology meant that few commodities except grain, tea and sugar could be imported on a viable basis. Other foreign grown items, including fruit and vegetables, were still rare outside London and only occasionally could they be afforded by the mass of the population. Indeed most family budgets indicate that the only vegetable purchased on a regular basis was the potato and there is not a single reference to fruit at this time.[4]

However it would be foolish to suppose that fruit and vegetables were not eaten at the height of their seasons or when gluts forced their prices down to absurd levels. In addition those with gardens or access to land would grow what they could and those in the rural areas would gather wild berries, fruits and nuts whenever possible.

During the remainder of the nineteenth century the forces which had created this situation were to be gradually modified and fundamentally altered. This was eventually to result in a substantial improvement in the nation's diet but their impact was to vary considerably with the social standing and income of the individual. For the upper and middle classes the changes served merely to add a few more exotic items to their menus and to extend the seasons of others. However the growing numbers of skilled artisans and their managers, foremen and chargehands, plus the increasing members of professional groups were to experience a steadily rising quality and quantity of food of all types as the century

From Orchard to Market

progressed. Unfortunately few of these benefits "trickled-down" to the mass of the population much before c.1850. Until the middle of the century both the urban and rural workforce lived in circumstances of real poverty with a diet of which the basic ingredients remained bread and potatoes. For these people life was a constant struggle to get enough of anything to eat and with their lack of purchasing power could offer no effective market for either imported or domestic fruit and vegetables.

Covent Garden Market in 1812

The conclusion of the wars with Napoleonic France in 1815 ended one artificial constraint on trade. Unfortunately, however, it was followed by a long period of depression which continued until the 1840s. Thus the purchasing power of most workers remained extremely low but this was counteracted, to some extent, by the doubling of the population from approximately nine to eighteen million in the period from 1801 to 1851. It should also be appreciated that while only one fifth of English people lived in urban areas at the start of the century this proportion had risen to half by mid-century and four-fifths by 1900.[5] It can reasonably be assumed that this development made some contribution to enhancing the demand for food as urbanization reduced the opportunities for growing food at home. The process of industrialization also ensured that the proportion of those engaged in the skilled trades and professions gradually increased and this section of the work force was able to make at least some small advances in their standard of living. Overall, therefore, the first half of the nineteenth century did produce a moderate

The Effect of the Industrial Economy

increase in effective demand for food even though large sections of its population continued to live in conditions of real want and deprivation.

These demographic changes provided a great challenge for British agriculture and this was met so successfully that, apart from the gradually rising trend in wheat and flour imports, the nation remained largely self-sufficient in basic foodstuffs until C. 1850. While the producers, aided by low wages, could claim a rise in productivity this was only a partial explanation for the achievement. It is clear that the tariff policies employed by the Government also played a critical role by making imports more expensive. However the advantages of free trade to a country leading the world in industrial technology meant that it was inevitable that the protection of the domestic producer would be steadily phased-out.

Until 1838 the duties on imported fruits were both substantial and varied. Thus a bushel of apples was charged at 4/-d while the rate for pears was 7/6d. These charges were then replaced by a uniform one of "£5 per centum ad valorem". As this amounted to only 3d or 4d per bushel the fruit trade was left virtually unprotected. This aroused considerable controversy and a Select Committee was set up "……to inquire into the state of the Fresh Fruit Trade".[6]

In the evidence given to the Committee it was stated that English apples were generally regarded as superior to those from France and Germany which were the principal foreign suppliers. Increasing demand for better quality fruit had led to a substantial planting programme after 1819 and these trees were now coming into full production at a time when they were to face a serious threat from poorer but cheaper imports. Statistics were then considered which showed that in 1837, when there was an abundant crop at home only 337 bushels were imported in London and these realised an average price of 2/3d. The following season saw a poor British crop of apples so 120,000 bushels were brought in and these achieved an average price of 4/9d. When these facts were taken in account the Report concluded that there was no case for additional protection. It was thought that the extra cost of transport and handling together with the small, remaining, duty would be sufficient to offset overseas competition except when domestic supplies were artificially low due to a very poor harvest. It was further stated that as pears and cherries were of such little importance that no action should be taken on their behalf.

This example surely indicates that the authorities at that time were certainly in favour of reducing or abolishing duties wherever they could. It was increasingly felt that whatever injury might be done to British agriculture would be far outweighed by the benefits which would accrue to British industrial exports. However as Customs and Excise duties made up nearly half of total national revenue it was not until income tax was re-introduced in 1842 that the levels on many imports could be significantly reduced or abolished. Thereafter the position of many local farmers and growers was to be seriously undermined while at the same time the potential for cheap food imports was to be greatly enhanced. However for a variety of reasons which will be considered later it was not until the 1870s that fundamental changes took place. It was only then that the basic weaknesses of British agriculture were to be fully exposed and the flood of cheap, foreign, imports, which they so greatly feared, was to become a reality.

Britain's commitment to free trade was symbolized by the abolition of the laws which protected the corn industry. Although this took place in 1846 many other items were still the subject of Customs and Excise duties and it was not until the 1860s that these were finally reduced to what proved to be their minimum level. (Some duties were, of course, retained to raise revenue). Thus one major hindrance to the import of foreign commodities was effectively removed but this was not, in itself, sufficient to promote the substantial quantities which might have been expected. The principal, though not the only, reason for this was because of the inadequacies of the international transport system.

The difficulties of moving large quantities of relatively heavy commodities of a high-bulk/low-value nature were well known to many growers who had aimed to supply the London market in earlier centuries. These found that once the Capital reached a certain size the cost of transport became prohibitively expensive. Thus the limited capacity of the horse-drawn wagons and the poor state of the roads then available meant that the carriage of fruit and vegetables over more than a short distance had the effect of pricing many of the items out of the market. Fortunately for the citizens of London and their suppliers the Thames and its tributaries were able to offer a viable alternative and the Kent fruit trade in particular, was able to prosper with the aid of an extensive use of barge traffic.

> "At the beginning of the eighteenth century there were about 1,160 miles of navigable river. Particularly important were the Thames, Severn, Warwickshire Avon, Mersey, Yorkshire Ouse and Tyne".[7]

The deepening of these and other rivers, the construction of artificial channels where these were necessary to overcome particular physical difficulties and the removal of man made and natural obstacles provided a considerable advance over road transport. As these river systems were linked by a rapidly expanding service supplied by coastal shipping the beginning of a national water-borne transport network can clearly be seen. However many areas of the country could not be satisfactorily served by these means and as the eighteenth century progressed it became obvious that economic development was being stifled by the high costs

The Effect of the Industrial Economy

of transport.

As coal was the major commodity to be affected by these constraints it is not surprising that attempts to overcome this bottleneck were first applied to its carriage from mine to customer. While the Sankey Brook navigation, which carried Cheshire salt to Lancashire coal (and coal from St Helens to the Mersey and Liverpool) is generally regarded as the first canal of the modern industrial era it was its successor which represents the real beginning of the "Canal Age". This was the Bridgewater Canal which carried coal from the Duke's colliery at Worsely into Manchester. The success of this venture, opened in 1761 - which had the effect of reducing the price of coal by half - then led to the construction of many more miles of canal. To a large extent these new waterways extended rather than replaced the existing river system and together they provided a vital ingredient into the process of industrialization. One aspect of this was to be the development of new inland towns such as Birmingham : another was the growth of those ports like Liverpool which became the focal point of combined river and canal networks. The net effect of these developments was that distribution and manufacturing costs were significantly reduced and markets were widened and the evolution of an industrialized and urbanized society was given an important boost.

From a rural point of view the areas served by the canals were able to enjoy cheaper bulk commodities like coal, bricks and fertilizers - in some districts this was the first time these items had been available at virtually any price! At the same time farmers and growers of all types were able to widen the range of their potential markets and the reduction in the cost of transport encouraged many to seriously enter the cash-crop business. Thus producers and consumers alike were able to benefit as local scarcities could be easily overcome and fresh opportunities became available. However it would be easy to over-estimate the impact on agriculture. While it is certainly true that the industry shared in the general price reduction of numerous items and that the demand for its products was increased the ability to respond to the fresh opportunities was greatly inhibited by the performance of the barges. While some special "express" boats, pulled by relays of men, did reach the giddy heights of three miles an hour and travelled throughout the 24 hours these were employed on only a few routes and could be used for only the most urgent and valuable of cargoes. The normal services were much slower. It is generally estimated that the average voyage, including the time taken to traverse the locks, achieved only one mile per hour and even this could only be completed during the hours of day light.

Unfortunately fruit, and especially vegetables could not be carried for any distance at high rates without becoming too expensive for the consumer to buy.

From Orchard to Market

As a result they were normally moved by the slower vessels. This naturally meant that many items, especially soft fruits, needed to find their markets within relatively short distances from where they were cultivated. Thus although canals and river improvements did make a useful contribution to the development of many aspects of agriculture and the feeding of the growing population these were severely restricted by the limitations of their technology.

Early enthusiasms and expectations led to the spreading of the canal network so that by 1800 it covered almost all of the non-mountainous areas south of a line drawn between Liverpool, Leeds and Hull. Many of these routes proved to be unprofitable - the seasonality of some trades including those in agriculture and horticulture being one significant factor. In fact it was only those services which carried substantial quantities of coal that proved to be viable in the longer-term. However in spite of some difficulties the system remained virtually intact until the mid 1830s when it was to come under serious attack from the first railways.

The railways were the result of a long series of innovations which had originated in the need to move coal from the mines to the nearest waterways. The difficulties of moving trucks over poor terrain led to the construction of wagon-ways made of logs. At a later stage wooden guides were attached to the edges of the logs to prevent the trucks from deviating from the path and these gradually evolved into rails on which grooved wheels could sit. At first these wagons were pushed to their destinations but over time horses began to be employed. This enabled the wagons to be made of iron and, in turn, the added weight and scale encouraged the use of iron rails.

Simultaneously with these developments came experiments designed to apply steam power to traction. At first these were mainly directed towards carriages designed for running on the highway but when it was understood that "smooth wheels would not slip on smooth rails"[8] then attention was gradually concentrated on what were then referred to as "tram roads". The marriage of steam propulsion and iron rails then led to the evolution of the locomotive and on Tyneside early models were employed to haul coal from c. 1810.

Further technical experiments which led to the exhaust steam being directed up the chimney of the boiler fire greatly increased the power to raise steam and for the first time it became possible to consider using locomotive for passenger transport. However when the Stockton and Darlington line was opened in 1825 it was decided to use stationary engines and cables as the principal source of power with locomotives and horses being used in a supplementary role. Thus it was not until the Liverpool and Manchester Railway Company began to operate in 1830 that the prerequisites for a new system were fully in place. The success

The Effect of the Industrial Economy

of this enterprise - 400,000 people travelled on this route during the initial year - then led to a rapid expansion of what quickly became a national network. This saw the 166 miles of track in 1832 growing to 1,497 miles in 1840 and to 6,559 miles in 1851.[9]

The development of an extensive rail system quickly destroyed all the long-distance coach routes and made most of the canal companies unprofitable. However the resulting combination of rail and canal. together with the ongoing contribution of coastal shipping, and the use of horse-drawn vehicles to operate feeder-services and for local deliveries, meant that Britain enjoyed a closely integrated and highly efficient transport network. The construction of the railways and the ongoing benefits enabled the expansion of the economy to continue and the process of industrialization and urbanization was given an enormous boost. From an export viewpoint British manufacturers were further cheapened by the ability to get them to the ports at low freight charges and domestic consumers also gained by this reduction in transfer costs. The new situation meant that rural areas had better communications with the rest of the country so domestic producers and growers had unimpeded access to all their markets. At the same time imports of foreign foods could henceforth be rapidly and cheaply dispatched from the ports of entry to any desired destination without difficulty. This of course, would have had little real significance or impact unless overseas suppliers could ship their cargoes at rates which would enable them to be competitive with local products. For this to happen required the kind of transport revolution which had occurred on land to be duplicated on the seas.

The types of ships which had evolved at the beginning of the nineteenth century were able to carry moderately sized cargoes at reasonable costs but were usually slow and frequently unreliable. For many commodities the speed and scale of these vessels may well have been adequate and even appropriate for the levels of trade then available. However the shipping industry of the day was poorly equipped to provide carriage for perishable items as these demanded rapid and constant voyage times as well as presenting major problems of stowage. Thus imports of all kinds of food were inhibited by these constraints and they were of particular importance in the fruit and vegetable trades. The inefficiencies of the ships were counteracted, to some degree, by the development of supplies from nearby producers - hence the reliance on apples, pears, soft fruits and onions from France, Germany and the Low Countries. In normal times these items were imported as part of general cargoes carried by a wide variety of ships but at the height of the season - or during periods of glut on the continent and shortages at home - many fishing vessels and other small craft were quickly pressed into service. However the demand for tropical fruits could not be solved so easily as even the nearest sources of supply necessarily involved long ocean voyages.

From Orchard to Market

In these circumstances individual shipowners and merchants reacted to the gap in the market and evolved vessels which maximised the available technology. While all tonnage was constructed of wood and driven by sail the designers and builders still retained many options. The principal decision to be made in the first instance was to balance the conflicting demands for speed and carrying capacity. This was, of course, greatly influenced by the character of the particular trade in which the vessel was to be employed. To some extent this determined the ratio of length and breadth and the weight of the timbers but a second decision then needed to be made in respect of the sail plan. By and large square rigged ships were faster than fore and aft rigged vessels but they were more expensive to build and maintain and required larger crews. These two considerations would certainly play an important role in deciding on the precise type of craft to be ordered but few extreme examples were forthcoming because it should be remembered that the majority of ships operating during this era would be expected to carry a wide range of cargoes over a variety of routes during their lifetime. Nevertheless while the typical merchant ship was essentially a compromise some vessels were built with heavy or bulky commodities in mind, such as grain or wine, while others were constructed more lightly with finer lines. It was the latter which were to be further developed and refined for the carriage of fruit over long distances.

In spite of the gradual evolution of fast, handy, vessels in the second half of the eighteenth century which could make rapid voyages from the Azores, the Mediterranean, Portugal and Spain the import of tropical fruit remained very limited. Volumes continued to be quite small and consisted almost entirely of various types of oranges, lemons and limes. These, of course, possessed relatively long shelf-lives but adverse weather frequently led to whole or part spoilt cargoes. As duty had to be paid on even rotten fruit this was a further inhibiting factor but after c. 1825 a steadily increasing demand encouraged many new operators to enter the trade. These were mainly based in South-West England and in their hey-day it has been estimated that they employed up to three hundred sailing "Fruiterers" [10] Almost all of these vessels fell into the eighty to one hundred and sixty ton category as experience indicated that this size was most appropriate for the business : ie craft of this type could enter the smaller harbours, more easily find a cargo ready for shipment and conveniently cater for a commodity which although packed in wooden boxes could readily be squashed.

Many examples of the speed and efficiency of these "Fruiterers" are provided by David Williams in his article entitled: The Citrus Trade to Britain in the 19th Century.[11]

> *"The extent and continued presence of so many small vessels is to be explained by the nature of the citrus trade, with its perishability and the*

The Effect of the Industrial Economy

requirement, above all, of a speedy transit. Because of this, the need to rapidly complete a sea voyage of around 1,200 nautical miles in the case of the Azores to London, quick sailing schooners were employed. The schooner rig, at the mid-century, was most effective for vessels up to and around 100-125 tons, thus speed took priority over capacity. And speedy these small vessels were. The Brixham schooner, Susan Vittery is listed as having made two runs out to St. Michaels (Azores) in six weeks, a schedule representing about 170 miles per day, if 5 days in port are allowed for loading and discharge. Similarly, in 1869, the Elinor of Salcombe sailed from London to the Azores and back in 17 days".

The cargoes landed in Britain by these "Fruiterers" together with consignments brought by other deep sea vessels and those imported from the Continent undoubtedly grew steadily throughout the first half of the nineteenth century. However as comprehensive statistics are not available until the Annual Statement of Trade and Navigation began to be published in 1853 details for earlier years can only be estimated.[12] Fortunately a retrospective view of 1840 was complied by a correspondent of THE LIVERPOOL COURIER and published on the 20th of February 1890 (p.4) and this gives what appears to be an accurate picture of all fruit and vegetable imports in that year:-

Imports of Fruits and Vegetables into Great Britain and Ireland in 1840

		Weight	Value £
Apples			33,627
Cherries			211
Dates	cwt	985	2,446
Figs	cwt	30,063	42,444
Grapes			32,108
Coconuts			4,486
	bushels	15,152	3,409
Oranges & Lemons	boxes	26,752	150,137
Pears			265
Plums			21,873
Potatoes	cwt	545,744	109,206

Although these statistics indicate that substantial quantities of fruit and vegetables were being imported they were still relatively small for a population which was

From Orchard to Market

to reach nearly sixteen million in England and Wales by 1841. Demand was, however, steadily growing for apart from the accelerating rise in the population and the beginning of a significant increase in the purchasing power of almost all those in employment, the reduction in import duties on fruit in 1838 (and their subsequent abolition in 1860) were all having a major impact. To some extent this additional demand could be met by domestic production but the changing situation obviously presented profitable opportunities for the importer. At the same time the rising efficiency of industrial production, supplemented by the improvement to internal transport were leading to lower unit costs and thus making British manufacturers ever more attractive in foreign countries. However at first many overseas clients lacked the purchasing power to satisfy all their requirements but as Britain came to buy more and more of whatever foodstuffs and raw materials were available a mutually advantageous situation began to evolve. For this to fully develop and reach its real potential it soon became clear that ocean carriage would have to be transformed in such a manner as to enable it to cope with bulk cargoes at very competitive rates

Landing Spanish Oranges and Onions by London Bridge 1874

This was, of course, a far cry from the traditional demands which had previously been made upon the shipping industry when both scale and distance were

The Effect of the Industrial Economy

quite small. The new situation meant that a series of technical and commercial problems needed to be solved so it was fortunate for the British shipowner and his customers that the process of industrialization enabled them to have ready access to the necessary technology. The development of a large scale industrial base had, in turn, encouraged the emergence of a commercial and financial structure which, with all its imperfections, was far in advance of any comparable institutions elsewhere so the necessary pre-requisites were also already in place.

The obvious technical answer to increasing demand was to construct larger and larger ships but this apparently simple solution conceals the many constraints which had to be overcome before it could be implemented. For a start it was not feasible to build wooden hulls over a certain size - 300 feet was regarded as the maximum - so the nineteenth century was to see the gradual adoption of iron and, later, steel for their construction. Furthermore while the uncertainties of wind power could be accepted when trade was of an ad hoc nature the need to provide regular, uninterrupted services led inevitably to the use of steam propulsion. Early engines, however were extremely wasteful of fuel and, apart from the cost of coal, this had the unfortunate effect of requiring that a high proportion of carrying capacity was occupied by non-freight-paying bunkers. It was only when a series of innovations reduced this disadvantage that steamers were able to make an effective challenge to sail.

Early experiments culminated in the establishment of a number of coastal and cross-channel services in the 1820s but is was not until the 1860s that all the technical problems had been solved so that iron steamships could undertake long ocean voyages at viable rates. It was then that Alfred Holt's first class of steamers were constructed with compound engines and high pressure boilers which enabled them to consume only 2 lbs of coal for each indicated horsepower. Economy of this scale them permitted Agememnon to steam from Liverpool to Mauritius - a distance of 8,500 miles - at a rate of ten knots without refuelling. Henceforth all routes were technically open to steam navigation but in view of the costs involved it was at first only taken up by those trades which carried the mail, passengers or perishable commodities where the benefits of speed and reliability made it worthwhile to pay an additional premium.

Of more relevance to the reduction in the costs of ocean carriage was the development of metal hulls. Iron enabled the average vessels to be up to 25% less in weight than its wooden counterpart. This meant that there was a corresponding increase in its cargo carrying capacity and thus greater earning power. However the main bonus of using iron and, later, steel for hull construction was that there were no artificial constraints on its dimensions. Therefore ships could be designed in response to commercial requirements and their scale was limited only by the ability of the merchants to fill them and of harbours to accommodate them.

The first iron steamship of note was Great Britain, built in 1843, and of 3,270 gross tons. Twenty years later Britannic at 5,500 gross tons was not only considerably bigger but with a speed of 16 knots she could complete almost twice as many Atlantic crossings each year. By the year 1907 the new Mauritania was 70,00 gross tons and achieved a speed of 25 knots.

While all of these vessels were passenger liners employed on the North Atlantic the increase in the size and performance of cargo tonnage followed a similar pattern. A single example will be sufficient to demonstrate the economics of scale which had been achieved by 1912. By then the typical, deep-sea, steamship of 7,760 gross tons would have a speed of 13 knots and capacity for at least 10,400 tons of cargo. However the overall benefit of the increase in the scale of merchant shipping can best be seen by reference to the Isserlis Index. This shows that in spite of improvement in both the quality of the ships and the regularity of service the level of freight rates fell from 100 in the base year of 1869 to only 49 by 1904.[13]

As this decline in freight rates was considerably more than the fall in the general price level the real cost of ocean transport was effectively reduced. This had the consequence of giving a huge boost to world trade with seaborne cargoes rising seven fold from 20,000 tons in 1840 to 140,000 tons in 1887.[14]

From the foregoing it is quite clear that economies of scale were able to significantly reduce the cost of ocean transport. Although this process had only made limited progress by 1850 the trends were already well established and with the culmination of the moves towards free trade it was fully expected that a flood of foreign imports would soon begin to supplement Britain's food supply. While this would certainly widen consumer choice and reduce retail prices its impact on domestic producers was regarded with much apprehension by all engaged in British agriculture.

3
Developing International Trade

The five decades from 1850 to 1900 were to witness many important changes in the supply of foodstuffs to the United Kingdom and these were to be especially significant in the case of fruit and vegetables. This was a response to the rise in demand which was brought about by the growth of living standards of the ever increasing population which in England and Wales was to expand from eighteen to thirty-two million during this fifty year period. The economic background to these events was that the benefits of early industrialization, aided by the policy of "Free Trade", had already led to such a degree of international specialization that:-

> "By the mid-nineteenth century 93 per cent of British exports were composed of manufactured goods and the same proportion of imports were primary, unprocessed, produce. By contrast only 7 per cent of imports were finished manufactured goods. This was at a point when Britain dominated the world economy, with over 40 per cent of the entire world output of traded manufactured goods produced within the country and about a quarter of the world's international trade passing through British ports". [1]

As a consequence of these developments Britain's balance of payments (though not her balance of trade) was to be in credit throughout the period from 1816 to 1913 so huge investments were built up in overseas countries. This meant that there were no financial constraints on the purchase of food from abroad. Furthermore the improvements in ocean transport enabled many commodities to be produced in far-distant parts of the world and yet be landed at British ports at prices which were frequently lower than local products. These factors also meant that tropical fruits and vegetables could be imported at prices which, for the first time, made them affordable to the general public. By 1850 it was widely anticipated that the scene was now set for a lengthy struggle between foreign and domestic producers but in reality this competition was not to begin on a serious scale until the mid 1870s.

Among the reasons for this twenty year delay was the fact that although the United Kingdom possessed a comprehensive network of internal transport in 1850 the communications systems on the Continent and in North America were still far from being fully developed. In addition while the cost of carrying goods by sea was beginning to decline this process was far from complete. However the

From Orchard to Market

major difficulty which compounded these problems was that a series of wars in Europe caused considerable dislocation while the American Civil War, 1861-65, delayed the opening-up of the prairies and limited the export of wheat. Thus although some foreign products including butter, cheese and eggs did grow at a rapid rate most imported foodstuffs grew so slowly that they did not keep pace with the demands of the expanding British market. This helped retail prices to remain stable and British farmers were so encouraged that they increased their production of many items. Later, looking back on the third quarter of the nineteenth century, many felt it was "the golden age of agriculture".

Although the competition from foreign suppliers was limited most food imports did increase at a steady rate. Thus in the two decades after 1850 shipments of wheat gradually doubled but as these were not sufficient to flood the market the average British farmer was able to cope. Imports of tropical fruits and vegetables also grew quite considerably during this period with currants from Greece and raisins from Spain more then doubling. At the same time shipments of oranges and lemons, mainly from the Azores, rose from only 814,065 bushels in 1854 to 2,385,160 bushels in 1872. Simultaneously imports of apples and other "raw fruits" principally from the temperate zones grew substantially in some years but demand for these items appear to have fluctuated enormously in response to the size of the British harvest.[2]

This was also true for a number of vegetables where overseas producers were quick to fill any gaps in the British market. Over time, however, imported vegetables gradually gained a rising share in each trade. Thus the consumption of non-domestic potatoes rose from under one pound per head in 1854 to over thirteen pounds per head in 1872. Beans from Egypt, peas from Canada, Denmark and Prussia together with onions from a wide variety of sources also supplemented domestic production on an increasing scale.

> *Among the first wholesalers to handle tomatoes was George Monro, who had started in business regularly handling produce on consignment for senders in 1871. Known as the 'Love Apple' the fruit was then regarded as a table decoration. Monro's business flourished soon handling every type of fruit and vegetables as well as flowers. In 1903 he was to be one of the founding members of the Wholesale Federation, and his company which remained in the family became one of the leaders of the industry*

Developing International Trade

In the final quarter of the 19th century the demand for foodstuffs in the United Kingdom continued to increase. This was partly due to the ongoing rise in population and also due to the ever higher level of expectations by those engaged in industrial activities. Unfortunately from the early 1870s the balance between domestic production and the impact of foreign foodstuffs gradually shifted in favour of the latter. This was because the improving efficiency of ocean carriage was at last being matched by comparable improvements in the internal transport networks of the overseas producers. Thus with the aid of the newly completed railways the wheat growers of North America were able to deliver their crops to Britain so effectively that their landed cost was only half the price of home-grown grain. This situation was made worse by Britain's retention of a "Free Trade" policy even though most European countries gradually re-adopted increasingly heavy protective duties. As a result, Britain not only became the market for most American wheat but also stimulated export production in other countries including India. Most food imports grew at a rapid rate including vegetables and fruit.

Growth of UK Food Imports

	1850	1868	1872	1896
Wheat (cwt)	16m	37m	42m	70m
Rice (cwt)	0.8m	4.7m	7m	4.5m
Potatoes (cwt)	1.3m	2m	6m	2.5m
Onions (bushels)	-	-	0.9m	6m
Oranges & Lemons (bushels)	-	1.8m	2.4m	8.9m
Apples (bushels)	0.5m	1.1m	-	6.2m

Items like citrus fruits and apples could, of course, be transported by traditional sailing vessels but, overtime, these were steadily phased-out by the more efficient steamships. This meant that all foodstuffs could be carried at lower units costs and, in addition, widened the range of sources from which the more perishable varieties could be shipped. Imports of peas, plums, cherries and grapes, mainly from the Continent, also rose significantly in response to the growing demand

In addition to these items which could have been produced at home the final quarter of the 19th century witnessed a substantial growth in the import of tropical fruits. Some of these, like oranges and lemons represented the expansion of an existing trade and the import of these citrus fruits rose from 814,065 bushels in 1854 to 102,422,216 bushels in 1899. At the earlier date the principal sources of supply were Portugal and Azores but by the end of the century Spain and Italy

From Orchard to Market

were the largest providers by far. However, throughout the period London and Liverpool remained the major ports of entry. [4]

Queen's Dock, Liverpool in the 1890's

While it was clearly felt by some commentators that the United Kingdom should produce a larger percentage of those fruits and vegetables which could be readily cultivated in this country there were no such reservations about the importations of tropical products. Here it should be remembered that from as early as the 17th century virtually all fruits and vegetables from warmer countries were occasionally and spasmodically brought into many British ports. These items were often imported on an ad hoc basis by individual members of ships crews when returning from the appropriate overseas voyages. Private trade of this nature was an ever-present aspect of the seafarers' life for whenever possible they would acquire any goods which seemed likely to have a higher value in Britain than where they were produced. These purchases were frequently inanimate articles such as wood carvings and native artwork but monkeys and parrots were also quite common on some routes. Tropical fruits and vegetables which were extremely cheap in certain foreign ports and which promised high returns because of their curiosity value were, of course, particularly attractive. They had the added advantages of being easily portable and could be obtained in small lots but, on the other hand, they were liable to go bad during a protracted ocean voyage. However experience gradually demonstrated that many varieties could

Developing International Trade

be successfully carried if picked before ripe and sufficient survived for a small, if intermittent, trade to develop.

These tiny imports were greatly restricted by the potentially lengthy voyage times of the sailing vessels then available. This disadvantage could be partly offset by ships which operated on the (relatively) shorter routes or on those where the prevailing winds favoured a rapid transit back to Britain. Thus although minute quantities of exotic fruits and vegetables were brought back from a wide range of sources, a majority of those landed in a saleable condition tended to come from the Azores, the Canary Islands, Madeira and the West Indies. The fruit which typifies this development most clearly was the banana. The opening of trade with Africa - especially the West Coast - led to an increasing number of small sailing vessels calling at the Canaries or Madeira while on their way home to Europe:-

> *"These visits were primarily to replenish water and provisions but officers and men would frequently take local products on board with a view to making a profit when they arrived home. These inevitably included some bananas and enough of these survived the rigours of an ocean voyage under sail for the fruit to become at least slightly known at a few British ports.*
>
> *With the introduction of steam and the consequent reduction in voyage times it became easier to carry the individually purchased bananas without deterioration. Consequently, by the mid-nineteenth century a tiny business had developed so that the London market was occasionally provided with what was regarded as an expensive luxury - a hand usually costing between 20 and 30 shillings depending upon availability and condition. It should be stressed, however, that there was no organised trade in bananas and the few bunches which arrived came entirely through the initiative of individually seafarers".* [5]

Other exotic trades which grew from small beginnings in the era of sail included both melons and pineapples. Increasing quantities of the former were added to the growing cargoes of citrus fruits which were transported to London by fast schooners from the ports of Spain and Portugal. However, as in the case of the banana, this was not a business which could really develop until steam vessels were employed on their respective routes. On the other hand the pineapple, with its longer keeping qualities, was able to evolve into a major trade. Thus shipments from the West Indies which commenced in the early 1840s had risen to over 200,000 pineapples per year by 1854. [6]

In spite of the exception of the pineapple trade the growth of fruit and vegetable imports into Britain was almost entirely dependent upon the transition from wooden sailing vessels to iron steamships. While this was not to be the whole explanation, for many commodities required the provision of artificial cooling to be carried successfully, it was the first essential step in transforming the business from a relatively small, luxury, trade to one which encouraged and catered for a mass market. In addition ships cannot operate without the appropriate shore facilities and although small craft can manage with a minimum of support the more sophisticated the vessel the more advanced were its needs. As most of the tropical producers of fruit and vegetables tended to be in the undeveloped parts of the world few could, at first, cope with the larger and more technically demanding steam tonnage.

Thus although the African Steam Ship Company began a service to West Africa in 1853 and its homeward routes passed close to the Canary Islands the inadequate and dangerous nature of its harbours meant that few of its vessels were prepared to stop in the archipelago. The ever increasing size of iron steamships further emphasized the deficiencies of the existing facilities and representations were accordingly made to the government in Madrid as early as 1852. Difficulties in attracting the necessary finance were then to delay the various proposals that were put forward but in 1884 the first phase of the improvements at Puerto de la Luz (adjacent to Las Palmas) was completed. The following year saw the opening of a new harbour at Santa Cruz de Tenerife and thereafter it was quite feasible for the largest vessels of the day to call at the Canaries.

Word of the completion of the construction at Puerto de la Luz quickly reached (Sir) Alfred Jones, the Senior Partner of Elder Dempster and Company in Liverpool. This firm was closely involved with the two British lines then operating to West Africa and Jones had long wished to establish a coaling depot in the Canaries that would enable his vessels to re-fuel during the course of their voyages. After a brief visit he accordingly made the necessary arrangements and coaling companies were rapidly established at the two new ports. This then led to Elder Dempster vessels calling at either Las Palmas or Santa Cruz de Tenerife for bunkers while en route to Liverpool:-

> "As a matter of normal policy their captains were instructed to purchase commodities which could profitably be loaded to fill any space which remained empty when a ship had left West Africa. It then became clear that a large market existed in Britain for bananas and tomatoes, but it was also apparent that a whole series of problems would have to be solved before this trade could really flourish. One major difficulty was that of distance, for Liverpool lay six days to the north, and during that period the fruit inevitably deteriorated even if it were not to spoil altogether. Small, experimental, shipments then showed that both bananas and tomatoes

Developing International Trade

could be carried on deck without the provision of special facilities. However, this required that the bananas (and to a lesser extent the tomatoes) needed to be picked before they were ripe so that they could mature en route. This skill was eventually acquired, though at some cost, and then a second important problem had to be solved. This occurred because bananas were virtually unknown to the Merseyside retailers and it took much effort to persuade them to handle this exotic and delicate fruit. Indeed the early, experimental shipments could not be disposed of via the normal channels at all and Alfred Jones had to resort to the expedient of dealing directly with the Liverpool "barrow boys". It is reported, in fact, that in the initial stages of the trade the fruit was actually given away with the suggestion that it be sold for what the market could bear". [7]

As a result of Elder Dempster's enterprise the quantity of bananas entering Britain rose from approximately 10,000 bunches (from all sources) in 1884 to about 50,000 bunches in 1886. [8]

Practically all of these bananas arrived at Liverpool which was the normal terminus of the Elder Dempster route so while the fruit began to be accepted as a cheap and useful addition to the diet of many who lived near to the port it remained a rare and expensive commodity in London. This situation began to change when, as a consequence of illness, the Fyffes' family were advised to take a lengthy holiday in a warm climate. Thus Edward Wathen Fyffe was to spend much of 1887 and the early part of 1888 in the Canary Islands. As a keen businessman who operated a small but profitable tea importing business in High Holborn he gradually became aware of the potential of the banana so before he returned to London he arranged to establish an agency which would cater for the fruit which was to be supplied by four of the principal Canary producers. In the absence of other real alternative it was arranged that these bananas would be shipped on board any vessel which called in Las Palmas on its way to the United Kingdom and the first consignment arrived at Fyffe's office in September 1888.

As ever larger quantities arrived on the Thames Fyffe evolved a comprehensive system for their disposal. Most of these bananas were sold by auction at Covent Garden but a wholesale business was created which sold directly to the many "high-class" fruiterers who catered for the needs of the more affluent in the capital. Fyffe also began the regular practice of selling the fruit which was ripe when landed to the "barrow-boys" so that it could be marketed while it still had a value. This tripartite system ensured that losses were kept to a minimum and the business prospered even though Elder Dempster opened a major branch in London during 1892. The trade grew rapidly and by 1900 over 1,500,000 bunches of bananas were being imported into the United Kingdom from the Canary Islands.

From Orchard to Market

The vessels engaged in the Canary banana trade used only the draught caused by their forward motion to keep their cargoes from ripening too quickly. While this was successful on a relatively short route with the aid of fast steamships this system could not cope with either more delicate and faster ripening fruits or with bananas from more distant sources. Thus, the carriage of perishable items over long ocean voyages could not be a viable under-taking until artificial cooling methods had been fully developed. Experiments in the shipment of meat received considerable attention and culminated in a cargo of beef, chilled with the aid of natural ice, being successfully transported from the United States to Britain in 1874. Although considerably more time and effort were to be required before large scale cargoes could be carried these voyages demonstrated that it could be practical to import meat over long distances. Further attempts from both Australia and Argentina also achieved some degree of success but it was not until 1880 that these were to be both technically and commercially viable.

The experience gained with the transport of meat might suggest that there would be no difficulty in shipping fruit and vegetables over similar distances. In fact, the carriage of "live" produce (typified by fruit) and of "dead" produce (typified by meat) require separate and distinctive forms of treatment during long ocean voyages:

> "The carriage of both of these groups have certain things in common, but there are also some wide differences. The major one being that in live cargoes - fruit and vegetables, the living process continues after harvesting and during this retarded ripening process, heat continues to be given off and the produce 'breathes' in oxygen and exhales CO_2 and other gases. With dead cargoes - meat and fish, on the other hand, the main requirement is to prevent the development of micro-organisms which live on the produce......".[9]

These differences naturally implied that the experience gained with meat did not mean that it was automatically appropriate for other items. In fact pears and green peas in their pods were reported to have been imported from Italy in a "refrigerated" state and sold in Covent Garden as early as 1880.[10]

Experiments such as this then persuaded other overseas suppliers to attempt to ship their products to Britain and those in South Africa were particularly tenacious in seeking an outlet for their fruit. The development of regular steamship services enabled them to send large quantities of raisins and other dried fruits but two cargoes of apples sent in 1888 arrived in poor condition and had to be sold at a loss. It was then felt that the provision of cool chambers was the only solution and that fitted to Grantully Castle was able to carry 21 tons of meat and fish to

Developing International Trade

the Cape without difficulty. However the grapes which were loaded for the return journey were largely spoilt - subsequent investigations indicating that they were of an unsuitable, thin-skinned variety and had been kept at too low a temperature. These were relatively easy matters to put right and after further experimentation Drummond Castle successfully carried a small quantity of peaches to London in 1892.

In addition to the traditional import of apples from Europe the cross-Atlantic business had grown enormously with the advent of fast steamship services. These apples, which originated in both the United States and Canada, were tightly packed in barrels and shipped without any form of artificial cooling. Over 400,000 of these barrels arrived in Liverpool in the 1889-90 season and as they were mainly of high quality and low price they provided a major supplement (and threat) to domestic producers. By then apples from Australasia were also developing into a substantial trade so it was clear that South African fruit would find it difficult to find a niche in this market. The situation for grapes was very similar. In the early 1890s these were principally supplied from Almeria, Malaga and Lisbon but as their shipments were confined to the period from September to November this did offer opportunities to those who could harvest at alternative times of the year. However the strength of the competition, plus the outbreak of the Boer War in 1899, meant that the rise of Cape fruit exports was not to become significant until the early 20th Century.

PEACHES, NECTARINES, APRICOTS, PLUMS, GRAPES, PEARS, APPLES, &c.

J. W. DRAPER & SON,

Fruit Brokers (Established 1807), Covent Garden, London.

RECEIVED the First Consignment of Peaches in fine condition from the Cape, in the Cool Chamber of the S.S. *Drummond Castle*. They included them in their Public Auction Sale of Friday, 5th February, 1892. The Peaches realised from 80/- to 49/- per case. The cases were 2 feet long by 18 inches wide and 6½ inches deep, and contained from 35 to 48 Peaches each. Each Peach was wrapped in a long strip of wadding, and packed in a single layer, so that no oscillation could occur.

J. W. Draper & Son will be pleased to receive Consignments, will gladly furnish any information to those who desire to ship.

It is clear therefore, that by the 1890s many fruits and vegetables which had previously only been imported in small quantities or for brief periods in the year were becoming available on a much larger scale. This was, of course, because the fall in freight rates and increase in speed of ocean-going vessels meant that commodities which had formally been confined to short-sea routes could now be economically carried from a more distant range of sources. While the traditional citrus and apple trades continued to expand and the banana business came into

From Orchard to Market

being the producers of many other varieties also took advantages of the new opportunities. Thus imports of tomatoes from Guernsey and the Continent were increasingly enhanced by shipment from the Canary Islands. Onions, which had usually been imported from Holland and Belgium were supplemented by those from as far afield as Portugal, Spain and Egypt. The reduction in the cost and time of sea transport also encouraged (usually in association with other perishable items) the carriage of coconuts from the West Indies, pineapples from the Azores, Brazil and Jamaica and pomegranates from Malaga. All of these fruits and vegetables were, however, still transported without the benefit of artificial cooling and until this could be provided there could be little further expansion of these trades.

The development of the railway network enabled the growing urban population to offer a huge, new, market for fresh milk, eggs and other dairy products. The rise in population and of the standard of living also provided further opportunities for the production of barley (for beer) while the growing of potatoes, beet and carrots in specially favoured districts like East Anglia continued to be important.[11]

The latter half of the nineteenth century saw the development and expansion of wholesale markets throughout the UK to cater for the growth in consumer demand which was met by the spread of retail greengrocers. This was the time when many of the future familiar names in the trade became established. The Pouparts, for example, were market gardeners as early as 1776, and took their own produce to market until 1895 when John Poupart, who did the selling was approached by several other market gardeners to sell for them as well. He took a shop in Drury Lane and started in business as T.J.Poupart. George Monro, son of a market gardener at Potters Bar, sold just his father's produce until he was asked by Joseph Rochford, a big grower in the same area to sell his produce as well. One of the most succesful of the early entrepeneurs Monro's business soon embraced overseas supplies and established branches around the country to sell his increasingly wide range. In a paper delivered to the Horticultural Club in December 1895 he said:

> "Foreign fruits are important both in our market and in the trade generally, as the continual supply from different parts of the world keeps many retail shops open which would be compelled to close if depending solely on home-grown supplies, and in many kinds we are entirely dependent on them, such as oranges, bananas, lemons, and of late years pineapples.
> Since the Duke of Bedford opened the Floral Hall for auction sales, the quantity of foreign produce coming to Covent Garden has very largely increased , and by bringing more buyers, and concentrating the bulk of both foreign and English fruit, has made our English trade stronger"

Developing International Trade

Although tinned vegetables and, later, fruits were imported from the United States from c. 1880 these did not offer a serious threat to the trade in fresh commodities.[12] In fact, vegetable production, either as mainstream farm crops or from the market gardens sited near all centres of population, provided a very helpful solution to the problems of many farmers. Another possibility for those in suitable locations, such as Kent, the Vale of Evesham and Dundee, was the growing of fruit. The acreage utilized for this purpose more than doubled in the period from 1873 to 1907 as it was greatly encouraged by the demand of the commercial jam manufacturers and, like vegetables, of the expanding canning industry.

The following tables indicate the twelve most important growing areas during this period and show the development of orchards and areas of small fruit :-

Twelve Largest Counties Containing Orchards in 1901

County	Acre	County	Acres	County	Acres
Kent	27,175	Worcester	21,414	Salop	4,758
Devon	27,161	Gloucester	19,806	Dorset	4,459
Hereford	26,987	Cornwall	5,252	Monmouth	4,027
Somerset	24,929	Middlesex	4,974	Wiltshire	3,774

[13]

Extent of Orchards in Great Britain 1887 - 1901

Year	Acres	Year	Acres	Year	Acres
1887	202,234	1892	208,950	1897	224,116
1888	199,178	1893	211,664	1898	226,059
1889	199,897	1894	214,187	1899	228,603
1890	202,305	1895	218,428	1900	232,129
1891	209,996	1896	221,254	1901	234,660

[14]

Areas of Berries & Currants in Great Britain, 1890 to 1901

Year	Acres	Year	Acres	Year	Acres
1890	46,234	1894	68,415	1898	69,753
1891	58,704	1895	74,547	1899	71,526
1892	62,148	1896	76,245	1900	73,780
1893	65,487	1897	69,792	1901	74,999

[15]

From Orchard to Market

Although these attempts at self-help provided some relief for a hard pressed industry they were totally inadequate to compensate for the decline of the wheat and meat trades. Thus from the early 1870s agriculture was a major victim of what became known as the "Great Depression" and this was only to end with the outbreak of the first World War in 1914. In the meanwhile the Government's adherence to a policy of "Free trade" meant that it could offer no real protection to its farmers. It was firmly believed that, on balance, Britain's interests were best served by a minimum of restrictions. Consequently priority was given to the promotion of industrial exports with the corollary that raw materials and food would be imported in return:-

> *"Free trade had halved the cost of living of the consumer and there were few before the First World War who dared oppose the almost axiomatic principle that Britain should export her manufactures and import her daily bread. Joseph Chamberlain and the Conservative party discovered in 1905 that to advocate the return of tariffs, even for the noble cause of Empire unity, was political suicide. The strategic implication of the policy of dependence was only realised in 1916 when German submarines threatened to starve us into surrender".* [16]

In these circumstances there was considerable distress and anger in the rural areas but little that could be achieved by political means. The view of successive governments was that agriculture should stand on its own feet and that it needed to find its own solutions via increased efficiency. However they did make a number of gestures to assist in this direction so that the Agricultural Holdings Act of 1875 enacted that tenants should be paid compensation for their improvements. This was followed by the re-establishment of a new Board of Agriculture in 1889 - the first had been dissolved in 1822 - and this was able to utilize a small development grant to finance experimental projects. A Small Holdings Act of 1892 (and a later one in 1907) was designed to encourage new entrants on to the land but largely failed due to the indifference of the County Councils which were to administer the scheme. The Agricultural Rates Act of 1896 then cut by half the rates payable by the occupiers of land but as this did not apply to farm buildings it had little real impact.

The relative failure of these official activities naturally encouraged the level of private attempts to alleviate the situation. It might, therefore, be thought that bodies such as The Worshipful Company of Fruiterers would play an important role but the ROYAL COMMISSION ON THE CITY OF LONDON LIVERY COMPANIES, [17] which reported in 1884 stated that:

Developing International Trade

> "The Company has not for many years exercised any control over the trade, though 50 years ago it was from time to time moved to call upon those carrying on the trade in the City to take up the freedom of the Company. The policy and spirit of modern times has, however, been opposed to any restriction on or qualification for trading".

It also made the point that:-

> "Since 1835 the freedom of a Company and the freedom of the City has not been convertible terms and the Municipal Commissions reporting to the Government in 1837 states that: 'the Corporation possesses a very slight, hardly more than a nominal control over the Companies".

The key to the loss of political influence as well as commercial control is then indicated in the following extract from the Commission's report:-

> "Prior to the Reform Bill (2 Will. IV, c.45) the Liverymen of the Common Hall constituted the Parliamentary constituency of London. Every voter had to be a freeman of the City and a Liveryman of a company......".

The loss of the Fruiterers' status and authority is reflected in the fact that in 1882 only 87 Fruiterers were freemen of the City and that the Company's income was a mere £470. However the loss of these roles was not to mark the end of its activities for they were replaced so that:-

> ".......the principal function of the Company is the encouragement and promotion of the study of fruit culture and marketing, and the granting of awards for education and excellence throughout the fruit industry".
> 18

As part of this policy a prize of twenty guineas was created in 1882 to be awarded for an essay on "The Profitable Cultivation of Fruit on English Farms" and a second prize of twenty-five guineas was set up in 1889 for an essay on "Profitable Fruit Farming for Cottagers and Others with Small Holdings". Another aspect of the Company's activities was instigated in 1890 when Sir James Whitehead, then Lord Mayor and also Master of the Fruiterers Company organized a major show in the Guildhall to demonstrate that hardy fruits could be successfully grown in this country. As will be indicated later in this study the Fruiterers have continued and extended this aspect of their work into the 21st Century.

From Orchard to Market

Many educational establishments which specialized in agricultural topics were also established during the second half of the 19th Century. Amongst the more prominent were the Royal Agricultural College at Cirencester, the South-Eastern Agricultural College at Wye and agriculturally based departments at Cambridge University and Reading University College. Their activities were supported by many external bodies such as The Royal Agricultural Society and The Royal Horticultural Society and by numerous private ventures. An outstanding example of the latter was the Woburn Experimental Fruit Farm, established in 1894 at Ridgmont by the Duke of Bedfordshire with the object of:-

> "......ascertaining facts relative to the culture of fruit, and to increase our knowledge of, and to improve our practice in, this industry". [19]

All of these activities represented attempts to come to terms and alleviate the changed and adverse conditions which faced most sectors of agriculture in Britain. While individually their impact may have been quite small collectively they promised to be extremely significant. For this potential to be realised, however, the new ideas and information needed to be made available on a national basis. Unless this could be achieved it would not be possible to influence state policy, diffuse expert knowledge and encourage the spread of the best practices.

The only practical way in which these objectives could be accomplished was via the public press and as early as 1800 the original *Farmers' Magazine* was being regularly published. This was replaced by the *Quarterly Journal of Agriculture* in 1828 and then supplemented by a series of evermore specialized weeklies and monthlies. These included *The Gardeners' Chronicle* (which for a few issues in 1826 provided market prices) and in 1885 both the *Horticultural Times* and the *Covent Garden Gazette* and *Market Record* were started. However these amalgamated within twelve months and soon afterwards disappeared from the scene. This then left the field clear for a new publication and on the first of January, 1890, the *Fruit Trade Journal* appeared to fill this gap. This was "edited and conducted" by Mr. P.H. Davis, a fellow of the Royal Horticultural Society, and also Editor-in-Chief of *The Confectioners' Union* and of *The Cigar and Tobacco World*. Unfortunately for Mr. Davis this *Fruit Trade Journal* (which had no connection with the later publication of the same name) failed to attract the necessary support and after circulating for only twelve months it was merged with *The Confectioners' Union* and had little further connection with the fruit business.

Its place was partially filled when the *Nurseryman and Seedsman* was published in September, 1894. It then seemed that it would be fully replaced by *The Fruiterer and Greengrocer* but this was only ran from January to September 1895, and

Developing International Trade

then closed down. This failed initiative does not appear to have dampened the enthusiasm of Messrs. Briggs and Company of Salisbury Court for this firm were by then long committed to the publication of a wide-ranging weekly that would provide comprehensive coverage of the fruit trade. Thus on Saturday, the 5th of October 1895 it launched *The Journal of Greengrocery, Fruit and Flowers* and, in spite of numerous difficulties it quickly found a permanent niche in the affections of the business community. The success of the venture can best be judged from the fact that this publication has been able to continue (under differing titles) from then to the present day. It is through its pages that the past one hundred years of the British fruit and vegetable trades will now be described and analysed.

From Orchard to Market

THE JOURNAL OF
GREENGROCERY, FRUIT, AND FLOWERS.

A WEEKLY PAPER DEALING WITH ALL THAT CONCERNS GREEN & DRIED FRUITS, FLOWERS, &c.

| No. 1.—Vol. I. | SATURDAY, OCTOBER 5, 1895. | Price 1d. |

SALESMEN.

LONDON.	LONDON.	MANCHESTER.
GEO. MONRO, FRUIT SALESMAN, COVENT GARDEN MARKET, LONDON, W.C.	**EDWARD B. ROSSITER,** Importer of every description of FANCY BASKETS. FLOWER-BASKETS, 2/3, 3/3, 4/3 & 5/3 per set of Six. FRUIT-BASKETS, 18/- per dozen. A TRIAL SOLICITED. ADDRESS: 67, Earlsfield-rd., Wandsworth, London, S.W.	**J. T. BECKETT,** FRUIT AND FLOWER SALESMAN, Smithfield Market, MANCHESTER; And at Covent Garden, London.
J. DAY DAVIS, POTATO, PEA, AND FRUIT MERCHANT, SPITALFIELDS MARKET, LONDON, E.	LIVERPOOL. **W. GLOVER & CO.,** RECEIVERS OF FRUIT AND VEGETABLES, 69, Cazeneau St., LIVERPOOL.	**E. HOLBROOK,** ENGLISH AND FOREIGN FRUIT AND FLOWER SALESMAN, SMITHFIELD MARKET, MANCHESTER.
FRANK WOODHAMS, FRUIT, PEA, & POTATO SALESMAN, BOROUGH MARKET, LONDON, S.E.	**F. & T. WATERWORTH,** English and Foreign Fruit Salesmen and Commission Agents, 17, QUEEN SQUARE, LIVERPOOL.	LEICESTER. **R. RATCLIFFE & CO.,** English & Foreign Fruit & Flower Merchants, Commission Salesmen & Auctioneers, 4, Midland Fruit Warehouse, Queen Street, LEICESTER.
A. & E. WHITTOME, HAY SALESMEN AND POTATO MERCHANTS, 357, LIVERPOOL ROAD, N. Fine Magnums, 45s. per ton delivered.	**SMITH & CROUCH,** FRUIT AND FLOWER SALESMEN AND COMMISSION AGENTS, 12, GREAT CHARLOTTE STREET, LIVERPOOL.	SCOTLAND. **WILLIAM NEWTON,** FRUIT, FLOWER, AND POTATO SALESMAN, AND AUCTIONEER, 7, East Market Street, EDINBURGH. 11, 12, & 13, Quality Lane, LEITH.

Cover of the first issue of "The Journal"

4
Dawn of a New Era

In its first issue on the 5th of October 1895 the editor of the *Journal of Greengrocery, Fruit and Flowers* laid out its aims quite clearly and also stressed the changing background against which their trades were operating:

> *"....The familiar name of 'Greengrocer' hardly indicates the scope of his business transactions, for to keep pace with the times he must supply his customers with the productions that modern civilisation demands. Few realise what a large part of the world is laid under contribution to supply this demand, yet the fact that so common a fruit as an orange being now available all the year round should show that many a land is called upon to send us supplies. We may look upon it, then, that the whole world is fast becoming England's kitchen garden".*

> *"This paper is not issued for philanthropic purposes, but with a view to business requirements. Growers want to know the state of the market - the quantities of goods coming from abroad; the wholesale trade wants to get as many customers from among the retailers as possible; and the retailers want to know exactly where to go for special goods. Middlemen are a necessity, but there is no reason for multiplying them, as is in many instances done here, because the final purchaser does not know the wholesale merchant who keeps a special line".*

The editorial also made it clear that it had been intended to commence publication at an earlier date and that the delay had encouraged a competitor to enter the same area. The second journal was duly published on the 4th of December, 1895, under the title of *The Greengrocer, Fruiterer and Market Gardener*. Although its first editorial claimed that it was the only magazine of its kind this was certainly not the case as the original *Journal of Greengrocery, Fruit and Flowers* was already undertaking the tasks which the new weekly now aspired to cover. Nevertheless the newcomer was able to obtain a moderate share of the business and remained a serious competitor until its demise under its final title, *The Fruit-Grower, Market Gardener and Glasshouse Nurseryman*, in November 1952 when it was subsumed into *The Commercial Grower*.

The original weekly, published by Briggs and Company, which had become affectionately known as the Yellow Back - to distinguish it from its competitor the Green Back - was also to change its official title several times. Thus on the 4th

From Orchard to Market

of April, 1903, it was renamed *The Fruit, Flower and Vegetable Trades Journal* and it was under this title that on the 29th of June, 1907, it was acquired by Mr Harvey Hope-Mason. The new proprietor, who also became editor, was born in India in 1866 where his father (formerly a Colonel in the Bombay Staff Corps) was then a Magistrate and Superintendent of Bazaars. After his retirement in 1877 the Hope-Mason family returned to England although Harvey subsequently spent some time in Australia. He later returned to the UK and worked as a journalist with his interests gradually tending to focus on various aspects of the fruit trade. Thus by the time he came to take control of the *Journal* he was well versed in its subject matter.

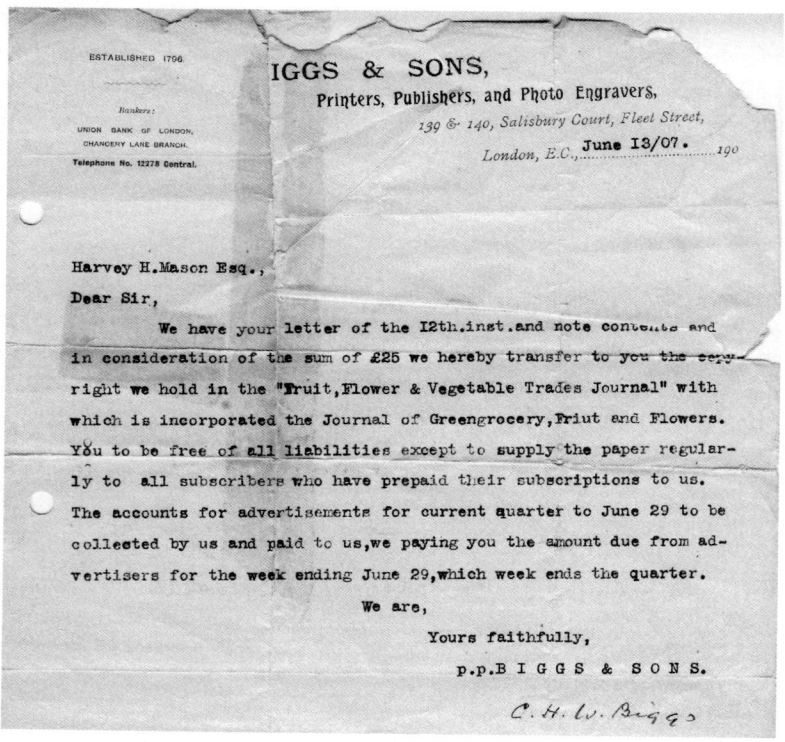

Letter confirming purchase of the 'Journal' in 1907

Mr Harvey Hope-Mason was to remain as editor for twenty-eight years and during this long period he introduced or enlarged many features which helped to make the *Journal* essential reading for all concerned in the fruit and vegetable business. The format which he laid down in 1907 was undoubtedly what the industry required and so was not only retained during his period in control, but has continued to form the basis of the Journal's philosophy to this day:

"A complete report of the markets up to their close on Thursday will be

Dawn of a New Era

given. The provincial as well as London markets will be treated with, the outlook reviewed by several market experts whose services will be secured, whilst special care will be given to trustworthy forecasts based on the actual statistical positions existing at the various sources of supply connected with each separate branch of the industry. Items of news of trade interest will be collated from all parts of the world, and, as the support forthcoming warrants it, the Journal will be materially enlarged and rendered in every way thoroughly worthy of the great industry it seeks to serve". [1]

As part of his desire to see the raising of the industry's status Harvey was an avid supporter of associations and cooperatives of all kinds and over the years was to play an important role in the establishment of the Retail Fruit Trade Federation and of the National Federation of Fruit and Potato Trades. He was also greatly concerned with the setting up and running of the Cheshunt Experimental Research Station and of the Essex Commercial Fruit Show.

FORMATION OF WHOLESALE ASSOCIATION

In April 1903 a number of leading members of the wholesale fruit and vegetable industry met in London and decided to form a national organisation.

It was realised that whilst a number of local organisations were already in existence in various towns throughout the country, there was no body available to co-ordinate their views on matters of national importance, and so the National Federation of Fruit and Potato Trades was born.

The first signatories to the Memorandum and Articles of Association were:

William Craze, Liverpool;   *Roger Ackerley, Manchester;*
Geo. Coleman, London;   *Louis Marks, Leicester;*
Geo. Monro, London;   *Michael Garcia, London;*
William Johnson, Leeds.

The membership comprised local Associations and their members (5s. per year subscription), and individual members (£1 1s. per year)

From Orchard to Market

However it was to be Harvey's success as Editor of the *Journal* that was to mark his real contribution to the gradual transformation of the industry. This can best be seen by policies that he adopted towards the vexed question of foreign imports versus domestic production for the *Journal* was always sympathetic to the plight of the domestic growers and took what action it could to help their cause. However this support was always balanced by the need to welcome the offerings of overseas producers when these were considered to be advantageous to the consumer. In general the Editor was critical of importing items which could just have easily been grown at home, but in the final analysis he appears to have been convinced that the future of the trade would be best ensured if the markets were supplied with the widest selection of fruits and vegetables, over the longest possible seasons, at the lowest practical prices. This attitude meant that imports would inevitably play a key role in the feeding of the British population and the *Journal's* policies reflected this view.

Imports of Fruit & Vegetables into the UK

	1896	1900
Apples	6,176,956 bushels	2,128,541 cwt
Bananas	-	1,287,442 bunches
Cherries	219,367 bushels	242,525 cwt
Grapes	883,244 bushels	592,857 cwt
Pears	483,823 bushels	476,901 cwt
Plums	560,245 bushels	436,708 cwt
Oranges and Lemons	8,890,887 bushels	6,038,277 cwt
Gooseberries		26,045 cwt
Strawberries		52,225 cwt
Onions	6,086,905 bushels	7,087,105 cwt
Potatoes	2,244,627 cwt	8,910,962 cwt

[2]

By the time of the establishment of the Journal the development of steam shipping and of extensive railway networks had already brought producers from many parts of the world in contact with UK markets. As a result a much wider range of fruit and vegetables had already become available and were being enjoyed by, at least, those in regular work! The principal ports of entry were London, Liverpool and Hull and these had their own distinctive markets to cater for their imports as well as for domestic products. Covent Garden, which served the affluent London population either directly or via its satellite markets, also catered for much of the

Dawn of a New Era

South and competed with Liverpool for the Midlands trade. The Stanley Street salesroom in Liverpool dealt with merchants from the Northern regions and secured much business from the Birmingham area - its facility of selling ex-quay giving a considerable advantage over London where every purchase had first to be taken to a warehouse. Hull, much smaller than either of its rivals, originally provided a service only to its own region, but by the 1890s was also acting as a national distribution centre for imports from the Continent.

While many other small ports, including Harwich and Newhaven, also dealt with fruit and vegetables from Europe it was London and Liverpool which became the major termini of most of the longer-distant shipping lines. Thus imports from Australasia, Brazil, Canada, the Canary Islands, the Mediterranean, Portugal, Spain, The West Indies and the United States, together with the beginnings of the trade with South Africa, all tended to be concentrated at these two ports. By 1895 the wide range of these producers was being increasingly matched by the diversity of their crops:

Sources of Fresh Fruit Imports (1902-1914)

	1902 - 1906	1907 - 1909	1910 - 1914
Apples	USA, Canada, Australia	+ France	No change
Apricots & Peaches	France	No change	+ South Africa
Bananas	Canaries, British West Indies	+ Costa Rica, Columbia	No change
Cherries	France	No change	No change
Gooseberries	Netherlands	No change	No change
Grapes	Spain, Portugal, Channel Isles	+ Belgium, South Africa	No change
Lemons, Limes	Italy, Spain	No change	No change
Oranges	Spain, Asiatic Turkey, British West Indies	+ USA	+ South Africa
Pears	France, Belgium, USA	+ South Africa, Australia	No change
Plums	France, Germany	+ Belgium	No German plums in 1914
Strawberries	France, Netherlands	No change	No change

[3]

From Orchard to Market

In addition to these staple items the old established trades in dried fruits still continued with currants coming mainly from Greece : dates from North Africa : figs from Turkey and raisins from Greece, Spain and Turkey. A number of other crops which were then regarded as exotics were also being imported in the 1890s. These included bananas, (still only from the Canaries and Madeira) custard apples, loquats, lychees and prickly pears. However the lack of a cost-effective system of artificial cooling still prevented the large-scale carriage of many crops from the more distant parts of the world.

In the early years of its circulation the threat posed by the rising scale and range of foreign food supplies found much space in the pages of the *Journal*. The other aspects of Britain's free trade policy and the consequent problems that were faced by the whole of British agriculture were also reflected in its editorials and articles.

While most farmers and market gardeners in Britain were able to establish direct relationships with their local retailers - and in some cases with the consumer - many of the larger producers found it necessary to make arrangements with the wholesalers in the bigger markets. These deals, like those for soft fruits and vegetables from the Continent, were usually fixed so that the consignment was sent at the owners' risk and he received the proceeds, less carriage and commission, only after the items had been sold. Individual arrangements were undoubtedly many and varied in different markets but in the case of Liverpool only potatoes and kitchen vegetables originated in the immediate vicinity. Kent and Worcestershire, in fact, provided most of the city's cherries, currants, gooseberries, pears and plums which were sent by the regular passenger trains on a daily basis during the growing season. These were usually consigned on a commission basis but other fruits, including strawberries from Cornwall or Cheshire, and damsons from Cheshire, Shropshire and Worcestershire were normally sold directly to the retailer or consumer.

All of these arrangements were, of course, highly dependent upon the railway network. By 1895 this amounted to approximately 20,000 miles and provided major links between the ports or production areas, and their markets in the growing towns and cities. By then virtually the whole of Great Britain was served by a series of private lines which supplied passenger and freight services to even quite small centres of population. While many places could be catered for by a single railhead the more substantial urban areas - especially London - needed several and the larger wholesale markets were usually provided with their own direct links. However transport from surrounding areas into city centres and the ongoing carriage of fruit and vegetables from the markets was essentially undertaken by road.

Dawn of a New Era

Covent Garden Market in 1910

At first road transport for the carriage of fruit and vegetables relied almost entirely on animal and human power ! Teams of heavy horses were employed to bring produce from outlying farms and market gardens while single, lighter, horses and donkeys - plus handcarts - were used to distribute these commodities from the railheads and wholesale markets. Although this system satisfied almost all needs within the urban area the situation for many rural producers was less happy. The reasons for this are made clear from the case:-

> "....of a successful florist and market garden grower in Sussex on a prolific little holding of five acres, who delivers his produce by road. His complaint to us when we inspected his gardens was that distribution by the ordinary cart was slow - very slow!; but as he sent his supplies to the village shops within a radius of 20 miles, no other method - not even the expensive railway service - was available". [4]

From Orchard to Market

It was for this reason that wholesalers and market gardeners took a very early interest in the development of the horseless carriage, and one reporter after visiting the experiments undertaken at Sydenham by the Daimler Company; claimed that their latest carriages would enable loads to be transported in one-third of the time and at one-third of the existing cost. However this very optimistic statement made in December, 1895, took no real account of the true cost of motor wagons and it was not for a further ten years that they were to become a viable proposition.

Over the next decade or so the reduction in costs and the improvement in reliability was such that the motor wagon was increasingly being regarded as a practical proposition. Thus by 1908 the railway companies had introduced road services which in some districts were already collecting agricultural produce within a twelve mile radius of their stations. However this development, which was to further enhance the central role of the rail network, was simultaneously being challenged by the emergence of direct carriage by road:-

> "In the Worthing district, growers complain of the exorbitant charges made by the railway companies for the carriage of produce to London. It may be mentioned that last season (1907) a Worthing grower hired a motor lorry for two weeks for the sum of £10 per week, which included all expenses, to go and return from London three times a week, making six journeys in all, and to carry five tons of fruit each journey, bringing empties back on the return journey.
>
> We have it upon the authority of one who travelled with the fruit to Covent Garden Market, that it arrived in better condition than when handled by the railway company, the grapes and cucumbers opening up as fresh as when cut. The time occupied on the journey was five hours while the cost was half that charged by the railway company.
>
> If one grower can do this, surely it is possible for a number to co-operate and establish a regular motor service worthy of the Worthing district, placing the fruit upon the early morning market within a few hours of it being cut or picked". [5]

The *Journal* certainly stressed the advantages of motor transport and by 1914 it was effectively competing with the railways around the periphery of London and other large cities. Outside these areas the rail network continued to provide long distance services although motor lorries were increasingly used to increase their catchment zones. There was little attempt to use motor vehicles on trunk routes on the other hand they were gradually replacing horse-drawn carts for shorter deliveries and collections. The latter were also being subjected to additional competition from a widening range of tradesmen's tricycles and carrier bicycles.

Dawn of a New Era

The "Ideal" Market Lorry

You need a "GARNER" for quick and easy delivery of your produce.

You can have any type of body, but we suggest the one as illustrated.

The proved best of the 30/40 cwt. type.

CHASSIS £595

(EASY PAYMENTS ARRANGED).

THREE LORRIES IN ONE.
1. Flat Platform.
2. With Hinged Sides.
3. With Crate Tops.

WRITE FOR PARTICULARS.

HENRY GARNER, LTD.,
MOSELEY MOTOR WORKS,
BIRMINGHAM.

While motor vehicles were gradually evolving into an important segment of the internal transport network another development, which was to be equally significant in the long-term, was taking place in the banana trade. As noted earlier in Chapter 3 the import of this delicate fruit had grown from only 10,000 bunches in 1884 to over 1.5 million bunches in 1900. The next stage in the expansion of the banana industry came in 1901 when the two firms Elder Dempster and Fyffe Hudson and Company - amalgamated to form Elders and Fyffes Ltd.

This merger was largely due to the British Government's desire to provide an alternative market for Jamaican bananas which up to then had been exported almost entirely to the USA and Canada. Alfred Jones, encouraged by the promise of a knighthood, agreed to market the fruit in Britain without fully realising the technical problems which would need to be overcome. The fact that bananas could be carried on the relatively short route from the Canaries utilizing simple methods of ventilation did not imply that this system would suffice for a two week voyage from Jamaica. A journey of this magnitude would clearly require some form of artificial cooling.

The commercial importation of frozen and chilled meat began in the 1880s. The type of machinery used for this purpose was subsequently refined by Messrs J and E Hall of Dartford and was then successfully adopted for the carriage of apples from Australia. Knowledge of this system then led to the first serious attempt to carry bananas from a distant source. This was made by the Jamaica Fruit Importing and Trading Company in 1896 and 1897. This was a small firm which chartered

From Orchard to Market

a number of old vessels (which had originally been used in the Australian meat trade) to bring bananas and some oranges from Kingston, Jamaica, to London. Four voyages were undertaken but only one could be regarded as moderately satisfactory. The difficulty appeared to be in controlling the temperature which in order to avoid premature maturing of the bananas needed to be kept between 12.5 C and 13.0 C. By the time that the necessary experience had been gained the enterprise had lost its credibility as well as its very limited amount of capital and what was really an experiment came to an abrupt end.

Elder Dempster appear to have taken no account of the failure of the Jamaican firm and it was only after a ten year contract had been signed with the British and Colonial Governments that serious attention was paid to the problem of actually carrying the fruit. By accident Mr Stockley then heard that a White Star ship fitted with a cool-air system for the carriage of apples from Australia had arrived at Tilbury. When he inspected this vessel he found that its equipment could readily be adapted to cater for bananas and was soon able to make satisfactory arrangements with its manufacturers Messrs J & E Hall. Proof of the efficiency of this system came with the first voyage of 'Port Morant' in February 1901. This was completed from Jamaica without difficulty and later deliveries by her and her sister ships to Bristol were also undertaken successfully. As a result all of Elders and Fyffe's fleet were subsequently to be fitted with this method of cooling and this was to mark the real beginning of the world wide trade in bananas.

The adoption of artificial cooling was also significant in the way that bananas had to be handled when they reached their port of destination. Canary bananas arrived in Britain when they were about to mature and so needed to be sold as quickly as possible from the ports of entry at Liverpool and London. The arrival of Jamaican bananas in a green condition was a different matter and required the creation of a national network of ripening rooms before the industry could reach its full potential. This, in turn, needed the provision of suitable transport from Bristol and, after some early problems, heated railway trucks were introduced and depots were then sited on rail sidings in most towns of any size. While the larger of these were usually operated by Elders and Fyffes many independent handlers and ripeners were appointed and a number of these were to maintain their links with the Company for many years. These included Thomas Dowd of Liverpool, George Jackson of Birmingham, Tom King of Nottingham and L & H Williams of Glasgow. Charles McCann of Dundalk was also appointed and in 1906 was the first firm to import bananas into Ireland on a regular basis.

Dawn of a New Era

s.s. Port Morant, carrying the first commercial cargo of bananas from Jamaica

In the years up to the outbreak of the first World War the import side of the industry, and the *Journal,* were able to make steady progress. The impact of free trade policies, allied to the continued improvement of shipping and cooling-techniques meant that Britain could take full advantage of the rise in world production. Thus in addition to an expansion of what were becoming traditional trades with old suppliers - Australasia, the Canary Islands, Europe, the Mediterranean - the North American apple business was increasingly being supplemented by citrus and other fruit imports from both California and Florida. Furthermore the changing conditions were ensuring that the links with the new entrants - Palestine, South America and, especially South Africa - were growing stronger every day.

The annual value of "fresh" fruit (which included raw currants, dried dates and nuts) rose from a total of £9.6m in 1902 to £12.1m in 1913. This trend was closely followed by fresh vegetables which increased from £3.7m to £5.4m during the same period. All of these items were imported free of customs charges as only a few dried or preserved fruits were then liable to duty.

In spite of the rise of protectionism in many countries the United Kingdom still maintained a virtually unchanged policy of free trade. This meant that market forces were almost entirely responsible for determining the sources of most of Britain's imports of fruit and vegetables. In practice this resulted in the great majority of cargoes originating in foreign countries in 1895 and this imbalance was to continue in the era up to 1914. British Possessions, including the Channel

From Orchard to Market

Islands, provided only fresh fruit to the value of £1.262m in 1902 while foreign growers supplied £8.369m. This pattern was to remain throughout the pre-war period with the British Dominions and Empire usually contributing about 20% of the total and amounting to only £1.671m out of £12.1m in 1913. _British Possessions were rather more successful in providing fresh vegetables for the home market with their contributions reaching a third in 1909. In that year they supplied £1.019m of produce while foreign countries were responsible for £2.958m. However as their share usually averaged nearer a quarter it will be seen that in both of the fruit and vegetable sectors the foreign grower continued to hold dominant positions.

In 1902 the most important fresh fruit imports were oranges, apples and bananas with grapes, plums, pears and lemons playing supporting roles. This order of magnitude remained largely unaltered to 1913 although bananas had almost caught up with apples and the values in each section had gradually increased:

Annual Value of Fresh Fruit Imports into the United Kingdom

	1902	1908	1913
Apples	£1.923m	£2.079m	£2.230m
Apricots and Peaches	.033	.060	.030
Bananas	1.060	1.769	2.172
Cherries	.216	.234	.123
Currants	.092	.121	.147
Gooseberries	.016	.025	.067
Grapes	.676	.728	.740
Lemons, Limes and Citrons	.417	.471	.477
Almonds	.554	.560	.888
Oranges	2.358	2.269	2.476
Pears	.439	.515	.650
Plums	.515	.427	.437
Strawberries	.058	.045	.025
Unenumerated	.308	.291	.325
Total (other than preserved) not liable to duty	£9.632m	£10.650m	£12.077m

Throughout the period from 1895 to 1914 the orange continued to be the most

Dawn of a New Era

important of Britain's fruit imports. Although Portugal and the Azores had originally been important suppliers Spain had come to dominate in the 19th Century and this position was to be maintained until the outbreak of the First World War. Another traditional supplier, Italy, retained a small niche in the British Market but it was the expansion of imports from Asiatic Turkey (which included Palestine) together with the gradual growth of cargoes from the British West Indies, the United States and South Africa which were the most significant aspects of the business at this time.

Fresh Orange Imports into the UK, £m.

	1902	1908	1913
Spain	£2.086m	£1.899m	£2.053m
Italy	0.053	0.055	0.057
Asiatic Turkey	0.115	0.159	0.258
British West Indies	0.024	0.073	0.052
USA	0.011	0.050	0.021
South Africa	-	-	0.016
Major Suppliers:	2.289	2.236	2.457
Other Suppliers:	0.069	0.033	0.019
Total Imports	£2.358m	£2.269m	£2.476m

7

The expansion of the new entrants was the more remarkable when it is appreciated that the demand for oranges in the United Kingdom showed little growth in this period yet Spanish production was steadily rising ! In the event Spain was obliged (or found it advantageous) to widen the range of its export markets and the UK's share fell from 79.1% in 1895 to 42.8% in 1913.

PACKAGING

In the early days, there was only one container, the basket supplied in three sizes: peck (IOlb), Half bushel: (28lbs), and bushel (40lb). Vegetables were sent loose in wagons and sold by the 'tally' a term meaning five dozen. Subsequently they were graded and packed in bags or nets containing about two dozen in each.

From Orchard to Market

Destinations of Oranges Exported from Spain
Quantities given in Spanish quintals - approximately English cwts.)

	1895	1900	1905	1910	1913
Germany:	8,056	149,384	302,613	865,293	1,125,133
%	0.3	5.7	9.6	17.4	19.8
France:	414,825	466,652	566,861	1,017,792	1,289,058
%	17.7	17.9	18.0	20.5	22.7
Great Britain:%	1,856,884	1,862,477	2,018,377	2,321,521	2,435,966
	79.1	71.6	64.1	46.7	42.8
Others:	67,423	123,744	259,225	764,464	840,493
%	2.9	4.8	8.3	15.4	14.7
Total Qn	2,347,188	2,602,257	3,147,076	4,972,070	5,690,664

With its thick skin and long shelf life the orange was able to survive the relatively lengthy voyage times imposed by the limitations of sailing vessels. On the other hand the more delicate apple could not be carried for any considerable distances until after the introduction of steam shipping in the mid 19th Century and the subsequent adoption of cooling-techniques c. 1880s. Thereafter the trade in apples rapidly emerged as the principal rival of the orange and in 1896 6.1m bushels of apples were imported against 8.9m bushels of citrus fruit. The progress of the apple was particularly impressive when it is considered that it also needed to compete with the long-established domestic industry - of which more later! The vast bulk of these shipments originated in North America but in the last quarter of the 19th Century cargoes from Australia, especially Tasmania, began to provide a degree of competition. This pattern was maintained until 1914 with France, Belgium, Portugal and the Netherlands supplying most of the remaining balance: -

Fresh Apple Imports into the UK, £m.

	1902	1908	1913
USA	1.004	0.693	1.000
Canada	0.569	0.836	0.730
Australia	0.187	0.305	0.296
Major Suppliers:	1.760	1.836	2.026
Other Suppliers:	0.163	0.243	0.204
Total Imports	£1.923m	£2.079m	£2.230m

Dawn of a New Era

As noted earlier the commercial importation of bananas from the Canary Islands began in 1884. This was only on a small scale but the trade received an enormous boost when (Sir) Alfred Jones extended his activities to include Jamaica in 1901. The subsequent establishment of Elders and Fyffes then marked the beginning of regular shipments to the United Kingdom where the organizational flair of Arthur Stockley was to quickly ensure the creation of an integrated system of shipping, distribution and ripening of the fruit. Unfortunately, Jamaica, which was really geared towards supplying the United States and Canada, found it difficult to serve these markets as well as the expanding demand in Britain. Elders and Fyffes was therefore obliged to enter into an agreement whereby half of its capital was acquired by the American United Fruit Company which in return agreed to supply whatever fruit was required for the UK.[10]

Jamaican bananas in Fyffes cellar at Neal Street in Covent Garden in 1905

In the absence of this arrangement it is likely that Jamaican production would have gradually risen so that it could, in time, have satisfied the needs of the UK market. However without a sufficient volume it seems quite possible that the trade could have become so unprofitable that Jones would have felt obliged to withdraw his support. In either case the growth of the banana industry in Britain would have been greatly retarded whereas, in the event, the value of imports rose dramatically and by 1913 were virtually equal to those of apple shipments. This was, of course, only achieved by the acquisition of cargoes from other sources and these were increasingly secured from the plantations of the United Fruit

From Orchard to Market

Company in Costa Rica and Colombia:

Banana Imports into the UK, £m.

	1902	1908	1913
Canary Islands	0.821	0.743	0.750
Costa Rica	-	0.804	0.681
Colombia	-	-	0.603
British West Indies	0.230	0.221	0.132
Major Suppliers:	1.051	1.768	2.166
Other Suppliers:	0.009	0.001	0.006
Total Imports	**£1.060m**	**£1.769m**	**£2.172m**

[11]

In addition to the three major imports of oranges, apples and bananas a number of other fruits were also of considerable significance in the pre-war era. Grapes, which had long been a welcome if expensive addition to domestic glass-house production, were valued at £676,000 in 1902 and this figure had risen to £740,000 by 1913. Throughout this period Spain and the Channel Islands were the largest suppliers with Portugal and Belgium providing smaller quantities. Surprisingly France contributed little at this time but there was a small but rising shipment of the fruit from what was then recorded as the Cape of Good Hope. Attempts to promote the export to grapes on the much longer route from Australia were also achieving some success by 1909:-

<u>Successful Experiment with Western Australian Grapes</u>

"The Acting Agent-General for Western Australia (Mr. R.C. Hare) has received from Mr. R.L. Gilbert, Officer-in-Charge of the Western Australian Government Agency in Melbourne, Victoria, particulars of an interesting and important experiment in connection with the cool storage of table grapes for export to London and other British markets. It will be remembered that sample shipments of Western Australian grapes sold in London a few months ago up to 1s. 4d. per lb. wholesale.

Mr. Gilbert informs the Agent-General that early this year he received a consignment of Western Australian grapes through the Department of Agriculture for exhibition at the Melbourne Government Agency. The grapes were packed in bunches in granulated cork dust in wooden cases, containing about 23 lbs. of fruit each, precisely similar to the shipments

Dawn of a New Era

which had been sent from Western Australia to the London market. The Melbourne consignment had been ten days in the steamer's hold before it reached Mr. Gilbert's hands, and it was placed by him in exactly the same condition in which it was received in the chambers of the Government Cool Stores, Melbourne.

There the grapes remained untouched for three months at the end of which period (on the 11th July last) the cases were brought out and opened in the presence of a distinguished company, including a number of members of the Commonwealth Parliament. The representatives of the three Melbourne Press present reported that the grapes were found, after their ten days' sea journey and three months' cold storage, in "perfect condition".

The varieties experimented upon were Almeria (known in Spain as Ohanez), Flame Tokay, and Purple Cornichou, and they were grown by Mr. Barret-Lennard, of Guildford, Western Australia, who was also the grower of a shipment which realised 33s. per case of 23 lbs. in London a few months ago. Mr. Gilbert writes:- "The Ohanez (Almeria) opened up absolutely perfect, and the same can be said of the Flame Tokay. With regard to the Purple Cornichou, although the berries were perfectly sound, some of them fell away from the stalks when the bunch was lifted'. The remarkable freshness and quality of the fruit excited great enthusiasm among those present, and it was unanimously agreed that the experiment had been a great success".

The grapes which came to England from Western Australia in April and May last were stored only a few weeks between the time they were gathered at the vineyards and the time they were marketed in London, but the Melbourne experiment indicates that even three or four months' storage does not induce deterioration, in freshness, firmness, flavour or appearance. That this was also the view taken by the trade in this country would seem to be indicated by the prices paid for the four shipments of grapes from Western Australia totalling over 4,000 cases. One shipment averaged 14s. per case of 23 lbs., another 19s., a third 23s. The cost per case, including all charges, was 4s. 5d., so that the net return to the growers was highly satisfactory.

The Victorian Government Viticultural Expert was so impressed by the success of the storage of grapes at the Melbourne Cool Stores that he is getting several thousand cuttings of Flame Tokay from Western Australia for, propagating at the Viticultural College in the State of Victoria, and an

From Orchard to Market

immense impetus has been given to the grape growing industry in Western Australia by the results of last season's London shipments". [12]

Until 1893 all citrus fruits were lumped together in the official import statistics but thereafter oranges were returned separately while lemons were included with citrons and limes. The good keeping qualities of lemons, like other citrus, meant that they could be successfully carried on relatively long ocean voyages and so their import into Britain had been possible at a very early date. By the 19th Century Sicily and the Azores were the major suppliers but by the beginning of the 20th Century Italy and, to a much smaller extent, Spain were the only substantial exporters to the United Kingdom. Sicily, in fact, had always been the principal producer and in the period 1902 to 1913 was contributing 90% of the Italian total:

Lemon, Lime and Citron Imports into the UK (£ ,000)

	1902	1908	1913
Italy	360	412	398
Spain	44	51	65
Major Suppliers:	404	467	463
Other Suppliers:	13	4	14
Total Imports	£417,000	£471,000	£477,000

[13]

The importation of pears was yet another trade of long-standing. Its origins lay on the Continent from where supplies were traditionally secured to supplement British production as and when necessary. By the 19th Century the principal sources were in France with the "Low Countries" playing supporting roles. This was still the case in 1900 when a total of 476,000 cwts were imported although by then pears from North America were becoming increasingly important. This trend continued up to the outbreak of the First World War with the growers in Europe being strongly challenged by cargoes from the United States and shipments from Australia, Canada and South Africa also making significant contributions.

The trade in plums followed a similar pattern in some respects with 436,000 cwt being imported in 1900. France was again the largest producer but although many other European countries shipped moderate quantities from time to time it was Germany that provided the most substantial and sustained competition. Unlike pears long-distant sources were slow to enter this activity and only the United States shipped plums to Britain on any scale. The modest nature of this

Dawn of a New Era

business can be seen from the statistics for 1913 when France supplied fruit to the value of £200,000 while that from America amounted to only £18,000.

The remaining imports of fresh fruits were of much smaller value and were greatly influenced by the fluctuations in British production and demand. Almost all apricots and peaches, together with cherries, originated in France with tiny but rising quantities of the former beginning to arrive from the USA and, especially, from South Africa. The Netherlands were largely responsible for gooseberries while France, plus the Netherlands, supplied virtually all of Britain's imported strawberries. The balance of fresh fruit which was recorded as unenumerated was shipped from a wide range of sources. In the prewar period Spain and Germany made the biggest contribution to this sector with the Azores, initially important, continuing to decline. Of more significance were the rise in cargoes from the Channel Islands, British West Indies and South Africa but it should be noted that the total value of this classification only averaged about £300,000 per year throughout this era.

In addition to fresh and dried fruits, a considerable quantity of fresh vegetables were imported into the United Kingdom in the prewar period. In 1900 the major commodities were potatoes, onions and tomatoes and these continued to dominate until the outbreak of the First World War.

Fresh Vegetable Imports into the UK, £m.

	1902	1908	1913
Onions	£0.999m	£0.993m	£1.035
Potatoes	1.589	1.967	2.589
Tomatoes	0.700	0.955	1.348
Unenumerated	0.468	0.371	0.519
Total Imports	£3.757m	£4.288m	£5.492m

14

As noted earlier only about a quarter of these vegetable imports originated in British overseas possessions and foreign growers were responsible for the balance. The major sources of potatoes in 1902 were France, the Channel islands and Belgium and these suppliers were able to maintain their shares until 1913 although by then the Canary Islands were becoming increasingly important. Over the same period Spain, the Netherlands and Egypt were the chief providers of onions, while the Canaries, the Channel Islands, Spain and France were the principal shippers of tomatoes in 1902. This continued to be the case in 1913 but

From Orchard to Market

by then the Netherlands had risen to become third in importance.

Competition for both the overseas suppliers of fresh fruit and vegetables and for domestic growers was provided by the increasing importance of preserved, mainly canned or bottled. The canned/bottled fruit was largely supplied by Spain although shipments from North America and Australia were beginning to develop. The other preserved fruits were almost entirely sent by Italy, Spain and Greece. Canned vegetables originated principally in Italy with France, Belgium and the United States also making substantial contributions. The much smaller quantities of dried (preserved) vegetables were provided by Germany and other continental suppliers.

A final import which should be mentioned was the trade in flowers. These were handled and distributed by many of the wholesale merchants involved with fruit and vegetables and provided them and their retailers with valuable additional revenue at certain times of the year:-

Fresh Flowers Imports into the UK (not liable to duty) £

	1902	1908	1913
Foreign Countries	167,139	117,025	181,952
British Possessions	100,142	112,777	106.776
Total Value	**£267,281**	**£229,802**	**£288,728**

[15]

At the beginning of the 20th Century most of the foreign flowers were provided by France and virtually all British supplies came from the Channel Islands. Although the Netherlands made some small contribution to the business imports from France and the Channel Islands continued to dominate the trade in 1913.

However it should not be forgotten that many flowers, as well, as fruits were also grown under glass. While the Channel Islands (whose production was included in the import statistics) was very significant, domestic output within the United Kingdom was also extremely important.

> *"The cultivation of fruit and flowers under glass has increased enormously since about the year 1880, especially in the neighbourhood of London, where large sums of money have been sunk in the erection and equipment of hothouses. In the parish of Cheshunt, Herts, alone there are upwards of 130 acres covered with glass, and between that place on the north and London on the south extensive areas of land are similarly utilized.*

Dawn of a New Era

In Middlesex, in the north, in the districts of Edmonton, Enfield, Ponders End and Finchley, and in the west from Isleworth to Hampton, Feltham, Hillingdon, Sipson and Uxbridge, many crops are now cultivated under glass. At Erith, Swanley, and other places in Kent, as also at Worthing, in Sussex, glass-house culture has much extended. A careful estimate puts the area of industrial hothouses in England at about 1200 acres, but it is probably much more than this. Most of the greenhouses are fixtures, but in some parts of the kingdom structures that move on rails and wheels are used, to enable the 'ground to be prepared in the open for one crop while another is maturing under glass. The leading products are grapes, tomatoes and cucumbers, the last-named two being true fruits from the botanist's point of view, though commercially included with vegetables. To these may be added on the same ground dwarf or French beans, and runner or climbing-beans. Peaches, nectarines and strawberries are largely grown under glass, and, in private hothouses - from which the produce is used mainly for household consumption, and which are not taken into consideration here - pineapples, figs and other fruit. Conservative estimates indicate the average annual yield of hothouse grapes to be about 12 tons per acre and of tomatoes 20 tons. The greater part of the space in the hothouses is assigned to fruit, but whilst some houses are devoted exclusively to flowers, in others, where fruit is the main object, flowers are forced in considerable quantities in winter and early spring. Tomatoes are grown largely in houses exclusively occupied by them, in which case two and sometimes three crops can be gathered in the year. In the Channel Islands, where potatoes grown under glass are lifted in April and May, in order to secure the high prices of the early markets, tomato seedlings are planted out from boxes into the ground as quickly as the potatoes are removed, the tomato planter working only a few rows behind the potato digger." [16]

The statistics of Britain's fruit and vegetable trade provided above indicates that virtually all of these imports continued to expand throughout the period from 1895 to 1914. The advance in steam shipping, together with the evolution of cooling techniques, had widened the range of sources so that every part of the world was now able to contribute to the British market and there were many new entrants into the business. It was a period when many traditional trades were able to grow and when the relatively new imports of bananas and tomatoes were consolidated into major enterprises. As a result the diet and choice of the British consumer was considerably enhanced but to some extent this progress was only achieved at the expense of the domestic industry.

It was not difficult for Britain to pay for the expansion of fruit and vegetable imports

From Orchard to Market

as these were more than counter-balanced by industrial exports and by the returns from overseas investments. However the situation of British agriculture and horticulture remained in a sad state due, it was claimed, to the unfair competition engendered by the ongoing policies of free trade. While the fortunes of market gardeners in favoured areas and for those engaged in growing specific crops for the rising number of canning and bottling factories, were moderately satisfactory in most years the bulk of the industry remained permanently depressed. Although the population of England and Wales grew from 32.5 million in 1900 to 36.1 million in 1911 this was not sufficient to offset the increasing level of imports. In addition the prosperity of growers was not helped by the reluctance of the general population to eat more than relatively small quantities of their products except for potatoes. In fact the total annual, average, consumption for the years 1909 to 1913 amounted to:- potatoes, 208 pounds per head: other vegetables, 60 pounds per head and fruit, 61 pounds per head. As these figures include imports it will be seen that it required a major change of attitude if demand was to be significantly raised. Such a transformation did indeed take place when the First World War broke out in 1914 and for the following five years all that could be produced could be sold without difficulty.

5
The Impact of War

The start of hostilities with Germany and the Austro-Hungarian empire in August 1914 saw the United Kingdom almost totally unprepared in many areas. This was especially true of agriculture as in the years prior to the war Britain was only producing about 42% of its food and was dependent upon overseas sources for the remainder.

While some of these overseas items could only be grown in tropical or sub-tropical areas many could have been produced in the British Isles. Of these wheat was by far the most significant as nearly 81% needed to be imported. This was, of course, due to the national policy of free trade which ensured that wheat was obtained from overseas sources, where it could be grown more cheaply - including the cost of shipping - than at home.

In a number of ways this suited the UK economy as food (and raw material) imports could be used by their producers to help finance the purchase of British industrial goods and coal. To a large extent this exchange was, therefore, of mutual advantage in the period up to 1914 but although it may have facilitated British exports it also led to a considerable reduction in the UK's arable land : this had amounted to over 24m acres in 1872 but by the outbreak of war only 19m acres were under cultivation in spite of a considerable increase in the population.

Britain's reliance on overseas fruit in the period 1909-1913 was even greater than upon wheat as approximately 84% needed to be imported. To some extent this can be explained by the purchase of substantial quantities of oranges, other citrus and bananas which could not be grown at home. However these cargoes were massively increased by large shipments of apples and pears - many of which could have been produced in the UK. On the other hand Britain was almost self-sufficient in potatoes and was normally able to provide up to 60% of its other vegetables of which onions and tomatoes were by far the most important.

In spite of the obvious deficiencies in home production only limited action was at first taken to safeguard the nation's food supply. However a Royal Commission on Sugar was established in August 1914 which was designed to offset the ending of imports from Central Europe. In addition an organization was quickly set up to secure meat for the Army and this then ensured that the Board of Trade was obliged to take control of most of Britain's refrigerated ships. At this time Government policy was to encourage farmers to produce more wheat and other

From Orchard to Market

foods but it was not prepared to offer any financial inducements. It was thought that market forces would provide sufficient incentives but there was in fact no overall improvement in output in the early years of the war.

The failure to raise domestic production was not a matter of immediate concern for shipping losses remained low for the first two years of hostilities. While some vessels were requisitioned and others diverted to carry troops and war supplies enough remained so that food imports were little affected. By 1916 this situation was beginning to change and with the onset of Germany's unrestricted submarine warfare campaign in February 1917 shipping losses rose dramatically.

Shipping Losses During World War I (gross tonnage)

Year	British Empire	World
1914	252,738	-
1915	885,471	1,312,216
1916	1,231,867	2,305,569
1917	3,660,054	6,078,125
1918	1,632,228	2,528,082

[1]

The first official reaction to the increased level of sinkings came in April 1916 when the use of cereals and sugar for the brewing of beer was greatly restricted. This was followed in October 1916 by a Royal Commission on Wheat Supplies (similar to that on sugar) and a month later the Board of Trade was authorized to:-

> "......introduce a complete system of food control, by regulating the importation, production, distribution, prices and quality of all kinds of food or articles necessary for the production of food". [2]

The appointment of a Food Controller was then followed, in January 1917, by the establishment of a Food Production Department. This, in turn, set up War Agricultural Committees in each county and these delegated their powers to sixty-one executive groups - each with specialized sub-committees - and down to district levels. Their aim was, of course, to encourage the farmers to produce the greatest possible quantities of food from their land. This inevitably meant that there would need to be a move away from the production of livestock and towards the cultivation of wheat and potatoes which supply higher yields per acre. Incentives were provided by the Corn Production Act of 1917 which guaranteed an agreed return to the grower. This was fixed so that the consumer paid a fair-price but also provided a reasonable profit for the producers in order to give a motive for higher output. As it was difficult to achieve both of these objectives simultaneously this policy eventually obliged the Government to directly subsidize the cost of bread

The Impact of War

Potential output was not only dependant upon the weather, goodwill of the grower or on government regulations. There were many difficulties which lay in the path of increased production of which the most important concerned the workforce. In 1914 this had included 800,000 men but by January 1917 this figure had been reduced to 562,000. The pressing need for food resulted in many ploughmen being given two month's leave from the Army. However the real solution to the labour shortage came from the recruitment of Prisoners of War, Public School boys, Boy Scouts and an increased employment of women who were normally resident in villages and rural areas. In addition the Women's Land Army was formed in 1917 and by the end of the war its 16,000 members were actively engaged in agriculture. Taken together these measures provided a basis for the industry to expand but many other problems remained to be solved. These included shortages of tractors, horses, fertilizers and seed potatoes and considerable ingenuity was necessary to overcome these obstacles to higher output. The extent to which they were surmounted can best be judged by the fact that 40% more grain was produced in 1918 compared with 1916 and that the total area under cultivation in the United Kingdom rose by 1.7m acres during the same period.

When this acreage is examined in terms of actual production the specific output of individual crops can be analysed in more detail. The figures for vegetables show a massive rise for potatoes with turnips, swedes and mangolds remaining virtually static. However, beans recorded a small decline with cabbages, peas and, especially hops falling to much lower levels than in 1909-1913. The statistics for fruit are only provided in general terms but the variation in annual amounts would appear to fall within the range of normal harvests and quantities were largely unchanged.

Agricultural Production of Selected Items (000 tons)

	1909-13	1914	1915	1916	1917	1918
Wheat	1,598	1,706	1,961	1,559	1,634	2,428
Beans (000 qrs.)	1,038	1,113	919	889	466	922
Peas (000 qrs.)	604	373	300	261	277	439
Potatoes	3,604	4,031	3,830	3,036	4,451	5,360
Turnips & Swedes	21,524	19,762	19,340	18,882	20,217	17,532
Mangolds	8,578	7,961	7,890	7,382	8,535	8,280
Cabbages	918	789	759	716	587	589
Fruit	365	405	365	330	400	270 [3]

From Orchard to Market

It has been estimated that the increase in British domestic output after 1916 resulted in the saving of 2.6m tons of shipping in 1918. Further savings of cargo-space were also made through the expansion of allotment schemes which saw individual plots rise to over 1.2m by the time the war ended for it is thought that they contributed an extra 800,000 tons of food in England and Wales during 1918. The policy laid down by the Food Controller which ensured that production was concentrated upon grain and potatoes was an additional factor of major significance for this resulted in the provision of substantially more calories per acre than meat or milk could have provided. In general terms:-

> "......It was calculated that 100 acres would maintain only 9 persons if used as meat producing pasture, and 41 if used as milk producing pasture; but they would maintain 172 persons if planted with oats, 208 if planted with wheat and 418 with potatoes". [4]

As a consequence of all these measures local farmers and growers were able to supply 47% of the (reduced) national diet in 1918 compared with only 41% in the pre-war era. [5]

Another way in which the limited supplies of wheat were made to go further was by the inclusion of the more plentiful potato:-

> *"BREAD AND POTATOES*
> *It is said that the use of potatoes in bread, at present encouraged by the Ministry of Food, will probably be enforced as soon as the necessary machinery for making potato flour on a large scale is available........*
>
> *The pity of it is that using potatoes in bread making was ever discouraged or prohibited. A quarter of a century or so ago there was no doubt many growers as well as the writer supplied bakers with potatoes which were used in the making of bread.*
> *The use of potatoes in bread-making is simply getting back to the old-fashioned way of making it, when it was far more palatable, digestible, and sustaining than the stuff we are getting today".* [6]

As a result of these sustained efforts to raise food production in Britain and of the changes in the pattern of consumption the need for imports was certainly reduced but considerable quantities were still essential. The limited capacity of the merchant fleet, which continued to shrink until mid-1918, meant that there was never sufficient tonnage to meet more that the most basic demands. Thus the requirements of the war-machine had always to be carefully balanced against

The Impact of War

the minimum quantities necessary to feed the population and as it was estimated that every 5,000 tons of civilian cargo meant 1,000 fewer American troops on the battlefield it will be appreciated that all food shipments were strictly limited.[7]

Two policies were therefore adopted to reduce the shipping needed for food cargoes to an absolute minimum. The first of these, as in the case of domestic production, was to see shipments concentrated upon those foods which would offer the best returns in terms of nutrition. The second was to ensure that whenever possible the nearest sources of supply were utilized to limit route-miles to their smallest levels. As a result of these twin considerations cereals and meat were imported at above their pre-war quantities and were mainly acquired in the United States and Canada. On the other hand most other food shipments declined by varying amounts with both vegetable and fruit cargoes being much less than in 1914. This may not be immediately apparent in financial terms as, due to a degree of inflation, the value of both vegetable and fruit imports actually rose. However when the quantities are examined it will be seen that substantial reductions did take place:-

Annual Imports of Fresh Vegetables into the United Kingdom

	1914	1915	1916	1917	1918
Onions (Bushels)	7,513	7,477	6,843	4,748	4,342
Potatoes (cwt.)	3,332	2,170	1,788	1,598	1,015
Tomatoes (cwt.)	1,576	1,394	1,649	519	516
Unenumerated (£)	475	318	233	177	96
Total value of all items (£)	5,022	4,821	5,760	5,500	7,002

[8]

In the case of vegetables it was not always possible for them to be obtained from the nearest sources. Thus in 1914 Spain and the Netherlands were the largest suppliers of onions with Egypt also shipping substantial quantities. Wartime conditions limited access to neutral Holland and so it was Spain and Egypt which provided virtually all of the reduced number of cargoes which were authorized. In the pre-war era imports of potatoes mainly originated in the Channel Islands, France and the Canaries but after the outbreak of hostilities shipments from both France and the Canary Islands gradually came to an end. Attempts to secure alternative supplies were only partly successful and had been terminated by 1918 so that Jersey and Guernsey became the sole providers of potatoes which then amounted to less than a third of those in 1914. Tomato imports followed a

From Orchard to Market

similar pattern with the Canary and Channel Islands normally supplying the bulk of cargoes. By 1917, however, tomatoes from the Canaries had been phased-out and Guernsey and Jersey were the only remaining sources of what proved to be small shipments on par with those of potatoes.

The total annual values of fresh fruits imported into the UK rose from a total of £10.6m in 1914 to £14.9m in 1918. However these figures are distorted by inflation and a truer picture is obtained from an analysis of the actual cargoes which were landed at British ports. These show that while nearly 12m cwt arrived in 1914 less than 5m cwt were received in 1918

Total Imports of Fresh Fruit into the UK (m.cwt)

	1914	1915	1916	1917	1918
Apples:	2.929	3.343	2.658	0.889	0.410
Apricots & Peaches:	0.030	0.009	0.010	0.002	-
Cherries:	0.167	0.027	0.014	-	-
Currants:	0.144	0.117	0.089	0.048	-
Gooseberries:	0.023	0.004	-	-	-
Grapes:	0.650	0.554	0.798	0.205	0.415
Lemons & Limes	0.830	0.775	0.691	0.495	0.792
Oranges:	5.108	6.006	5.875	2.818	2.640
Pears:	0.409	0.210	0.160	0.059	0.002
Plums:	0.207	0.137	0.061	0.047	-
Strawberries:	0.030	0.012	0.001	-	-
Bananas (m bunches)	9.007	8.143	6.095	2.230	0.729
Total: Million cwt	11.975	12.968	11.818	5.269	4.835

9

From the above table it is clear that fruit followed the general pattern of food and vegetable imports. Thus quantities were maintained at high levels until 1916 but then, as the sinking of merchant vessels increased, came a very rapid reduction in the quantities of almost all items. This is very apparent from the statistics for the "big 3" - oranges, apples and bananas - although grapes and other citrus fruits continued to arrive in reasonable amounts. Spain was the traditional supplier of oranges to the British market and this was sustained throughout the war even though cargoes declined to less than 50% of their pre-war average. However even this reduction was small when compared to that of the other two, main, fruit imports.

The Impact of War

By the outbreak of war the banana was well established in the UK with Messrs Elders and Fyffes being responsible for more than 90% of the business. In 1914 121,700 tons (approximately 9m bunches) were landed with Costa Rica, the Canaries, Colombia and Jamaica providing almost all of these shipments. Thereafter quantities fell steadily, especially after 1916 and in 1918 less than 10,000 tons were imported.

There were two explanations for this enormous decline. In the first place five of Elders and Fyffes vessels were immediately requisitioned by the Admiralty and a further ten were to be taken over at later dates. In addition the Company suffered the loss of another ship even before the war was officially declared:-

> *"Elders and Fyffes announce that their steamer 'Nicoya,' of which the firm had been without news for several days, has been detained in Hamburg. The crew managed to make good their way to Copenhagen. On board was a cargo of 63,000 bunches of bananas destined for Hull which has now been commandeered as food for the German troops."*
> [10]

This meant that only two ships of the original fleet were left to continue the trade. A further four vessels were completed during the war but losses by enemy submarines ensured that sufficient tonnage was never available to maintain a regular service.

In these circumstances it would have been helpful, and in line with Government policy, if it had been possible to develop the existing trade with the Canary Islands from where the voyage times were relatively small. Unfortunately this route became so dangerous that it had to be suspended in December 1916. As a result those bananas which were imported needed to be carried over the much longer distances from the Caribbean and this, together with the shortage of ships, ensured that the Company was never able to maintain adequate supplies in the later years of the war.

Until 1914 apples had been largely provided by North America and Australia with smaller quantities originating in Portugal, the Netherlands and France. The wartime policy of utilizing the nearest sources whenever possible then saw a great decline in American cargoes and an end to those from Australia. At the same time shipments from France expanded substantially but overall total apple imports amounted to only 15% of the pre-war average in 1918. To some extent this was because the apple, unlike the orange and banana, could be produced in the UK and domestic growers might be expected to fill at least some of the deficit. This was an opportunity which appears to have been taken in 1917 but was unfortunately prevented by bad weather in 1918. As a result of the anticipated shortage the Government found it necessary to introduce regulations to control the sale of

From Orchard to Market

both apples and pears:-

> "ORDER CONTROLLING PRICE OF APPLES AND PEARS
> An Order controlling the price of apples, and perry pears has been issued by the Food Controller. This came into force on Tuesday, September 24th, 1918, except that apples and pears actually sold and delivered by the grower before that day might be sold without restrictions up to Friday, the 27th inst. By this Order the Small Apple (Temporary Prices) Order, 1918 is cancelled. The Order does not affect Cox's Orange Pippins which will not pass through a 2in. diameter ring, or apples of the other varieties named in Part 1 to the order which will not pass through a 2in. diameter ring, provided that these apples are separated out by the grower and sold and invoiced wholesale under their proper names and ticketed and sold retail under their proper names.
>
> The perry pear Blakeney Red is also excluded from the Order. All apples which will pass through a 2in ring (except apples of the varieties named in Schedule 1, Parts 1 and 2) are designated 'jam apples', and may not be sold except to manufacturers of jam pulp or cider. A grower of more than 5 cwt. of apples or perry pears can only sell to a recognised fruit salesman, or to a jam manufacturer or pulp manufacturer licensed under the Soft Fruit (Sales) Order, 1918, or to a cider manufacturer licensed to purchase fruit for cider making. The maximum prices at which apples and perry pears may be sold by the grower are set out in the second column of the second schedule. To these prices may be added the railway carriage to the buyer's premises, 40s. per ton for the use of pecks, strikes, half-sieves, and bushels, 10s. per ton for the use of bags, and 25s. per ton for other packages. The salesman's commission or profit is fixed at 20s. per ton of small apples and perry pears and 40s. per ton of other varieties controlled by the Order. Market tolls and porterage may also be added when these charges have been actually paid". [11]

The *Journal* played a full role during the war in spite of the inevitable shortages of labour and scarcity of newsprint. It duly published all Government regulations which affected the industry and was very active in promoting domestic production.

The Editor was always prepared to support unpopular measures when they were thought to be in the national interest but, on the other hand, was very critical of bureaucracy and inefficiency wherever it was to be found. This may be seen by

The Impact of War

reference to the Apple Order which was regarded by him, and many others, as a terrible indictment of state interference:-

> "THE APPLE ORDER
> Whatever food control may have done by way of helping the public to get through a tight period is beyond our province to discuss, but so far as State interference with fruit and vegetables is concerned it has certainly imposed upon traders one difficulty after another. From potatoes to onions, from onions to soft fruit, then to blackberries, round to potatoes again, and now, to render 'confusion worse confounded,' we have the Apple Order." [12]

In the pre-war era the service and rates of the railway companies were a constant bone of contention. There can be little doubt that the large scale and bureaucratic nature of some of the larger firms meant that they frequently operated without too much attention to many of their smaller customers and this created great difficulties were perishable items were involved. These criticisms were repeated by the Editor throughout the war years although it may be thought that he took insufficient notice of the external factors which lay behind the Government's decisions:-

> "DANGEROUS AND DAMAGING DELAYS: ARE THEY NECESSARY?
> Since the outbreak of the war and the commandeering of the railways by the Government great inconvenience and loss have been incurred by growers and salesmen in the course of their business. Most people will say that loss and inconvenience at such times of national stress ought to be endured without murmur, and we agree, provided that such are unavoidable in the general welfare. To some extent, at least, we think the action of the railway officials and the dock companies might be modified in connection with the transport of perishable supplies. We are prompted to touch upon the subject because the situation, instead of improving, shows signs of getting worse, and when the time comes for the transport of Kitchener's Army, now in training, across the Channel, which is expected to take place in early spring, just when the fruit trade ought to be getting busy, matters will indeed be serious unless the rights of the traders and the interests of the general community receive better recognition at the hands of the transport companies then present indications lead us to expect. An equally bad, or worse, state of affairs exists at the docks, where ships remain for days without getting their cargoes discharged. Here, unless we greatly mistake, the labour unions have some bearing on the situation. If so, it is surely up to the Board of Trade authorities to take such steps as may be necessary to

> *uphold the rights of those willing to make good any shortage of labour, the rights of traders and the rights of the public to access to necessary supplies."* [13]

This opinion, expressed at near the beginning of hostilities, can be partly justified by the contemporary belief that the country would be best served by a policy of business as usual. However reasonable this viewpoint may have seemed at the time it was soon to be overtaken by the developments which led to the concept of a total war.

The Editor of the *Journal* may well have been justified in pointing-out the deficiencies of the railways for it was certain that both the fruit trade and the war effort would benefit from a more efficient transport system. However his comments on the possible ending of all fruit imports, made in August 1917, can be regarded as somewhat partial. These indicate that even at this acute stage of the war Harvey Hope-Mason still felt an over-riding obligation to protect the fruit distribution system and its overseas suppliers. However it could be claimed that he was also arguing for the public good as he genuinely believed in the health-giving aspects of fruit eating:-

> "THREATENED PROHIBITION OF OVERSEAS FRUIT
> *It is incumbent on all engaged in the fruit trade to look well ahead, and so it is that to-day, when for the first time for many months past salesmen and retailers alike might be happy in the immediate prospect of ample supplies of home-grown fruit supplemented with some bananas, their joy is tempered with doubts and anxiety regarding the future. Owing to a variety of causes which need not be enumerated here, supplies of English fruits have never been anything like up to the maximum limit of production, and large quantities of overseas fruits, hardy fruits as well as tropical and semi-tropical products, have been needed to keep the public adequately supplied. It is no exaggeration to say that but for these substantial imports the retail fruiterer would long since, like Othello, have found his occupation gone, and the market salesman hard set to tide over the long period intervening the sale of the last English-grown apple and the return of the soft fruit season.*
>
> *It is, therefore, with the utmost concern the trade has recently heard ugly rumours regarding the intention of the authorities to extend the restrictions which have been in force for some time past, under which limited quantities only of overseas fruit have been allowed to be imported, and to totally prohibit the importations of apples and other fruits from abroad. Now, although the prospects for English fruits*

The Impact of War

> *this season are distinctly good it so happens that the later and best-keeping varieties of apples are likely to be short, and if the authorities carry out the threatened embargo upon overseas fruits we are face to face with an apple famine for the six months from December to June. A very serious matter for the public, and as we have stated, nothing short of disaster for those whose living consists in the useful work of distributing this most healthful of foods. Nor is it our own people alone who stand to suffer. Our kith and kin in Australia, Tasmania, New Zealand, Ontario, British Columbia and Nova Scotia all stand to suffer material loss should their supplies be shut out of this market. By the irony of fate it happens that abundant crops are everywhere reported from Greater Britain across the seas. Considerably over a million barrels, we hear, are estimated to be ready for shipment from Nova Scotia in September! British Columbia reckons its crop to be fully 25 per cent. above last year's, whilst our good friends, and now Allies, in the U.S.A. would be ready to send over big quantities of their choice apples from the Yakima Valley......".* [14]

Although the policy of a total ban on all fruit imports was never introduced the limitations imposed by the shortage of shipping and the concentration upon other items of food did result in a considerable decline in landings. Thus in the last year of the war only oranges, other citrus, grapes and dates arrived in any reasonable quantities as Britain struggled to survive the crippling and cumulative effects of Germany's submarine campaign.

The Food Controller was a key figure in these events for under his guidance 85% of all the food eaten by British civilians came to be purchased and supplied via the Ministry of Food. This included imported apples, dried fruit and oranges and, in 1918, home-produced potatoes. The only significant omissions which then remained were fresh fish and milk and most locally-grown fresh fruits and vegetables. Ultimately 94% of all food items were subject to fixed maximum prices but even this proved to be insufficient to control the shortages which had emerged by the end of 1917. By then food stocks were down to emergency levels and in January 1918 it became necessary to ration sugar. This was quickly to be followed by meat, butter, margarine, jam, tea and finally bacon.

In effect the war period saw a reduction in the consumption of butter, meat and sugar of approximately 40% while fresh milk supplies fell by about a quarter. This was partly offset by a growth in the eating of bacon, ham, lard, margarine and, especially, of bread and potatoes. The two latter items were never rationed and came to form the most important times in the national diet. This can be seen very clearly from the fact that weekly consumption of potatoes rose from

From Orchard to Market

on average 3.67 pounds per head in the pre-war years to 5.26 pounds per head by 1918. As most of these potatoes were produced in the UK and as more wheat was grown in Britain during 1918 than in 1914 it will be appreciated that domestic agriculture and horticulture played a vital role in preventing the country from being starved into submission.

Much praise has already been given to British producers for expanding their output in spite of fewer or poorer imputs of labour, fertilizers, seed, machinery, power and transport. However little credit has so far been given to the importers, distributors, wholesalers and retailers who did their best - also with denuded resources - to satisfy the conflicting demands for their increasingly limited products. At first those involved in the fruit and vegetable trades were merely asked to continue with their traditional businesses and to contribute to worthy causes of which the Covent Garden Committee of the Charing Cross Hospital Fund was an obvious example:-

> "PRO PATRIA
> *At this time, when everybody throughout the land is burning with zeal to do what he or she can in support of Mother England and her allies, organisation is an all-important factor. It is most desirous that there should be no wasted effort, no overlapping, and as little cost in the way of administration as possible. Those connected with Covent Garden, and that means directly or indirectly everybody engaged in the fruit, flower and vegetable industry, have an admirably managed organisation at their hand. We allude, of course, to the Covent Garden Committee of the Charing Cross Hospital Fund. Owing to the proximity of this hospital to the terminal station, it is almost certain that many gallant fellows who have suffered in their country's cause will be brought there for treatment. Thanks to the spirited action of two ladies bearing names respected throughout the length and breadth of the trade, Mrs. Monro and Mrs. Medlock respectively, opportunity is given for women workers to render their services in full knowledge that what they do will be certain of use. With long active experience in municipal work, Mrs. Monro brings a practical mind to bear on the situation, and the first move on the part of these ladies has been to interview the Matron and Council of the Hospital to learn exactly what is wanted in the way of garments. The course is thus made easy for any woman worker to lend a hand in no matter how humble a capacity. Full particulars can be obtained by addressing a card to Mrs. Monro, 99 Haverstock Hill, N.W. or to Mrs. Medlock, 110 Haverstock Hill, N.W.. Money, of course, is needed, and it is with pleasure we record that the employers and the employés of Convent Garden Market and its environs, as is ever their wont in a good cause, are taking up the matter with full-hearted vigour. The following is the first list of donations and subscriptions received:-*

The Impact of War

W. Medlock & Son (special donation), £5 5s.
Mr. Geo. Monro (special donation), £5 5s.
Messrs. Elders & Fyffes, Ltd., £5 5s.
Mr John Sullivan, £5
Messrs Dan Wuille & Co., £2 2s.
Messrs. Watkins & Simson, £2. 2s.
Mr. T. J. Poupart (annual donation), £2 2s.
Messrs. E. A. O'Kelly & Co., £2 2s.
Messrs. Parsons & Co., (annual donation), £2 2s.
Mr. J. Rouse, £2 2s.
Mr. C. H. Deakin, £2 2s.
Mr. A. Saltwell, Upminster, £1 1s.
Messrs. Butler, McCulloch & Co., £1 1s.
Anon (per Mr. H. Baker), £1 1s.
Mr. J. Sweet, £1 1s.
Messrs. Lowe & Shawyer, Ltd., £1 1s.
Messrs. Thomas Bros., (annual donation), £1 1s.
Mr. J. B. Wright, (annual donation), £1 1s.
Messrs. Thos. Rochford & Sons, Lts., £1 1s.
Mr. Geo. Monro, Junr. (annual donation), £1 1s.
Mr. Robert Robinson, (annual donation), £1 1s.
Mr. R. Levy, 10s. 6d.
Mr. Mark Woolf, 10s. 6d.
Mr. Geo. Walker, 10s. 6d.
Mr. C. Ullmann, (annual donation), 10s. 6d.
Mr. J. Sawbridge, 5s.
Total, £48 6s.
15

Almost immediately, however, a more significant demand was to be made upon the trade as reservists were called to the colours and as civilian workers were asked to volunteer for active service. This had a rapid impact on the labour market as all volunteers were accepted without reference to their existing occupations. Thus less than three weeks after the outbreak of war the Journal was already commenting on the difficulties this was creating for some aspects of the fruit and vegetable business:-

> "THE CALL OF WAR
> *We hear of several instances of which considerable loss and inconvenience is being occasioned to nurserymen through numbers of their men being called up, or enlisting to join the fighting forces. Such losses and inconvenience are inseparable in times of national*

From Orchard to Market

crisis, and are invariably borne without a murmur of complaint. Our neighbours and allies are, however, in a much worse plight, to judge by the experiences of the great French house of Vilmorin, who have had 400 of their staff of 700 called up for action at the front. We wish them and all others a safe and speedy return to their normal, peaceful occupations". [16]

The conflicting demands for more and more men for the Army and the necessity to retain skilled personnel in key industries was well illustrated by the experience of agriculture and horticulture. In the early years of the war, when food production was not seen as a particularly high priority, a quarter of the work force left to join the armed services or to find better paid employment in other occupations. Although regulations to control these movements were gradually introduced it was not until November, 1915, that a comprehensive system was put into place. By then much of the exodus from the countryside had already occurred so when it became essential to boost domestic output other forms of labour had to be arranged. These were mainly women, prisoners of war and children but some specialists were released from the Army on working leave for limited periods.

It should be understood, of course, that the needs of the Army were always paramount. Thus not only were these men to be recalled when necessary but others, from reserved occupations, were called-up for the first time when the military situation made it essential. Many arbitrary decisions were therefore made - frequently at short notice - which seriously affected the running of efficient businesses and it became almost impossible to plan for the future.

Allied to the shortage of labour was the question of pay. The immediate effect of the war was to mop-up much of the existing unemployment and wages quickly began to rise. However the onset of inflation meant that in real terms, wages were to decline over the war years even though earnings (which included overtime, night-work, bonuses and piece-rates) did rise sufficiently to keep pace with the cost of living. In addition the growth of full employment enabled many workers to enjoy regular wages for the first time and so did much to head off any potential industrial unrest.

This was fortunate for the fruit and vegetable trade had been seriously affected by industrial disputes in the pre-war era. This was because in addition to internal, usually local, difficulties in individual markets and companies every dockside or transport stoppage had a major impact on perishable commodities. These problems may have continued but for an agreement reached by the Government with the trade unions in March, 1915. In return for an assurance that this would not prejudice their post-war position and other concessions there were to be

The Impact of War

few official strikes but after May, 1917, many stoppages were organized by the emerging shop stewards' movement. These were principally in the engineering sectors but a railway strike in September, 1918 was an unwelcome addition to the problems of the trade:-

> *"The railway strike has had a very bad effect on trade since Tuesday last, as from this centre produce is despatched to all parts of the country. More particularly is this so just now with the increased populations on war work in various towns. It is out of our province to argue the why or the wherefore of the case, but a more selfish or unreasonable strike we cannot imagine, apart from the loss in perishable food entailed".* [17]

The extent to which labour problems together with shortages of fertilizers and seeds, were overcome can best be judged by the reports published in the *Journal* each week on The Week's Market. These, of course, are also a very useful guide to the availability of imported fruits and vegetables and their prices!

> *"MARKET NOTES*
> *Covent Garden*
>
> *Thursday, August 19th (1915)*
>
> *Trade is not what it would be under normal conditions, but those who grow and handle choice fruits such as peaches, nectarines, melons, etc., are feeling the want of trade more than those who grow and market the usual run of produce, such as apples, pears, plums, etc. The trade as a whole, however, may congratulate itself upon trade being better than at this period last year, when owing to the outbreaks of war many people lost their heads, to use a common expression, money became scarce, and those of a panicky nature lost their appetite.*
>
> *A twelvemonth of war, however, has altered the state of things generally. The growers and salesmen of special items, and also the high-class fruiterers, have had the worst time for the simple reason that we have very few foreign visitors at the large hotels, in addition to which all social functions, garden parties, dinner parties, and at-homes have been tabooed, which were the backbone of the high-class fruit trade. It was also possible for some of the barrow men in the City to obtain fourpence each for peaches, but these men will tell you now that their customers who bought peaches now purchase plums at fourpence a pound.*

From Orchard to Market

Purveyors of fruit and vegetables to middle and working classes, however, have not been so badly hit. Some thousands of the latter are earning double and treble the wages they were getting previous to the outbreak of war, and as they are a class who believe in well stoking the inner man, so that the bodily strength may be equal to that required of it in its laborious work, the sale for the ordinary run of fruit and vegetables has therefore been greater than in some years of peace. Apart from this, we must not forget the absence of foreign competition to a considerable extent, whereby better clearances have been effected of home-grown produce. We have only to mention tomatoes, which throughout the season have been an excellent trade at very good prices, and continue to sell and clear well. In fact, most wholesale houses in Covent Garden Market, where thousands of packages exchange hands in a few hours daily, are cleared by mid-day, and can only supply from next morning's consignments; that is how we find it on our round of the market.

With some other items, perhaps, trade is not so satisfactory. Take apples for instance; trade is bad in this item on account of the inferior quality of the majority of samples arriving; in fact, we never remember during our 20 years' round of the markets seeing such a scrubby lot of Worcesters, Beauty of Bath, and Quarrendens as are on the market at the present time; half the stuff is unsaleable, not fit to be fed to pigs. But any real good clean samples are making money, and growers having fruit answering the latter description will do well to market it". [18]

From the above report it is clear that the war was having a mixed effect on supplies after a year of hostilities and that there were many gains as well as losses to the business. By 1917 the situation had worsened but even then there were some welcome bright spots which provided some relief:-

"MARKET NOTES
Covent Garden

July 19th (1917)

Bananas - Owing to the arrival of two boats the trade have been able again to handle this popular fruit, which in spite of arriving in the middle of the soft fruit season have been in great demand and sold well at about double the usual prices. The last shipment,it may be mentioned, consisted of Jamaica fruit, this being the first consignment

The Impact of War

since the great hurricane of 1916. The trade generally are well pleased with the condition and size of the fruit; one salesman termed them Goliaths. A few red-skinned fruit were also included in the shipments.

Owing to the absence of some and the very limited supplies of other foreign soft fruits, the home-grown supplies are selling well including cherries, red and black currants, ripe gooseberries and raspberries. There are also a few strawberries still about the market, which meet with a special trade at good prices. In ordinary times we have at this period much larger supplies of French and Dutch produce, and also larger quantities of oranges, pines, Australian and Tasmanian apples; special lines in the way of granadillas, loquats, mangoes, and other items, thus giving who could afford it a much wider choice. None of these items being on the market gives the grower a chance of marketing selected and well-graded samples of home-grown fruit, which a number of growers are doing, for choice dessert fruit and some very fine samples of red currants, ripe gooseberries and raspberries are to be seen in high-class shops in punnets, ticketed at one shilling per lb. and upwards". [19]

Twelve months later the trade was in a poor state. In the first place this had been caused by the commandeering of the soft fruit crop for jam making:-

"MARKET NOTES
Covent Garden

June 20th (1918)

The talk of the market is, of course, the commandeering of the soft fruit crops, more especially strawberries, at the present time, when fruiterers and others were expecting to make up for the deficiency of the foreign supplies, which the fruiterers have been deprived of since our own crops finished last autumn with the exception of apples. Oranges, it is true, have been on the market throughout the winter months, but in greatly diminished quantities, and realising such high prices that only the high-class stores, retailers, and restaurants could afford to sell and the rich or well-to-do afford to buy. Medium class traders, having with difficulty tided over the winter and spring months of the year, are now debarred from selling the home fruit crops just as the season is commencing. It would be interesting to know who are the advisers to the Ministry of Food, and how many have a practical knowledge of fruit-growing or the fruit trade? An Advisory Committee was

From Orchard to Market

appointed some time ago, consisting of some of the most experienced and reliable members in each branch of the industry, with a view to their being consulted upon matters in connection with the trade. It would be also interesting to know if this Advisory Committee were consulted before the Order commandeering the soft fruit was issued?

Before the war thousands of tons of fruit pulp for jam-making were imported into the country from Holland, our Colonies and America, and although we are well acquainted with the difficulties of transport, one would have thought some arrangements could be made for a supply from one of the sources named, to be used with the second quality of home-grown fruit generally bought for jam-making, without commandeering all the dessert fruit of home growers for this purpose. Spain having done so well over oranges is now forwarding orange and apricot pulp, the only neutral country, we believe, from which pulp is arriving, the same being consigned to a large firm of jam boilers.

The result of the Order has been to give Covent Garden the appearance of a deserted market at a period when it should present a busy scene, the market being bare of one of the most popular fruits of the season. In other places, viz., Portsmouth, Bournemouth, etc. Strawberries, it is stated, were being sold in the shops after the issue of the Order, which, to say the least, was unfair to the London trade and the public.

As regards other fruit, grapes, melons, peaches, nectarines, and figs are a good trade, the effect of the Order being to create a better demand." [20]

The second major factor which inhibited trade was the failure of the English fruit harvest which was compounded by the inability to import alternative supplies from overseas:-

"MARKET NOTES
Covent Garden
July 25th (1918)

The far-reaching effects of the failure of the English fruit crops is now being felt by the growers, pickers, wholesale salesmen, retailers and public alike, and 1918 is likely to stand out for some time, as one of the most unprofitable seasons within recollection. Hothouse fruit is being forwarded to make up the deficiency to some extent, but can only be purchased by the few. Many people who find employment during the

The Impact of War

summer months in fruit picking are this year without their customary work, but many have found employment of a different nature, and are probably earning a good deal more money than they would be picking fruit, but not in such healthy surroundings. In ordinary times hundreds of tons of plums, pears, apples, etc., would be coming across the seas to fill the gap, but there is no such luck as this at present, although we believe very great efforts are again being made to modify the embargo placed upon foreign fruit. Partaking of fruit has become such a habit with the people and is conducive to the health of the nation, and unless something is done to make up for the deficiency illness and epidemics are likely to follow.

For comparison to this year's failure as regards the fruit crop in this country we must go back fifteen years, to 1903. But in that year our shortage was made up by immense shipments from the Continent. The receipt of currants, cherries, plums, etc., were enormous. Over 80,000 packages of French fruit being out on our markets in one week. More than 60,000 came from Germany, and some 25,000 bushels of apples reached us in the same period from America, Spain and Russia. 45,000 packages of bilberries arrived from Germany and Holland. In six days 16 steamers brought 124,000 packages from Spain, consisting of grapes, melons, tomatoes, pears and plums, and over one million packages, chiefly fruit, were exported to England from Guernsey during the first eight months of the year.

With the imports almost entirely cut off and the failure of our own crops the study of these figures give some idea of the state of affairs in the fruit trade at the present time, which we do not think even the Minister of Food, or some of his staff realise, for the simple reason that many of them, have had no experience of the trade". [21]

The final straw to many traders at this difficult time was the consequences of the Apple Order reported in the *Journal* on the 28 September 1918:-

"MARKET NOTES
Covent Garden

Apples - 'Confusion worse confounded' sums up the situation in this article. In another part of the journal we give the new Order in extenso as issued by the Ministry of Food. The daily Press have given excerpts and different interpretations, with the result that grower, salesman, or retailer, to use a Chevalierism, 'Dunno where 'e are'. That a further

From Orchard to Market

Order would be issued was expected, but it was also expected that the trade would receive due notice. This, however, does not appear to have been given, and even the Advisory Committee do not appear to have had notice of the Order. Members of the trade desirous of obtaining complete copies applied to the Ministry of Food, but they could not be supplied, while some of the officials were ignorant of the issue of the Order. The result has been stagnation of trade all round in this particular article. On the other hand, it is rumoured that the Order has been rescinded, and where there is any sale the fruit is being sold at the previous market prices. Surely the least that could be done in issuing direct or through the trade papers, allowing a reasonable time before the Orders come into operation, so that the information comes directly under the notice of those chiefly concerned".

Throughout the conflict the flower business continued albeit on a much reduced scale. In the later stages of the war the trade was almost entirely dependent upon home-produced items and supplies for Christmas, 1917, were distinctly thin! However they still played an important role in maintaining civilian morale at a time when other traditional, seasonal, fruits and vegetables were very limited indeed:-

"The Flower Trade. - In our last issue we gave some forecast of the Christmas flower trade, and here there is very little to add. The situation remains the same. Chrysanthemums will be the main feature. Carnations and roses will be very short and there will be very little, if any, French flowers on the market. Lilies are on the short side. What flowers there are it would appear the London markets are getting, as quite a large number of country orders are going out at this week-end. Foliage is a very good trade both in holly and mistletoe, and although a Government order has been issued to stop railway consignments of these emblems of the festive season, they were just too late again, as large quantities had already arrived on the market. But the serious part of the whole business is that while the railways have been dealing with holly, etc., there has been the greatest difficulty in getting empty baskets conveyed, with the result that there is a shortage of empties on the market, thus preventing produce, otherwise food, from being conveyed to various parts of the country where it is required. Apart from which for the London markets a large quantity arrives by road, while country towns get their supplies locally. One of the daily papers, of course, came out with the scare heading, 'NO HOLLY!' but, of course, no one takes the daily papers' information on the fruit trade seriously.

The Impact of War

The holly is well berried, and there is some very pretty bunches of English-grown mistletoe on the market; slender branches, well-berried, and the boughs of medium-size, much prettier than some of the coarse stuff we get from France. There is a fairly good trade in foliage, and Golden Euonymus are a bright spot in the market.

Covent Garden Foreign Auction Market.
December 19th (1917)

There has been but little alteration in our market, and owing to the short and irregular supply prices in general have been maintained. Unfortunately the boats which should have been here with Xmas supplies have either not yet arrived or have arrived in other ports than London, and at such time that, with the want of railway facilities, the bulk will not reach the London market for the Xmas sales.

Salads are in very small quantities. Of walnuts there are only the dried on the market (Cornes). Fewer French apples have reached London. Oranges are in irregular quantities, and, contrary to expectation, no mandarines have yet come to hand. The value of onions is slightly lower, and the prices of grapes are irregular and according to quality and condition.

Prices:- Lettuce, 1s. Endive, 2s. Sprue, 1s. 3d. Paris Green, 6s. Walnuts (Cornes), 90s. per cwt. French apples : Red, 18s.; Russets, 29s. to 30s. per case. Dates, 1s. 3d. per carton. Grapes, 40s. to 60s., according to quality. Oranges, 140s. to 200s. per case. Lemons, 30s. to 70s. per box. Onions, 32s. to 35s. per case". [22]

In spite of all these difficulties the Great War was brought to a successful conclusion in November, 1918, and within a week the *Journal* was already looking to the future. In acknowledging the nation's debt to British producers during the previous four years the Editor now expressed the need to place the industry on a really sound basis so that it could compete more effectively. At the same time he made it clear that in his view it would be unwise to seek too high a degree of self-sufficiency in peace time:-

"FORWARD HORTICULTURE

A great deal has been said and written during the war period about the need for growing vastly more foodstuffs than in the past, so that we may be much more self-sustaining than since we adopted free imports

From Orchard to Market

as the national policy. Unfortunately, the production of foodstuffs cannot be determined by political chatter or academic theories. The essentials are soil, climate, labour, and last, but certainly not least, sunshine. Bonaparte is said to have regarded General Winter as the most redoubtable of his adversaries. In like manner General Sol is the most potent and, likewise, the most unreliable of all the commanding forces in the service of British farmers." [23]

6
Problems of the 'Twenties'

The ending of hostilities did little to relieve the chronic shortages of virtually all types of food within Britain and Christmas 1918 was an affair of some austerity for most of the population. However home-produced holly and mistletoe were available and the special service for the delivery of cut flowers from France had recommenced albeit on a small scale. The chief difficulty which faced the suppliers of these, and other items, was one of transport for the military and naval authorities were attempting to grant leave to large numbers of their personnel while the process of demobilization was also beginning to make heavy demands on already over-stretched rail and shipping facilities. The trade was further handicapped by the continuation of government regulations although some controls on apples and potatoes had by then been lifted. In addition the plentiful supply of money ensured that virtually every thing that reached the markets could be sold without difficulty so the year closed with a feeling of great optimism.

This post-war boom was to continue until wartime prices fell sharply in early 1921. In the meanwhile high levels of domestic production were maintained and imports of both fruit and vegetables rose dramatically to offset the shortages which had developed during the last years of hostilities:

Summary of Fruit and Vegetable Imports

FRUIT	1918	1919
Apples: (m. cwts)	0.410	2.969
Oranges: (m. cwts)	2.640	5.200
Total quantities (m. cwts)	4.835	12.287
Bananas: (m. bunches)	0.729	4.896
VEGETABLES		
Onions: (m. bushels)	4.342	6.932
Potatoes: (m. cwts)	1.015	0.988
Tomatoes: (m. cwts)	0.516	1.306
Unenumerated: (£m.)	0.096	0.484
TOTAL VALUES (£m.)	7.002	9.284

[1]

From Orchard to Market

During this period the wartime debt which it was felt was owed by the nation to its domestic food producers was fully acknowledged by many important individuals and institutions including the Prime Minister. In what was regarded as a major statement of policy in October, 1919, Mr Lloyd-George spoke of the need to ensure that agriculture was never again to be neglected:-

> *"....The Agricultural industry is the greatest industry in the State. It ought therefore to be a primary concern of every Government and of every Statesman to do what in them lies to promote that industry. I regret to say that in no civilized country has the State done so little during the last generation to foster agriculture. I hope that record will now be rolled-up and that there will begin a new era in the relations of the State with the greatest and most important of its industries.*
>
> *The question is 'Are we going back to the dismal pre-war conditions or are we merely going to maintain the progress which has been made?' 'Are we not going further?' There can be but one answer from every man who loves his country! We must go forward. How is it to be done? You must have a settled policy with regard to agriculture. The first condition is security to the cultivator; security in the first place against ruin through the violent fluctuations of foreign agriculture".* [2]

These views were not, of course, universally held. In the special circumstances which prevailed from 1916 to 1918 every scrap of food which could be produced at home was of major importance and many believed that without the enormous contribution of British agriculture the population would be been starved into surrender by the German U Boat campaign. However accurate this opinion may have been it was also true that pre-war output had been allowed to decline in the first two years of the war and that the considerable efforts made after 1916 had merely restored production to the 1913 level [3]. It was also thought that many small-scale producers had seldom suffered from any real shortages and that practically all sections of the industry had enjoyed high levels of prosperity throughout the war. This view that the growers had already been sufficiently rewarded was further reinforced by the fact that husbandry, including fruit and vegetable production, had been especially excluded from liability under the Excess Profits Tax [4].

However the decision not to follow the policies advocated by Mr Lloyd-George was not to be taken because of any sentimental feelings of obligation towards or against the domestic producers. Nor was it to be taken on strategic grounds for it was recognised that Britain would benefit from having a strong industry which could provide protection in the event of future emergencies. This argument was

Problems of the 'Twenties'

largely discounted due to the belief that agricultural output would always respond positively if, as in 1916, the appropriate conditions and incentives were provided. The final outcome was, in fact, to be decided by two separate and distinct factors - the continued belief in free trade, and, most importantly, the cost of subsidizing British farmers and growers over long periods.

In the first place it was widely believed that for the previous hundred years or so the UK had enjoyed considerable advantages by exporting her manufactures and importing raw materials and food. Tropical products - especially fruit and vegetables - had, of necessity, to be purchased abroad as they could not be produced in Britain's moderate climate. Of much more significance were the huge quantities of apples and pears, onions, potatoes and tomatoes which could have been grown at home. A proportion of these could be regarded as seasonal additions which merely supplemented domestic output at certain times of the year but these shipments were only a small part of the total trade. The real attraction of the remaining imports was that they were not only cheaper than many locally grown items but were also, in numerous cases, of higher quality and better presented. In addition it was generally understood that it was only by accepting these overseas cargoes that their countries of origin could afford to buy British exports. The fact that there was little correlation between these separate transactions was seldom appreciated at this time!

The other major consideration and the one which was eventually to prove decisive was the expense of supporting domestic producers. The Corn Production Act of 1917 had guaranteed minimum prices for wheat and oats and had also set up Agricultural Wages Boards which had then fixed minimum rates of pay. However the rising levels of wartime prices and wages had meant that these guarantees had cost nothing even though they had generated a considerable degree of confidence and , hence, output. The ending of the war saw the Board of Agriculture transformed into the Ministry of Agriculture and this, at first, pursued an active policy which required all County Councils to set up Agricultural Committees. These were to provide a forum for discussion and to advise the Minister but a dispute with the National Farmers' Union reduced their effectiveness. The Agriculture Act of 1920 then introduced a new scale of guaranteed prices for wheat and oats which was based on the average returns for 1919. Provision was then made for these figures to be reviewed and adjusted on an annual basis and when the fall in prices came in 1921 the Exchequer was obliged to pay £15m to growers in England and Wales and a further £4.4m to those in Scotland.

Although this was exactly the situation for which the system had been devised the high cost to the government at a time of financial retrenchment rapidly led to a repeal of all the relevant legislation. This included the abolition of the Agricultural

From Orchard to Market

Wages Board and thus, for all practical purposes the industry had been returned to the un-protected and unregulated position which had existed in 1914.

While the decision to end support for agriculture was essentially made on grounds of cost the policy of continuing with Free Trade was taken in the belief that this would help the UK to return to the dominant trading position it had enjoyed in 1913. Unfortunately the ending of the brief post-war boom was to be followed by a period during which international commerce grew only slowly. This expansion was insufficient to cope with the manufactured goods then becoming available from both new exporters - especially the United States and Japan - as well as cater for the return of the traditional suppliers of which the UK had been by far the most important. In addition many countries including those in the Far East, Canada, India and Latin America, which Britain had been obliged to neglect during the war had either began to develop their own industries or had been forced to rely upon other nations for their needs. Thus when Britain was ready to resume its shipments it found that many of its previous markets had disappeared or were being supplied by its competitors. As a result Britain's share of world exports fell from approximately 14% in 1913 to less than 11% in 1929.[5]

The changing condition which had caused British exports to decline also led to a steady increase in her imports. In response to wartime demands many primary producers had expanded their output and now found it necessary to lower their prices in order to try to maintain their sales. In many instances this proved ineffective because a number of the world's principal countries were protected by high tariffs. Thus the UK, as the biggest remaining free market for raw materials and food, became increasingly attractive and ever-larger shipments arrived at British ports. Fortunately this cheapening of imports meant that Britain benefitted from more favourable terms of trade so that in effect a greater return was obtained from the sale of her manufactured goods. As a result and with the aid of her invisible exports (returns from banking, insurance, shipping and of overseas investments) it was possible for the UK to maintain a positive balance of payments up to 1929.

The net effect of these developments in overseas trade was two-fold. The reduction in the export markets for coal, heavy engineering, iron and steel, shipbuilding and textiles led to ever-growing unemployment in these industries so considerably decreased the purchasing power of their work forces. On the other hand the lowering in cost of many imports (and the knock-on impact on home produced prices) provided a rising standard of living for those (the vast majority) who were in work even though their wages remained static. Amongst those commodities which were much in demand were imported fruits and vegetables for, as the following table indicates, although quantities rose during

Problems of the 'Twenties'

the period from 1920 to 1928 this was not matched by a corresponding increase in total values:-

Summary of Fruit and Vegetable Imports for 1920 - 1928.

FRUIT	1920	1924	1928
Apples: (m. cwts)	4.620	7.232	6.089
Oranges: (m. cwts)	4.401	7.519	7.760
Pears: (m. cwts)	0.663	1.324	0.859
Bananas: (m. bushels)	8.057	11.307	12.965
TOTAL VALUES OF IMPORTS (not subject to duty) £m	£40.153	£33.094	£33.929
VEGETABLES			
Onions: (m. bushels)	7.980	9.510	10.154
Potatoes: (m. cwts)	5.210	9.009	9.521
Tomatoes: (m. cwts)	1.616	2.437	2.804
Unenumerated (£m)	0.732	1.045	1.564
TOTAL VALUES OF IMPORTS (£m)	£13.770	£12.353	£13.359

Unfortunately the expansion of fruit and vegetable imports after 1920 had the effect of reducing the returns obtained by many sections of the domestic industry. This was not only due to the increased volumes which arrived in the UK but was because of their cheaper costs which inevitably led to a lowering of the general price level. From 1920 prices were consistently below that of the cost of living and, apart from 1922 and 1923, also beneath the cost of labour. This tendency gradually accelerated throughout the 'Twenties' so that by 1928 the differential was so substantial that many farmers and growers were in serious financial difficulties. These problems inevitably resulted in a significant decline in the acreage devoted to the land under cultivation together with a relatively small increase in the area of permanent grass:-

From Orchard to Market

**Total Acreage of Principal Crops
in England and Wales (000 acres)**

	1922	1928
Wheat	1,966	1,395
Beans	284	169
Peas	173	114
Potatoes	561	489
Small Fruit	74	64
Total Arable	11,310	10,108
Permanent Grass	14,715	15,396

[7]

This reduced acreage of arable land led to a gradual decline in the value of agricultural and horticultural produce sold off the farms of England and Wales and the total fell from £235m in the 1924-25 season to £221m in 1928-29. However this reduction was quite small in the horticultural sector with the value of fruit only falling from £7,260,000 to £6,940,000: glasshouse production coming down from £5,050,000 to £4,970,000 and vegetables actually increasing from £10,280,000 to £10,470,000 during the same seasons. When the decline in the price level is taken into account these statistics indicate that output was little changed but the fact remained that in most cases the activity only provided very modest returns.

This sad picture inevitably aroused much serious comment in the trade press. Thus at Christmas, 1922, it was reported that:-

> "....With the year practically at a close the fruit trade as an industry will hope that it has seen the last of superabundant supplies of fruit and vegetables, accompanied by a scarcity of customers. The latter half of the year has been deplorable from a trade point of view. There have been gluts and gluts and gluts on top of gluts and produce has had to be sold at giving-away prices and vast quantities have gone to waste. Even before Christmas trade was as dead as the proverbial ditch-water. Generally speaking, the year, taken as a whole, has been far from profitable for growers".[8]

The following year, 1923, was to be just as bad or even worse due to adverse weather which seriously limited fruit production. Most varieties of pears were a failure and the apple harvest included far too many on the small side. Eating

Problems of the 'Twenties'

apples, especially Worcesters, did well when available but in many places the crop was almost non-existent. As Continental outputs were also below normal huge quantities of apples were imported from Canada and the United States and shipments rose by more than a million boxes and 700,000 barrels over the previous season. This over-reaction to domestic shortages helped to keep prices low and the situation was not improved by the presence of large quantities of Spanish oranges which, although small, were being sold at 30% less than in 1922. Fortunately for the domestic grower vegetables provided a reasonable crop even though potatoes were rather lighter than usual but moderate prices and rising costs ensured only low profitability.

Newly arrived Nova Scotian apples awaiting distribution in 1923

In an attempt to improve this difficult situation the Conservative Government of the day proposed to introduce a limited number of protective measures, which included the imposition of a tax of 5/- per cwt on foreign, but not Empire, apples. However this legislation was rejected by the electorate in the General Election of December 1923 for the Liberal-Labour opposition which won the contest had fought on a platform of Free Trade. The subsequent first Labour Government was in an overall minority and came to an end in October 1924. Although this was then replaced by a Conservative administration with a large majority it was felt that it would not be advisable to re-introduce the measures to protect the domestic producer. Instead it was considered that Britain's interests would be best served by a return to the Gold Standard which had been suspended in 1914. This, in itself, was not critical but the decision to return at the pre-war parity of

From Orchard to Market

US $4.86 to the pound was to have serious consequences.

The overvaluing of the pound had the effect of raising British prices and thus played a significant role in reducing exports. It was also important in creating the financial circumstances in which it quickly became necessary to increase the Bank Rate from 4% to 5%. These two factors accentuated the problems of the coal industry as the cost to its overseas customers was increased by approximately 10%. By 1924 foreign demand had already fallen by 7% from its peak in 1909-1913 and the new rise in prices led to it becoming 22% less in 1925. This fresh difficulty led to the miners' strike and, in turn, to the General Strike of May, 1926.[9]

These industrial problems resulted in much disruption and inevitably led to decreased demand and profitability in many areas. Those trades like fruit and vegetables whose products were mainly of a perishable nature were, of course, especially vulnerable to any hold-ups in distribution or transport. There were many of these in the early 'Twenties' with numerous stoppages at the ports and on the railways. In addition the fruit and vegetable business suffered from many specific strikes at the wholesale markets with London and Liverpool being amongst those usually worse affected.

The net effect of the retention of Free Trade and the consequent rise in food imports; the subsequent decline in prices and the impact of industrial disruption meant that profitability throughout British agriculture and horticulture was very poor. In these circumstances few producers could hope to do little more than survive.

While the gradual rise in real incomes for those in work could do little to aid the domestic growers of grain the markets for milk, eggs, poultry and high quality meat continued to hold-up moderately well. These, like fruit and vegetables, were the very commodities which were given some degree of protection by distance from foreign suppliers and so offered the home producer an opportunity to compete on more satisfactory terms. Even so the financial returns from these items continued to be considerably constrained by potential imports from a wide range of overseas sources. These, in turn, were, of course, to be greatly influenced by the transport facilities then available and during the 1920s these were to be steadily improved.

If anything these developments tended to aid the importers rather more than the local producer. One of these improvements was new but the others marked the evolution of trends which had existed for some time. The importation of perishable items by air was commenced by Flying Transport Ltd in 1919 when it inaugurated a service from Paris to London. This was used to carry tiny quantities of fruit on

Problems of the 'Twenties'

an *ad hoc* basis and during the following season Messrs Charles Wilkinson and Company of Covent Garden began to bring strawberries from Paris on a regular basis. Their example was emulated by many other firms and a small-scale trade began to emerge. The high cost of this form of transport meant that this was almost entirely confined to early and expensive fruits and, later, to the carriage of flowers from Holland. However at this stage the expense and limited cargo capacity of the available aircraft ensured that other forms of income was actively investigated and it was quickly discovered that they could play a useful role in facilitating business meetings between, for example, continental growers and their wholesalers in Britain.

Of much greater significance for most importers were the improvements to shipping and to the distribution system within the UK. In the case of the former the 1920s was to see only minor modifications to the various types of tonnage which served the British market. The growing number of specialized fruit-carriers, which catered mainly for bananas, continued to consist almost entirely of single-temperature, refrigerated vessels driven by triple expansion steam engines. During this period the use of coal was steadily being replaced by oil and the average speed gradually rose so that by 1930 it had reached 13 knots. The hold capacity of newly constructed ships also tended to increase but apart from the limited adoption of steam turbines there were no other major innovations. This was also true for most of the cargo liners and tramp ships which brought the bulk of food imports into Britain although by the end of the decade a few were being fitted with diesel engines. However both cargo and passenger vessels were increasingly being built with refrigerated spaces which could be utilized for perishable items so that a wider range of options was made available for the shipper.

Typical examples of the way in which these latter developments were utilized involved the importation of citrus fruit from California. The opening of the Panama Canal in 1914 meant that a direct water route from the Pacific Coast to Europe had become available for the first time. Due to the outbreak of the Great War this potential was not to be exploited until 1920 when boxes of lemons and oranges began to be shipped from Los Angeles to Atlantic ports for onward transmission to Europe by other vessels. As shipping rates had already returned to their pre-war levels while rail charges remained at approximately 67% above those of 1914 the savings were obvious and helped to make these fruits more competitive in the British market. Further advantage of the Panama Canal was taken in April 1921 when the first direct shipment was sent to London via the Holland-America liner 'Eemdyke'. This consisted of ten carloads of oranges and a hundred boxes of lemons and was moved from Los Angeles to London in 25 days. As this was at least three days less than if the cargo had been sent by rail and shipped via New York and was less subject to damage from double-handling the overall cost was considerably less than with the previous system.

The net effect of these developments were that Californian citrus was enabled to strengthen its position in the UK but the quantities remained quite modest throughout the 1920s with Spain and Palestine remaining the major suppliers. Of more importance to the British consumer (and producer) were the vast cargoes of apples and pears which arrived on a massive scale throughout the decade. While these had been successfully imported from Canada and the United States (at first with no artificial cooling) and from Australia and New Zealand with relatively simple cooling systems from the 1880s much work remained to be done. There was, for example, much discussion and experimentation with pre-cooling on the longer Australian routes and although this was found to be advantageous in small chambers its use for whole cargoes remained debatable. As late as 1922 the results for pre-cooled pears was very variable for a while:-

> "....One line of 750 cases of pre-cooled apples had arrived in England frosted while unpre-cooled fruit arrived sound". [10]

By then, however, a much more scientific approach was being undertaken by the Australian Fruit Council, the Tasmanian Fruit Advisory Board and the US Department of Agriculture. Some of these investigations were directed specially at the elimination of brown heart which affected many apples in transit, while others were aimed at securing the most efficient systems of cooling and stowage. Although these were primarily concerned with the carriage of apples and pears, it was anticipated that they would also play an important role in enabling other items including oranges, grapes, peaches and tomatoes to be transported over long distances on a large scale.

While many of the innovations and changes mentioned above may have been small in themselves their net impact was cumulative and resulted in rising efficiency and a corresponding reduction in costs. These developments placed further pressure on the domestic producer by lowering the overall price level for fruit as well as providing direct competition for some of their products. Importers of fruit and vegetables using the shorter routes from the Continent were also aided by the general improvements in shipping and some were particularly helped by the introduction of train-ferries designed to cater for goods wagons. The first service was commenced between Zeebrugge and Harwich in 1925 and its success led to plans to establish a second link from Dunkirk to Dover. It was not until 1936 that this became operational due to the need to construct a special dock at Dover which could cope with a 25 feet tidal range. Thereafter three major routes converged at Dunkirk coming respectively from Chiasso on the Swiss-

Problems of the 'Twenties'

Italian border via Basle; from Lyons via the Rhone Valley, and from Hendaye and Cerbère in Spain via Perpignan. With the aid of blocks of ice virtually all types of produce including apples, dates, lettuce, nuts, peaches, potatoes and soft fruits, could then be viably moved to the UK entry ports.

The system which evolved from the mid-twenties was that once the wagons had been landed in Britain those for the London markets were taken directly to depots at Gravel Lane or Battersea Wharf while those for the provinces were moved to Hither Green for onward transmission. Although the chief advantage of this scheme was that it did not require the double handling needed by normal shipments it also benefitted from its linkage with the British rail network which remained the principal form of distribution throughout the 1920s and 1930s.

The First World War had placed a tremendous strain upon the railways and had left them in need of much repair and replacement. Government action designed to assist them took the form of compulsory amalgamations and four new systems were established. These were then operated by the London and North Eastern Railway: the London, Midland and Scottish Railway: the Great Western Railway, and the Southern Railway at prices which were fixed at too high a level. Although the arrangements provided some economies of scale and the railway companies introduced containers, door-to-door services, better railhead facilities and a limited amount of electrification and dieselization its role declined steadily due to its expensive charges and, especially, to the growing competition from road transport.

From Orchard to Market

The technical efficiency of motor vehicles had, of course been significantly raised during the war and these improvements were to be further developed during the following decade. Thus a steadily widening range of lorries, trucks, vans, three-wheelers and motor cycle combinations were offered each year. With greater production all of these vehicles became progressively cheaper and thus more readily available to all sections of the industry. This, in turn, led to road transport taking an ever rising share of the market and into direct conflict with the railway companies. Government policy was always constrained by the need to assist the railways which were regarded as an essential national asset. At the same time it was not thought to be desirable to inhibit a promising new activity. Thus is 1928 a reduced scale of motor taxation was introduced under which special concessions were made to farmers, market gardeners and growers - these included a 20% reduction if pneumatic tyres were fitted instead of solids - but although this was undoubtedly a helpful measure its impact was small in an agricultural and horticultural industry which remained depressed and largely un-profitable.

In the absence of the scale of government assistance which was required to offset these nationwide problems the industry was obliged to turn to other bodies and methods in order to try to remain in business. One was in which it was hoped that British producers could be helped was through the establishment of co-operative societies. The obvious advantages of co-operation in buying and selling on a wholesale basis and its success in many overseas countries like Denmark had long been recognised and had resulted in the creation of the Agricultural Organisation Society in 1900. This was set up:-

> *"....for the purpose of advocating the principles of co-operation amongst agriculturalists and giving advice and assistance in the formation and organisation of properly registered co-operative agricultural societies in suitable districts. The society does no trade and makes no profit and is supported almost entirely by voluntary contributions. The agricultural co-operative societies formed in different localities are entirely self-supporting and self-governed. The principal objects of these local societies are to obtain for its members their manures, seeds, feeding stuffs, implements, etc, from the manufacturers, importers or large wholesale merchants at first cost, charging its members a small profit to cover management expenses. To enable the farmer to secure the best market for the sale of his produce......"*

and:-

> *"....By grading and packing fruit in similar depots, so that it is placed on the market in a fresh and attractive condition and more suitable to*

Problems of the 'Twenties'

> *the requirements of the consumers. To open up remote districts by motor goods wagons and to establish agricultural banks".* [11]

There had, in fact, already been a number of attempts to organize the co-operative marketing of fruit and vegetables of which the East Anglian Farmers' Co-operative Society formed in 1897 was an early example. However the work of the Agricultural Organisation Society accelerated their proliferation and, amongst others, co-operative bodies of various types were set up to form the Bewdley Agricultural Supply Association, Worcestershire, in 1902 : the Evesham Growers Association in 1903 : the Hereford Co-Operative Fruit Grading Society in 1905 and the Avalon Fruit Grading Society of Somerset in 1906. A further development came in 1909 with the establishment of a co-operative auction market at Pershore. At about the same time the East Anglian Farmers Co-operative Society opened a branch at Covent Garden and undertook to sell on commission produce sent to it by smaller societies or by their individual members.

Similar arrangements were made in many other different parts of the country while new functions were taken on board by some societies. Thus in 1910 the Worthing and District Market Farmers Association was formed primarily for the purpose of reducing rail charges by bulking consignments and for the recovery of claims and debts on behalf of their members. The Swanwick and District Fruit Growers Association was also set up in 1910 and undertook the distribution of information regarding markets and salesmen, the collection of debts and negotiation with the railway companies re the general needs of the fruit trade:-

> *"....This Society was also instrumental in securing the use of baskets of a uniform size, containing a standard weight of fruit. In 1913 it established the Swanwick and District Basket Factory to meet the difficulty of securing, at a reasonable price, an adequate supply of the chip baskets in which the members were accustomed to market their strawberries".* [12]

From the foregoing it would appear that co-operative marketing was making significant progress in the pre-war period but, in fact, only ten societies dealing in fruit and vegetables were in operation in December 1913. This was partly because a number of ventures had already failed as some societies suffered from a shortage of first-grade fruit when their members found it more profitable to dispose of it elsewhere. Nevertheless their value was fully appreciated during the First World War and with the aid of state subsidies a further twenty-three societies were created. However the abnormal failure of the fruit crop in 1918 and the subsequent return to peace-time conditions had a dramatic effect on their viability and by the end of 1923 only eighteen remained in business.

From Orchard to Market

Thus although the Agricultural Organization Society had much initial success, especially with dairy products and eggs, the harsh economic climate of the 'Twenties' meant that many societies failed and those that did succeed tended to be bought by commercial firms when they achieved a certain size. Even the provisions of the Agricultural Credits Act which supplied loans equal to the member's share capital did not help very much although a few, like the Eastern Counties Co-operative Society at Ipswich, did develop into strong trading corporations. As a result the Agricultural Organization Society was eventually dissolved and its functions were taken over by the National Farmers' Union.[13]

Of more success was the development of grading and packing stations following the lead by French and South African growers who were placing increasing emphasis on quality control and grading The first of these in the inter-war period was opened by the British Fruit Packing Company in 1924. This was a public company which provided facilities at East Peckham in Kent before moving to East Farleigh and setting-up a branch at Faversham. This firm then undertook to grade, pack and sell at a fixed charge all fruit delivered to its premises so the growers were relieved of these tasks although they still shared in the goodwill attached to the Company's label. They also enjoyed the advantage of having their products dealt with by the Company's skilled personnel and with their aid a total of 60,000 bushels of apples were handled in 1925.

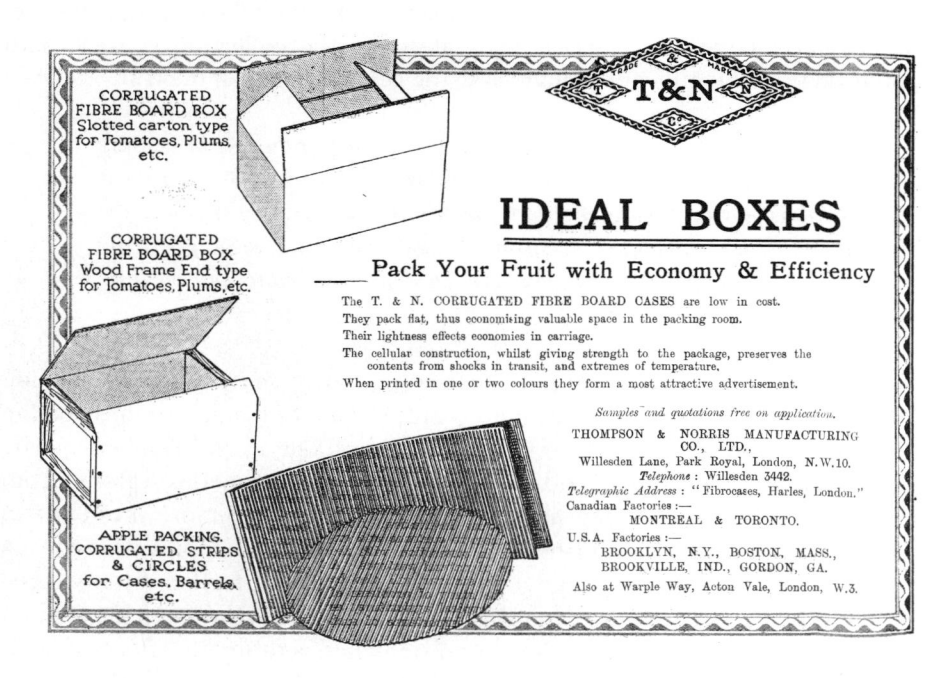

T & N

IDEAL BOXES

Pack Your Fruit with Economy & Efficiency

CORRUGATED FIBRE BOARD BOX
Slotted carton type for Tomatoes, Plums, etc.

CORRUGATED FIBRE BOARD BOX
Wood Frame End type for Tomatoes, Plums, etc.

APPLE PACKING.
CORRUGATED STRIPS & CIRCLES
for Cases, Barrels, etc.

The T. & N. CORRUGATED FIBRE BOARD CASES are low in cost.
They pack flat, thus economising valuable space in the packing room.
Their lightness effects economies in carriage.
The cellular construction, whilst giving strength to the package, preserves the contents from shocks in transit, and extremes of temperature.
When printed in one or two colours they form a most attractive advertisement.

Samples and quotations free on application.

THOMPSON & NORRIS MANUFACTURING CO., LTD.,
Willesden Lane, Park Royal, London, N.W.10.
Telephone : Willesden 3442.
Telegraphic Address : "Fibrocases, Harles, London."
Canadian Factories :—
MONTREAL & TORONTO.
U.S.A. Factories :—
BROOKLYN, N.Y., BOSTON, MASS.,
BROOKVILLE, IND., GORDON, GA.
Also at Warple Way, Acton Vale, London, W.3.

Problems of the 'Twenties'

A similar station was established at Cottenham in Cambridgeshire during 1925 through the combined efforts of the local fruit growers. This business was conducted on co-operative lines so was assisted by a loan from the Ministry of Agriculture which was used to buy the grading and packing machinery which came mainly from the United States. In its first year over 10,000 bushels were handled but the failure of the apple crop in 1926 and 1927 prevented the station from reopening and the enterprise came to an end. However this example was to be repeated elsewhere and, over time, was to become an accepted feature of the rural economy. [14]

The limited success of agricultural co-operatives during the 'Twenties' and the failure of the Government to give more than token assistance led to even greater reliance on voluntary bodies and trade associations. The Worshipful Company of Fruiterers continued to be active in promoting the cause of domestic fruit production in government circles and maintained its close links with a number of educational institutions. These included Wye College and what was to become the University of Bath which taught specific courses on horticulture as well as with the research stations at East Malling and Long Ashton. In March 1918 it sponsored a conference convened by the National Fruit Growers' Federation to investigate ways in which potential post-war problems could be resolved.

In addition the Fruiterers' Company pursued its policy of awarding prizes to encourage the growing of fruit and in December, 1918, it helped to ensure the creation of the Chamber of Horticulture. This acted as a central body which could speak with a single voice on behalf of all sections of a very diverse industry and which could help to correlate all new developments in the general interest.

The Chamber of Horticulture gets a royal send-off in 1921 from H.R.H. The Prince of Wales, with its first President, Mr George Monro, on the left.

From Orchard to Market

The National Fruit Growers' Federation mentioned above was formed in Maidstone in 1902 and quickly attracted a considerable amount of support from both growers and other members of the industry. It emerged as a major voice on items of general concern to the trade and was particularly active in negotiating with the Joint Railway Committee and with government departments on matters of principle. In the following year a number of leading members of the wholesale fresh fruit and vegetable industry met in London and decided to form their own national organization. It was appreciated that whilst a number of local organizations were already in existence in various towns throughout the country there was no body to co-ordinate their views on items of national importance. Accordingly the National Federation of Fruit and Potato Trades, Ltd was established in 1903 with William Craze of Liverpool as its first President and was soon to be representing its members on a number of key issues. These included the Lincolnshire Potato Rebate Case (which was lost!), the subsidy on Jamaican bananas, the publication of standard net weights to be known as *The National Federation Standard Weights* and opposition to the proposal to operate a closed salesroom in Liverpool.

The wartime conditions of 1914-1918 saw the Federation take over the responsibilities of the United Apple Committee and this, in turn, led to a decision to extend its activities to all imported green fruits. Then in 1918 a new Potato Crop Order was introduced which cancelled all existing wholesale licenses. Thereafter these licenses could only be issued to the Co-operative Wholesale Society and to members of the Federation. This development was to be very important for although price control was soon to be ended the licensing system was to continue for some time. Partly, perhaps, because of this situation the Federation, through its Associates and direct membership, then came to represent up to 90% of the wholesale distributive trade during the early 1920s. This strength provided added weight to its consideration of many matters of concern which at a typical Executive Committee included the legality of Commission Accounts, deposit charges on empties, the need for fast goods services, the reduction in railway rates, the opposition to the railways carrying goods in their motor vehicles which have not been previously transported by rail, the need for promotion and the conditions for the sale of seed potatoes.[15]

The retail side of the trade also attempted to protect its interests by joining together to form its own organizations. At first there were a number of separate bodies but in 1901 the five leading local associations came together to create the National Federation of Retail Fruiterers, Florists and Fishmongers. As this failed to obtain the support of retailers in the South of the country it opened its offices in Liverpool. Later, in 1910, the latter joined to form the London and Home Counties Retail Fruiterers and Florists Association - a title which was subsequently changed to

Problems of the 'Twenties'

the Retail Fruiterers' and Florists Association. After some early hostility the two bodies began to work harmoniously together and the difficult trading conditions of the 'Twenties' helped to strengthen their mutual interests. As a result and, following much delicate discussion, the two organizations came together in 1934 and the Retail Fruit Trades Federation came into existence.

Although the Chamber of Horticulture, the National Fruit Growers' Federation, the National Federation of Fruit and Potato Trades and the two main retail organizations had many specific and individual concerns they were all united by their belief in the value of publicity as a means of alleviating many of the industry's problems. Attempts to influence the public by this means were to take two separate forms. The first of these included the general activities organized by the Fruit Trades Federation's (Retailers' Propaganda Association) which was typified by the Eat More Fruit campaign and the wholesaler's advertising of home-grown fruit, vegetables and potatoes. This was financed by a per package levy on growers and wholesalers and although this was later abandoned for non-proprietary items it was to be subsequently to be utilized for encouraging the sale of foreign and commonwealth fruit. This section should also include the promotions undertaken by major companies of which Elders and Fyffes were the most innovative. Their slogan: "Bananas: The All-Food Fruit", backed by strong campaigns which stressed its health-giving qualities and its cheapness were very successful and in spite of the depression imports rose from 127,400 tons in 1921 to 151,600 tons in 1924 and to 170,200 tons in 1927. [16]

From Orchard to Market

The second aspect of publicity involved support for the provision of fruit exhibitions and demonstrations of all kinds. For many years a number of local fruit shows had been held in the major fruit growing districts especially at Maidstone, Worcester and at Wisbech, and the Ministry of Agriculture had come to the conclusion that something on a national scale would be more appropriate. Such a project was in process of preparation when the Daily Mail suggested an even larger event and thus the first Imperial Fruit Show came to be held at the Crystal Palace in November 1921. This was followed by a second, also sponsored by the Daily Mail and held at the same venue, but although both were regarded a valuable "showcases" for the trade they were not financially viable and were in danger of being discontinued. At this point the Ministry of Agriculture decided that in view of the good that had been achieved it would be wise to continue and with its aid a third show was held at the Belle Vue Gardens in Manchester. Subsequent annual Imperial Fruit Shows were then to held at Birmingham and London before returning to Manchester and all had a considerable impact in raising the quality of British products and thus enhancing the image of the industry.

The *Fruit, Flower and Vegetable Trades Journal* did what it could to aid these attempts at self-help by supporting these major exhibitions as well as sponsoring many local ones.

In addition it made its pages available to both the wholesale and retail associations and the Editor spent a great deal of his time in pressing a reluctant government to do more to control unrestricted foreign competition. However the measures which were taken by the state, plus the efforts made by the industry itself, were then to be assisted by a gentle improvement in the national economy and by 1928 a feeling that "trade had turned the corner" was beginning to permeate many activities. It was at this point and against this background that the events of 1929 were to lead to the worst depression that agriculture and the country had ever experienced.

Problems of the 'Twenties'

OPENS ON FRIDAY, OCTOBER 26th

IMPERIAL FRUIT SHOW

BELLE VUE, MANCHESTER

THE IMPERIAL FRUIT SHOW will be opened at Belle Vue Gardens, Manchester, at 2-30 p.m. on Friday, 26th October, by the Lord Mayor of Manchester.

IT will remain open until Saturday, November 3rd, daily from 10 a.m. to 10 p.m.

THE EXHIBITION has been entirely organised and financed by the Fruit Growing and Allied Industries. Prizes totalling over £2,000 are to be competed for by Fruit Growers in all parts of the British Empire in the commercial competition for Apples, Pears, Grapes, Tomatoes, Oranges, and Grape-fruit.

EXHIBITS representing every section of the Industry are being staged—Horticultural Implements and Machinery; Insecticides and Fruit-tree Washes; Apple Grading Machines. There will also be exhibits by Fruit Salesmen, Distributors, and Growers.

THE numerous special attractions include a daily demonstration of Apple Packing, with a competition for expert packers, for which prizes and diplomas will be awarded; Free Tasting of many varieties of fruit; Guessing Competitions in aid of Manchester Hospitals; Cooking demonstration of Fruit and Potatoes; Free Distribution of Recipes.

IN the Conference Hall matters vitally affecting Fruit Growers and Traders will be discussed.

THIS EXHIBITION will prove an education, not only to the General Public, but also to Fruit Growers and Fruit Traders themselves.

THERE are many other attractions at Belle Vue Gardens—every Monday, Wednesday, and Friday, at 8-30 p.m., Grand Spectacle "The Redskins," and Firework displays. Zoological Gardens. Music. Dancing. Refreshments daily.

ADMISSION to the Gardens and Fruit Show 1/-, including tax.

The famous Besses-o'-th'-Barn Band on Saturday, October 27th, and Saturday, November 3rd, from 2-30 till 4-30, and from 6 till 8 p.m.

Enquire at your Local Station for particulars of Excursion Trains.

From Orchard to Market

7
Depression and Recovery

Until 1929 the UK had been struggling with only moderate success to adapt to the changed circumstances of the post-war world. This task had been made the more difficult because of her too-large export industries and her over-valued currency but had been assisted by the gradual improvement in the level of international trade and prosperity. The ending of American foreign loans in 1928 : the impact of the collapse of Wall Street in October 1929 and the subsequent fall in US imports rapidly worsened this environment and it was replaced by a situation in which all countries attempted to restrict their imports and expand their exports by virtually any means. The proliferation of tariffs, quotas and financial barriers which followed was to hit British commerce especially hard for while its exports were significantly reduced its position as the only remaining free trade market ensured that it received an ever-growing glut of cheap imports.

In the absence of any real controls these imports inevitably included a rising tide of fruit and vegetables:-

Summary of Fruit and Vegetable Imports: 1928 - 1931

FRUIT	1928	1929	1930	1931
Apples (m cwt)	6.089	5.757	6.171	7.598
Oranges (m cwt)	7.760	9.263	10.207	10.391
Pears (m cwt)	0.859	1.078	1.029	1.237
Bananas (m bunches)	12.965	14.936	14.989	16.161
Total value imports (£m) Not subject to duty	£33.929	£36.235	£34.181	£34.675
VEGETABLES				
Onions (m bushels)	10.154	10.685	10.783	10.170
Potatoes (m cwt)	9.521	5.869	5.781	16.653
Tomatoes (m cwt)	2.804	2.751	3.052	2.936
Unenumerated (£m)	1.564	1.576	1.713	1.691
Total value all imports	£13.359	£11.226	£10.530	£14.972

1

From Orchard to Market

These statistics demonstrated quite clearly that while the shipments of fruit and (to a smaller extent) vegetables into Britain rose quite significantly during this period their overall cost tended to fall. Thus the average price of most imported items steadily declined and this, in turn, had the effect of further lowering the level of returns which could be earned by many domestic producers:-

> *"The estimated total value of the agricultural produce sold off farms in England and Wales in 1930-31 was £197,400,000 and is thus £18,830,000 less than in 1929-30. The fall is mainly due to livestock and livestock products, which were valued at £13,760,000 less than in the previous year, while fruit and vegetables were valued at £3,880,000 less.*
>
> *The relatively smaller reduction, viz, £1,190,000 in the value of farm crops is consequent on the higher figure estimated for potatoes and sugar-beet, - the total value of corn sold off farms being estimated at about £6,000,000 less than in 1929-30".* [2]

These falls should be placed in perspective by an examination of the changes in the level of prices for the previous decade:-

Percentage Increase in Prices as Compared with 1911-13. 1913=100

Harvest year, Sept - Aug	Cereals and Farm Crops	Fruit and Vegetables
1919-20	197	202
1920-21	120	252
1921-22	64	192
1922-23	28	73
1923-24	45	114
1924-25	53	75
1925-26	31	94
1926-27	39	59
1927-28	39	73
1928-29	25	77
1929-30	11	55
1930-31	1	23
1931-32	8	37

[3]

Depression and Recovery

From the above it will be seen that once the rapid fall from wartime heights had taken place the 1920's were to witness a gradual decline in the levels of agriculture and horticulture prices. This overall picture was less true for fruit and vegetables which enjoyed some welcome, upward, fluctuations but all shared in the misery which followed the catastrophic collapse which was triggered by the Wall Street Crash. These trends were parallelled, and even exceeded at times, by the reductions in the general wholesale commodity index. Thus inputs into domestic growers cost less but this beneficial effect was almost entirely offset by the climate of fear which was engendered by the difficulties of the other sectors of the economy. As a result profitability and investment were either at very low levels or were negative and survival became the limit of many producer's aspirations. In many cases therefore the decline in the unit cost of most varieties of fruit and vegetables led many growers to attempt to raise their output but this inevitably encouraged prices to fall still further.

The culmination of these difficulties in 1929 led the level of returns to fall to the lowest point since 1915:-

> "Between January and December, 1930, agricultural prices in this country fell by 15% and in 1931 the corresponding fall was 10%. Taking the two years together, coming as they did at the end of a period in which the trend in prices had been downwards for several years, this rapid decline was probably the most disastrous for which we have modern records. During the past 100 years it was parallelled only by the fall in 1921 and 1922 which, though actually considerably heavier, followed immediately upon the spectacular rise in prices during the war period and on this account was probably less injurious to farmers". [4]

This enormous fall in prices had the inevitable consequence of reducing the area under cultivation. Thus the overall arable total for England and Wales fell from an average of 10.64 million acres in the years 1921 to 1930 to 9.58 million acres in 1931. This represented a loss of approximately 10% but this global figure included many variations. At one end of the range were beans which lost 25.3% and turnips and swedes which declined by 20.3%. Potatoes lost 10.2% while "small fruits" (strawberries, raspberries, currants and gooseberries) fell by 9.8%. On the other hand peas lost only 4% while "orchards" (which produced apples, pears, plums and cherries) actually increased over the period by 1.9%. However the extreme conditions which developed at the end of the "Twenties" meant that orchard fruits declined by 2,201 acres and small fruits by 4,186 acres in the twelve months from 1930 to 1931. Thus although these variations were largely dictated by reductions in price and demand it should be noted that they were also influenced by the speed at which changes in crop patterns could be introduced.

From Orchard to Market

In addition to the shrinking arable area the other major impact of the depression was on employment. The decline in the number of agricultural employees clearly accelerated after 1929 and this was particularly serious at a time when unemployment in other industries was also rising dramatically. This had been running at about 6%, or 1.16 million persons out-of-work, in 1927 but by December 1930 had reached over 20% - or almost 3 million unemployed.

The economic situation which had faced the incoming Labour administration in 1929 was a serious one but it had not yet reached crisis proportions. However once the Wall Street Crash had occurred the rapid decline in world trade which followed was bound to have a major impact on Britain's foreign trade. Thus the UK's exports declined from £839 million in 1929 to £666 million in 1930 and to only £461 million in 1931. While it is true that the overall cost of imports also fell this was at a lower rate due to the open nature of the British market.

"*Not worth the* PICKING — — *owing to* FOREIGN DUMPING"

VOTE FOR THE NATIONAL GOVERNMENT AND GIVE OUR OWN FOLK FAIR PLAY.

The ensuing economic crisis led to the formation of a second National Government with a commitment to examine all aspects of fiscal policy and with its huge conservative majority the introduction of tariffs was just a matter of time. Dumping was the major concern and within a few weeks of the election the Abnormal Importations bill was approved. This gave power to place up to 100% ad valorem duties on any manufactured goods which were deemed to be arriving in excessive quantities. In fact duties of 50% were immediately charged on a wide range of goods. This legislation was quickly followed by the Horticultural

Depression and Recovery

Products (Emergency Duties) Act which gave the Ministry of Agriculture similar authority to limit the importation of fresh fruits, flowers and vegetables. These temporary expedients were followed in February, 1932 by the introduction of the Import Duties bill. In general terms this imposed a general customs levy of 10% on almost all items except those placed on a free list or already liable to existing duties. However those goods which originated in the Empire were to be excused from payment until an Imperial Economic Conference could be held. In addition the Act also established an Imports Advisory Committee and it was to be its recommendations, implemented by the Treasury, which were formed the basis of import control throughout the remainder of the 1930s

It should be remembered that the vast majority of customs receipts arose from charges which were imposed - and had been for many years - to raise revenue rather than to protect the home producer. It was the responsibility of the Chancellor of the Exchequer in his annual Finance Act to fix these revenue duties each year but it was the role of the Imports Advisory Committee to provide a flexible system of protective tariffs which could be commenced or altered on an almost day to day basis.

However such rates were regarded as provisional until the Ottawa Conference could be held in July and August of 1932. The discussions which ensued were designed to provide British manufacturers with concessions in the Dominions while in return their foodstuffs and raw materials were to be granted special exemptions from duties when imported into the UK. Unfortunately it was not to be quite so simple for the Dominions were anxious to protect their own infant industries while Britain wished to support its own farmers and growers. In the event agreements were made with all of the Dominions, except the Irish Free State, which attempted to achieve these objectives at the expense of foreign suppliers. Thus British exports continued to be charged existing rates when the Dominions raised these to even higher levels for other nations. At the same time Dominion products were granted an imperial preference which resulted in these being either admitted free or at the reduced rate into the UK. The net effect of these measures, plus the licensing schemes and quotas which accompanied them, were that empire-producers of many items were placed at a considerable advantage over their foreign rivals.

To some extent these benefits were reduced by the seventeen trade agreements which Britain made with other countries such as Argentina and Denmark in the period from 1932 to 1935. In spite of these arrangements there can be no doubt that the National Government did replace free trade by a substantial degree of protection which effectively refocussed Britain's overseas trade:-

From Orchard to Market

The Effect of the Ottawa Agreement on Import Tariffs

	1930	1932 Before Ottawa	1932 After Ottawa
Percentage of imports free of duty:	83	30.2	25.2

The consequences of these events, plus the move off the gold-standard and towards a balanced budget, were certainly beneficial to the UK economy and that of her Dominions and Colonies. However it is difficult to assess the extent of their assistance as compared with that provided through the improvement of world trade after 1933 and the re-armament boon which helped to complete the recovery after 1937. It would seem to be unwise to attach too much significance to the imposition of protective duties for as late as 1938 they were producing less then £50m per year. On the other hand the revenue duties, which included items such as tobacco, petroleum, sugar, spirits and dried fruit was then raising over £214m. Even so the measures taken did seem to have a definite impact on the origins and destinations on much of Britain's overseas trade:-

Proportions of British Trade with Empire and Foreign Countries
(Note that trade with the Irish Free State is not included)

	1929 (%)	1931 (%)	1932 (%)	1938 (%)
Imports:				
From Empire:	25.7	24.5	31.6	37.9
From Foreign Countries:	70.6	71.3	64.6	59.6
Exports:				
To Empire:	39.6	35.9	38.2	45.6
To Foreign Countries:	55.5	56.3	54.7	50.1

These general trends in Britain's overseas trade were also noticeable in the importation of raw fruits and nuts and, to a lesser extent, of vegetables. The statistics for this period indicate very clearly that from the low points of 1930 (by value) and 1931 (by quantity) the landings of the major fresh fruits tended to rise even though this fact was not always apparent from its cost. The table below also shows that while the value of fruit and nut imports from British possessions was less than 28% of the total in 1931 this proportion had risen to 54% by 1938. From this single detail it seems certain that the adoption of protection, together with

Depression and Recovery

the introduction of imperial preference, was having a significant effect on the sources of these items:

Annual Imports of Fresh Fruits (1930 - 1939)
Million cwts except for bananas (m. bunches)

	Apples (cwt)	Bananas (bunches)	Oranges (cwts)	Pears (cwts)
1930	6.171	14.989	10.207	1.029
1931	7.598	16.161	10.391	1.237
1932	8.090	17.107	9.342	1.112
1933	7.450	15.907	11.554	1.133
1934	5.892	17.053	10.404	1.008
1935	7.241	20.063	10.305	1.272
1936	5.627	20.442	9.535	1.153
1937	5.479	22.571	12.461	1.113
1938	7.067	22.178	10.765	1.348
1939	4.684	20.836	11.266	1.207

Value in £m

	Imports from Foreign Countries	Imports from British Possessions	Total Values of Imports
1930	22.498	11.683	34.181
1931	25.012	9.663	34.675
1932	18.065	11.522	29.587
1933	16.983	11.514	28.498
1934	15.079	11.426	26.505
1935	16.368	13.775	30.144
1936	13.745	12.873	26.619
1937	11.746	15.512	27.258
1938	12.688	15.341	28.010
1939	10.702	14.756	25.458

From Orchard to Market

When these aggregated figures are broken down into their constituent parts it is clear that the principal fruits - apples, bananas and oranges - were all increasingly being acquired from within the Empire. A major factor in this change was the duties imposed at Ottawa and the preferential entry granted to the producers in the Dominions and Colonies. Thus while in 1930 only just over 37% of apples were imported from British possessions this proportion had risen to over 70% by 1938. This was mainly because of the much smaller, though still substantial quantities arriving from the United States. In addition only France of the other, former, foreign suppliers were able to maintain much of their previous market shares. Over the same period Canadian apples had increased significantly while both Australian and New Zealand were also able to raise their shipments. However exports from South Africa grew only slowly and remained relatively small in 1938 by which date imports were marginally less than they had been in 1930.

At the beginning of the "Thirties" most of Britain's bananas originated in foreign plantations with Columbia, Costa Rica and Honduras, together with Brazil and the Canary Islands providing over 60% of the total. At this time Jamaica was the only important banana grower within the Empire and this supplied virtually all of the balance. The adoption of protective duties and, following the Ottawa Agreement, the remission of £2.50 a ton for bananas produced within British possessions, was to transform this situation. As a result, by 1938, Jamaica was providing over 85% of a greatly enlarged UK market: total banana imports having risen from 195,000 tons to 305,000 tons over this period. These developments inevitably meant much smaller shipments from elsewhere with Brazil being the only foreign supplier to hold its market share. The Canaries, which had been a major force in the "Twenties", was badly hit by the emergence of other, more efficient, producers and then by the consequences of imperial preference. Thus its banana exports to the UK steadily declined during the decade and were almost terminated as a result of the outbreak of the Spanish Civil War. However any shortages could always be offset by supplies of the previously dominant "dollar" fruit from Central America - an arrangement which was readily facilitated by the links between Elders and Fyffes, the principal British importer, and the American United Fruit Company of which it was a wholly owned subsidiary.

The sources of orange imports into Britain were also to change rapidly during the "Thirties". Historically Spain had been the UK's major supplier and this continued to be the case up to 1930. In that year it provided over 70% of British requirements but by 1938 this had fallen to only about 14%. While the disruption caused by the Spanish Civil War was part of the reason for this enormous decline another fundamental factor was the opportunity provided by import duties and imperial preference. Thus while Palestine and South Africa had together only contributed about 23% of Britain's needs in 1930 their combined share had risen

Depression and Recovery

to over 52% of a demand which had expanded only slightly by 1938. Of these two major Empire producers it was Palestine which had made the most rapid progress and at this latter date was enjoying a 36.7% market share while South Africa's exports by then represented a little more than 15% of the total. However it should be noted that in spite of imperial preference both Brazil and the United States had also been able to expand their shipments to the UK and from small beginnings in the "Twenties" had both secured 14% shares by the last full year of peace.

Although the provisions of the Imports Advisory Committee and the subsequent Ottawa Agreement applied equally to fruit and vegetables they were to have a different impact on the principal vegetable imports - onions, potatoes and tomatoes. The total value of fresh vegetables landed in the UK changed very little from 1930 to 1938 being £10.5m and £9.6m respectively. In the case of onions foreign countries continued to provide virtually all of Britain's overseas requirements which, over this period, declined from approximately 5.39m cwts to 4.57m cwts. However within this total the contribution of Spain, formerly the market leader, had been temporarily curtailed - no doubt due to its internal problems - and by the end of the decade it was the Netherlands and Egypt which provided the UK with the bulk of its needs.

The volatile nature of potato imports can be judged by the rise from 5.7m cwts in 1930 to the 16.6m cwts of 1931 and by the less violent fluctuations of the later "Thirties". As these showed a decline to under 3m cwts in both 1938 and 1939 it is clear that protective duties, plus other measures, were having their designed effect! The introduction of imperial preference was also working as intended by changing the former patterns of trade. Thus foreign nations had provided 78% of the total in 1930 but by 1938 this proportion had been reduced to 50%. This was largely due to the reduction of shipments from the Continent and although there was a small rise in cargoes of new potatoes from the Canaries the real beneficiaries were the Channel Islands which steadily increased their market share of this product.

In some respects tomatoes were to follow a similar pattern. Thus foreign countries provided about 71% of the UK imports in 1930 but only 50% in 1938. However with this product there was no decline in imports and the overall level of shipments continued to average just under 3m cwts throughout the decade. The rise in the share of Empire tomatoes in the UK market was almost entirely due to the growth of exports from the Channel Islands. With imports static this ensured that foreign growers found it difficult to compete and only the Netherlands of the former Continental suppliers managed to keep much of its market share. On the other hand the Canary Islands, with the advantage of their early season, continued to satisfy their British customers at a time of the year when other supplies were not available.

The imposition of import duties, plus the adoption of imperial preferences, undoubtedly changed the pattern of Britain's overseas trade so that a much larger proportion of her fruit and vegetables were acquired from within the Dominions and Colonies. In addition the continued operations of the Imports Advisory Committee ensured that throughout this period licensing schemes, quotas and prohibitions could be arranged at short notice so as to prevent dumping or to protect the domestic producers. This, of course, meant that the concerns of overseas suppliers, import merchants, the local growers and the consumer all needed to be balanced in what was considered to be the National Interest. These powers were then instrumental in securing a series of bilateral agreements made soon after the Ottawa Conference. As these were made from a position of strength, rather than weakness, they were only concluded when they were thought to be to Britain's benefit.

When this was not the case, as with Eire, a lengthy trade war ensued and this lasted until a satisfactory deal could be negotiated in April, 1938. In the same year an agreement was also concluded with the United States which directly affected Canada. One of the results of this was that while Canada gained more access to the American market she lost some of her preferences with the UK. Thus the duty on wheat was abolished and the concessions granted on Canadian apples and pears (amongst other items) were reduced.

From the foregoing it should be appreciated that Britain's protective policies were both complicated and constrained by many external factors. Nevertheless they were successful in achieving one major objective in that trade to and from the Empire was considerably increased. Of equal importance was the need to restrict imports where these could be satisfactorily produced at home. Tropical varieties could not, of course, be economically grown in the UK so the fact that more bananas were landed and that shipments of citrus continued at previous levels was not of direct concern to British fruit growers. However the small fall in apple imports over the decade when compared with 1930 and the subsequent decline compared with 1932 did offer some useful opportunities to the domestic industry.

A similar situation developed in respect of vegetables. Almost all of these previously imported could have been grown in the UK but were frequently acquired when British crops were out of season. Others were purchased on grounds of cost or quality while large quantities were sought on occasion to fill in temporary gaps when the domestic yield was poor. In fact, shipments of these three major items - onions, potatoes and tomatoes - were all reduced by various amounts during the

Depression and Recovery

"Thirties". This was partly because of the import restrictions introduced by the state and partly due to market forces but while these reductions gave some relief to local producers they were to be only one aspect of British agriculture's gradual return to prosperity.

In many respects the most important factor in the recovery of agriculture and horticulture was the general improvement to the UK economy which began in 1933. While the return to protection had some impact on this development it was the growth of world trade and other international events which were the prime reasons for the ending of the depression.

These movements ensured a rising standard of living for those in work so the "Thirties" were to see a considerable boom in the building of houses together with a rapid spread in the ownership of motor vehicles and electrical appliances. Another important consequence was on the diet of the population.

Trends in UK Food Consumption (lb per head per year)

	1909-13	1924-28	1934-38	1941	1947	1950	1960
Meat	131	129	129	99	96	112	135
Poultry & Game	5	6	9	6	7	7	9
Fish	41	41	26	16	32	22	21
Eggs	16	15	28	25	25	31	33
Butter	16	16	25	10	11	17	18
Margarine	6	12	9	18	15	17	15
Sugar	79	87	98	67	82	83	115
Potatoes	208	194	182	188	286	246	220
Other Vegetables	83	106	127	123	142	132	107
Fruits	69	118	104	30	89	86	149

8

These statistics make it clear that there were significant changes in the pattern of consumption when the years 1924-28 are compared with 1934-38. As these take no account of the depths of the depression in 1931-32 they are really contracting one peak with an even higher one a decade later. To some extent these trends are characteristic of a rising standard of living with a decline in the eating of bread, margarine and potatoes and a rise in the use of butter, eggs,

From Orchard to Market

poultry and sugar. The consumption of vegetables was also significantly greater but the eating of fruit appears to have declined from the very high levels of the previous era. However it is quite possible that these figures may be somewhat distorted by the very poor fruit harvest in 1938. In addition the extent to which farm-gate sales and household production and consumption were recorded is not known and may have varied from period to period. What is certain is that these developments provided an increasing market for many items and that due to government policies this meant that considerable opportunities were created for local growers.

Even prior to the ending of Free Trade domestic producers were already being assisted in a number of small ways. As noted earlier a subsidy on beet sugar had commenced in 1924 and agricultural land had been exempted from local rates in 1929. Farmers also enjoyed a privileged position in respect of their income tax assessments but it was not until the adoption of protection that their plight received serious attention. A deficiency payment scheme for wheat was then introduced while the Agricultural Marketing Acts of 1931 and 1933 give authority for the establishment of organized marketing arrangements when these were requested by two-thirds of those engaged in a particular trade. Over the next few years a number of bodies were set-up to deal with hops, barley and oats, fat cattle, pigs and bacon and - most importantly- for milk and for potatoes:-

> *"The Potato Marketing Board, set up in 1934, dealt with a crop which had little to fear from imports, except for earlies, but had suffered in the past from a highly variable yield as against a most inelastic demand. Of all the marketing schemes it was the most successful. It succeeded in stabilizing the acreage grown by a penal levy on excess acreage, it administered a quantitative control of imports from 1934 onwards, and it regulated the seasonal variations in supply by a simple method of control, the riddle: by varying the gauge of the riddle through which all potatoes had to pass before sale, it could vary the share of the crop sold for human consumption".* [9]

With the aid of these measures there was a general increase in agricultural and horticultural output which rose in volume by one-sixth in the period from 1931 to 1937. At the same time, although prices to the consumer remained fairly constant, the higher level of activity helped to raise the value of land and rents and provided more employment for those who chose to remain in the industry. However in spite of the implementation of minimum wage legislation the decline in the workforce still continued. Thus while 925,000 were employed in agriculture in Great Britain during 1925, this had fallen to 829,000 in 1931 and to only 708,000 in 1939. In view of the substantial increase in output this suggests that the productivity of

Depression and Recovery

each worker must have risen quite sharply !

Fruit, flowers and vegetables were not included in any statutory marketing schemes as it was thought that they were already given adequate protection by the Import Duties Act of 1932. Apart from items on the free list all commodities imported from foreign countries and the Irish Free State were liable to a basic 10% ad valorem duty. In addition various extra duties were also imposed - usually for specific periods.

Many of these duties were supplemented by the Ottawa Agreements Act (also of 1932). This had the effect of raising the rates for specific periods on foreign products but from which the Dominions, Colonies and India were to be exempted. Thus an imperial preference was established for a whole range of imports which included apples and pears (4s 6d per cwt), bananas (2s 6d per cwt), grapefruit (5s per cwt), oranges (3s 6d per cwt), peaches and nectarines (14s per cwt) and plums (9s 4d per cwt). As noted earlier it was these remissions which effectively increased the share of the Empire in Britain's imports while reducing that of foreign supplies even though some of these arrangements were liable to be modified by bilateral agreements.

It should also be noted that for the remainder of the "Thirties" the Imports Advisory Committee was empowered to alter and amend the level and duration of many duties whenever it was felt to be necessary. Thus imports could be effectively controlled in the interest of the domestic producers of fruit, flowers and vegetables who were then able to share in the overall expansion of British agriculture:- *(see p 136)*

The table indicates that in terms of value all sectors, except fruit, had successfully recovered from the very low levels achieved in the 1932-33 season. The exception to this progress was due to the particularly unfavourable weather in 1938 which resulted in orchard fruits, apples and pears, producing less that half of their average for the previous ten years. In addition the outturn for virtually all small fruits was severely curtailed with blackberries, cherries and gooseberries being the lowest recorded since returns were first collected in 1923. However in spite of this poor year the overall trend for all sectors, including fruit, was clearly favourable especially at a time of constant or declining prices. Thus the industry as a whole had made a remarkable recovery from the difficulties of the early "Thirties" and with the growing prospect of war was set for a further period of rapid expansion.

There can be no doubt that the introduction of tariffs and other protective measures was widely welcomed by most members of the trade. This view was reflected in the Journal, when, on the occasion of King George V's jubilee in 1935, a comparison was made by the Editor with 1910 when he ascended the throne.

From Orchard to Market

"We imported annually fresh fruit to the value of £10,700,000 of which our contemporary of that date, The Globe, estimated the following might have been grown in England - (thousands of pounds) apples, £2,231 : cherries, 199 : gooseberries, 26 : nuts, 800 : pears, 478 : plums, 345 : strawberries, 54 : unenumerated, 190 - making a rough total of £4,323,000 or, as our contemporary put it at that time, a sum equivalent to the cost of three new up-to-date Dreadnought cruisers goes into the foreign fruit growers pockets each year, of which amount if employed on the land at least 70% would be paid in wages.

As may be gathered from this brief retrospect, the tariff reform agitation was at that time being pursued with vigour. Well the reform has since taken place and nobody to-day can say that either the Trade or the community at large have in any way suffered......." [10]

From the foregoing it will be appreciated that the policies adopted by the National Government provided considerable opportunities for British growers. These were to be continued by another National Government which was elected in November 1935. This also had a large conservative majority so Stanley Baldwin replaced Ramsay MacDonald as Prime Minister. Although Baldwin was to resign in May, 1937, he was then succeeded by another conservative, Neville Chamberlain, and so continuity of policy was assured until the onset of the Second World War.

In spite of this greatly improved situation the UK growers of fruit and, to a lesser degree, of vegetables still faced many serious problems. The fact that cargoes from the Empire were steadily replacing those from foreign countries was of little real comfort to local producers who had to face the competition of these shipments wherever their origin. Not all of these items were, of course, direct substitutes for home products and in any event they were aided by the overall reduction in the level of overseas supplies. Both local producers and importers were, of course, helped by the increase in consumption and this expansion was assisted by various forms of publicity. The first, major, generic campaign was that directed by George Boggan in 1923 under the slogan of Eat More Fruit and which was regularly re-launched throughout the "Thirties". While this may be said to have benefitted both overseas and domestic suppliers the former were also strongly supported by a number of specific promotions which could not be readily duplicated by local growers.

Elders and Fyffes were the trend setters in this respect and followed their Bananas: The All-Food Fruit campaign with one introducing their Blue Label in 1929. This proved to be so successful that this symbol was to become a permanent feature of their advertising and did much to establish the Company's brand

Depression and Recovery

image. Fyffes' example was then to be followed by a number of their suppliers including Pagoda oranges (Welly, Welly, Good) in 1930 : Three Ring oranges and grapefruit in 1935 (this was later included with other South African citrus under the title Outspan) and the very effective Juicy Jaffa promotion which helped to make Palestine citrus a major ingredient in the British diet. Of course all of these campaigns were extremely expensive so branding could only be undertaken by the largest of concerns. As this was not possible for most individual producers the task increasingly fell upon national bodies which were originally established to consolidate exports and often to exercise quality control, as well as undertake promotional activities. These included the Australian Apple and Pear Export Council (1931) : the Canadian Horticultural Council (1922) : the New Zealand Export Control Board (1926) : the Citrus Marketing Board of Palestine (1927) : and the South African Citrus Exchange Ltd together with the South African Co-operative Deciduous Fruit Exchange Ltd.

Domestic producers could not hope to match the scale of these operations which until 1933 had the additional support of the Empire Marketing Board. At first this worked in conjunction with The Merchandise Marks Act of 1926 which attempted to ensure that the origins of all products were properly indicated. At the time it was hoped that this system would work to the advantage of the Empire and Home-grown items. Later, after the introduction of protection, its emphasis appears to have changed so that all imports (but especially those from foreign suppliers) could be identified for the benefit of the home grower. In practice, however, the labelling of apples and tomatoes - the main products involved - were widely evaded and did little to offset the advantages of the overseas producer.

As a result British growers were obliged to look to other measures to help them maximise their share of the UK market. These included the promotion of shows, demonstrations and exhibitions which, as in the 1920s, undoubtedly helped to publicise their products. Unfortunately these events were frequently also supported by the major importers and with their greater financial strength they may well have been the principal beneficiaries on many occasions. Attempts by domestic producers to use their membership of the main trade organizations was rather more successful. Thus the Chamber of Horticulture, the National Fruit Growers' Association and the National Federation of Fruit and Potato Trades, were generally supportive. However the Retail Fruit Trades Federation, created by amalgamation in 1934, was more concerned with the direct welfare of its members and most of their fruit, flowers and vegetables were sold on their merit - ie price and quality - irrespective of their place of origin.

In these circumstances domestic producers attempted to strengthen their position by whatever means were at their disposal. One of these was to join together to form co-operative societies of various kinds. This was, of course, an extension of earlier activities which had been encouraged by the Agricultural Organization Society. Although this body had been dissolved in 1924 some of its functions had been continued by the National Farmers' Union. Thus by 1935 there were:-

> "......apart from the small holding and allotment societies, about 230 co-operative societies in England, 81 in Wales and 88 in Scotland, with a total sales of £12.6 million. Most of them were purchasing societies, buying in feeding stuffs, seed and other requirements of their members. Many of the remainder were organized to pack and sell co-operatively their members' produce, mainly eggs, dairy produce and meat......". [11]

However in spite of this expansion, and further growth which took place later in the "Thirties", the contribution of co-operative societies to total output remained very small. Of much greater significance, perhaps, were the efforts made by the educational authorities in undertaking research and encouraging the spread of the best practice. A Research and Experimental Station had been established at Rothamsted as early as 1843 but although this proved to be highly successful it was greatly limited by a lack of funds. This was also the case in the few other establishments where research was carried out and it was felt that the UK was lagging behind other nations in this respect. Accordingly the Development Fund Act was passed in 1909 with the object of providing finance to re-structure the organization of agricultural and horticultural research:-

> "......After some discussions to the method to be followed, it was decided to divide the very wide field of investigation into subjects and to set up for each of the chief branches a Research Institute as the main centre for work of that description. Thus Rothamsted was recognised as the centre for the investigation of soil problems and the nutrition of the plant, at Cambridge two Institutes dealing with Animal Nutrition and Plant Breeding respectively were set up, the Dairy Research Institute was associated with the College at Reading, an Institute for investigation into Agricultural Economics was founded at Oxford, and the Fruit and Cider Institute at Long Ashton was enlarged to deal with investigations on fruit growing". [12]

These arrangements remained largely unaltered until 1930 when the Agricultural Research Council was established. This took control of the situation and under its guidance Rothamsted remained the largest of the British research stations. Other existing bodies were also supported including those concerned with fruit and vegetables at East Malling, in Kent, and Long Ashton, near Bristol, as well as the Experimental and Research Station at Cheshunt which concentrated upon

Depression and Recovery

the growing of crops under glass. While the Agricultural Economics Research Institute at Oxford continued to expand other, new, centres were also being created and supported. These included a Plant Breeding Institute and the National Institute of Botany - both at Cambridge - while smaller units were established at Aberystwyth, Aberdeen and Liverpool.

This pattern of research served the industry well and undoubtedly helped British growers to remain competitive. However as much of the practical information was made available to Dominion and Colonial producers this could not be be regarded as a major advantage. The provision of suitable training courses was also essential for the creation of a well-informed workforce. This had been pioneered by the South Eastern Agricultural College at Wye which was re-opened in 1894 so as to provide a wide range of full and part-time courses. Five years earlier a similar college had been set up at Swanley in Kent. At first this catered for both sexes but in 1913 it turned into a women only establishment and then became in effect a sister centre to Wye College. Both of these institutions continued to provide high-class educational facilities for agricultural and horticultural students throughout the "Thirties". By this time the research centres were usually attached to, or formed part of, university departments and over the period these gradually introduced courses which were also helpful for those who intended to follow careers on the land.

Thus on both the research and training fronts domestic producers were reasonably well served by the educational establishment. The fact that the labour force was better skilled than its predecessors, that management were more efficient and that yields had been improved while pests were being more successfully controlled were all important factors in the rise of productivity mentioned earlier. Another, equally significant, contribution was the progress of mechanization. While steam driven machinery had made some impact in the later 19th Century it was the development of oil and petrol engines that was to be really significant. Of even greater importance was the introduction of the tractor. Although the construction of these began in Britain in 1897 it was not until the labour shortages of the First World War that they were used in any real numbers. The low wages of the "Twenties" were then to slow their expansion but, even so, their number had increased to 16,000 in 1925 and by 1938 had reached a total of 60,000.

The net effects of the improvement in the productivity of British agriculture and horticulture were to enable it to remain competitive with the importers. In this respect the consumer was the chief beneficiary but the domestic industry also gained by securing slightly higher returns and a degree of security. Its main difficulty was, of course, that many of the actions which were taken benefitted imports just as much as home-grown items. This was certainly true of internal

From Orchard to Market

transport where the increasing cost-effectiveness and convenience of the motor vehicle demonstrated in the "Twenties" was further emphasised during the "Thirties". This led to road transport taking a rising share of the market including, for the first time, a move from short to medium hauls and even, for some items, to the longer routes. These activities brought the motor carriers into direct conflict with the railway companies which made every effort, including political pressure, to maintain their increasingly difficult position.

Government policy at this time was constrained by the need to assist the railways which were regarded as an essential national asset. However it was not thought to be desirable to inhibit a promising, new industry and so a number of minor concessions were granted to those vehicles carrying agricultural and horticultural products in 1928. Unfortunately the harsh economic climate of the following years plus the need to raise revenue and resolve conflicting interests led to a further consideration of this problem. The result was the Road and Rail Traffic Act of 1933 which was bitterly opposed by the Road Transport League. This claimed that the rail interest was not so concerned with the 20% of vehicles operated by road haulage contactors but wished to eliminate the ancillary users! These were, of course, those who employed motor vehicles as a means of transport in connection with their main business. This was undoubtedly an exaggeration but the Act did establish very strict controls on vehicles constructed or adapted for the carriage of goods. A licensing scheme was introduced which, in general terms, was to last until 1970. This provided for 3 types of licence:

> "A" for general carriers who ply for hire to carry goods anywhere for anybody.
> "B" allows the carriage of your own goods and those of a "neighbour".
> "C" limits you to the carriage of your own goods.

The Act proved to be something of a compromise. Thus road transport continued to develop albeit at a slower pace in a more controlled environment. Simultaneously the railways were empowered to expand their own interests in road haulage and, over time, were to be relieved of some of their more onerous duties as common carriers. However, while these legal matters were still being resolved, the Journal dated 27 November 1937 was reminding its readers that horses had many advantages for certain purposes and that motors were frequently more expensive unless used extensively.

In practice the rail network continued to carry the vast bulk of most cargoes throughout the "Thirties". This was less true for the fruit and vegetables produced domestically as their growers found motor vehicles to be more and more convenient for most short and medium length journeys. However imported

Depression and Recovery

items like bananas were still usually moved from the ports to the urban centres by rail although road transport may well take them to their final destination.

Bananas being off-loaded at a regional depot in the 1930's

The opening of the second train-ferry route from Dunkirk to Dover in 1936 further strengthened the role of the railways in respect of continental produce. As noted earlier the wagons landed at Dover or Harwich were subsequently moved on to London from where those not scheduled for the capital were taken to the main provincial stations.

While these innovations may be thought to have aided importers and domestic producers in equal measure there can be no doubt that improvements to external transport were only of advantage to the overseas supplier. The main innovation of the inter-war period was the introduction of the motor-ship and by 1939 the British merchant fleet included 25% of this type of vessel. However the banana carriers constructed for Elders and Fyffes up to 1930 were all of about 5,4000 gross tons, powered by triple-expansion steam engines, with a service speed of 13 knots. As this Company had virtually replaced its fleet by this date no further tonnage needed to be ordered during the difficult trading years which followed. Thus it was unable to benefit from the latest technology even though most of its vessels had been converted to oil-firing (instead of coal) by the outbreak of war.

In spite of the problems caused by the Wall Street Crash some shipping firms were

From Orchard to Market

able to invest in new tonnage and these vessels increasingly provided refrigerated holds for the perishable items. In addition many existing cargo-liners were updated to provide extra facilities for this type of cargo. The growth in the availability of ships with this capacity and the difficulty of obtaining sufficient freight made the entire trade very competitive. As a result many special arrangements were made between the shipping companies and the growers - one typical example being the relationship between the Union Castle Line, the South African Citrus Exchange and the port of Southampton.

Early example of containerisation improving efficiency in transport around 1930

Another was the agreement made in 1936 for the carriage of New Zealand exports - including fruit - to the UK. This was negotiated with a consortium of British firms - Blue Star Line, Commonwealth and Dominion Line, New Zealand Shipping Company and Shaw, Saville and Albion - and was stated to be worth £3.6m per year for a three year period. Although London and Liverpool continued to be the main ports of entry for all but continental imports other smaller centres were able to attract some direct services. Thus from 1930 seven of Glasgow's principal importers made an arrangement with the Blue Funnel Line for the carriage of apples from Australia to the Clyde. This was followed in 1934 by an agreement with the Fruit Express Line whereby its vessels began to land oranges and grapefruit as part of a regular service to Glasgow from California.

Depression and Recovery

Air transport developed only slowly after its introduction in 1919 and during the "Twenties" it was mainly confined to short range flights to the continent. Due to the relatively high cost of carriage this business was largely restricted to passengers and mail but early and expensive fruits gradually found a niché. This trade was at first operated almost entirely on the Paris to London route but other services also evolved over time. Amongst these were those from Holland arranged by International Air Freight Ltd for the carriage of flowers. This company began to operate c 1935 and by 1938 was employing four Curtis-Condor planes which had a capacity of 800 cubic feet or two tons. The flights from Amsterdam to Croydon took an average time of one hour, fifty minutes and a sophisticated organization then ensured the flowers rapid dispatch by road to their final destination.

The Union-Castle R.M.M.V. "Richmond Castle"
one of the several 'Castle' boats engaged in the South African trade.

At the same time the technical improvements to aircraft meant that services over longer distances could be gradually introduced. In the case of Britain these were principally organized by Imperial Airways which had been established in 1924. Using Cairo as its focal point this subsidized firm began a regular service to India in 1929. At first part of this journey was made by train and it was not until 1937 that these sections were eliminated. In the meanwhile a route to Singapore was opened in 1932 and in the same year a weekly service to Capetown was inaugurated - the initial schedule for this being 11 days! Two years later a service to Brisbane was commenced and, apart from trans-atlantic flights, a world-wide system was beginning to take shape. All of these developments were almost entirely concerned with passengers and mail and only a few, high/value, low/bulk items were carried. However a notable indication of future trends came early in 1939:-

From Orchard to Market

"EGYPTIAN PEAS BY AIR

> *Two hundredweight of fresh green peas from the fertile delta of the Nile were on sale for the first time in history at Covent Garden Market on Tuesday morning (February 14).*
>
> *They were brought by Imperial Airways to demonstrate that fresh garden produce from the Empire is available in winter to British housewives.*
>
> *The peas arrived in good condition, but were too advanced in growth to be young and tender, and their appearance left a good deal to be desired, with the result that they had to be 'knocked out' at very poor prices.*
>
> *The experimental shipment was divided into three lots. There were two sacks of peas in the pod, one box of shelled peas packed in dry ice, and one box of shelled peas without ice."* [13]

Clearly, although the improvements to shipping may have given some small advantage to overseas producers, the impact of air transport during the period was quite negligible. Thus the domestic growers of the majority of crops found that the protection given by government measures was adequate to secure them a moderate living. The contrast with the last days of free trade, when many were in despair or bankrupt, was remarkable even though the competition with Empire products ensured a highly competitive situation.

This was also true of the structure of the distributive trade which was only modified to a small extent during the inter-war period. Importers and growers tended to supply wholesalers and these, in turn, provided the retailers with their requirements on a daily basis. Thus most items passed through the market system which in London still utilized the increasingly inconvenient Covent Garden with Borough, Brentford, Greenwich, Spitalfields and Stratford playing supporting roles. The main provincial markets continued to include Belfast, Birmingham, Bradford, Bristol, Dublin, Edinburgh, Glasgow, Hull and Leeds while Liverpool was not only an important market but was also, with London, the largest of the long-distance import centres.

In the retail sector multiples such as J Sainsbury, founded in 1870, continued to expand while Waterworth Brothers were operating 106 shops when the enterprise was floated as a public company in 1936. However most of the retail outlets for fruit and vegetables still consisted of small firms with many single person, or family, operators and it was in this sector that competition was at its keenest. This was because the barriers to entry were very low - a rented shop, a hand-barrow plus credit from an equally desperate supplier - so the frequent

Depression and Recovery

bankruptcies were rapidly replaced by ever-hopeful new entrants.

For more than a century Pudding Lane, close to London Bridge was the selling centre by auction of all imported fruits, but on the opening of the new Spitalfields Market in 1928 a new Fruit Exchange was opened seen here in 1930.

These difficulties at the lower end of the chain of distribution were made considerably worse by the activities of the street traders. All levels of established retailers greatly resented the need to compete with a group of individuals who (it was said) paid no rents, rates, taxes or insurance. It was not just that the pressure of alternative suppliers tended to reduce the prices which could be secured : it was also because of their effect on opening hours. In many working class areas the poorer buyers had adopted the custom of waiting until the last possible moment before making their purchases. This was in the anticipation that the retailer would lower his price rather than keep a perishable item for longer than necessary. This was specially evident on Saturdays - the usual pay day - and it kept many shops open to very late in the evening. Of course the knowledge that street traders provided a substitute service helped this process and was extremely damaging when they chose to operate on Sundays as well as all hours of the week.

Sunday Trading was strongly denounced by the Government, the Church, the Trade Union movement and the Trade but it could only be stopped by the local authorities via their bye-laws. These increasingly chose to turn a blind eye and so it gradually spread especially when times were hard. Thus many retailers found

From Orchard to Market

it necessary to follow the example of the street traders if they were to survive. The improvement of the overall economic situation after c 1935 did not seem to reverse this practice and as late as 1939 Leeds Corporation decided to permit Sunday opening of its fruit and greengrocery outlets on its housing estates. The Journal campaigned against Sunday Trading for a long period but when it was clear that it could not be restricted it urged that those who decided to open should contribute a proportion of their profits to their Trade Benevolent Fund. [15]

This was not the only difficulty to beset the hard-working retailer during the "Thirties". The moves towards more hygienic premises and better washing facilities were generally welcomed as a major step towards preventing the contamination of the items they sold. These legal requirements, as codified by the Food and Drugs Act of 1938, had been building up over the previous two decades and would have been happily accepted if they had fallen equally upon all sections of the trade. Unfortunately it seemed certain that the provisions would not be followed by either the street traders or by those operating mobile shops thus giving these outlets a further competitive advantage.

Of course not all developments were adverse and from c 1935 the retail traders in most areas benefitted from the reduction in unemployment and the subsequent rise in the consumption of most fruits and vegetables. Some also attempted to protect their businesses by the introduction of Trading Stamps while most were able to take some advantage from the retail price maintenance schemes which were covering an increasing range of branded packages and tinned goods. Another innovation which promised much for the future of the retailer was reported in the Journal on the 7th of May, 1938. This described a meeting arranged by Mr SW Smedley at which he gave a demonstration of Wisbeck Instant-Frosted Fruits and Vegetables. Although frozen fruit packages had made much progress in the United States they were still in their infancy in the UK. Thus Smedley's plans for a national distribution system for quick-frozen foods had much to commend it and was to mark the beginning of a new era. Unfortunately the moves towards a wartime economy meant that these plans could not be fully implemented until the 1950s.

All of these events were accurately reflected in the *Fruit, Flower and Vegetable Trades' Journal*. This had gradually increased in size and status since it was originally acquired by Mr Harvey Hope-Mason in 1907. At that time it consisted only of a cover and sixteen pages and its advertising revenue was less than £5 per issue. Many firms still did not believe in advertising as they maintained that they had built-up profitable business without its aid. Even the much admired Market Price List had its critics for in some sellers' eyes it "gave the show away" and prevented them from earning windfall profits. The Editor mounted a vigorous

Depression and Recovery

campaign to overcome these objections and then, over the ensuing 28 years, introduced or enlarged many features which helped to make the Journal essential reading for all concerned with fruit and vegetables. Proof of the success of the format he adopted throughout this period can be seen from the fact that when he retired in 1935 the publication amounted to 36 pages of text, plus 16 or 18 additional pages of advertising, and that the revenue totalled several hundreds of pounds each week.

This progress was marked by a rise in price from one penny per issue in 1916, to three pence in 1931. The fact that circulation continued to expand indicated that the industry accepted that this was a price well worth paying for what had become essential reading. Much of this expansion was due to the efforts of Harvey Hope-Mason who, as Editor, throughout this period, had actively directed its policies. By 1936, however, he was playing a less demanding role and, although he continued as the Managing Director of Lockwood Press which published the Journal, Mr Wilfred A Jeffs was appointed as Editor. Sadly Harvey Hope-Mason was only to enjoy a few years in semi-retirement for he died in May, 1939, at the age of 73.

Harvey's only son was Gordon Hope-Mason who attended Haileybury College before joining his father in what was now always referred to as the *Fruit Trades' Journal*. After less than a year, however, he left to gain experience on a fruit farm in South Africa but returned in 1936 when his father's health began to fail. Gordon was then to spend the next three years working within the firm and learning at least some of the intricacies of the fruit trade. During this period the Journal continued to prosper and was also able to improve its technology. Thus in the issue dated the 20th of February, 1937, a four-coloured circular insert was produced on behalf of Batchelor's Peas Ltd : it is believed that this was the first time this had been undertaken in any trade magazine. However most of Gordon's activities were influenced by the shadow of the approaching war as the Journal did what it could to reflect government policy and regulations. Editorials such as Food Supplies in Wartime, Reserve Food Supplies and How Trade will be affected by the Militiamen convey the ever increasing tension of the era and there is no doubt that Gordon did whatever he could to assist in this vital work. Nevertheless, once war had been declared in September, 1939, he immediately volunteered for the Royal Artillery and was subsequently to see much action in France and, later, with the Eighth Army.

From Orchard to Market

Estimated Value of the Output of Agricultural and Horticultural Produce in England and Wales (£000)

	1930-31	1931-32	1932-33	1933-34	1934-35	1935-36	1936-37	1937-38	1938-39
Farm Crops:									
Potatoes	11,680	15,900	9,060	8,490	11,620	13,820	14,460	11,940	11,370
Other Farm Crops	21,540	17,060	17,300	21,940	24,280	22,150	25,370	23,390	20,430
Total	**33,220**	**32,960**	**26,360**	**30,430**	**35,900**	**35,970**	**39,830**	**35,350**	**31,800**
Fruit and Vegetables									
Fruit	7,800	5,600	7,100	8,200	10,510	4,990	8,330	7,250	5,640
Vegetables	12,270	15,150	12,940	16,820	13,340	15,000	15,370	17,770	18,650
Total	**20,070**	**20,750**	**20,040**	**25,020**	**23,850**	**19,990**	**23,700**	**25,020**	**24,290**
Glasshouse Produce									
Open and Nursery Stock	7,120	7,000	7,805	7,680	8,075	8,515	8,770	8,770	8,780
Grand Total	**60,410**	**60,710**	**54,205**	**63,130**	**67,825**	**64,475**	**72,300**	**69,120**	**64,870**

Based on Table 29 M.A.F Agricultural Statistics, LXXII, I, 6

8
The Shadow of War

As the shadow of war again descended over the country preparations were being made to ensure regular supplies of food.

> *"The aim of the preparations as a whole is (a) to secure an uninterrupted supply in the United Kingdom of all essential foodstuffs; (b) to reduce to a minimum the inconvenience and delay caused by any dislocation in the movement and distribution of food stuffs in this country which may result from war conditions; and (c) to ensure that supplies of essential foodstuffs at controlled prices are available to meet the requirements of all types of consumers and in all parts of the country, if, and when, an emergency arises. To secure these objects, food control, i.e., the organisation of supplies and regulation of consumers' demands, is essential".* [1]

The general principals on which the plans were based included the guarantee of regular supplies: the limitation of prices and profits, and equality of sacrifice in the event of shortages. Of equal importance was the decision to exercise the necessary control through machinery which was to be operated, so far as was practicable, by the food industry itself and each proposal was to be considered and developed with the active participation of members of the relevant trades.

It was then proposed that Great Britain be divided into 15 Divisions (plus London and the Home Counties) These were to act on behalf of a Food Controller in co-ordinating the work of local Food Control Committees which would be responsible for:-

(1). The registration of all consumers in their areas.
(2). The licensing and registration of retail dealers in essential foodstuffs in their areas.
(3). The issue of rationing documents to consumers within their areas if it should be decided to ration consumers.
(4). The adjustment of retail supplies to the aggregate requirements of retailer's registered customers.
(5). The consideration of applications by consumers to change their registered retailers.
(6). The adjustment of supplies to catering establishments, hotels

(7). *and other institutions.*
(7). *The collection of such returns and information as the Food Controller may require.*
(8). *The inspection of records of dealings in, and prices charged for, controlled commodities.*
(9). *The enforcement of Orders relating to food control.*

²

The Report estimated that home producers were currently only able to meet in full the demands for fresh milk and potatoes. As a result more than 50% of meat: about 70% of cheese and sugar: nearly 80% of fruit and approximately 90% of cereals and fats needed to be imported. This meant that in terms of energy value (or calories) domestic output was providing about 40% of total consumption. In addition almost 25% of the home production of meat, eggs and dairy produce was dependent upon imported feeding-stuffs and this was a further factor which would need to be considered in the event of war. The Report therefore concluded that the maintenance of adequate supplies would require a three-fold strategy- action to safeguard the importation of staple foods, the stockpiling of essential stocks and the expansion of the growing of certain crops within the UK.

The Report's detailed recommendations for ensuring a fair distribution of whatever supplies were available were paralleled by similar arrangements made for the transport of food (and other commodities) from overseas. An inquiry into the problems associated with the storage of food had also been commenced and the Food (Defence Plans) Department was actively considering schemes to requisition suitable facilities as well as to construct new ones. However this body was not to be concerned with any aspects of domestic production as these were to be the responsibility of the three Agricultural Departments which respectively covered England and Wales, Scotland and Northern Ireland. Government control in this area, already strong after the events of 1931, was further strengthened by the Agricultural Development Act of 1937 so the Ministry of Agriculture and Fisheries was in a strong position to plan for the wartime expansion of output which was clearly going to be a crucial factor in the feeding of the population.

The obvious decision to enlarge the arable area was taken by the Ministry at an early stage. However it was not until after the final blow which ended Czechoslovakian independence in March 1939, and made war inevitable, that positive action was taken. This took the form of a subsidy of £2 an acre which, from the following June, became available for the tilling of land which had not been ploughed for the previous seven years. The encouragement of arable at the expense of grassland which was to form the basis of government policy for the next decade, was complemented by arrangements for the detailed supervision

The Shadow of War

of all aspects of agriculture and horticulture. These were based on County War Agricultural Committees similar to those employed during the First World War and were designed to provide the essential link between the Ministry and the grower - the strength of these bodies being that they were mainly staffed by individuals who knew the practical difficulties of the business!

While these arrangements were being finalized during the last year of peace the customary work of the fruit and vegetable industry continued in a nearly normal manner. However all sections of the trade were affected by the introduction of numerous regulations which either required immediate action or preparations for possible contingencies. These included the construction of air raid shelters in the principal markets and the "provision of shelter against blast, splinter and falling debris" in all commercial premises where more than fifty people were at work. As this total referred to a whole building - not individual concerns - almost all firms and shops needed to comply. Participation in the Air Raid Precautions organization: negotiations re changes in the schedule of Reserved Occupation and their impact on those which wished to volunteer for the armed services, and attempts to prepare for the restriction implicit in the wartime lighting of commercial buildings were just a few of the myriad tasks which faced those in business at this difficult time.

It should be remembered that those obligations went hand-in-hand with the annual trade events and both the National Wholesale Conference and the meeting of National Retailers were held as usual early in April 1939. As many individuals were also engaged in a variety of civil defence and other part-time causes this meant that most firms were fully stretched and this situation was worsened by the absence of a rising number of young men. Some of these were volunteers but the majority were Militiamen who were called up to undertake military training. While their departure pressed most heavily on family and other small enterprises they also had an impact on the larger concerns which found it difficult to recruit adequate replacements in what was becoming a more competitive labour market. However most employers were able to console themselves with the thought that the military training was for only a limited period - unfortunately the outbreak of war meant that many of the Militiamen were to be away for over six years!

As the international situation worsened the British Government quickened its preparations and on the 24th of August enacted an Emergency Powers (Defence) Bill. This enabled the armed services to call up their reserves and placed civil defence on full alert. Thus when Germany invaded Poland on the 1st of September preparations were at an advanced stage so that Britain was able to enter the conflict only three days later. A large number of other statutes were also quickly authorized so that several new Ministries were created and the scene was

From Orchard to Market

set for the mobilization of all aspects of the economy. This was certainly essential for the neglect of the inter-war years had left the country ill-prepared for a major war and it was necessary that industry be converted to its new tasks as quickly as possible.

Fortunately for Britain its still small, though increasing, armed forces were not called upon to undertake immediate large-scale action. Once Germany had successfully completed its three weeks campaign against Poland a long lull was to occur during which Britain and France merely faced the Third Reich on the Western front. Thus the Winter of 1939-40 was to be a period during which the economy and society were moved from a peace to a war footing. This process was at first very uneven so that while the personnel in the services rose from under half a million in June 1939 to nearly two million by March 1940 there were still about one million registered as unemployed. Over the same period some non-essential industries continued with little change while those vital for the prosecution of the war had not yet been fully expanded.

All sections of the food industry were seriously affected by this time of change and uncertainty. This inevitably included the fruit, flower and vegetable sector which had the added complication of being dependent upon both imported and home produced items. The Fruit, Flower and Vegetable Trades Journal did what it could to reduce this confusion in spite of having immediately lost its Managing Director (Mr Gordon Hope-Mason), its Editor (Mr WA Jeffs) and its contributor Vigilant to the services. Its first wartime headline appears to have summed-up the situation very accurately : Present Conditions - Business as usual as far as possible! In the same issue it was announced that the Retail Fruit Trade Federation's weekly bulletin, which had appeared in the Journal for many years, would be replaced by a Weekly Emergency Bulletin in which all official notices were to be incorporated. Its policy of making its pages available for government communications can also be seen from the issue of the 30th of September 1939. This gave details of the Minister of Agriculture's advice to the County War Agricultural Committees in respect of the changes to horticultural crops which he thought needed to be introduced as soon as this could be arranged.

While the interregnum known as the "phoney-war" continued the trade was obliged to adapt to a whole series of changing conditions. Apart from the obvious difficulties caused by the loss of key men and the "Black Out" it was the gradual tightening of government control and the increasing spread of state interference which characterized this period. This began immediately on the 3rd of September when the importation of most fruits and vegetables was prohibited except under licence. As these needed to be authorized by the then small staff of the Import Licensing Department of the Board of Trade many initial problems emerged and

The Shadow of War

HORTICULTURE IN WARTIME
Ministry's Suggestions to Producers

'Although it is obvious that unlimited scope in wartime cannot be given to what might be called the luxury horticultural crops, such as asparagus, chrysanthemums or carnations, yet it is important that valuable stocks of these plants and bulbs should be retained, for they will be required again for expansion after the war. But more food is now our paramount need.

The Ministry of Agriculture has informed the County War Agricultural Committees of the changes in horticultural crops that he thinks necessary at the present time. This is what he advises:-

TOP FRUIT

a) Derelict orchards should be grubbed up and the land made avaible for the production of potatoes.

b) Since trees take several years to come into bearing no land should be planted to further trees except with the consent of the War Agricultural Executive Committee and this generally should not be given.

c) Since the labour available for fruit farms will in all probability be restricted, there would be no advantage in under-cropping the land beneath the trees.

During the period of war the amount of fruit imported will be below normal and growers should be encouraged to produce the maximum crops from established trees. Growers should be urged to make full use of "sprayings" and tree nutrition.

SOFT FRUIT

With lesser quantities of butter available larger supplies of jam will be needed and also canned fruit to offset reduced imports. The acreage to raspberries, currants, gooseberries and loganberries should, therefore, be maintained, but not increased without the special consent of the Committee.

Strawberries present a special case because of the number of poor and unproductive stocks in the country and the luxury character of the crop. Unthrifty beds and beds of three years of age and over should be grubbed and the land freed for potatoes or cereals. The occupier should be given permission to replant an area of land not exceeding 75% of the grubbed, provided the Committee approve the strain worthy of planting.

VEGETABLES

The acreage of most kinds of vegetables should be maintained at existing level; for other kinds of actual increase will be essential as imports decline. In a few cases a decrease would be necessary.

Increases in acreage are considered desirable in the West Country and the Isles of Scilly for winter broccoli, spring salads, early potatoes and early vegetables, and in other districts for carrots and onions. In past years imports of carrots and onions have been heavy, and some shortage may be experienced unless there is increased home production'.

F.F.V.T.J Sept 30, 1939

could not be speedily resolved. This was of major significance where perishable items were concerned yet the original bureaucracy was so cumbersome that it inevitably led to much confusion and delay. With the benefit of experience many of these difficulties were reduced and the entire system was overhauled in March 1940 so that the Ministry of Food took a more prominent role. Of even greater importance was the appointment of a Controller of imported fruit and vegetables, especially as Mr CH Lewis of Covent Garden was chosen to fill this vital position.

The inevitable delays caused by the increasing levels of control were not helped by the decision of many firms and organizations to move away from their traditional offices into new premises in safer areas - the Journal moving to St Albans at a later date. This was particularly unfortunate at a time when negotiations in respect of such necessities as War Risks Insurance and the establishment of the Emergency Scheme for Road Transport needed to be quickly finalized. The latter was of special importance as it required operators with 'A', 'B' and 'C' licences to register their vehicles and join into groups as an essential precursor to obtaining fuel when it became rationed. However these, and other difficulties, appeared to be gradually being brought under control as the bureaucracy became more efficient. Thus although agricultural workers were being steadily called-up for military service the creation of the Women's Land Army and the issuing of substantial contracts by the Ministry of Food meant that by April, 1940, it was generally felt that the overall situation was much improved. It was at this point that the war in Europe exploded into action.

The invasion of Denmark and Norway on the 9th of April 1940 was to have two highly significant consequences. In the first place it was to mark the beginning of a series of German victories which were to transform the war in Europe and, secondly, it was to have a major impact on the leadership of the British Government. The failure in Norway was an immense blow to public confidence so after a bitter debate in Parliament Winston Churchill replaced Chamberlain as Prime Minister. At almost the same time the Germans commenced an attack on the Low Countries which was ultimately to lead to the evacuation of the British Army at Dunkirk. The obvious weakness of the Allies then led to the entry of Italy into the war and on the 17th of June France decided to sue for an armistice. This left Britain (and her Commonwealth and Empire) alone to face the two Axis powers with few military resources but with the strength of a united nation fighting a just cause. While this situation was extremely dangerous, with the possibility of invasion being only narrowly averted by the Battle of Britain, it also presented many long-term threats to the United Kingdom's food supply.

The German occupation of much of Western Europe had considerable economic consequences. The UK was, of course, denied access to many former imports

The Shadow of War

from the Continent of which Scandinavian high-grade iron-ores and timber were the most significant. On the other hand this disadvantage was partly offset by the ending of Britain's obligation to supply her friends and allies with coal and other essential items. In normal times the Continent was also an important source of fruit and vegetables for the British market while only very small quantities were exported in return. Thus prior to the war the Low Countries supplied large quantities of carrots, cucumbers, endive, lettuce, onions, potatoes and tomatoes together with smaller amounts of pears and strawberries. Italy was a major provider of cherries, peaches, pears and plums together with green peas and lettuce: France was important for strawberries, asparagus and lettuce with smaller amounts of apples, while Poland shipped substantial quantities of onions.

The loss of these supplies was a major blow to Britain especially as it was compounded by the total cessation of imports from the Channel Islands. These were occupied on the 30th of June, 1940, and thereafter the UK's principal sources of new potatoes and tomatoes were no longer available. Spain had also been another major exporter during the "Thirties" although the civil war had caused some disruption. Nevertheless until 1939 she supplied Britain with substantial amounts of onions and potatoes and large quantities of apricots, grapes, plums and (particularly) oranges. The outbreak of hostilities then created many problems. These were partly due to the restrictions placed on the cross-channel train-ferries which had previously carried some of this trade and also because of the distinctly hostile attitude adopted by the Franco Government in the early years of the war. As a result Spanish exports to the UK were at very low levels until 1943 but once it became clear that Germany was unlikely to win cargoes of oranges and onions began to be shipped on a much larger scale.

Once Continental and Channel Island supplies were cut off the British Government faced a difficult dilemma. The nearest alternative sources to fill the gap were in North America but these would need to be purchased in hard currency. Other potential supplies lay in Australia and New Zealand which could be paid for in sterling but which required much more tonnage to provide equivalent levels of cargo. Thus a balance needed to be reached between the need to conserve Britain's shrinking financial resources and to make the best use of the scarce shipping space which could be spared to provide for the home market.

In some respects it was the adverse balance of payments which posed the greatest threat for Britain's ability to survive. Although imports of luxury goods were restricted as soon as war was declared it took a long time for effective measures to be imposed on other items. Thus it was not until March 1940 that the Ministry of Food took control of all food imports and constraints on financial transactions were not complete until the following month. However even when all these measures had been fully implemented the cost of imports continued to rise due to the increasing expenditure on war materials. At the same time the value of British exports steadily fell as industrial production was concentrated upon equipment for the armed services and civil defence. The net result was that the UK's deficit on visible items rose from £400m in 1939 to £767m in 1941 and reached £994m in 1943. Although these annual losses were slightly reduced by her invisible earnings Britain's total deficit at the end of the war meant that all of her pre-war assets had either been sold or were mortgaged to cover outstanding loans made by the USA and Canada.

These financial problems meant that as early as December 1940 Britain was already becoming illiquid and was only able to continue with the aid of the Lend-Lease arrangement made with the still neutral United States. This aimed to provide, free of charge, all the goods and services required by Britain that were available in America for the duration of hostilities. However competition from other potential consumers at first ensured that many items could only be supplied to the civilian market on a limited basis. In any event, even when food and other commodities were readily available, the volumes which could be transported to the UK were restricted by the ongoing shortage of shipping space.

The total dry-cargo merchant fleet available to Britain in September 1939 amounted to 18.7m deadweight tons. In spite of the gradual reduction of UK registered vessels as losses from enemy action were not made up by new buildings the addition of Norwegian, Danish, Dutch, Belgium, French and Greek ships ensured that by the end of 1940 the fleet had risen to nearly 22m tons deadweight. As it was to remain at about this size for the remainder of the war it might be thought that this total was adequate to meet most demands. This was not the case for two principle reasons. In the first place the use of a convoy system added greatly to voyage times while the need to avoid the English Channel and the Mediterranean considerably increased the mileage on many routes. Secondly the task of transporting and supplying huge armies in distant places as well as building up the resources and manpower necessary for the attack on Hitler's Europe both placed large, additional, tasks on the available tonnage. Thus it was not until 1944, when large numbers of American built Liberty ships became available, that the chronic shortage of merchant tonnage could be finally resolved.

Thus the Ministry of Shipping (incorporated into the Ministry of War Transport in 1941) always needed to make the best possible use of whatever vessels were at its disposal. Priority was, of course, given to the armed services with the importation of raw materials for war production a close second. As imports for civilian use were strictly restricted they were kept to the lowest possible minimum. This policy resulted in considerable shortages of a whole range of

The Shadow of War

unrationed items from razor blades to kitchen utensils. Fuel was also in very short supply so that although the meagre ration for coal was to be maintained the small petrol allowance for private motoring was ended in 1942. The government policy for the provision of food was even more important and most foodstuffs were gradually rationed by the use of coupons. These entitled each citizen to a certain value or weight of each commodity at a controlled price. In addition each ration-book holder was allocated 20 points per month which could be used to obtain scarce items. This system gave the consumer a degree of flexibility because while dried peas might be rated as one point per pound the luxury of a tin of salmon would take 32 points. It was also decided at the highest levels that bread, fish and potatoes and - most significantly - fresh fruit and vegetables were not to be rationed. Of course the levels at which both rationed and uncontrolled foods could be maintained were entirely dependent upon the supplies which could be imported or produced at home.

Until 1941 the import-mix was partly influenced by the cost of individual commodities but the introduction of Lend-Lease removed this constraint so that the only consideration was the best use of the limited shipping space that was available. The policy which was then adopted was for concentrated, high-energy, foods like meat and eggs (later joined by dried egg and milk powders) to be imported while the more bulky items like grain, sugar and feeding-stuffs were greatly reduced. This system also ensured that shipments of fruit, nuts and vegetables were all considerably restricted:-

Annual Imports of Fresh Fruit and Nuts (m.cwt)

	1939	1940	1941	1942	1943	1944	1945
Apples	4.684	1.840	0.323	0.412	0.159	0.402	0.605
Bananas	5.751	3.862	0.002	-	-	-	0.022
Oranges	11.266	8.262	1.684	2.094	0.905	3.313	5.828
Pears	1.207	0.302	-	-	-	-	0.002
Nuts	1.196	0.692	0.072	0.094	0.044	0.035	0.024
Total	27.619	16.511	2.284	2.621	1.550	4.247	7.932
Total (£m)	25.458	20.292	3.768	5.075	2.181	7.275	14.153

These statistics indicate very clearly the enormous decline in the landings of fruit and nuts during the war period. Thus total imports fell from over 27m cwts in 1939

From Orchard to Market

to a low of only 1.55m cwts in 1943. They also demonstrate that these cargoes had a very different composition than in pre-war days. Thus apples and pears, which could be grown in the UK, were shipped in only tiny quantities and nuts followed a similar pattern. It will be seen that the import of oranges did continue - albeit on a much reduced scale - but bananas were totally excluded after November 1940. Although this provoked strong accusations of partiality it seems certain that the embargo was introduced for purely practical considerations:-

> *"In the first year of the war most of Elders and Fyffes' vessels were able to sail independently, for their relatively high speed was considered to be a useful defence against German attacks. Following the capture of Norway and the fall of France the wider range of bases and airfields which became available to the Germans enabled the submarine campaign, aided by aerial reconnaissance, to reach a new intensity. The growing losses sustained by the company's fleet in the autumn of 1940 meant that independent voyages were no longer safe. Most of Britain's merchant ships were then being grouped together in convoys, but this solution was not really appropriate for banana carriers. The level of technology at the time had been developed to cope with voyage times of approximately twenty-one days, but escorted convoys tended to be slow and were subject to many delays and diversions. Thus the fear that cargoes of bananas might overheat and be ruined was one of the major factors which lay behind the ban......"* [4]

It could also be argued that these specialized vessels were better employed in bringing refrigerated cargoes of meat, eggs and bacon across the North Atlantic - as some did - than in maintaining their existing trade. Nevertheless the absence of the banana (plus the reduced availability of other fruits) meant that the nation was almost totally dependent upon indigenous production together with the relatively small quantities of oranges which could be imported. Fortunately this potentially unhealthy situation was partly resolved by the acquisition of substantial quantities of unsweetened orange juice. This could, of course, be carried in a wide variety of ships and did not require any special handling facilities. As a result the importation of fruit juice was largely maintained at pre-war levels. However the composition of these shipments was drastically changed so that the vast bulk was made up of concentrated orange juice. Although this went much further than its peacetime equivalents it was still only sufficient to provide adequate amounts for pregnant women and for children up to five years of age.

The importation of fresh vegetables was to be even more limited than that of fruit and nuts:-

The Shadow of War

Annual Imports of Fresh Vegetables (000 cwt)

	1939	1940	1941	1942	1943	1944	1945
Asparagus	5.4	3.7	-	-	-	-	-
Broccoli and Cauliflowers	202.0	8.2	0.1	0.1	-	-	-
Cabbages and Sprouts	34.2	15.6	1.9	1.7	0.8	0.2	-
Carrots	238.9	133.6	1.9	0.5	-	1.7	0.7
Cucumbers	33.6	0.4	0.1	-	-	-	1.0
Green Beans	11.5	0.9	-	-	-	-	1.5
Green Peas	19.1	0.9	-	-	-	-	-
Lettuce, endive, chicory	211.0	10.2	-	-	0.1	-	-
Onions	4,985.9	2,776.6	197.6	99.5	2.2	557.9	924.3
Potatoes	2,923.0	2,097.9	69.19	360.2	134.8	162.8	157.7
Tomatoes	2,839.5	1,163.2	36.9	-	-	-	147.3
Turnips	7.8	15.3	2.3	2.3	1.6	0.5	-
Total	11,626.8	6,243.4	819.9	475.7	145.3	732.9	1,237.0
Total (£m)	9.533	6.945	0.600	0.341	0.100	0.753	1.748

From the foregoing statistics it will be seen that vegetable imports fell quite dramatically in the years after 1940 and were thus only able to play a minor role in feeding the nation. When this decline is added to the fall in landings of fresh fruit and nuts the combined totals represent the difference between over 38m cwt in 1939 to under 2m cwt in 1943. At a time when so many other foods were in

From Orchard to Market

short supply this meant that unless domestic producers could fill at least some of this gap many British citizens would go hungry as well as lacking vital vitamins !

In broad terms the volume of UK food imports amounted to an annual average of more than 22 million tons during the period 1934 to 1938. This represented approximately 70% of the nation's then requirements. During the years 1942 to 1944 these shipments fell to approximately 11 million tons but because of the concentration on high-energy and dehydrated items these cargoes still provided 60% of Britain's more limited food supplies. The remaining balance needed to be produced at home and output was progressively raised so that it eventually made up 40% of a total which was, of course considerably restrained by the impact of rationing.

The principal way in which domestic production could be improved was by increasing the area of arable land under cultivation. As noted earlier a subsidy of £2 an acre was introduced in June 1939 for the ploughing-up of grassland. The impact of this, and other measures was that arable (including clover and rotational grasses) rose by 6m acres to reach 19.2m acres in 1944. This rise of 50% was used to double the area devoted to wheat and barley while that for oats rose by a half. The acreage for potatoes was also doubled while that for sugarbeet and flax increased by very significant amounts:-

Increase in Production of Field Crops: 1939 to 1944 (000 tons)

	1939	1944	Increase
Wheat	1,645	3,138	1,493
Barley	892	1,752	860
Oats	2,003	2,953	950
Potatoes	5,218	9,096	3,878
Turnips and Swedes	10,315	12,224	1,909
Mangolds	4,069	5,560	1,491

[6]

This tremendous expansion could only be achieved with the aid of a larger workforce. However although the total employed on the land rose by 172,000 to 975,000 its composition was gradually changed as regular male workers were called-up for active service. This loss was largely offset by the recruitment of casual male labour and then expanded by the addition of large numbers of female workers. Some of these were members of the Women's Land Army but most were country women attracted by the new opportunities which were created.

The Shadow of War

By 1944 the workforce was also being strengthened by the presence of more than 31,000 prisoners of war. Surprisingly, perhaps, this less experienced labour did not result in any general decline in the average yields per acre. This was due to a combination of factors which included the support given by Agricultural Executive Committees which advised on the selection of fields to be ploughed and on the crops which were then to be grown. Of equal importance was the increase in the use of agricultural machinery of all types - tractors rising from 120,000 in 1942 to over 180,000 by 1944 - for this encouraged the best use to be made of the less-skilled labour which was available. A further factor which enabled yields to be largely maintained throughout this period was the state's encouragement of the use of fertilizers. Thus domestic supplies were obtained to replace those which could no longer be imported.

The growth in the output of field crops was not duplicated by an expansion in livestock. The numbers of sheep, pigs and poultry were greatly reduced because of restrictions on the import of animal feedstuffs as well as the ploughing-up of grassland. The latter also led to a fall in the production of hay from 7.7m tons in 1939 to 5.6m tons in 1944 and this decline was reflected by a reduction in the numbers of horses used for agriculture as well as those kept for other purposes. However the need for milk, which was given a high priority, ensured that the size of the dairy herd rose by 7%. This was also true for both vegetables and fruit as the government fully appreciated the contribution which these products could make to providing the nation with a healthier diet. As a result the volume of domestically grown fruit was considerably above the pre-war average in each of

From Orchard to Market

war years except 1941. The pattern for vegetable production was also encouraging with output rising by more than 50% over pre-war days in 1942 and 1944:-

Output of Fruit and Vegetables in the UK (000 tons) (excluding potatoes)

	Fruit	Vegetables	Total
Pre-War	452	2,370	2,822
1939-40	824	2,402	3,226
1940-41	583	2,617	3,200
1941-42	321	2,883	3,204
1942-43	749	3,690	4,439
1943-44	657	3,143	3,800
1944-45	666	3,422	4,288

Although the total output of domestic fruit rose significantly when compared with the pre-war average the estimated number of orchard trees in England and Wales remained little changed. However in the period 1939 to 1944 the area utilized for the production of small fruit fell by 10,000 acres down to approximately 40,000 acres. Thus while apples and pears, on which most efforts were concentrated, were able to show important gains most other fruits tended to decline by varying amounts:-

Fruit Production in England and Wales (000 tons)

		1934-43 (Average)	1944
Apples:	Cider	70.8	131.7
	Dessert and Cooking	246.3	282.2
Pears:	Perry	6.2	11.5
	Dessert and Cooking	23.3	23.4
Cherries		16.7	17.0
Plums		107.7	99.4
Currants:	Black	9.3	6.4
	Red and White	2.7	2.2
Gooseberries		15.3	11.0
Loganberries and Blackberries		3.2	2.2
Raspberries		4.3	2.0
Strawberries		18.7	14.9

The increase in the output of vegetables was based, as indicated earlier, by an expansion in the area devoted to these crops in the UK and this rose from

The Shadow of War

280,000 acres in 1939 to over 466,000 acres by 1944. The biggest growth was in the acreage provided for peas, but there were also substantial increases for beetroot, broccoli and cauliflower, carrots, lettuce, onions, parsnips, tomatoes and turnips and swedes. Those items whose acreage was little changed included beans, Brussels sprouts, celery and rhubarb while asparagus and most bulbs and flowers were considerably reduced.

The net effect of these great efforts by all engaged in agriculture and horticulture was that by 1944 the domestic production of barley and oats had doubled when compared with pre-war : wheat had risen by 90% : potatoes by 87% : vegetables by 45% and sugarbeet by 19%. This meant that at least part of the gap created by reduced imports could be offset so that the level of the food ration could be maintained at an acceptable standard. The increased output also helped to ensure that many items including bread, flour, oatmeal, potatoes, fish, fresh vegetables and fruit (other than oranges) were not rationed although their prices were strictly controlled so as to bring them within the reach of all consumers.[9] It should also be noted that the national diet was considerably aided by the efforts of many individuals who planted their gardens and allotments with potatoes and other vegetables. These were later aided by government campaigns such as "Dig for Victory" and as a result many families were able to supplement their meals in a substantial and healthy manner.

The pattern of agricultural and horticultural production was significantly influenced by a combination of direct Government control and a range of financial inducements. The most important of the latter was the provision of guaranteed prices which ensured that revenue rose faster than costs. In order to prevent these increases being passed on to the consumer (and thus raising inflationary pressures) a comprehensive system of food subsidies was introduced and subsequently extended:

Agricultural Returns : 1939-1945

Year	Official Cost of Living	Retail Food Prices	Agricultural Prices
1936-38	100	100	100
1939	104	103	103
1941	130	123	172
1943	130	121	186
1945	133	125	196

[10]

As agricultural prices rose much faster than the cost of living and as retail food prices rose slower than this official index both producers and consumers were given considerable support. There was, however, no such aid for the food distribution network within the UK which was obliged to do the best it could - in the national interest - with whatever resources it could muster. The major difficulty for many firms was, of course, the shortage of labour. At first "key" men of under 30 engaged in the fruit and vegetable trades could be reserved from conscription if their work was classed as essential and could not be undertaken by women or by men over military age. The age for exemption was raised to 35 in April, 1941, but it was then proposed that there should be a complete ending of all reserved occupations within the retail sector by the first of June. It should be remembered that these decisions were made when Britain's fortunes were at their lowest point but nevertheless it still posed the very serious question of whether the task of fruit and vegetable distribution was a matter of national importance?

> *"We do not have to look far for the answer. The contractual activities of the Ministry of Food alone in regard to three vegetable crops - potatoes, onions and carrots - involving a sum approaching £20,000,000 pay ample testimony to the importance of vegetable supplies. It must be apparent that production in itself is insufficient and that this only serves its vital purpose of feeding the people when it has been efficiently distributed throughout the length and breadth of the land".* [11]

Fortunately it was possible to convince the Government that this policy was likely to lead to a breakdown in food distribution and some reservations were retained. However in March, 1943, it was decided that there should be a further transfer of labour from the retail trades. These proposals included provisions for the move of both men and women to the Armed Forces and vital war industries. In the case of retail grocers and provision merchants the basis for the retention of staff involved the number of consumer registrations possessed by each establishment and there were special arrangements for multiple organizations. Unfortunately it was not necessary for customers to register with retail fruiterers or greengrocers and so this important factor could not be taken into account in these trades. The criteria which was adopted then resulted in the loss of a number of experienced individuals but, even so, the fruit and vegetables sector was required to lose even more staff in the following September. The arrangements for these transfers were made between the Ministry of Food on behalf of the Ministry of Labour and the National Federation of Fruit and Potato Trades and the blow was partly softened by the assurances that this was likely to be the final demand for manpower from this part of the distribution network.

In addition to these compulsory losses of labour it was also difficult to retain or attract alternative employees. While wages rose steadily on the recommendations

The Shadow of War

of such bodies as the Agricultural Wages Board and the Retail Food Trades Joint Industrial Council they were frequently less than could be earned in other industries. Thus many retail outlets found themselves almost totally dependent on semi-fit or elderly staff with youngsters awaiting their call-up providing much of the necessary muscle. Both public and family companies were greatly aided by experienced, former, staff who returned to help and by individuals who chose to work past their retirement dates. This undoubtedly, mixed, workforce was then obliged to operate under a myriad government orders and restrictions with the sometime awkward prices fixed by the Ministry of Food being a particular bone of contention:-

> *"Let us examine some of the fractional prices scheduled for the fruit and vegetable trade. First and foremost we have the Potato Prices Order which in some cases introduced the fraction of one-fourteenth of a penny on lb. sales. In carrot control the farthing has frequently made its appearance, although an attempt is now being made to disguise its presence by scheduling prices for 2 lbs. instead of for single pounds. Also, in the vegetable field is the onion price of 4¼d per lb. in certain districts, with large green onions at this price in all districts, and also subject to measurement 'at right-angles to the axis'!*
>
> *On the fruit side we fare little better. In the North of England this season, such awkward prices as 4¼d., 8¼d., and 5¾d. per pound. were scheduled for plums. In other cases the 'odd half-penny' has been conspicuous by its presence in practically every instance thereby introducing the inevitable farthing when half-pound or quarter-pound sales are made. And when, as frequently happens in the case of apples and oranges, odd weights have to be sold, the calculation of the correct price becomes something of a teaser".*
>
> [12]

The adoption of Maximum Price Control of a commodity in short supply created another, much more important, problem. This first showed itself in respect of imported cargoes where it was discovered that because no allowance was made for transport costs that distribution tended to be confined to the centres nearest the ports. It was also found that in these more convenient areas many persons and firms which had not previously handled oranges, lemons and onions had somehow gained a share of these scarce items. In addition it became clear that there were tremendous inequalities in the quantities received by well established firms. These difficulties caused much criticism and led to demands that 'The Distribution Muddle' be quickly resolved. Thus, in March, 1941, a scheme was devised under which the UK was divided into nine sections each of which was linked with a primary port. Special Committees were then given the task of ensuring that each wholesaler in their area received a fair proportion of the supplies allocated to the population in its region. The wholesalers, in turn, were to divide those supplies which arrived proportionately amongst their retailers. At about the same time the Government set up the National Vegetable Marketing Company which was designed to be the sole purchaser of all bulb onions and carrots grown on holdings of over one acre. At that stage Great Britain was divided into selling and production areas with each selling centre being linked with one or more of the producing regions.

Both of these attempts to provide a more equitable system of distribution were rendered much less effective by the activities of some growers, especially of tomatoes, who chose to by-pass the regular marketing channels. Furthermore the attractions of the Black Market continued to divert many supplies from their official outlets. Prior to August, 1941, only potatoes needed to be handled by specially licensed wholesalers but in that month the scheme was extended. Thereafter all wholesalers dealing in onions, tomatoes, soft fruits, apples, oranges, lemons and dried and canned fruits could only operate under a Ministry of Food licence. These changes did much to restrict the leakage to the Black Market, while the creation of a register of retailers, categorized according to size, was another step in the right direction for it will be readily understood that during times of shortage it was easy to sell whatever produce was available. Accordingly, so as to ensure that all outlets received a fair share, a series of Retail Distribution Committees were set up in all the major areas. These bodies were clearly vital to the livelihood of all engaged in the business so it was fortunate that the Ministry agreed that they should be largely organized by the trade itself. Their very nature required that the individuals chosen to serve on these bodies needed to be scrupulously honest as well as knowledgeable and their chairmen had to be men of absolute integrity. In the case of the Merseyside and North Wales area the person chosen to be the leader of its Committee was James Waterworth, Chairman and Managing Director of Waterworth Brothers Ltd, and the allocation system which he subsequently devised was later to be adopted throughout the country.

The success of these arrangements led to a gradual increase in the range of fruit and vegetables controlled by the Ministry of Food. In January, 1943, this was further extended to include green vegetables so in spite of their more perishable nature cabbages, Brussels sprouts and sprout tops, cauliflower and broccoli, sprouting broccoli and kale all became subject to Government regulation. Thus the "official" distribution network became responsible for the marketing of almost all of domestically grown produce while still retaining its role in respect of imported items. This function was, of course, of little importance during the period from 1941 to 1943 when landings reached their lowest levels but changes in the overall military situation were then to reactivate this side of the business.

The Shadow of War

Germany's attack on Russia in June, 1941, and the bombing of Pearl Harbour by the Japanese six months later brought two powerful allies into the war and thereby transformed Britain's prospects. One aspect of this was the successful conclusion of the fighting in North Africa in May, 1943, and this, together with the subsequent Allied advance up the Italian mainland meant that the Mediterranean could again be used by merchant shipping. Arrangements were quickly made for the purchase of Sicilian lemons and Palestinian oranges (at first in juice form) and for Egyptian onions but shortages of tonnage kept quantities quite small. The increasing likelihood of Allied victory also encouraged Spain to resume its exports and early in 1944 both onions and oranges began to be landed in ever-rising quantities. However the extent of these welcome shipments should be kept in perspective for the amounts were only tiny in relation to the British population. Thus it was estimated that in January, 1944, there would be a one-off allocation of one-third of a pound of lemons per ration-book and it was hoped to make one pound of oranges available to each ration-book holder in the period from January to March or April. Unfortunately the distribution of these oranges, and of a one pound allocation of onions, were delayed by the discovery of time-bombs on board some of the vessels bringing these cargoes from Spain.

Further signs of the relaxation of the restrictions on imports came in November, 1944, when an allocation of South African oranges was announced. At the same time it was stated that substantial quantities of apples had been secured in the United States and Canada and that a ¼lb of nuts would be available for Christmas. These cargoes were extremely welcome and did much to raise morale but they also placed still more strains on a distributive system already fully stretched and under-manned. The passage of time had enabled a reasonably efficient bureaucracy to develop by the later stages of the war but the lack of maintenance and replacement of physical facilities meant that many items were worn out and at the end of their economic life.

This was particularly true of the railways whose pre-war role as the principal form of long-distant transport was further strengthened during the period of hostilities. This was because while the quantity of goods and numbers of passengers which needed to be moved rose substantially the use of both private and commercial motor vehicles was being severely curtailed in order to save imported fuel. Pressure on the railways was also increased by the lengthening of former supply routes due to dislocation and military activities. This was mitigated to some extent by zoning arrangements and both coastal shipping and the canal network were used wherever possible. However the ending of private motoring in March, 1942, and the decision to concentrate road haulage on the shorter routes ensured that rail continued to carry the major burden.

From Orchard to Market

The movement of fruit and vegetables from the ports or the growing areas to where they were required was thus the main responsibility of the railways which had come under state control in 1939. The need to economize on the use of transport quickly led to attempts to cater for each market from the nearest source of supply. This proved to be moderately successful in reducing the lengths of many journeys but this still left the ongoing distribution (or collection) to motor vehicles in many areas. In order to reduce their use to the barest minimum the number of railway depots and halts was increased and a road haulage organization was established to co-ordinate all trips of over 60 miles. When this was fully working in 1943 this ensured that most lorries operating under 'A' and 'B' licences could be employed on the shorter routes while the 'C' licence holders (who could only carry their own goods) were gradually confined to only the briefest and most essential of journeys. It should also be noted that the conditions upon which all these licenses were issued were greatly modified during the war and this was an important factor in permitting the organization of pooled delivery and similar joint services. This proved to be some slight compensation to many traders who needed to cope with the ever-growing shortages of petrol, spare parts and tyres.

All of the difficulties experienced by the industry were, of course, greatly aggravated by the enemy. Ports and railway centres were obvious targets for German bombers while administrative offices, storage facilities and shops were frequently damaged as a result of air raids on the major cities. One of the worst incidents during the early part of the war came on the 11th of January, 1941, when the Covent Garden area was devastated. This included a direct hit on Elders and Fyffes' headquarters in Bow Street which led to the death of thirteen members of staff and of nine members of the public who had been given permission to use the firm's air raid shelter.

These were, of course, just a few examples of the heavy damage and many casualties suffered by members of the industry during the first phase of the enemy's aerial assault. As the Germans concentrated their efforts on the Russian front these raids were considerably diminished. At a later stage of the war, beginning in June, 1944, the attacks were resumed with the aid of Flying Bombs and, after September, by V2 rockets. These jointly also caused enormous destruction and loss of life especially in the London region. The worst incident took place at Smithfield Market where 115 persons were killed and 123 were seriously injured. In addition there was the potential loss of much foodstuffs which was stored in what became damaged premises. By the end of 1944 this amounted to over 112,000 tons but, fortunately, all but about 2,000 tons were subsequently to be salvaged.[13]

The Shadow of War

In spite of all these problems the fruit and vegetable industry undoubtedly played a significant role in helping to ensure that the British population received an adequate diet during the Second World War. This had provided an average of at least 3,000 calories a day [14] and much of the credit for this must go to the farmers and growers who expanded their production to offset the shortfall in imports. The fact that the maximum possible quantity of this increased production was encouraged to leave the farm and enter the general pool and that whatever supplies were available were distributed on an equitable basis says much for the system which evolved and how it was made to work efficiently. This involved the goodwill and hard work of all concerned with administration, storage and transport as well as the actual importers, wholesalers and retailers. Of course it could be argued that this activity was in the financial self-interest of those firms engaged in the trade. While this is certainly true it should be remembered that the fixing of maximum prices for most fruit and vegetables left only small margins for those in the business. On the other hand it is clear that most items could be sold without delay so even with higher overheads a steady return could be achieved. However the imposition of Excess Profits Tax, which was based on the more uncertain years of 1937 and 1938, meant that the scope for profiteering was very limited. When the compensation received for war damage is included in the overall equation and this is balanced against the costs of reconstruction it will be seen that many firms did little more than break-even over the period.

The real reward for the tremendous efforts made by all involved in the industry came with the German surrender on the 8th of May, 1945. Victory in Europe day was then quickly followed by the welcome news that the Channel Islands had been liberated. As this announcement was accompanied by the news that the basic petrol ration was to be restored to private motorists and that more liberal allowances would be made for commercial vehicles it seemed to many that the trade would soon be able to return to peace-time conditions. Unfortunately this euphoria was soon to end in disappointment.

From Orchard to Market

9
Peace and Recovery

Almost as soon as the immediate military threat to Britain had been overcome much consideration began to be given to the nation's future in the post-war era. Some of these discussions involved social security, health and full employment and these culminated in the Beveridge Report during November 1942. Other internal matters were concerned with the development of education, the provision of housing and with planning for the reconversion to peace time production. External affairs were also of crucial relevance in view of the UK's financial weakness. Thus the arrangements made with the United States at Bretton Woods were clearly of immense importance as they established both the International Monetary Fund and the Bank for Reconstruction and Development. These certainly offered substantial advantages to the debtor nations but, in return, the UK and other potential borrowers were obliged to agree to the eventual ending of tariffs and other restrictions on international trade : these were to lead to the General Agreement on Tariffs and Trade in 1947. While these developments were thought to be generally beneficial to Britain in the longer-term they presented major short-run problems by limiting its immediate freedom of action. This was of particular concern to an economy which it was anticipated would have a deficit of £750m in 1946. [1]

This figure assumed that the war with Japan would go on for some time after the ending of hostilities in Europe and that lend-lease would then continue to provide at least a brief breathing-space. In the event the dropping of the atomic bombs forced Japan to surrender on the 15th of August 1945 and lend-lease was abolished only three weeks later. Thus the new Labour Government, elected in July, was faced with overseas liabilities estimated at £3.5 billion with reserves of less than £500m together with a massive balance of payments problem. In these circumstances it was clear that it would be essential to increase British exports as rapidly as possible while at the same time imports - especially from dollar sources - needed to be limited to the bare essentials. This situation ensured that domestic food production would have to be maintained at near wartime levels and that whatever imports were allowed would need to be acquired from soft-currency producers. These two principles were to guide British policy for most of the ensuing decade even though this period was to see international trade move from a period of great shortages to one characterised by one of surplus in most commodities.

From Orchard to Market

The UK's economic problems left no choice but to secure a substantial loan from the United States. Although this was granted on relatively favourable financial terms it brought with it further restrictions on Britain's freedom of movement in many areas. However the absence of foreign competitors in a world starved of both consumer durables and capital equipment meant that virtually everything that could be produced could be sold at good prices. As a result British exports (and re-exports) rose from only £281m in 1944 to £1,135m in 1947 and to £1,818m in 1949. Unfortunately the value of imports, in spite of many curbs and restrictions, also continued to rise and it was not until 1949 that a small, favourable, balance of payments could be achieved. In the meanwhile the economy remained under enormous pressure and even with the help provided by the Marshall Plan, which gave breathing space in 1948, the UK was obliged to devalue sterling from US $4.03 to US $2.80 in 1949.

On the international level this was an era which was dominated by the cold war between the two super powers, the Soviet Union and the United States. Thus the UK was obliged to adjust to a lesser role in world affairs and this was symbolized by its gradual withdrawal from its overseas commitments. The granting of independence to India, Ceylon and Burma during 1947 and the return of the mandate for Palestine the following year marked the beginning of the end of the British Empire even though this may not have been fully appreciated at the time. This was partly because of the attention attracted by the enormous legislative changes being introduced by the Labour Government which resulted in the nationalization of many industries and the formation of the Welfare State. In addition, the ongoing shortages of many commodities meant that it was necessary to retain many existing controls and most foods and other consumer items continued to be rationed in various ways. The need to add bread to this list from July 1946 to July 1948 was a considerable blow to morale as it had been possible to avoid this drastic step throughout the war. Further restrictions on supplies of coal, fish and potatoes during the severe Winter of 1947-48 deepened the discontent as the nation failed to receive the fruits of victory it felt it deserved. In these circumstances Britain's changing status in world affairs received rather less publicity than any moves which promised a return to normality at home.

The Government was, of course, well aware of this discontent and within its overall balance of payments constraints did what it could to alleviate the situation. Although the accumulation of wartime balances and credits meant that many countries were well capable of paying for British exports in the short-term it was appreciated that they would only be able to sustain these purchases if the UK was to buy the commodities which they produced. As Britain needed to acquire large amounts of raw materials and food in any event these two factors ensured that a steadily rising level of cargoes were shipped to British ports. Although part of

Peace and Recovery

these imports were utilized to maintain the export drive the balance was used to meet the demands of the domestic consumer. These items naturally included substantial quantities of fruit and vegetables and as financial and shipping shortages eased these gradually increased in both range and quantity.

As the dollar loans negotiated with the United States and Canada were quickly exhausted most fruit imports needed to be secured from soft-currency areas. Thus there were very real financial limitations on the sources from where supplies could be obtained until at least 1951. However the distinction between supplies from British possessions and Foreign countries does not appear to have been significant during this period. This was because in the difficult days following the war non-dollar fruit was welcome from virtually any source:-

Origins of Fresh Fruit and Nut Imports (1945 - 1951) £m

Year	Foreign Countries	British Possessions	Total
1945	8.173	5.979	14.152
1946	25.834	13.470	39.304
1947*	30.979	23.387	54.366
1948	31.389	27.269	58.531
1949	38.937	17.407	56.344
1950	36.308	25.482	61.790
1951	45.285	24.796	70.081

When these statistics are broken down into the principle fruit categories it will be seen that all expanded rapidly from the low point of 1945:-

Annual Imports of Fresh Fruits and Nuts 1945-1951 (m.cwt)

	1945	1946	1947	1948	1949	1950	1951
Apples	0.605	1.836	1.490	1.950	1.761	2.342	3.882
Bananas	0.022	2.031	2.097	2.977	3.056	2.758	3.270
Oranges	5.828	5.129	8.089	9.306	5.855	6.333	7.465
Pears	0.002	0.920	2.093	1.529	2.129	1.636	1.348
Nuts	0.024	0.519	0.559	0.857	1.786	1.404	1.038
Total (m.cwt)	7.932	12.805	18.370	20.849	19.080	18.856	20.600
Total(£m)	14.153	39.305	54.367	58.531	56.217	61.288	70.081

From Orchard to Market

As noted earlier only small quantities of fruit and nuts were imported into wartime Britain. As these included no bananas after the ban in November 1940 the resumption of shipments was eagerly awaited once hostilities had ceased. Thus the arrival of Fyffes' s.s. Tilapa with ten million bananas on board in December 1945 was seen by many as the start of a new era of plenty but, in fact, it was not until 1955 that the pre-war peak of 305,000 tons could be equalled. This process took much longer than in either France or Germany and was in spite of much unsatisfied demand. The explanation for the delay was partly due to the continued control of food imports exercised by the Government and of the general need to husband Britain's limited quantities of foreign exchange. These factors were, of course, significant for many products but the banana was to carry an extra burden.

Following the Ottawa Agreement, which introduced a remission of duty of £2.50 a ton for bananas produced within the Empire, Jamaica became the major source for the British market. This situation encouraged the colony's industry to expand and so it was badly hit when this outlet for its fruit was closed for most of the war. The imperial government therefore undertook to purchase any bananas which could not be sold locally or shipped to North America. Although the price which was guaranteed was low it was sufficient to maintain most of the plantations and in 1945 an agreement was made so that all Jamaica exports would be sent to the UK. Unfortunately the Island's production was slow to recover and could only provide moderate quantities for shipment. As a result Britain was obliged to seek other sources of supply and limited amounts were obtained from Brazil, the Cameroons, the Canary Islands and the Gold Coast. By 1951 Jamaican exports to the UK were still very low, partly due to a series of hurricanes and 'blow-downs', and could contribute a paultry 40,600 tons - a far cry from the 233,000 tons sent in 1938. Thus in that year a total of only 163,700 tons reached British ports but these, significantly, included approximately 6,000 tons from the Windward Islands.

The importation of apples and pears had also been considerably reduced during the war on the grounds that moderate quantities could be produced at home. Thus less than 10% of peacetime shipments of apples were received in 1944 and 1945 was only marginally better. Thereafter landings steadily increased but were still well below the pre-war average in 1951.

> *New Zealand Apples Arrive*
>   CONDITION PERFECT
>
> *Trade opinion is unanimous regarding the excellent condition in which the first post-war consignments of New Zealand apples are reaching this*

Peace and Recovery

country.
First of these cargoes (79,228 cases) arrived at the London docks on Monday last in the ROYAL STAR for distribution in the London area. Varieties include Cox's, Jonathans, Golden Delicious, Red Delicious, Kidd's Orange Red and Cleopatra.
To complete the London allocation a further 20,000 cases will be discharged from the HORORATA, prior to her docking at Avonmouth with a balance of some 90,000 cases.
The CORDILLERA, with 59,239 cases arrived in Glasgow on Wednesday.
[4]

This was partly due to the shortages of shipping which at first restricted cargoes from Australia and New Zealand while the scarcity of dollars limited supplies from the United States to the barest minimum. However Canada continued to provide substantial amounts and after 1948, many European countries - including Belgium, Italy and Switzerland - began to supply the British market. These were later joined by the Netherlands and Denmark and by 1951 the Argentine and, to a small extent, South Africa had also entered the trade. Pears followed a rather different pattern. The import of this fruit declined to even lower levels than apples but its recovery was to be much more rapid. Thus landings quickly overtook the pre-war average of 1.2m cwt as both Italy and Holland were able to resume their exports in 1946. These supplies were at first strengthened by shipments from the United States but these cargoes were then gradually replaced by the growth of others from Australia and South Africa.

The need to make the best possible use of the available shipping meant that concentrated orange juice was the main substitute for fruit for most of the war. However, as noted earlier, some oranges continued to be imported and by 1945 about half of the pre-war average of 11m cwts were again being received. This rapid recovery continued until 1948 when over 9m cwts were landed but totals then declined and only 7.5m cwt reached Britain in 1951. Part of the reason for the failure to maintain the early progress which had been achieved was due to the changed status of Palestine. The introduction of Empire Preference and the problems caused by the Spanish Civil War ensured that this mandated territory had been the UK's largest source of oranges in the late "Thirties". The creation of the state of Israel in 1948 and the disruption which followed meant that these shipments fell to a third of their previous peak. Spanish and South African exports gradually rose to fill the gap and smaller quantities were obtained from Brazil, Cyprus and Italy but shortages of dollars prevented any imports from the United States during this period. Spain and Italy continued to monopolize the supply of bitter oranges and by 1951 these amounted to approximately 400,000

From Orchard to Market

cwts per year which was in addition to the statistics of sweet oranges, clementines, mandarins and tangerines given above.

Thus orange imports, like those for apples and bananas, had still not reached their pre-war levels by 1951. It was thought by many engaged in the Trade that this was mainly because of the system of bulk-buying operated by the Government at this time. However true this may have been for these particular controlled items it does not appear to have been the case for other fruits and for vegetables - many of which could be imported under licence by private firms. Pears, for example, had already well exceeded their 1930's average and grapes, grapefruit, melons, peaches, pineapples and many varieties of soft-fruits and nuts had all rapidly increased in quantity during this period.

The shortages of most types of fruit imports in the early post-war years meant that existing controls were largely retained. In the case of apples a maximum price order - especially for home produced crops - had been introduced in 1940 and this was soon followed by other orders which covered the distribution and transport of all fruit produced by growers with more than one acre under cultivation. These arrangements were paralleled by controls over imports which were prohibited except under licence. For most of the war the level of shipments was relatively small and so were easily handled by peacetime firms acting on behalf of the Ministry of Food. The resulting landings were then supplied to licenced retailers through a number of Grading and Allocation Committees which operated via a version of the pre-war wholesale system.

Allocations to retailers of imported produce were granted on the basis of their trade in the year preceding the outbreak of war. Although this provided a guaranteed income for those outlets fortunate enough to be thus licenced this caused little resentment during a period of very limited supplies during the war itself. However as supplies began to become more readily available this attitude gradually began to change. Partly to offset this criticism the Government decided to add to the number of retailers on the allocation registers and in October, 1946, these rose from about 100,000 to approximately 120,000. This development was received with mixed feelings by the trade. Many growers and wholesalers welcomed the increase in potential customers but existing licence-holders regretted the move as they felt that they could easily cope with any additional quantities. However this expansion in their ranks was to be more than compensated for by the gradual expansion in the supplies of apples, bananas, pears and oranges. Thus even though total throughput remained below pre-war levels those in receipt of substantial allocations of scarce fruits were able to reap handsome rewards.
In 1949, when supplies of most imported items were becoming more plentiful and prices were falling below their controlled levels, the Government began to loosen

Peace and Recovery

its grip on the trade. As a result 'Open General Licences' replaced the individual open licensing system for most imports of fruit and vegetables from non-dollar sources in October that year. This quickly led to the abolition of wholesalers' and selling agents' licences and to an end to the retail licensing arrangements although not to an immediate end to the methods of allocation of some fruits and vegetables. However it was then announced that oranges and grapefruit would be "freed" from May 1950. This provoked the following editorial in the *Journal* dated the 24th of December 1949:-

> *A Welcome Step*
> "Welcome Christmas news for the Christmas trade: oranges and grapefruit are to be 'freed' next May when trade will once again be able to buy and distribute without restriction from practically all, save dollar, areas. But is it so welcome to those whom have grown accustomed to the idle, easy luxury of a guaranteed allocation margin based on a liberal grading for services rendered and work done in the distant, pre-war past? How many, we wonder, will be jolted from their easy-going security when the mad May scramble comes?"

This movement towards almost complete decontrol was taken a further step in January 1951 when the Ministry of Food decided to admit all apples on open general licences. While this was to be limited to countries with whom the UK had no balance of payments problems it was a major step forward. In effect the only fruit which then remained subject to direct regulation was the banana!

Vegetable imports followed the same general pattern as fruit. Their lowest point came in 1943 when practically nothing was landed and even in 1945 only about 10% of their pre-war average was received. Thereafter shipments quickly increased and after 1948 were regularly larger than their previous, peacetime, totals:-

Annual Imports of Fresh Vegetables 1945-1951 (000 cwts)

	1939	1945	1946	1947	1948	1949	1950	1951
Onions:	4,985	0,924	1,547	3,855	3,150	4,319	3,794	4,518
Potatoes: New	2,659	0,010	0,028	0,570	1,555	1,538	2,292	3,380
Potatoes: Other	0,264	0,146	0,125	2,091	3,487	0,524	0,400	0,334
Tomatoes:	2,839	0,147	1,928	3,803	4,102	4,688	3,851	3,755
Total (m cwt)	11,626	1,237	3,874	11,142	12,961	12,305	12,064	9,634
Total (£m)	9,533	1,748	11,137	27,613	35,841	34,350	33,191	28,943

5

From Orchard to Market

From the above it will be seen that the quantities of new potatoes rose at a steady rate from their wartime low to eventually exceed their 1939 total. At first these vegetables were mainly imported from the Channel Islands but by 1951 Algeria, the Canaries, Italy, Morocco and Spain had also become quite important. Other types of potato increased in a more fluctuating manner but quickly rose above the usual levels of pre-war shipments. The reasons for the differing fortunes of these two, very distinctive, products was that while seasonal factors ensured a permanent role for new potatoes much of the mainstream crop was acquired to make good whatever deficiencies occurred in domestic production. However seasonality was of major significance for both onions and tomatoes so both were able to retain substantial niches for themselves in the British market. Thus landings of onions rose steadily and by 1949 were close to their pre-war average. Throughout this period up to 1951 Egypt, The Netherlands and Spain were the principle providers with smaller contributions being made by Italy and Chile. Tomato imports were also quick to revive largely due to the rapid resumption of production in the Channel Islands. These continued to be a major source but were soon overtaken by the Canaries. These two producers were then to dominate the trade, with only limited competition from Holland and the 1939 shipments into the UK were then to be exceeded on a regular basis.

Victoria Street, Liverpool in 1951, a hub of the imported fruit trade

The quantities of fruit and vegetables that were imported in the early post-war era were, of course, greatly influenced by government policy. In view of the need to conserve foreign exchange every effort was made to limit landings to what

Peace and Recovery

were regarded as essential levels and these restrictions were applied with special zeal to supplies from dollar-sources. To some extent the amounts which were permitted were also modified by the quantities which could be grown within the UK. Thus the wartime legislative framework was largely retained while further regulations were introduced which were designed to increase the output of items which were thought to be especially desirable but which were in short supply. The Agriculture Act of 1947 placed these arrangements on a more permanent basis by following a system of guaranteed prices and deficiency payments which helped the domestic production of nearly 75% of all food crops. Although very expensive to the state, this policy was extremely successful in stabilizing the level of cheap imports and in the circumstances this expenditure was generally felt to have been fully justified.

The wartime period had seen home produced food rise from approximately a third to a half of total consumption. The 1947 Act them aimed to raise output by a further 20% so as to achieve a 150% increase over pre-war levels. By 1950 this target had been virtually reached as can be seen from the following statistics:-

Crops Harvested in Great Britain (m tons)

	1938	1946	1950
Grains	4.95	7.22	7.78
Potatoes	5.11	10.17	9.51
Fruit & Vegetables	2.33	3.67	3.85

[6]

These substantial increases, plus comparable ones for livestock, were made possible by the incentives provided by the government which made agriculture and horticulture profitable activities. These enabled the industry to retain much of its wartime labour so that the 1945 total of 681,000 was little changed by 1951. However over this period the number of female employees declined by about a third as males returned from the armed services. Government policy also ensured that the process of mechanization which accelerated during the war was encouraged to continue. Thus from 1944 to 1952 the number of tractors more than doubled while those for combined harvesters rose from only 2,500 to more than 17,000.

These developments helped to improve productivity and to meet the buoyant demand generated by full employment. In the case of fruit and vegetables the limited supply or rationing of many substitutes like sweets and chocolates was an additional factor which encouraged an increase in output.

From Orchard to Market

Fruit Production of the UK (ooo tons)

	1945	1946	1947	1948	1949	1950	1951
Apples	317.7	470.5	700.7	478.0	622.1	557.6	698.1
Pears	38.5	34.0	46.1	33.8	44.5	24.5	33.0
Plums	76.7	121.9	144.8	155.8	115.6	64.9	108.6
Cherries	17.5	23.9	26.9	24.0	25.1	15.3	17.1
Total Orchard Fruit	450.4	651.5	919.9	692.1	808.0	663.4	857.9
Total Small Fruit	37.9	52.7	63.1	71.5	89.5	78.0	97.9

The production of vegetables also rose substantially during the second world war and continued to rise in terms of value during the early years of peace. However, although the actual output of most items was at first maintained at wartime levels, the gradual increase in imports lead to a modest decline:-

Vegetable Production in the UK (000 tons)

	1944-45	1945-46	1946-47	1947-48	1948-49	1949-50
In the Open						
Roots and Onions	853	842	892	734	799	686
Brassicas	1100	1179	1000	1125	1101	729
Peas (harvested dry)	56	80	95	68	86	133
Other Legumes	190	227	213	130	208	165
Other Vegetables	530	444	393	340	350	276
Under Glass						
Tomatoes	113	103	98	106	110	114
Other Vegetables	3	7	14	25	28	33

The ending of hostilities in 1945 left an impoverished Britain in a disturbed world with innumerable financial, economic, political and social problems. These difficulties ensured that wartime shortages were to continue well into the post-war era and so many regulations and restrictions could only be gradually relaxed. Global scarcities of shipping and output meant that food imports into the UK were inevitably of major concern and even when these had been resolved the balance of payments remained an important constraint. In these circumstances Government policy aimed to increase domestic output as far as practicable and the output of fruit and vegetables rose significantly. The level of fruit shipments

Peace and Recovery

into Britain also steadily increased although they had not reached their pre-war quantities by 1951 and some sources could still not be used because of the need to save hard currency. This factor was less critical in the case of vegetables as they could be mainly acquired from non-dollar producers and their landings returned to near former levels at an early stage.

Pear harvesting in Kent in the 1950's

While this bare outline of a gradually improving supply of fruit and vegetables is basically correct it provides only a very limited picture of the difficulties of the early post-war years. All sections of the Trade - importers, growers, wholesalers and retailers - as well as those concerned with ancillary activities such as marketing and transport were therefore obliged to struggle against a whole range of problems. These included the shortages of labour and the consequent need to pay higher wages and made inevitable the industrial strife which disrupted the markets and the transport network on many occasions. Other irritations concerned the leakage to the 'Black Market', the shortages of fuel and building materials and the ongoing restrictions caused by government interferences and price control. The licensing system did, of course, provide healthy returns for those firms fortunate enough to receive supplies of scarce items and all sections benefitted from the rising demand encouraged by full employment. Thus most concerns were able to adapt to the changing market conditions and with the very real shortages which continued to at least 1950. They were, however, constantly frustrated by official bureaucracy and there was little that they could do on an individual basis against Government inefficiency and mis-management.

These tasks were in practice largely undertaken by the various trade associations and by the *Fruit, Flower and Vegetable Trades' Journal*. The ending of the war had seen Gordon Hope-Mason return to the Lockwood Press and it was under his guidance that the Journal, in spite of the continuing shortage of newsprint, was able to highlight many of the absurdities and abuses which beset the industry. Numerous examples of these activities will be seen in the pages which follow which will also illustrate many of the criticisms of state policy made by the major organizations involved in the business. During the national emergency the Government had worked very closely with the National Farmers' Union, the National Federation of Fruit and Potato Trades, the Retail Fruit Trade Federation and other trade associations. However in the changed circumstances of the post-war era what was perceived as the sectional interests of these bodies made this co-operation much less effective and so made the role of the *Journal* even more essential. This was especially true of the Retail Federation which was given its own space and which by 1955 had contributed over 1,000 weekly articles.

Self-Service Comes to Town
A.E.Hammond comments

The self-service selling of fruit and vegetables has started in this country, in quite a small way, it is true, but it is a significant and important pioneering step, taken long before most people expected.

Last week I saw many scores of people shopping by this method, as a matter of course, in a section of a Marks and Spencer store in Wood Green, a north London suburb. About one fifth of the store has been converted into a self-service food department, and one counter is given up to fresh produce.

The range of produce on sale the day I visited the store comprised cauliflower, Brussels sprouts, South African peaches and plums, mandarines, apples, tomatoes, chestnuts, and walnuts. Some of it was put up in brown paper bags, some in transparent cellulose film, and some left unwrapped. The packaging was done on the spot by two girls behind the counter.

F.T.J Oct 15, 1949

Peace and Recovery

Typical of the causes which were championed by the Retail Federation concerned the provision of more staff for retail outlets. At a time of ongoing scarcities an important characteristic of the period was the need for the consumer to queue for almost every necessity. This was an inevitable consequence of the Government's desire to secure a fair and just distribution of whatever was available for this led to a proliferation of ever-changing rules and instructions from the Ministry of Food. In many instances it was very time-consuming to implement these measures and as it was frequently not possible to retain adequate staffs delays were unavoidable. As a result many retailers were heavily criticized by the public and less informed sections of the press.

As the early post-war era was to be characterized by full employment the shortage of labour was to become a near permanent feature for many years. Thus the Agricultural Wages Board was obliged to make a series of orders raising minimum and overtime wage rates while holiday and other entitlements were gradually improved. Until 1950 a degree of wage restraint was encouraged by the Trades Union Congress but moves towards a "Five Day Week" could not be resisted and this created major difficulties for many growers. In addition, although this was not a period of large-scale industrial action, a number of unofficial stoppages by dockers, transport workers and market porters badly affected distribution from time to time. This disruption, allied to ongoing scarcities of many items, encouraged the growth of illegal trading which took a number of different forms. One aspect concerned allegations of conditional sales at some wholesale markets:-

> "......A small greengrocer goes in to buy four sacks of potatoes, and he must at the same time take a sack of savoys at very high prices, and a case of grapes at an even higher range. He wants neither, but is told that he must have both if he is to get his potatoes".

The consequence of this type of activity was that:

> "......at almost every street corner hawkers are selling fruit at well above controlled prices. For sweet oranges, which should retail at 8d. per lb., 1/3d. is being charged. For bananas that are controlled at 1/1d. per lb., 6/- is being asked by these black market traders.
>
> We know, the trade knows, and the public knows, that such unlawful dealings are happening every day within the industry, but whose responsibility is it to stop it? The retailer argues he is victimised if he lays information against a wholesaler - the wholesaler blames the sender or importer, who says unless he pays a higher price he'll lose the consignment".[9]

From Orchard to Market

This argument was compounded by the feeling that the Ministry of Food's enforcement officers did little to prevent this abuse especially where street hawkers were involved. There is, in fact, considerable evidence to show that many prosecutions were undertaken and some cities, like Manchester, made great efforts to resolve the problem. However there did not appear to be any lasting impact and the trade felt that the officers spent too much time investigating 'technical' offenses and enforcing petty regulations. Nevertheless it is clear that many firms did flout the controls in an attempt to offset what they regarded as Ministerial inefficiency:-

Heavy Fines

> "Found guilty of 34 offences relating to the Potato Control and Prices Order, 1943, Joseph Mealor, potato merchant of Hawarden, a magistrate and chairman of the Hawarden Rural Council, was fined a total of £380 at the local magistrates' court recently. He was also ordered to pay £100 toward the expenses of the prosecution. It was alleged that between January and May of last year he sold potatoes at a price exceeding that fixed grower's prices. Mr. Mealor said that at the time his lorries made futile journeys to Liverpool docks where the potatoes could not be obtained because of the congestion. There were claims that the potatoes were frosted and there were losses on various transactions". [10]

While most of the difficulties faced by the industry were essentially caused by shortages of supplies and labour many believed that political considerations were making matters worse. These ideas hinged around the wartime development of bulk purchasing and central distribution which it was widely agreed had conveyed many advantages to the nation. By 1947, however, these systems were being heavily criticized on the three grounds summarized in a letter sent to the Ministry of Food by the Fruit and Vegetable Trade Association of Importers, Distributors and Salesmen quoted in F.F.V.T.J., dated 15 February 1947. In the first place it was claimed that the re-emergence of other countries meant that Britain was no longer in a monopoly position so was finding it increasingly difficult to acquire adequate quantities at reasonable prices. Secondly, as many of the finest executives - largely seconded from the Trade - had now left the Ministry and returned to private firms, the degree of knowledge and expertise was much less than during the war. Thirdly, the system of distribution, being based on an "area population basis" took no account of "consumer choice". This had been of no importance when supplies had been limited to small allocations entirely provided by the Ministry and had ensured a fair share of whatever was available. However as by 1947 some private importations were being permitted the public were being given a basis for comparison and it was alleged that they were becoming increasingly resentful over artificial controls.

Peace and Recovery

Then in January, 1946, price control was lifted for all green vegetables, leeks, rhubarb, soft fruits, cucumbers and root vegetables excepting cooked beetroot. In the following twelve months the prices of all these items either rose or, at best, remained static.

In spite of price increases demands for a relaxation of control continued unabated largely because of the administrative inefficiency which saw many headlines in the Journal expressing the concern felt in the trade at Government policy. These included Import Muddle, A Disastrous Decision, Market Planning and Ministry Ostriches, No Wonder the Housewife Protests and The Potato Muddle (A Story of Waste and Incompetence).

Since 1934 the Potato Marketing Board had regulated supply and demand by varying the "size of the riddle" so that small potatoes could not be retailed. The surplus was then either fed to stock or ploughed back into the land and little provision was made for a reserve to be carried over for future years. These arrangements were greatly modified during the Second World War when every effort was made to increase production. While this was very successful it was only achieved by a multitude of controls, a vast army of officials and a large statistical department which, sometimes belatedly, produced estimates of future requirements. This system was continued into the post-war era but failed to appreciate that the world-wide shortage of wheat and the rationing of bread which followed would inevitably lead to an increase in demand for potatoes. When this incompetence was compounded by severe weather in the Spring of 1947 a crisis was only just averted. This was bad enough but the events which followed were even worse.

> *"The spring of 1947 was put down as an "Act of God," but no act of man seemed to be called for in 1947/8. What if exchange resources were falling fast, what if bread rationing should continue, what if bad weather should come, our potato potentates were reared and bred for restriction. Instead of a sharp step-up in acreage, and a concentration on production by the more skilled and better equipped growers, an amazing programme was issued allowing a continuing run-down in the potato acreage over the next few years.*
>
> ### *Delayed Action*
>
> *This season's potato crisis was predicted by many as far back as June, 1947 -it was clearly visible to everyone in the industry by October. But 'not until the complete census returns are to hand' could the Minister act: If rationing had to come, and everyone in the trade knew that it must, it would have been effective in August to October, by checking both waste*

From Orchard to Market

and hoarding. When the Census Department of the Potato Division finally told us what we all knew months before, it was too late for the ration to be maintained without imports, and very expensive imports at that. But it was not until January that the Ministry took fright, and Sir John Mollett was sent to scour Europe for the potatoes which under free enterprise would have been secured in August by private traders at much lower prices. Today, while the Potato Division is frantically importing old potatoes from as far afield as Australia (what the freight alone will be is a frightening thought), another section of the Ministry is lavishly issuing licences ad lib. for private importation of so-called 'early' potatoes. Two thousand tons of Egyptian 'Hardskins' at £28 per ton f.o.b. are a poor substitute for a few hundred thousand tons of Majestics which a fair price system and less red tape would have ensured at home. Altogether a sorry record of 'too little and too late' of which we have not heard the end by any means. [11]

While the Administration were able to put forward a number of reasons for the failure of its policies there can be no doubt that it received much adverse publicity. Thus in an attempt to improve its image as well as to seek to overcome these problems the Government decided to establish the Fruit and Vegetable (Marketing and Distribution) Organization. This, it was claimed, was designed to help the trade to bring these items to the consumer in the best possible condition at the cheapest possible price. Unfortunately it was conceived as only an advisory body and as its functions overlapped with those of both the Ministry of Agriculture and the Ministry of Food it proved difficult to reconcile conflicting interests. As a result only bland generalizations were produced and no new legislation was introduced. However the Journal also concluded that the Minister of Food had finally appreciated that there were no easy solutions to the ills which beset horticulture:-

> *"In a word Mr. Strachey is beginning to realise that the evils are not so glaring, the present marketing and distribution methods not so inefficient, the abuses and waste not so eradicable, as popular belief implies. He has therefore preferred to maintain on the subject an indefinite and hopeful silence which his deputy, Dr. Summerskill would be wise, on occasions, to emulate."* [12]

In practice it seems that bulk purchases and centralized distribution could only work with the co-operation of all concerned. This was forthcoming during the war but was increasingly rejected once peace had returned so that more control often provided less for the consumer in many cases. There was also great anxiety in the trade over Labour's plans to nationalize the transport sector. During the Second World War the state had imposed strict controls over road transport by

Peace and Recovery

extending the 1933 Act and had arranged for it to work closely with the railway companies. The post-war Government thought this co-operation should continue and nationalized the railways and the larger road haulage contractors. However those who operated "C" licence vehicles were allowed to continue - partly because of the campaign mounted by the Journal to have the fruit, vegetables and potato trades excluded. An unseen consequence of this concession was that "C" licence holders expanded at such a rate that the Railway Executive claimed that their business was being affected and wished the government to impose a 25 mile radius on all their journeys:-

> **Rail and Road Transport**
> "The campaign against those who carry their own produce in their own vehicles (a description which appears, rightly or wrongly, to include many wholesalers who carry goods belonging to growers) is mounting in strength, and we make no apology for returning so soon to the subject of the threatened "C" licensee. For the first time a senior official of the nationalised Railway Executive has said bluntly (in Rome) that the welfare of the railways is being threatened by the number and growth of "C" licensees, and that the Government should take steps to limit their activities - presumably by imposing (as the Government has always retained the right to impose) a 25-mile radius limit on the journeys of such vehicles. The havoc this would cause in the fruit and vegetable distribution trade is not difficult to envisage: not so much because nationalised road haulage would prove incompetent to do the job itself - that is a debatable point - but because the railways who really want this lucrative trade have shown themselves quite inadequate for the task. If present experience is any criterion (and why shouldn't it be?) the extent of delays in delivery, missed market arrivals, and broken and pilfered consignments, to say nothing of higher freight charges, will add noticeably to the already high cost of distribution.
> The railway authorities doubtless supported the general view that the siting of new wholesale markets must of necessity be adjacent to rail termini. Most people appear to have accepted this as an indispensable condition of re-siting. But prevalent trade opinion, certainly in some quarters, considers such a pre-requisite quite useless; because the vast majority of produce is sent by road. Why? It is cheaper, quicker, and less troublesome in most cases for fairly short hauls. The railways should be aware of imposing arbitrary and dangerous restrictions on their rivals. It cannot help them in the long run." [13]

From Orchard to Market

In the event this restriction was never imposed and the election of a Conservative administration in 1951 effectively ended this possibility. It also led, in the longer term, to the final denationalization of the haulage industry.

The technical evolution of the motor vehicle during the Second World War was such that it was eventually able to compete with the railways on even the longest of routes. This was certainly not the case in the early days of peace when, apart from the statutory limitations, there were considerable shortages of vehicles, fuel and labour. Many roads were still suffering from a lack of maintenance and although this was gradually rectified the national network was barely able to meet the growth in demand before the construction of the motorways began in 1958. The railways were, of course, also in a deplorable condition when hostilities ceased and the entire network required a considerable degree of renovation and investment. These difficulties ensured that Government controls continued until the British Transport Commission was established in 1947. Separate Executive Boards were then deputed to run the nationalized railways, canals and long-distance road services and it was hoped that a fully integrated system would gradually evolve. However the administrative structure which was set up made little provision for coordination at regional level and virtually all decisions had to be referred to London. The resulting bureaucracy, together with ongoing shortages and the need to justify individual projects, encouraged many local and area units to go their separate ways. As a result competition between the different modes of transport continued and the share of the railways steadily declined. [14]

Although British Road Services developed some interconnected, regular, long-distance routes which proved to be generally satisfactory rail continued to provide the best option for trunk journeys. This was also the case for the overland route from the Continent. The train-ferries reopened in 1947 and gradually built up their traffic to pre-war levels. At first they continued to be hindered by the fact that Spain and Portugal (as well as Russia) operated different gauges on their railways so that any freight needed to be trans-shipped on their borders. However the Transfesa Company, formed in Madrid in 1943, for the carriage of livestock within Spain, appreciated the potential of handing goods for export and in 1951 devised a system whereby axles could be rapidly changed. Border points at Hendaye and Cerbère were fitted with this apparatus and this enabled trucks loaded with fruit and vegetables to be loaded in Spain and taken directly to their destinations in Europe including the UK. In that year the rail service carried 31% of the Spanish citrus crop while 69% was moved by sea - significantly none was transported by road at that time.

Almost simultaneously British, French, Dutch, Belgium, Swiss and Italian railways established Interfrigo to provide for the carriage of perishable commodities on

Peace and Recovery

their networks. It was organized on a co-operative basis with its headquarters in Switzerland, although registered in Belgium and began to operate in 1950 utilising its members own wagons. It was soon constructing its own, specially designed, trucks and, over time, extended its membership to include Denmark and Western Germany while links were established with most other countries in Western (and later) Eastern Europe.

The arrangements with Transfesa and Interfrigo were not affected by the emergence of British Rail. This was also the situation when civil aviation was nationalized. In 1939 Imperial Airways and British Airways, which had been subsidized for sometime, were bought out by the Government and combined to form British Overseas Airways. In 1946 this was re-organized as a state corporation for long-haul routes while British European Airways was established for continental services. Later, in 1974, BOAC and BEA were combined to form British Airways and this was privatized in 1986.

The Civil Aviation Act of 1946 effectively reserved all scheduled routes for the two nationalized corporations. Private firms were not even allowed to offer regular services if the nationalized airlines choose not to operate particular routes themselves! Thus all developments on scheduled services were the responsibility of BOAC or BEA and, over time, they carried ever increasing quantities of fruit and vegetables from a wide variety of sources. However private airlines were able to operate on a charter basis and they rapidly responded to the demand for soft fruits and other perishable items when it was profitable to do so. This business, greatly aided by the new air market at the Baltic Exchange, quickly became quite substantial although it began on a very moderate scale.

As early as April, 1947 charter flights were bringing strawberries and cherries from Verona and Bari in Italy. These were mainly carried by converted Lancaster and Halifax bombers but Skymasters and Dakotas were also to engage in this trade. While this business, together with the carriage of asparagus, worked well in a technical sense it was less successful commercially. Nevertheless a wide variety of experimental flights continued, and after the Berlin airlift, was continued on a larger scale. At one stage flying-boats were considered and the Journal dated 18 June 1949 reported that six tons of apricots were brought from Spain to Southampton by this type of aircraft. However land based planes were clearly more convenient and in the same year grapes from Malaga, greengages and apricots from France and tomatoes from Amsterdam to London were all imported. Later that same year BEA brought in grapes and mushrooms from Gibraltar, Italy and France while BOAC imported half a ton of pineapples from Nairobi.

From Orchard to Market

In order to maximise the limited capacity of the planes then in use French fruits such as peaches, plums and apricots were taken overland to Le Touquet and then flown to Lympne Airport in Kent. Other short-distance routes were subsequently developed by Silver City Airways from Guernsey to Eastleigh Airport and by Channel Air Bridge from Rotterdam to Lydd and Southend: by 1959 the latter catered for over 7,000 tons of freight which was largely fresh fruit. The merger of Silver City and Channel Air Bridge to form a part of British United Air Ferries marked the increasing scale of the organization required to cope with ever-bigger quantities. This was reflected on the technical side by the replacement of Bristol Freighters with their 5 ton payload by Carvairs (a modification of the DC4) which could carry up to 9 tons of freight.

Flowers from Guernsey are unloaded at Eastleigh, Southampton in 1956.

In spite of this considerable progress it should be remembered that air transport, either as part of scheduled services or via special charters, still only catered for the carriage of early, out-of-season and the more exotic varieties of fruit and vegetables. Some of these, together with a number of mainstream crops, were also imported from the Continent via the train-ferries, but many items from Europe continued to be brought to Britain by sea in traditional style vessels. MacAndrew's, for example operated services to all the major Spanish fruit ports including those in Almeria, Burriana, Gandia, Malaga, Seville and Valencia. The Norwegian Fred Olsen Line and the Spanish Naviera Aznar Line imported substantial quantities of produce from the Canary Islands and, like MacAndrew's, many of their voyages terminated at either Liverpool or London. However they, like many smaller companies frequently used other British ports which were more convenient for particular purposes. Thus Boston, Dover, Portsmouth, Sheerness and Shoreham

Peace and Recovery

- to name just a few - were found to have many advantages especially during an era when industrial disruption was common at those harbours subject to the National Dock Harbour Scheme.

Ships were, of course, also responsible for bringing the vast bulk of fruit and vegetables from the more distant sources of supply. Some of these cargoes came in the holds of fast, passenger liners but most were transported in specialized vessels which had their origins in the meat carriers of the late 19th century which were subsequently adapted for the carriage of bananas. These can best be described as single temperature refrigerated ships which catered for a homogenous cargo which was cooled at an appropriate, uniform, rate depending on its particular needs. Vessels of this type were in short supply in 1945 but then rapidly increased in number to cope with the growing demands of world trade. These were largely constructed to pre-war designs with either steam turbines or diesel engines replacing triple expansion steam. There were few other innovations until the 1960s - the only real changes before then were to speed and scale.

It is generally accepted that by 1950 the abnormal conditions caused by the Second World War were coming to an end. The process of deregulation was making good progress with the termination of both the petrol and points rationing schemes while oranges and early potatoes had been freed from control. The Imported Deciduous Fruit Order and imported apple schemes were also withdrawn and replaced by allocation schemes so that by the end of the year only bananas and potatoes were still subject to direct regulation.

These events were, to a large extent, a reflection of the recovery of the British economy since 1945. The pent-up demands from overseas countries had enabled British exports to grow rapidly while imports had been restricted to some extent so the Balance of Payments situation had gradually improved. The ability of the UK industry to take advantage of this opportunity had been greatly assisted by the breathing space provided by the North American loans and the aid provided by the Marshall Plan. In addition, production had been considerably encouraged by a Bank Rate of only 2% so both the older, staple, industries and the newer, science-based firms were better able to cope with the back-log of demand from both home and abroad. One major effect of these developments was that unemployment fell from a bare 2.2% in 1946 to less than 0.91% of the insured population in 1951. Although wage levels were limited with the active support of the Trades Union Congress these conditions of full employment inevitably led to an increase in consumer demand and thus placed pressure on Britain's competitive position.

The growth of disposable income naturally led to a rise in the demand for whatever items were available and thus the market for both fruit and vegetables was considerably enhanced. Government support then helped to ensure that domestic output rose to meet as many of these requirements as possible and, in spite of scarcities of labour and materials, most growers were able to enjoy a reasonably profitable era. The situation of the distributive network was much less sanguine. Importers, wholesalers and retailers as well as the transport and marketing sectors continued to be affected by the ongoing shortages and the minutia of state regulation without the compensation of any state subsidies. However by 1950 most of these initial problems had been largely overcome even though wage differentials with other industries made it hard to retain the more skilled of the workforce. Even so, after all the difficulties were taken into account, the ability to sell to a willing public made sure that most firms were not only busy but also made substantial profits.

The overall strengthening of the British economy was hindered by the growth of imports and although the Balance of Payments gradually improved it was badly affected when costs and prices in the United Sates rapidly declined. As a result it was thought necessary to devalue in 1949 and this led to a temporary, comparative, advantage for British exports. As they became cheaper they were able to expand very quickly but, on the other hand, imports became more expensive and it became much more difficult to maintain a policy of wage restraint.

This unpalatable fact tended to be obscured by the immediate success of the devaluation which helped to secure a favourable balance of £306m in 1950. Thus the economic environment in which the fruit and vegetable industry operated appeared to be reasonably bright even though the rise in costs was beginning to cause some anxiety. These conflicting signals could not disguise the moderately prosperous state of all sectors of agriculture and horticulture and that the Government had played a significant role in improving their situation. In spite of this, as the General Election approached in February, 1950, the trade was almost unanimously opposed to the return of a second Labour administration.

This was principally because of the universal dislike of the enormous bureaucracy which had continued since 1945 without, in the opinion of the trade, the previous justification. It was generally believed that this retention of wartime policies fitted in very conveniently with the ethos of the Labour Party and that it would wish these controls to became a permanent feature of its administration. The fact that restrictions were slowly being removed was lost in the overall debate in respect of State Control vs Private Enterprise and some of the advantages of bulk buying were quickly forgotten. Thus as late as August 1948 it would seem that this system had much to commend it:-

Peace and Recovery

Ministry imported fruits: Prices per cwt
(Prices realised in home markets)

	1938 (Average)	1948 (August)	Increase by
Grapefruit	14/-	35/-	150%
Bananas	16/-	52/-	225%
Lemons	17/-	28/-	70%
Oranges	14/-	39/-	180%
Apples	17/-	56/-	230%
Average			171%

Privately imported fruits: Prices per cwt

	1938 (Average)	1948 (August)	Increase by
Apricots	34/-	166/-	360%
Grapes	40/-	194/-	385%
Peaches	44/-	140/-	220%
Pears	23/-	67/-	200%
Plums	33/-	119/-	260%
Onions	8/-	21/-	162%
Tomatoes	32/-	142/-	340%
Average			275%

15

Later, however, the increasing provision of items such as onions, lemons, nuts, mandarins, dates, clementines, grapes and peaches by the private sector was making the Government's bulk buying and allocation system very difficult to operate. Matters came to a head in December, 1949, when following a period when few controlled fruits were distributed several allocations were made almost simultaneously:-

> "In the larger towns, some of our wholesalers have found themselves with 2,000 boxes of oranges, 2,000 to 3,000 packages of apples, Scotian or Italian, 500 or 800 grapefruit, and a full allocation of bananas, all more or less simultaneously. Not only have their retail customers been unable in many cases to take up all these commodities in "dollops" (as we say in the North of England); but very many distributors in the wholesale markets have found it physically impossible to store and deal with these

From Orchard to Market

quantities on a market that is already supplied with a very wide range of attractive fruits, nuts and vegetables by private enterprise".

"The shopper is no longer willing to buy so many pounds of oranges, grapefruit or Ministry apples when issued. She freely recognises the advantages of a free system of distribution, in which she can buy one lemon, a pound of onions, or a pound of English (free enterprise) apples as and when she want them - as opposed to the "scientific" method of our Socialist theorisers, which decrees that each person holding a ration book shall receive one pound of grapefruit, whether she wants it or not, in week 29 in Area One, but no housewife shall have that opportunity in other Areas until week 30 or week 31; or that housewives in Area 3 shall have Scotian apples while those in other Areas shall have Italian apples, whether they like those particular apples or not.

The breakdown in London, when the price of Italian apples was reduced from 25s. 9d. to 20s. 9d. to wholesalers in order to effect any movement at all; and the offer in other areas to charge out these Italian apples as "four chalks" (although they were quite sound) - but with no extra profit to the wholesaler, the extra 5s. being a concealed bribe to the retailer to induce him to continue working a bankrupt policy, have finally brought out into the clearest daylight the fallacy both of bulk buying and of allocations when supplies get anywhere near the parity with demand". [16]

The problems led the trade to largely accept the view put forward by Mr CH Lewis that the bulk distribution and allocation system no longer served the needs of the consumer. Most in the business were also concerned by the way that sudden allocations of controlled items tended to disturb the working of the free market. While a few of the established companies who helped to run the scheme were content to see it continue the vast majority - especially those who had entered since 1939 and had no official role - felt that all non-dollar products should be made the responsibility of private enterprise via an open general licence. This strength of feeling, together with the nearness of the General Election, then encouraged the Ministry of Food to announce that it would abandon the bulk purchase of oranges and grapefruit with effect from May 1950. The Conservatives subsequently fought on a platform which promised more incentives for individual effort and enterprise and this was clearly more to the taste of those in the industry. In the event the Labour Party was successful but its majority was so small that it was certain that a further election would not be long delayed.

Peace and Recovery

Although the country's economic situation did not appear to be critical at the time of the election the outbreak of the Korean War in June 1950 was to have severe consequences for the UK. In the first place it helped to move the terms of trade against Britain so import prices began to rise and, secondly, it led expenditure on defence to be more than double than that which had originally been planned. In addition other countries gradually reacted to the British devaluation and the combination of these events meant that the positive balance of 1950 was replaced by an adverse balance of payments of £365m in 1951. This catastrophic change was accompanied by the beginning of inflation and by the TUC refusing to continue its co-operation in holding down wage levels. In turn these difficulties led to internal divisions and the growth of rivalries within the Labour Party and to a public lack of confidence in its policies. On the other hand more people began to believe in the greater financial competence and flexibility of a Conservative Administration and felt that it could be better trusted in this difficult time. The General Election of October 1951 reflected these beliefs and Mr Churchill was returned as Prime Minister. While his majority was only small - the Conservatives obtained 321 seats against Labour's 295 - he and his successors were to spend the next thirteen years in power. Thus this event was to prove highly significant for both the nation and for its fruit and vegetable industry and could be regarded in many respects as the start of a new era.

From Orchard to Market

10
Fruits of Freedom

With a Conservative Government in office for the greater part of the two decades after 1951 they first used their authority to accelerate the process of decontrol and by 1954 virtually all vestiges of rationing and wartime regulation had been eliminated. The process of nationalization was also halted and in the cases of long-distance road haulage and the steel industry was partly reversed. However the Conservatives made little attempt to return these industries to the private sector and largely accepted and extended the welfare services introduced by the post war Labour administration. In turn, when Labour came back into office it was mainly content to maintain the status quo and there was no serious effort to extend the role of the state beyond existing boundaries. The prime reason for these policies being continued was that both parties found that much of their energy was devoted to combating the recurring crises which continued to beset both Britain's national interests and its economy throughout this period.

The major financial difficulties of successive administrations were those caused by Britain's balance of payments. The resulting fluctuations naturally led to a degree of uncertainty about the strength of the British economy and to a loss of confidence on many occasions. The need for the Government to respond to the subsequent speculation then led to a series of "Stop-Go" policies which effectively prevented industry from reaching its full potential. In addition these financial difficulties not only made it essential to limit expenditure on desirable projects and defence they also helped to sour industrial relations and encourage the growth of inflationary pressures.

To some extent it could be argued that the growing freedom of the market place - encouraged by the Conservatives - was a major factor in strengthening the demand for higher wages. The defeat of the second Labour administration in 1951 had coincided with the virtual ending of official trade union support for any real form of wage constraint. However this was not so important as the rise of the shop steward and the interdependence of industry was already shifting the centre of union power. Nevertheless, the change in "official" policy did lead to the beginning of annual wage bargaining and, without corresponding increases in productivity, this raised costs and helped the inflationary circle. Government and employers resistance to growing demands meant that strikes, which had lost an average of two million days in the early post-war years rose to 3¾m in 1955. As the stoppages tended to be concentrated in the transport sector - railways, docks and shipping - the whole economy was badly affected with the food industries being especially at risk. The failure of successive Governments to come to terms with this problem exacerbated this situation and when Labour returned to power in 1964 it was immediately faced with a severe run on the pound. While this was successfully resisted (and Labour was again elected in 1966) this was only achieved at the expense of deflationary policies and led, in November 1967, to the devaluation of the pound from US$ 2.80 to US$ 2.40. While this had some obvious beneficial consequence it also had the effect of making food imports more expensive and thus could have had a long-term impact on the sources of Britain's fruit and vegetable supplies.

In practice technical developments in the transport industry were already doing much to reduce the consequences and cost of poor labour relations and were beginning to play an important role in off-setting the higher prices of overseas products. This was because the late 'Fifties' and early 'Sixties' were to see the start of what was to become a "transport revolution". Although this was ultimately to result in an integrated, door-to-door, service this had its roots in shipping where it was designed to reduce both the labour necessary for the handling of cargoes and the amount of time which vessels needed to spend in port. These objectives were first to be achieved by the use of pallets - either returnable or non-returnable - which increased unit loads and speeded-up the loading/unloading process with the aid of specialized cranes and fork-lift trucks. This process was greatly aided when a standardized size of pallet was agreed and their use rapidly became widespread for many items of dry, general, cargo. Their obvious potential for perishable commodities then encouraged many experiments with fruit and vegetables and these gradually developed into formal, long-term, arrangements.

Throughout the 1950s virtually all perishable cargoes continued to be carried in single temperature refrigerated vessels. These were steadily replaced by multi-temperature refrigerated ships which could simultaneously cope with a number of different products. At the same time the internal layouts of existing tonnage was modified and new buildings designed so as to be pallet compatible. Typical vessels constructed a this time included four sister ships operated by Safmarine in 1963 and 1964 on the South African/UK route. Not all routes were able to accommodate the new changes so comfortably. For example the wide range of loading facilities and varieties of horticultural exports from the Canary Islands meant that many different types of ship were still employed in 1964. Thus individual boxes of fruit and vegetables continued to be stowed by hand although there was some specialized carriage of bananas and tomatoes.

However, by 1968, both of the main companies serving the Canary fruit trades had largely converted to the pallet. In that year the Aznar Line, working in conjunction with their agents - Yeoward Brothers - the Importers Association, the Port of

Fruits of Freedom

Liverpool Stevedoing Company and the Mersey Dock and Harbour Board had introduced a fully palletized service to Liverpool. Later, in 1971, the Fred Olsen Line made it clear that their future fruit carriers would all use standardized pallets. These were to be loaded via automatic elevators and side ports and then moved entirely by machinery to their final position.[1] Given the expense of the structural alterations which were necessary to cope with pallets and the fact that less boxes could usually be carried, it is not surprising that operators on short-sea routes were rather slow to provide purpose-built facilities. Thus while pallets were gradually introduced on cross-channel ferries as part of general cargoes specialised arrangements for fruit and vegetables were slightly delayed. Nevertheless, in March, 1965, the Trafrume Line's 'Amelia de Aspe' brought the first part-cargo of palletized oranges from Spain to London's Millwall Wharf.

This successful experiment was soon to be followed by many others and the pallet became an essential ingredient in the transport of most fruit and vegetables. One of the more significant ways in which it was integrated into larger units was organized by Westland Imports Ltd.

This involved the adaption of their vessels to ship Dutch and Italian fresh products in what were described as "open-sided containers". This system had the very desirable object of raising the size of the individual loads moved by the mobile cranes so that very rapid turnrounds could be achieved. As a result their two vessels were able to maintain a six-days-a-week service between Holland and Whitstable.

First cargo of palletised fruit 1965

"Containers" of many kinds had already possessed a long history for they had been used in the UK railway network from the early years of the Century. However it was the development of landing craft, allied to roll on/roll off methods, evolved by the United States during the Second World War that was to prove the real impetus to commercial progress. A number of American road haulage and trailer concerns subsequently adopted the concept and two firms began to utilize "boxes" on short-sea routes in the late 1950s. Both the Matson Navigation Company and Pan Atlantic (later renamed Sea-Land Services Inc) extended their operations to deep-sea trade and when the latter decided to inaugurate a North

From Orchard to Market

Atlantic service in 1967 the transformation of the international transport system may be said to have really begun.

Westland Imports' new open sided containers carrying Dutch salads being off-loaded at Whitstable in 1967

As might be expected these events stimulated many experiments elsewhere. The venture organized by Westland Imports was only one such example but the general success in reducing costs and raising efficiency ensured that others quickly followed. These were to reach their logical conclusion in 1967 when British Rail ordered two 4,000 ton cellular container ships. These were planned to operate between the Hook of Holland and Harwich and were each to carry 148 "boxes" built to the specifications laid down by the International Standards Organization. It was then arranged that these containers were to continue on via a fleet of specially designed rail wagons to a terminal at Stratford where those not destined for London would move on through the national Freightliner network. The essence of this scheme was that once the containers had been filled at their port of departure the entire operation utilized mechanical handling so little labour was required until they reached their final destination.

Arrangements of this type, which integrated shipping with ongoing land networks, were to become a major feature in the carriage of most non-bulk commodities. While the advantage of these methods was apparent for the movement of fruit and vegetables it was also clear that they would need some form of specialized treatment. Thus a wide variety of ventilated, insulated and refrigerated containers were steadily evolved so that different items could be kept fresh. On the shorter, European, routes "boxes" mounted on trailers proved to be a viable alternative to those delivered to the port by rail or road, but this style of Roll on/ Roll off system did not lend itself to the deep-sea trades. However it was gradually accepted

Fruits of Freedom

that even on these routes containerization was the most economic format for the majority of cargoes. As a result Associated Containers Transportation was established and ordered an initial fleet of three cellular vessels specifically for the Australian Fruit trade. These were each equipped with 327 refrigerated and 897 general containers and *'ENCOUNTER BAY', 'ACT I'* and *'FLINDERS BAY'* commenced their service in 1969. In that year they lifted more than 250,000 bushels of apples and 93,000 bushels of pears to the UK and their success ensured that there were to be many similar developments on other routes in the following years. On the other hand the improvements in multi-temperature refrigerated vessels, mentioned earlier, meant that there was to be no large-scale carriage of tropical fruits in containers until after 1972.

Not all fresh fruit and vegetables were imported via mainline shipping services, of course, and in the 'Fifties' and especially, the 'Sixties' ever increasing quantities began to arrive by air. The pioneering flights of the early post-war years gradually gave way to those operated by larger aircraft capable of coping with heavier loads over longer distances and this encouraged the emergence of a new commercial structure. These arrangements involved the use of any spare capacity on scheduled BOAC routes where their VC10s could carry up to five tons while the development of the Boeing "747" promised much greater loads in the future. BEA undertook the same task on European scheduled services and both companies (as well as their international rivals) began to evolve a number of purely air-freight flights. In this respect they were following the example of many private airlines which rapidly grew to satisfy the demand for chartered freight flights.

At first various ad hoc methods of loading were employed depending on the type of aircraft and the product to be carried. Over time, however, there was a general move towards the use of pallets and lightweight materials. Thus heavy, wooden, pallets designed to be used with fork-lift trucks were replaced with a much flimsier construction which was all that was necessary with roller-bed handling systems. At the same time there was a steady replacement of trays and half-trays by cardboard cartons of many kinds. There was also a gradual introduction of containers - some tailor made to fit the fuselage - and in 1967 the KLM company began experiments with refrigerated units. By 1970 this innovation had been further developed by BOAC and was being widely adopted by other airlines.

These technical innovations enabled an ever widening range of items to be carried over longer distances at increasingly viable rates. Inevitably those growers nearest to the UK were the first to benefit with rising amounts being brought by air from the Continent. The Channel Islands were also helped by the establishment of new links : Silver City Airways (see above p178) for example, providing a 50-minute flight to Eastleigh airport from 1956. While this service became very useful for many products including tomatoes and early potatoes it was especially helpful for cut-flowers. With its aid these could reach Covent Garden market by midnight on the day they were picked and thus be available for distribution in a really fresh condition. However not all such developments were as welcome as this one. Thus when BOAC issued a circular letter in November 1959 inviting recipients to order exotic flowers from Singapore, East and South Africa to be delivered just before Christmas it raised a storm of protest from the British Flower Industry Association. This criticism was based on the assertion that BOAC were "entering the trade in opposition to the established members of the flower industry".[2] However this seems to have been a short-sighted view which subsequently disappeared when it was appreciated that such action was encouraging a year round market for flowers in Britain and that it was also creating opportunities for British roses, snowdrops and daffodils to be exported to expatriates serving overseas.

Minor difficulties such as this were gradually reconciled and by 1962 Spain was contributing to the growing UK flower market by sending considerable quantities of roses and carnations to the UK at certain times of the year. As flowers could not stand up to the strains of a lengthy rail and ferry journey and yet had the advantages of being relatively light, non-bulky and of high value they clearly fell into one of the categories which were necessary for air transport to be viable. The principles which regulated the use of this method of carriage were carefully spelt out in an article published by the Journal on 12 May 1962:

> *"A high value needed"*
>
> *"To qualify however for air transit, produce must be of sufficiently high ad valorem value to stand the cost of higher freight rates, yet making a profit for, in theory, at all events, for the shipper and importer. This obviously golden rule of profit and loss must be the guiding factor in any business, especially when high freights are concerned.*
>
> *It would appear that this statement is conclusive enough in itself, but on a review of the services, and demand which is available, there are of course many other factors which define whether produce sent by this method is a paying proposition.*
>
> *These fall into two categories, primarily that produce which cannot stand up to shipment by sea, rail or other form of slower transport, due to the high perishability, and the fact that even limited travel will affect the condition on arrival.*
>
> *Obviously such an example is strawberries, which are susceptible to fluctuating temperatures amongst other things, and cannot stand the rigours of trans-shipment and more than a certain amount of swaying*

Fruits of Freedom

and bumping.

In this case air transport is the obvious and indeed the only answer, and to this end many companies have concentrated on developing such a service which it is hoped will eventually bring down prices, with lower inducement freight rates and create a regular demand, other than for the luxury clientele.

The second category is one which includes produce which although not luxuries in the accepted sense are flown over in bulk during a season merely to capture an early or late market."

With the aid of these general principles and the improvements in aircraft technology the carriage of many types of produce changed from small, experimental, packages to regular, substantial, cargoes. Thus as early as 1956 consignments of between 100 and 200 cartons of six "Queen" pineapples were being received within 30 hours of packing in Kenya by S J Parsons Ltd of Covent Garden. This was, of course, an item which could command a high price in hotels and restaurants. Other products which could not attract such a substantial premium sometimes proved to be too expensive to be profitable. By 1962 this was still the case with Tunisian and French asparagus which was only viable before and after the British season and efforts to import grapes and peaches throughout the year needed to be restricted because the market could only absorb a certain quantity of luxurious fruits and vegetables at the existing level of prices.

These drawbacks proved to be temporary setbacks in most cases for the public was slowly beginning to appreciate the convenience of year-round supplies and were accepting the extra cost which this entailed. To give a few examples, in 1964 air freight from South Africa and Israel was assuming significant proportions while produce from Holland was also arriving in large quantities - over a million heads of winter lettuce were flown over in that year. At the same time Canary tomatoes began to be carried to the UK by air and in spite of the need to charge an extra 10p per pound over fruit sent by sea the trade made steady progress. By 1966, for example, between 150 and 500 cartons each of 15 pounds were being flown five days a week - the advantages of extra freshness clearly offsetting the additional cost. This expansion can be further seen in January, 1967, when an airlift of 2,700 cartons of Canary tomatoes arrived at Liverpool airport. This flight was arranged by Bonny and Company and the time in transit was only 5½ hours compared with four or five days by sea. As a result the fruit was in excellent condition and was quickly disposed of to twenty buyers from the North of England.

These substantial trades were aided by the construction of specialized aircraft. Thus while standard VC10s could carry five or six tons of cargo in addition to their full complement of passengers the VC "freighter" had a capacity of up to sixteen tons even on the long South African route. Another indication of the growth of

From Orchard to Market

air freighting services can been seen from the following extract from the Journal dated 6 August 1966:-

> *"BC cherries arrive by air"*
> "For the first time a shipment of plum-sized cherries was transported from the orchards of B.C.'s Okanagan Valley by Air Canada's air freight service to London last week.
> The consignment consisted of 450 boxes, weighing a total of 10,400 lb., with the fruit carried in the lower cargo holds of a regularly scheduled Air Canada DC-8 Jet Trader.
> The shipper was British Columbia Tree Fruits Limited, and the parcel was consigned to several well-known wholesalers in the London markets with prices between 4s. and 5s. per lb. being made for the fruit."

A further indication of the growth of air transport concerns the shipment of Californian strawberries. In 1964 approximately 13% of the crop was moved out of the state by aeroplane but this had risen to 26% by the following year. Although only a small proportion of these strawberries were sent to Europe the actual quantities rose from 9,000 to 36,000 boxes over the same period. This expansion, plus that of other fresh fruits and vegetables, then encouraged the trans-Atlantic airlines to provide many more dedicated services and by 1966 BOAC, SAS, TWA and PAN-AM were all actively involved - BOAC, stressing their one day freight services from New York to Glasgow, Manchester and London, with the latter also receiving many regular flights carrying produce from many separate centres including California and Florida. One major firm which quickly took advantage of this situation were American Fruit Importers Ltd (a subsidiary of American Foods Inc) who opened premises in Brentford Market in May 1966. They specialized in providing many out-of-season lines such as strawberries, spring onions, radishes, and asparagus from the United States as well as early peaches and plums from South Africa.

The net effect of this growth in air transport can best be judged by the reaction of the airlines in providing freight services. These, in turn, promoted the construction of many facilities which were necessary to cater for the increasing flow of cargoes in both the supplying countries and in the receiving markets.

It will be seen that by the beginning of the 'Seventies' quantities of Britain's fresh fruit and vegetable imports were arriving by air. By then it was certainly providing a useful supplement to mainline shipping but the cost of air transport meant that it was still mainly limited to the carriage of exotics and to extending the seasons of other items. Its role would undoubtedly have been even greater but for the other alternatives which were available to potential importers.

Fruits of Freedom

Israeli exporters were quick to utilize regular charter flights to the UK and Europe.

The re-opening of the cross-channel train ferries in 1947 and the subsequent expansion of Transfesa and Interfrigo services were one such option. This possibility was further widened by the creation of dedicated routes from Holland and elsewhere by British Rail and these systems had the advantage of limiting handling to a single loading and discharging of the freight - a process which was made especially attractive by the extensive nature of both the European and British Rail networks at this time.

The increasing efficiency of these combined rail-sea services can be judged by the fact that although Spanish oranges took six days to reach London in 1939 this time had been reduced to just over three days in 1956. This was partly due to the measures taken to reconcile the Spanish 5'6" gauge to the 4'8½" European (and British) gauge as well as to improvements to rolling stock and management. This system enabled loads of up to 28 tons to be carried as far as the Channel but British loading restrictions kept wagons to a maximum of 20 tons. Nevertheless by the early 'Seventies' over 1,500 normally ventilated trucks, specially designed for the UK market, were in use. This was out of a total of approximately 5,000 of which 15% were refrigerated.

While the Transfesa Company organised these services in Spain, STEF and Transthermos undertook similar arrangements in France and Germany respectively. In addition the Interfrigo co-operative provided a system for the optimum use of the available refrigerated wagons for the international trade in perishable items. By 1972 this organisation was operating 20,000 refrigerated trucks on behalf of its members as well as the 8,000 which it owned. These were employed by a number

From Orchard to Market

of countries - principally Italy, France, Rumania and Hungary - to forward their products to their respective markets including the UK. At that time fresh fruit represented 43% and vegetables 32.5% of the totals carried by Interfrigo.

Since the beginning of the cross-channel rail freight services in the mid-twenties those wagons destined for London were sent to either Battersea Wharf or the larger depot at Southwark Goods Yard (usually known as Gravel Lane). In the same period those trucks for other regions were re-directed from Hither Green where no discharging facilities were then available. Both London railheads provided facilities for unloading and also sent wagons to be dealt with at other depots within the capital - these included Bishopsgate which was by far the most important. The growth in trade meant that by 1956 both continental railheads were being overwhelmed by the increases in throughput and a number of temporary expedients needed to be adopted. Thus provision was made for unloading at Lenham in Kent and plans were made to develop the existing site at Hither Green. This become operational in October 1960 and thereafter was the main centre for the overland route from Europe. Although designed to have an unloading capacity of 100 trucks per day it was not until December 1963 that even 95 wagons per day could be discharged. As a result the depot was greatly congested at weekends and, especially, during the run-up to Christmas each year. These problems were exacerbated by the practice adopted by some importers of leaving their produce in the wagons until it was required as this naturally worsened the situation. The construction of new warehouses at Hither Green helped to alleviate this congestion but further pressure arose in 1964 when a fire at Bishopsgate destroyed its continental freight terminal.

British Rail took the opportunity to develop a new facility at Stratford and the London International Freight Terminal was opened in July 1967. This was to play a significant role in reducing the difficulties at Hither Green for it subsequently catered for all fruit and vegetables arriving via the Zeebrugge/Harwich and Dunkirk/Harwich train ferry services.

A major advantage of the train-ferry services was that their cargoes could be distributed to the principal markets via rail without the need for double handling. This system was, of course, totally dependent upon the efficiency and extent of Britain's railway network which had amounted to over 20,000 miles in 1938. It had then been the principle form of transport for freight but throughout the early post-war years it had declined and had been reduced to under 11,000 miles by the late 'Sixties'. This had enormous consequences for the carriage of both imported fruit and vegetables and of those that were produced domestically. The reason for the decline was the growth of road haulage which had evolved from merely providing feeder services to and from the nearest station to competing directly

Fruits of Freedom

with rail for the complete journey. At first this competition had been restricted by technical factors to short and medium length routes but as soon as the immediate post-war difficulties had been overcome it was extended to include the longest of journeys for some commodities. Thus while in the 1948/9 season the railways were responsible for moving 99.4% of Scottish seed potatoes to the South this figure had fallen to 76.4% by 1954/5.

British Rail was to be more successful in retaining its role in carrying the more perishable items and in 1957 it claimed to be still moving one and a half million tons of fruit, flowers and vegetables each year. By then it was supplementing its ordinary, scheduled, freight services by a number of special express trains which ran daily when required to London and the provincial markets moving:-

> "Strawberries from Hampshire and the Wisbech area; plums from the Vale of Evesham; soft and hard fruit from Kent; new potatoes from principal growing areas; tomatoes, cucumbers, celery, lettuce, mushrooms, etc., from West Sussex, the Lea Valley and Cambridgeshire, and the Fylde district of Lancashire; broccoli from Cornwall; rhubarb and peas from the West Riding; flowers from the Scilly Isles and imported produce from Europe and many overseas countries".[3]

Although reassuring at the time these details were misleading as the prospects for rail were already being further undermined by the construction of motorways. In 1958 the first 8½ miles were opened and sections reached 350 miles in 1965 and 800 miles in 1971. These developments gave a huge boost to road transport as the following statistics reveal:-

Changes in the distribution of freight traffic

	1952	1960	1970	1980
Rail:	54%	38%	24%	14%
Road:	46%	61%	73%	77%

[4]

The extension of the motorway system encouraged the production of ever more efficient vehicles and by 1963 it was being forecast that the combination of these two factors would enable door to door deliveries between London and Glasgow to be regularly undertaken in twelve hours. By that date trucks such as the Foden turbo-charged eight-wheeler had a maximum speed of over 80 mph and could move 17 ton loads at more than a 60 mph average when utilizing the new motorways. Plans by Scammel Lorries Ltd to produce tractor units which, with their trailers, could carry loads of up to 75 tons were also well advanced. However the technical improvements which characterized the industry throughout the post-war era were limited to some extent by the legal restraints and changes imposed by successive governments.

The nationalization of long-distance road services undertaken by the Labour Government in 1947 was reversed by the following Conservative Administration. These arrangements were introduced by the 1953 Transport Act which provided for the disbanding of the Road Haulage Executive and the disposal of its assets.

The return of a Labour Government in 1964 brought a different approach to the nation's transport system. It was believed that the rapid growth of road haulage under private ownership was providing a major threat to the retention of a viable rail network. In addition, in spite of the contraction organized by Dr Beeching, the railways continued to record heavy deficits. The Administrations' answer was incorporated in the Transport Act of 1968. This set up a new National Freight Corporation which was designed to improve overall efficiency by co-ordinating rail and road transport. Great hopes were placed on the expansion of the Freightliner Services which were already in limited use carrying containers and full wagon loads between strategically placed terminals by rail and on to their destinations by road. This concept was a key aspect of rail operations and was gradually developed to cater for a wide range of whole train, bulk, cargoes. Unfortunately a number of teething problems, including a lack of flexibility and poor labour relations, meant that the system faced an ever increasing struggle against the cost effectiveness of road haulage.

A prime example of the difficulties which beset the early Freightliner service concerns the carriage of bananas which the railways had monopolized from the beginning of the trade. By 1967 Southampton was the sole port of entry used by Elders and Fyffes and although road transport was used for deliveries to nearby towns such as Portsmouth and Salisbury the railways were responsible for all more distant destinations. These arrangements meant that it took 36 hours for the fruit to reach Glasgow so when British Rail proposed a new system the Company was happy to agree. This meant that the bananas, prepacked in cartons, were offloaded from the ship to a container alongside, moved by road to the nearby terminal and thence to Scotland by Freightliner. As transit times were reduced to 18 hours by this method it was regarded as a considerable success but an eight month strike by shunters at Southampton in 1969 forced the Company to make other arrangements. Then, when this dispute came to an end, Elders and Fyffes found it convenient to continue to utilize motor vehicles for the bulk of their distribution and rail was only used to supply Scotland. The further extension of the motorway network and the technical improvements to lorries and

Fruits of Freedom

trailers made even this service redundant and after 1979 Fyffes' bananas were carried exclusively by road.

The Transport Act of 1968 also envisaged the relaxation of controls over the lighter types of goods vehicles and it was proposed to replace carriers' licences (A,B and C) with an operators (O) licence. In an attempt to aid British Rail, however, it was decided to give it a prior claim on traffic carried for over 100 miles if it could show that it could handle it with equal speed, economy and efficiency. Thus special restrictions were retained to control lorries of over 16 tons gross and plans were made for the introduction of vehicle testing and a Heavy Goods Vehicle driving licence. While many of these clauses were sensible and desirable that concerning the "100 mile rule" proved to be difficult to interpret and it was repealed when a new Conservative Government came into power in 1970. Arrangements were then made for the complete abolition of the carriers' licensing system and its replacement by operators' licences was greatly accelerated.

The building of motorways, the increases in the technical efficiency of motor vehicles and the reduction in legal restraints thus enabled road transport to provide ever more effective services for the carriage of fruit and vegetables within Britain. It was also beginning to supply a comprehensive distribution network for any cargoes which were imported by lorry from Europe. The post-war development of cross-channel (and other) car ferries provided increasing opportunities for vehicles to be loaded by a grower on the Continent and be subsequently unloaded at its ultimate destination in the UK. Quick delivery, minimum handling, less damage and enhanced freshness meant that this system was especially suitable for perishable items. As a result it grew from catering for small amounts carried in boxes and trays to larger, palletized units and eventually to full container loads. In the 'Fifties' the overland road route was employed mainly by producers in France and the Low Countries but greater distances to the port of embarkation gradually became viable. This process was extended so that by 1967 experimental journeys were being made to bring Turkish soft fruit and vegetables over the 2,000 mile trip to the UK. These cargoes were carried in a single refrigerated and insulated unit and took between four and five days in transit. The cost of 3d a pound compared very favourably with the 12d a pound by air even though more expensive than the 2d a pound for the slower delivery by sea. A similar plan to bring tomatoes from Malta was proposed in 1970. This envisaged a roll on/roll off sea passage to Marseilles, and a route through France to the Channel with a total time to the UK of five days. It was thought that this would cut freight charges in half but developments in other forms of transport appeared to make this unlikely as competition in one sphere triggered more cost-effective systems elsewhere. However by the early 'Seventies' roll on/roll off services were making considerable progress even though their major expansion was still to come.

From Orchard to Market

As a consequence of the depreciation of sterling and of the adverse movements in the terms of trade the cost of many imports rose steadily throughout much of the 'Fifties' and 'Sixties'. Fortunately the simultaneous reduction in the cost of transport was sufficient to offset most of these increases so that a complete range of fresh fruits and vegetables remained within the pockets of almost all British consumers. As a result both the quantity and value of imported items continued to grow during the entire period although there were to be many variations within the individual sectors:-

Annual Imports of Fresh Fruits and Nuts (1951-1971)

(000 cwts)	1951	1961	1971
Apples including Cider	3,862	4,535	5,706
Bananas	3,263	7,290	6,278
Oranges (all types)	7,748	7,897	8,955
Grapefruit	0,783	1,120	
Lemons	0,551	0,710	3,529
Limes	0,457	-	
Pears and Quinces	1,332	1,273	1,068
Grapes (including hothouse)	0,808	1,013	1,411
Melons	0,119	0,548	
Fresh Fruit not specified elsewhere	0,082	0,112	1,351
Tropical Fruit (excl. bananas)	-	-	0,233
Nuts: Edible	1,038	0,943	1,137
Total: 000 cwts	20,385	26,232	30,394
Total: £000	69,177	104,548	162,839

As the statistics above indicate the apple, banana and orange remained the backbone of the trade throughout this period. However while the landings of oranges and other citrus grew only slowly those of apples grew at a more rapid rate and banana cargoes more than doubled. In addition the more expensive fruits such as grapes and, especially, melons made particularly substantial progress in the UK market and by the end of this period in 1971 there was already a small but discernable increase in the demand for the more exotic tropical fruits. Other items including pears and edible nuts grew at a slower pace but like all other

Fruits of Freedom

imports shared in the evolution of what was becoming a year long market.

While the extension of the seasons was partly due to the improvements in transport and storage facilities it was also due to the availability of supplies from different geographic regions. In the case of the apple Australia and New Zealand remained the major source with Canada, the United States and Argentina providing declining quantities. At the same time the development of shipments from South Africa provided a further option for importers while domestic production was increasingly complimented by supplies from France which were gradually replacing those from Italy.

As banana shipments from Jamaica, the largest exporter to the UK in 1938, had failed to recover after the war it was necessary to obtain supplies from wherever they were available. Thus as late as 1951 bananas were being imported from Brazil, the Cameroons, the Canaries and the Gold Coast but overall quantities remained at less than half the pre-war peak. This situation was partly due to the dollar-shortage which prevented the fruit being obtained from Central or South America but it was also compounded by the system of bulk buying and control which the government had imposed on the industry. These arrangements began to change in 1951 when restrictions on retail sales were ended and complete deregulation had been achieved by 1953. As a result shipments were encouraged from many sources and total UK imports rose from 163,700 tons in 1951 to 315,700 tons in 1956. This progress was then to be seriously threatened by the raising of the duty on non-commonwealth bananas for this had the effect of ending landings from the Cameroons when it became an independent state and the same factor led to Canary bananas becoming too expensive and shipments ended in 1965. The loss of these two major producers led to a further increase in Jamaican exports but these were insufficient to fill the rising demand for bananas in Britain. Fortunately Geest Industries decision to develop a new source of supply in the Windward Islands meant that substantial cargoes were available just when they were most needed. Thus from the mid 'Fifties' onward Geest were to play an important role in the British banana business and Elders and Fyffes and Jamaican Producers found that they had acquired a new and serious competitor. [6]

The third and, in this period, still the most important fruit import was the orange. By 1951 landings had not yet reached pre-war averages mainly because of Israel's inability to regain the production levels achieved by the British Protectorate of Palestine. The next two decades were to see these problems overcome and Israel became Britain's largest supplier of oranges although not to her former domination of the trade. This was to some extent due to the competition provided by Spain with whom long standing links had been re-established during the time of shortage. It was also because of the additional production encouraged in South

From Orchard to Market

Africa and the new sources of supply which had emerged in Cyprus and Morocco. Limited quantities of oranges were acquired from Brazil when supplies were short but little came from the United States at this time as they needed payment in hard currency.

Imports of fresh vegetables had already exceeded pre-war averages by 1951 and were to remain on a plateau of about nine and a half million cwts for the next twenty years. Throughout this period onions and tomatoes (together with potatoes recorded separately) were to continue as the principal shipments. Other fresh vegetables including broccoli, cabbages, carrots, cucumbers and lettuce were landed to extend the British season and to cover for the shortages which inevitably occurred from time to time. Although there were some changes within the various categories the annual total for these items remained fairly constant. In this they differed from the imports of dried peas, beans and lentils which expanded until the late 'Fifties' and then tended to decline as frozen and other prepared vegetables extended their share of the market. The statistics for new potatoes show a gradually increasing demand for the whole period and seed potatoes appear to follow a similar trend. "Other" eg maincrop potatoes formed only a small import in the years under examination as demand could normally be entirely satisfied from domestic production. On occasion, however, when the UK crop was damaged or below average imports were utilized to ensure that adequate supplies were maintained. Thus while substantial quantities were brought into Britain during 1955, 1956, 1958 and 1959 little was required from overseas during other years.

Annual Imports of Fresh Vegetables (1951-1971)

(000 cwts)	1951	1961	1971
Onions	4.518	4.419	3.985
Tomatoes	3.755	3.152	3.198
Broccoli and Cauliflower	0.838	0.583	0.754
Cabbages	0.042	0.098	0.111
Carrots	0.142	0.375	0.380
Cucumbers	0.058	0.142	0.491
Lettuce and Endive	0.159	0.266	0.053
Total: Fresh	9.634	9.323	9.766
Potatoes: New	3.380	4.962	5.147
Other	0.334	0.074	0.002
Seed	0.052	0.185	0.174

Fruits of Freedom

At the beginning of this period in 1951 the Canary and Channel Islands together with Italy, Spain, Algeria and Morocco provided the majority of new potatoes required by the UK. Over the ensuing twenty years it is certain that the Channel Islands continued to ship substantial quantities of new potatoes to Britain but after 1956 these are regarded as part of the UK domestic production so no comparative statistics are available. Over the same period it is clear that the Canaries and Spain maintained their position as major suppliers whereas other countries appear to have failed to retain a serious interest. This was probably due to the rise of two new competitors - Cyprus and Egypt - who were together satisfying over 50% of the import market by 1971.

Imports of tomatoes followed a similar pattern to those of new potatoes. The early part of this period saw the Canary and Channel Islands dominate the trade with only limited quantities arriving from the Netherlands. This situation clearly continued over the next two decades although no comparative statistics are available for the Channel Islands after 1956. However by the beginning of the 'Seventies' the Netherlands appears to have secured a larger share of the business than previously and Spain was also contributing significant quantities to the UK market.

The other vegetable import of major importance was the onion. Egypt, Spain and the Netherlands were the largest suppliers for most of the 'Fifties' and 'Sixties' although only Spain retained its market share up to 1971. This was because both Egypt and Holland found it difficult to resist the challenge posed by many new entrants to the trade. Some of these, like France, Hungary, Italy, Malta and South Africa were only moderately successful but Chilean, Polish and North American onions found a growing niche in Britain. As result Egypt and Holland, while remaining large suppliers, had to be satisfied with a smaller share of the British market.

The 50% increase in the weight of annual imports of fresh fruits and nuts in the period 1951 to 1971, together with the relatively high level of fresh vegetables that were landed placed considerable pressures on domestic producers. This situation was to be further aggravated by the changes introduced by successive governments. Until the price review of 1952 Labour policies had been designed to raise agricultural and horticultural output so as to help reduce the strain on the balance of payments. The new Conservative administration, although still subscribing to these aims, adopted a different philosophy which sought to replace controls and incentives by market forces wherever possible. However, although those producers who were deemed to be in direct competition with importers were to be supported by the continuation of a system of "deficiency payments" these were to be adjusted on a regular basis so as to reflect changing conditions.

From Orchard to Market

In addition it was arranged that milk, potatoes and eggs would also be subsidized as necessary and be sold only via official marketing boards. This system resulted in supply and demand helping to fix prices at levels that were acceptable to British consumers while at the same time the cost of subsidies declined from the £382m of 1950 to less that £300m for most of the 1960s.

One of the major reasons for the success of the new arrangements was that the competition which it engendered helped to promote productivity. This can be clearly seen by the fact that the output of many items actually rose although agricultural land remained constant at about 48 million acres, while the labour force continued to decline from its wartime peak:-

Workers Employed in Agriculture (000)

	Regular Workers			Regular, Casual & Part Time		
	Male	Female	Total	Male	Female	Total
1951	621	69	691	750	131	882
1961	438	40	479	545	115	661
1971	231	30	261	309	108	417

[8]

As these figures demonstrate full-time, regular, staff employed in agriculture fell quite sharply while even when casual and part-time employees are included the total work force was reduced by more that 50%. Over the same period the overall domestic output increased from an index number of 88 in 1950 to 129 in 1966. [9]

The fact that reduced amounts of labour were producing more from the same quantity of land was a consequence of the new regime which obliged growers to utilize the most efficient methods and machinery. Thus the numbers of tractors rose by over a third, pest control and selective breeding techniques were improved and the average size of holdings increased significantly so as to take advantage of more capital intensive systems. As a result of this rise in productivity domestic growers were able to remain largely competitive with many imported items and the UK was still able to provide 55% of its food requirements in the early 1970s.

The period from 1951 to 1971 was characterized by a change in the world situation which saw post-war food shortages replaced by over-production of many items. When this development was allied with the steady reduction in the real cost of transport the net effect was to provide an ever rising flood of cheap fruit and vegetable imports. As existing state support proved to be inadequate further legislation including the Horticulture Act of 1960 and the Agricultural and

Fruits of Freedom

Horticultural Act of 1964 provided some additional assistance. Unfortunately this proved to be insufficient to combat the expanding shipments of cheap imports so domestic fruit production began a steady, though slow, decline:-

Fruit Production in the UK (1952-3 to 1970-1) 000 tons

	1952-3	1962-3	1970-1
Apples (Dessert and Cooking)	492.9	477.2	472.2
Pears (Dessert and Cooking)	46.0	51.8	67.7
Plums	121.5	68.3	45.5
Cherries	37.2	21.7	12.5
Total Orchard Fruit including Cider Apples and Perry Apples	795.3	726.3	663.5
Total Small Fruit	103.6	88.4	98.8
Grand Totals	899.1	814.7	762.3

[10]

In the case of vegetables the situation was rather different. The relatively high weight / low value of many varieties meant that the cost of transport and handing gave a degree of protection from overseas producers. Imports, therefore, tended to be largely complementary to British crops and were mainly utilized to extend their seasons. In addition imports were usually available to fill in any gaps in supplies as and when they occurred and, over time, some were able to develop special niches in the UK market. Nevertheless as a result of these constraints it was possible to maintain domestic production at a high and stable level and any changes in output were mainly caused by variations in the weather or by alterations in the taste of the consumer.

Repacking and sorting fruit into retail prepacks in the 1970's

From Orchard to Market

Vegetable Production in the UK : 1950-2 to 1970-1 (000 tons)
(not including field crops of potatoes and turnips-swedes)

	1950-51	1960-61	1970-71
Beetroot	87	132	115
Carrots	409	577	540
Parsnips	61	56	62
Turnips and Swedes	189	106	120
Onions (Dry Bulb and Green)	77	41	113
Brussels Sprouts	154	189	268
Cabbage	945	633	676
Cauliflower and Broccoli	248	271	291
Asparagus	2	2	1
Beans, Broad	24	27	39
Beans, Runner and French	54	69	105
Peas, Harvested Dry	116	46	86
Peas, Green for Market	164	101	40
Peas, Green for Canning	30	113	200
Celery	62	112	73
Leeks	19	22	31
Rhubarb	59	36	51
Tomatoes (in the open)	24	3	*
Lettuce (in the open)	73	109	149
Tomatoes (under glass)	102	87	106
Lettuce (under glass)	6	10	22
Cucumbers (under glass)	31	34	33
Other Vegetables (in the open and under glass)	165	170	180
Estimated Total Production	3,103	2,957	3,301
Estimated Cropped Area (000 acres)	533	467	543

* Included with "Other Vegetables".

The twenty years from 1951 to 1971 were to witness tremendous changes in the range, quality and seasonality of the fruit and vegetables imported into the UK. Over the period the gradual reduction in the real cost of these items encouraged larger and larger quantities to be landed and they were able to secure a major share of the British market. The difficulties which this growing tide of imports created for the domestic producer then led to a number of initiatives

Fruits of Freedom

by successive governments. Given that membership of GATT prevented many direct restrictions on imports these were necessarily limited to the support of the industry within Britain. At first these measures were based on the continuation of the wartime subsidies which aimed to maximise output at all costs but they then evolved to help develop a more efficient system which was better able to compete with overseas suppliers. While these later policies certainly encouraged a considerable rise in productivity the advantages possessed by many foreign growers meant that their progress could only be slowed and not halted.

The problems caused by the increase in imports were not, of course, the only ones which concerned British agriculture and horticulture. Like other sections of industry, domestic growers, as well as all involved with the import, distribution and retailing of fruit and vegetables, were significantly affected by the numerous changes in the environment in which they were obliged to operate. The key to the financial difficulties which emerged was inflation which averaged 3.8% between 1950 and 1967 before rising to over 7% from 1968 to 1973. This inevitably led to high interest rates and to price rises which frequently lagged behind the increase in costs. As a result many small firms - and some larger companies - became illiquid and were ultimately found to be insolvent. Inflation was also an important factor in the breakdown of industrial relations which led to numerous strikes which were particularly damaging to those interested in the production and handling of perishable items. The damaging effects of inflation to the nation's economy were then regarded as being so insidious that it became - along with the balance of payments - a major pre-occupation of successive British Governments.

Thus both Conservative and Labour Administrations found it necessary to adopt "Stop and Go" policies in order to combat external deficits. Both were also prepared at first to utilize differential rates on distributed and undistributed profits to help promote investment and control inflation. These were subsequently to be supplemented and then replaced by various forms of investment allowances and, after the mid 'Sixties' by a number of new impositions. These included Selective Employment Tax, Capital Gains Tax and Corporation Tax and all imposed their own particular stresses and strains on all those working in the industry. However, it should be noted that Income Tax remained fairly constant at about 8/- (40p) in the £ for most of this period and that Surtax was greatly reduced in 1961.

There were also a number of other factors which were to the advantage of those engaged in the business. The low level of unemployment - under 2% up to 1961 and less than 3% in 1970 - demonstrates that this was a period of some prosperity. Although Macmillan's statement, made in 1957, that "most of our people have never had it so good" may have been something of an exaggeration there can be little doubt that the general standard of living did rise considerably for many

From Orchard to Market

families. As a result the consumption of most types of fruit, nuts and vegetables rose steadily and thus provided a larger market for both imported and locally grown produce. The growth in the UK population from 50.2m in 1950 to 55.1m in 1967 was also a helpful factor in this respect:-

UK Food Consumption per head

		1944	1965
Vegetables, Fruit and Nuts	kg	87.1	106.4
Potatoes	kg	124.8	100.9
Liquid Milk	litres	139.7	141.7
Meat	kg	51.7	69.1
Eggs	number	78.4	250.0
Butter	kg	3.6	8.8
Margarine	kg	8.2	5.4

As the statistics above indicate the period was characterized by a move away from the cheaper foods and the consumption of margarine, potatoes and flour declined by substantial quantities. At the same time the purchase of the more expensive commodities all increased at varying rates - in the case of vegetables, fruit and nuts this amounted to an additional 19.3 kg per head annually. However in spite of this trend towards a superior diet the nation's expenditure on its food actually fell from 29.1% to 26% of its total budget. This was not only an indication of the UK's rising Gross Domestic Product and the growing affluence of the population. It was also a reflection of the lower world price for most foods and the consequent reduction in the cost of Britain's imports and thus of its domestic competition. Nevertheless it should be noted that the total spent by the British public on its fruit and vegetables did rise considerably over the period. Thus the potential for profitable trade was always present for the more efficient firms:-

Consumers' Expenditure at Constant Prices

	1951	1961	1971
Fruit	£170m	£282m	£415m
Potatoes and Vegetables	£324m	£482m	£785m

Fruits of Freedom

The rise and changing patterns of consumption which took place in the 'Fifties' and 'Sixties' needed to be supplied via what was essentially the pre-war distribution system. This might best be described "as a collection of private firms whose activities are for most part co-ordinated by a market mechanism". [14]

The two sources of supply had many features in common but also many differences. Overseas producers arranged for the collection of their products so that they arrived in the UK in bulk. These cargoes were then available to be distributed either via the importers own networks or through the primary (wholesale) markets. It is no coincidence, therefore, that the major ports of entry for fruit and vegetables (London, Liverpool, Southampton, Hull, Bristol and Glasgow in 1954) were also the sites of the major wholesale markets for these commodities at that time. However by 1970 the correlation was much weaker due to the changes in the methods of shipping which resulted in Dover, Felixstowe, Newhaven and Portsmouth becoming important landing ports without becoming significant distribution centres.

The pattern for the collection and distribution of domestic crops was rather more complicated. The trade was largely organized on a regional basis so that growers found it most convenient to supply their nearest centre whenever possible. However many specialized items needed to be sent to other major wholesale markets - especially those in London - and these included the large inland facilities at Birmingham, Leeds, Nottingham and Sheffield in addition to those at the ports. Thus the bulk of most produce was usually disposed of via wholesalers who arranged for its sale in either the national or rural markets although some items might be sold directly to local retailers or through a growers own outlets. Some output was always acquired by manufacturers for canning, bottling, chilling, freezing and pickling and in these cases this avoided any need to involve the trade network.

There were also important differences in the ways in which overseas and domestic trades were arranged and financed. More than 50% of imports were provided by "producer boards" which usually financed cargoes in transit and storage and then extended varying degrees of credit to their chosen agents. During this period these included the Australian Apple and Pear Board, the Citrus Marketing Board of Israel, the New Zealand Apple and Pear Board and two separate South African Boards which were responsible for citrus, and deciduous fruits.

From Orchard to Market

BRITAIN'S WHOLESALE MARKETS IN 1952

		Private or Municipal	Approx. no. Wholesalers	Auction Days	Main Ports of Supply
BELFAST	St Georges Market	M	16	-	Liverpool, Glasgow, occasional direct boats
BIRMINGHAM	Smithfield Market	M	55	-	All Principal Ports
BRADFORD	St James' Market	M	60	-	Liverpool / Hull
BRENTFORD	Brentford Market, Middx	M	120	-	London
BRIGHTON	Circus Street	M	30	-	London / Southampton
BRISTOL	Nicholas Street	M	30	-	Avonmouth
CARDIFF	Custom House Street	M	30	Tues or Wed	Cardiff / London
COVENTRY	Barracks Square	M	16	-	All Main Ports
EDINBURGH	Market Street	P	9	-	Glasgow / Leith
GLASGOW	Candleriggs	M 40% P 60%	56	Vary	Glasgow
HULL	Humber Street	P	50	Mon Wed	Hull
LEEDS	Kirkgate	M	55	-	All Ports
LEICESTER	Halford Street	M	20	-	All Ports
LIVERPOOL	North Market	M	70	Mon Wed	Liverpool / London / Hull
	Queen Square	P	30		"
LONDON	Borough Market, SE1	P	110	Tues Thurs	London
	Covent Garden, WC2	P	250	-	London
(excludes commission buyers and importers)	Greenwich Market, SE10	P	20	-	London
	Spitalfieds Market, E1	M	190	Mon Wed	London
	Stratford Market, E15	British Rail	55	-	London
MANCHESTER	Smithfield Market	M	250	Tues/ Thurs	Liverpool / Manchester
NEWCASTLE	Green Market & St Andrews	Both	36	Vary	Newcastle / Hull
SHEFFIELD	Castlefolds Market	M	90	-	Hull / Liverpool / London / Manchester
	Wholesale Market	M	12	-	London / Liverpool / Southampton / Cardiff / Bristol

Fruits of Freedom

Although these bodies each had its own individual characteristics they all aimed to organize the growing, grading, packing and inspection of their shipments. They sought to market their products by employing systems that would both maintain their quality and reputation as well as maximizing their returns. These objectives required close control of all activities so relatively few agents were appointed and these were always firms of the highest standing. These received their supplies on a commission basis and disposed of them in the primary markets, or via their own branches, by auction or private treaty. As the quota of produce received by the agent was allocated on the basis of previous performance the system incorporated a highly competitive element. This was heightened by the knowledge that there were always many firms waiting to become agents if a vacancy occurred.

Other importers of fruit and vegetables were less rigid than the Boards and utilized a wide range of buying and selling techniques. Many firms developed long-standing arrangements with their suppliers and these resulted in methods of payment and remuneration which suited their particular needs. In general, however, most items from Australia and North America were purchased outright but those acquired elsewhere tended to employ a system of advanced deposits and commission with a reconciliation of accounts when the final result was known. This was also the usual method used for home grown produce. Apart from the innumerable special agreements made with local or favoured outlets the bulk of these items were financed by their producers until sold on a commission basis by their wholesalers.

There were, of course, two domestic producers' boards but these had different objectives than the overseas boards. Thus the Tomato and Cucumber Marketing Board was intended to provide help to producers by improving the quality of their cultivation, grading and packing. It was also designed to aid their negotiations with government departments and in presenting their image to the public. The Potato Marketing Board, which was only concerned with "old" potatoes, had a different function as it was made responsible for equating UK production with estimated demand. This was secured by the control of the acreage put down to potatoes, as this was a crop with a guaranteed minimum price overproduction could have been a serious problem. The resulting output could then only be handled by licensed merchants who were not permitted to operate on a commission basis. The Board was also at this time required to advise the Government on levels of imports which might be necessary to ensure satisfactory supplies.

Although some of the wide variety of fruit and vegetables which arrived at the primary markets was destined for direct sale to manufacturers, caterers and the small, but growing, supermarket sector most produce was sold either to secondary wholesalers or to independent retailers who were to satisfy the needs of the

From Orchard to Market

consumer. The relative scale in each aspect of these complex operations can best be judged by the following statistics:-

Number of Firms and Persons Engaged in the Fruit Trade in Great Britain (1950)

	Number of Firms	Number of Branches	Persons Engaged*
Domestic producers	-	70,000	-
Primary wholesaler	300	450	7,200
Importers	140	160	
Others (wholesaling)	50	100	4,800
Commission buyers	100	100	
Secondary wholesalers	2,400	2,800	26,000
Greengrocers and fruiterers†	40,000	45,000	115,000
Total retail outlets selling fresh fruit and vegetables	-	150,000	-
Total (wholesaling and importing only)	3,000	3,600	38,000

* Includes persons engaged part-time.
† Figures adjusted to take account of response rate of only some 90 per cent.

This structure was to remain largely unaltered during the following twenty years. There was, however, some consolidation in the retail sector with chains of fruiterers at first expanding rapidly and coalescing into ever larger groups. Sam Cook and Gerrards in the South, Waterworths in the North West, and Malcolm Campbell in Scotland were examples. Waterworths by 1964 was operating 250 fruit shops and 5 food markets. By then, however, it was becoming clear that the future lay with the supermarket type of business and this presented the choice of heavy investment or selling out to realise property values. Waterworths were one of the firms who wisely took the latter option and thus avoided being squeezed between the large-scale activities of Tesco and Sainsbury's and the low-cost operations of individual retailers. The latter continued to survive, if not prosper, with the aid of pre-packaging but were hindered by the growth of self-service facilities elsewhere and by the ending of retail price maintenance in 1965.

Both large and small outlets were also concerned by the expense of coping with the demands of successive Food and Drugs Acts which required ever higher standards

Fruits of Freedom

of hygiene. This was further emphasised with the rapid rise of expenditure on quick-frozen foods - the total spent on all foods increasing from only £2m in 1950 to over £60m in 1962. However while technical changes of this nature caused proportionately more difficulties to the small operator the ease of entry to the retail trade and the optimistic attitude of many individuals ensured that any failures were quickly replaced.

The demands for improved hygiene allied to ever increasing traffic congestion emphasized the overcrowded nature of Britain's primary markets. This resulted in over thirty schemes of improvement being proposed for the provinces in the early 1950s but the most pressing problem was in London. The largest wholesale market was at Covent Garden but its site in the centre of a busy, built-up area meant that its functions were increasingly impaired. As a result in 1957 the Runciman Report recommended that it should move to an entirely new location and it re-opened at Nine Elms in 1974. This, and developments at other markets in the capital, went some way towards alleviating these long-standing difficulties but partly because of the limited extent of Government support they were not to be fully resolved until the 1980s.

This was a period when the trend towards de-regulation meant that government agencies took a less active part in controlling the economic environment. Consequently the role of trade associations, co-operatives of various kinds, and the Fruit Trade Journal became more significant. However although this was mainly an era of buoyant demand and moderate prosperity for the trade as a whole the forthcoming changes in Britain's relationship with Europe cast a long shadow over the 1960s. When the Treaty of Rome established the European Economic Community in 1957 the UK declined to join. Following the rejection of British proposals for an industrial free trade area by the EEC Britain led the way in establishing the European Free Trade Association. This included Austria, Portugal, Switzerland and the three Scandinavian countries and proved to be a valuable customs union of over 100 million individuals. Nevertheless it gradually became clear that this was no real substitute for membership of the EEC but applications to join were rejected in both 1961 and 1964. Further negotiations followed and were to be successfully concluded in 1972. Although this was to prove a great advantage to Britain's economic progress and overall trade it also posed enormous questions for the nation's food importers and producers. These concerns were naturally reflected throughout the entire fruit and vegetable industry.

From Orchard to Market

11
Europe - Opportunities & Threats

The return of the Conservatives to power in June, 1970 saw Edward Heath finally negotiate Britain's entry into the European Economic Community. The subsequent trebling of world commodity prices and massive rises in the cost of oil then led to the floating of the pound and by 1975 it was to lose a further 26% of its value. The inflationary pressures which were created then stimulated serious industrial unrest, the introduction of a Three Day Week and, eventually early elections. The ensuing Labour Administration was then to organise a referendum which confirmed membership of the E.E.C. and when, following the Winter of Discontent, Margaret Thatcher was elected in 1979 she also accepted - with some reservations - that Britain's future lay in what was to become the European Community.

The terms on which Britain, together with Denmark and Eire, were admitted to the European Economic Community from January 1973 provided for transitional periods during which the necessary harmonization would be progressively achieved. Thus British tariffs against the former "six" were to be removed in the five years from 1973 to 1977: the Common External Tariff was to be incorporated in the four years from 1974 to 1977 while the Common Agricultural Policy was to be adopted over the five years from 1973 to 1978.

The method of agricultural aid which had evolved in the UK had two distinct elements. The first of these consisted of direct grants which were available for capital improvements and machinery. The second guaranteed the payment of minimum prices to the producers of specified commodities. Market forces then set actual prices and if the level was below what had been approved the difference was made-up by the state. Under this system cheap foreign and, especially, Commonwealth food could be imported fairly freely so that the British consumer had the benefit of world prices. As an annual review adjusted the level guaranteed for each item it was also relatively simple to encourage or discourage the production of whatever was deemed most desirable.

The support system developed by the CAP ostensibly aimed to promote regular supplies and stable markets with reasonable prices for consumers and a fair income for the producers. However as the farming and horticultural community in the European Community (EC) formed a much bigger section of the population and produced a larger proportion of food requirements than in Britain a different format had evolved. Thus while the UK held food prices down to international

From Orchard to Market

levels and subsidized its farmers the CAP set "targets" for prices which were based on the cost of production. As many of the European units were small they tended to be inefficient and hence their prices needed to be high for them to remain viable. Imports were then subjected to duties which brought them up to the EC level and so the prices to the consumers were usually well above those ruling elsewhere. A degree of flexibility was provided by setting an "Intervention" price just below the "Target" level. If the market fell this was the point at which the CAP would step in and provide support by purchasing whatever was necessary to restore the situation. Unfortunately this system did little to improve efficiency and led to the creation of huge surpluses which then had to be stored at great expense or sold cheaply to the Third World.

The net effect of the CAP was to limit the importation of cheap, external foodstuffs (and so denied a market for many developing countries) and instead provided the consumer with expensive though home produced items. While there is clearly some merit in safeguarding home industries - there are equally compelling arguments against it - the CAP took these principles to extreme lengths. As a result since its inception many traditional producers in Europe had been able to largely ignore economic forces. Of course this was only achieved at enormous cost with expenditure on agriculture distorting the entire EC budget. In 1978 for example nearly 74% of all outgoings were spent for this purpose.[1]

This vast expenditure was partly financed by the levies on imports and partly by contributors from the member states based on 1% - later raised to 1.2% - of Gross Domestic Product. This system meant that Britain with its large level of imports and relatively small though efficient agricultural sector was obliged to pay in more than she was able to claim back. Although Mrs Thatcher was subsequently able to remove some of this anomaly it was to remain a lasting irritant for the whole of this period. On the other hand, as noted later, it is also clear that the CAP has had some beneficial consequences for British production so that its degree of self-sufficiency was encouraged to rise substantially.

All sections of the fruit and vegetable industry had, of course, to work within the changing economic environment in which they operated. This was largely determined by successive governments which all had an ongoing concern to maintain a viable balance of payments. Thus all aspects of external trade needed to be carefully monitored but the Administration's freedom of action was itself greatly constrained by its obligations under the General Agreement on Tariffs and Trade (1947) and by the restrictions imposed by the International Monetary Fund (1944). The difficulties which persisted for most of this long period resulted in much state intervention in the economy and "Stop-Go" policies seriously affected trading conditions. Firms within the industry consequently found it necessary

Europe - Opportunities & Threats

to cope with the inflation which reached a peak of 22% in May 1982: with rising unemployment, major industrial disputes and volatile interest rates. Activity and profitability was also influenced by changes in both the level and format of taxation. So in addition to the many variations in the rate (and allowances) of taxes on income those engaged in business were obliged to take account of the imposition of Capital Gains and Corporation Tax - both introduced in 1965. Other complications which beset those in the trade were caused by the replacement of Purchase Tax (which originated during World War II) and Selective Employment Tax (1966) by the time consuming Value Added Tax which commenced in 1973 when the UK joined the EEC.

While most, if not all, of these impositions were bourn patiently by the trade there was a considerable degree of apprehension in respect of the consequences of a possible link-up with the Common Market. It was generally understood that while all parts of horticulture might be threatened by membership those crops which needed to be grown under glass were particularly vulnerable. This was because of their high capital and running costs which would not be required in regions with more favourable climates. Thus as early as July 1961 the Tomato and Cucumber Marketing Board published an article which quoted items from THE OBSERVER and THE FINANCIAL TIMES which suggested that:-

> "......the growers of tomatoes and early vegetables are among those farmers who may be ruined...."

and that competition from Europe:-

> "....cannot but be serious for the least efficient section among British tomato growers and there can be little doubt that they will be one of the worst-hit sections of horticulture..." [2]

The more general concern was for the future of what was certainly a large and highly successful industry. Its importance can be clearly judged by the statistics for 1961 which indicate that the net value of horticulture output (including flowers) was about 15% of total agricultural production:-

> "Home sources (then) supplied about 75% of the flowers and bulbs, 70% of the vegetables (excluding potatoes) and some 35% of fruits consumed in the U.K. The home fruit output represents more than half the total of fruit which could possibly be grown in our climatic conditions". [3]

Those in the industry therefore kept a close watch on the progress of agricultural integration within the EEC and took a special interest in its proposals for the

From Orchard to Market

import and export of fruit and vegetables to and from external countries. A provisional agreement was made to cover these items from the early 1960s. This was in anticipation of Britain's expected entry into the Common Market and when this did not materialize further *ad hoc* arrangements had to be negotiated until membership was achieved in 1973. In the meanwhile there was much discussion of contentious issues which included that of the ongoing status of the Channel Islands. These were incorporated within the UK's application but it was feared, at one stage, that they could have been regarded as separate entities and thus excluded if the member states had so wished. If this had taken place Guernsey and Jersey would have been liable to full payment of the Common External Tariff once it was introduced. Other countries, especially Spain and Israel, were also deeply worried about ongoing access for their products to the EEC. While temporary agreements were made to protect these trades and those of some other external producers all remained extremely vulnerable throughout this interim period.

Particular concern was felt by the primary producers of the Commonwealth. This was because if Britain joined the EEC without making special arrangements for the preference area exporters of fresh fruit - especially apples, pears, bananas and citrus - they would lose the small concession now given by the UK and would also have to pay whatever Common External Tariff was decided upon for these commodities.

By 1970 when British entry seemed likely apples were paying a duty of 8% : pears 10% : bananas 20% and citrus between 4 and 8%, and in addition any imports would have to conform with the Community's fruit regulations which might be used to limit access whenever this was thought to be desirable (eg to protect internal production). If these tariffs were to be imposed on the fruit from the Commonwealth and other traditional sources it would, of course, raise its price at precisely the time when EEC members would be able to enjoy unrestricted, duty-free, entry into the UK.

Fortunately for existing suppliers the interim period (1973-1978) was to see many transitional arrangements which helped Britain and the other new entrants adapt to the common agricultural policy. Thus the common external tariff was only gradually introduced. The method for calculating this rate was to utilize the arithmetic average of the various customs duties of the "Six". In the case of oranges in 1971 this amounted to 20% during the Winter months and 15% in the Summer whereas Britain was only charging 5%. In practice, by then, many of the Mediterranean producers had achieved some form of associate status and so were able to enjoy varying degrees of preferential treatment. As a result the actual rates paid for citrus at this time were Greece, 0% : Morocco and Tunisia, 4% :

Europe - Opportunities & Threats

Turkey, Israel and Spain, 12% : Cyprus and others, 20%. It should be noted that the actual valuation for the collection of these duties was fixed in Brussels every 15 days - a different value being assessed for each variety and country of origin. In addition to coping with these tariffs external - as well as internal - producers were obliged to comply with compulsory common quality standards. These had been introduced in 1962 and had then been steadily extended so that by 1971 they included almost all fresh vegetables and fruits.

These controls imposed by customs duties and quality standards were supplemented by a market stabilisation scheme which had been first introduced in 1967. This covered only a limited number of products - apples, pears, peaches, grapes, citrus, tomatoes and cauliflower - and was designed to even out any fluctuations in supply and demand. In the case of these items an annual basic price and buying in price was established and then used to assess the real intervention price. This was the level at which produce could be drawn off and utilized for non-commercial purposes. Another aspect of this policy involved the need to invoke compensatory levies when the import price was lower than the reference price. This, in turn, was supported by attempts to prevent structural surpluses and in the 1970-1972 period a grubbing up scheme had already removed 100,000, mainly apple, trees. [4]

It should be remembered that in 1961 the common agricultural policy for the marketing of agricultural products covered only 52% of produce. By 1976, however, it had been gradually extended to over 91% and was then including most items. At that time a major omission was the potato but this was already regulated on a voluntary basis by the Union Europeene Du Commerce de Gros des Pommes de Terre. This had been established in 1952 and was subsequently accepted by the EEC as representing the whole of the potato wholesale trade. The British Potato Trades Consortium, which had been set up in 1969, accepted an invitation to join the European Union of Potato Merchants in 1972 so was able to play a significant role in framing the regulations which after 1976 were to control most aspects of the business.

Until the 1st of January 1978 many of Britain's traditional suppliers of fruit and vegetables had been protected from the full force of EEC policies by a number of transitional arrangements. Once the UK became a full member of the Community these agreements were increasingly difficult to maintain and great concern was expressed by a number of producers including South Africa, Israel and Cyprus:-

From Orchard to Market

> "From last Sunday, when the UK completed its five year transition to full membership of the EEC, South African exporters will have to pay the full European Common External Tariff, which, for fruit, ranges as high as 25%"

> "The Tariffs on apricots, peaches and grapes are extremely high.....and they don't seen all that logical. There is no alternative supply within the Common Market during our season, so that the only effect of the full tariff - other than to limit imports - will be to make the European consumer pay, either in the form of artificially high prices, or in lack of choice".

> "It's not protection. It's a wealth tax. It will undoubtedly hinder the development of South African fruit production". [5]

The Greek Cypriot industry was also gravely concerned about the future of its exports to the EEC. The main products which it feared would become uneconomic were potatoes, carrots, citrus and, especially, table grapes. The latter faced a tariff of up to 22% when the transitionary period came to an end. Fortunately for Cyprus, and for British consumers, further provisional arrangements were made which provided some concessions to most non-member countries. However these were all of a grace and favour nature and as they were only continued while they were felt to be in the Community's interest there was much apprehension amongst many producers.

Israel was another nation which was particularly anxious about its future trade with Europe. Israel had made considerable progress in diversifying its output so that citrus which had at one time been its only major product comprised only 50% of its shipments in 1980. This widened range of exports helped to enhance Israel's appeal within the Community and its position was further strengthened by the trade inbalance which saw Europe selling Israel over a billion dollars more than was bought from them in the same year. Consequently a modus vivendi had evolved which apparently suited both parties but this was perceived to be under serious threat when a second expansion of the Community was planned.

The proposed enlargement was to see Greece become a member in 1981 and Spain and Portugal join in 1986. Details of their exports to the EEC indicate the products which posed danger to external producers:-

Europe - Opportunities & Threats

Community Imports from Greece, Spain and Portugal in 1976

	Greece	Spain	Portugal
Early potatoes	31,595	35,501	2,701
Cucumbers	22,322	2,399	-
Oranges	22,934	752,639	-
Lemons	6,926	131,688	-
Table grape	31,456	95,946	-
Raisins	82,289	361	-
Apricots	19,262	8,649	-
Peaches	52,991	16,428	-
Melons	17,460	87,757	-

However an even greater threat was the rise in self-sufficiency which these new members brought to the enlarged Common Market:-

Percentage Self Sufficiency within the EEC

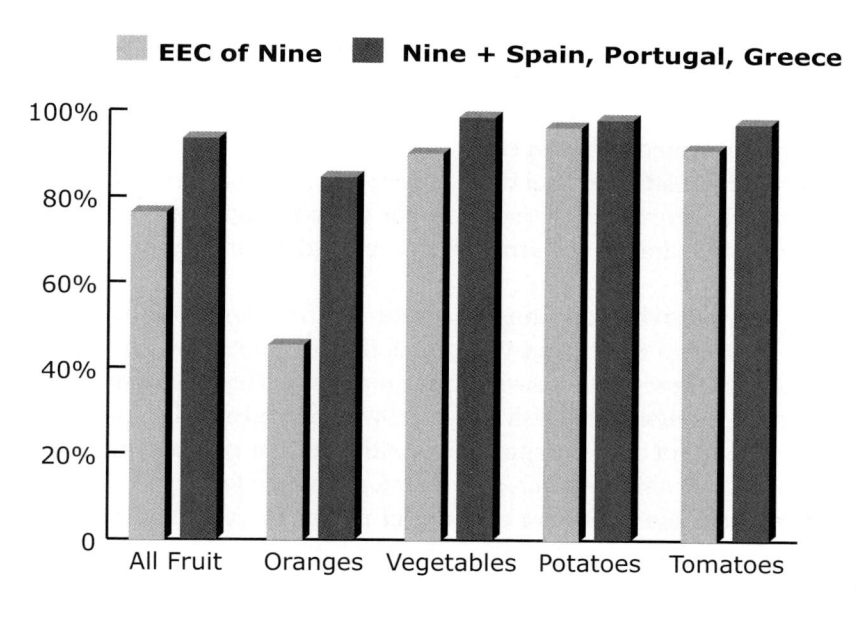

(Bar chart comparing EEC of Nine vs. Nine + Spain, Portugal, Greece across: All Fruit, Oranges, Vegetables, Potatoes, Tomatoes)

It was generally felt that third countries would not be adversely affected by the increased size of the EEC and may, in fact, benefit from it. On the other hand it was also understood that the Mediterranean countries, which mainly export farm products and textiles to the Community, would find their markets more

From Orchard to Market

difficult. Those particularly at risk in these respects were Cyprus (which sent 68% of its exports to the EEC), Morocco (which sent 51% -mainly citrus, tomatoes, canned fruit and vegetables) and Israel (which sent 33% - of which 21% were farm products). Although Israel pressed for a free trade area in agricultural commodities this was never a real possibility. Instead a series of special arrangements were completed and these culminated with a package in 1985 which was of special value to Israel and Morocco. The timing of these concessions was highly relevant as Spain, in spite of being still outside the EEC, was already second only to Italy as a supplier of fruit and vegetables. It was also known that Arab interests were actively financing plantations of flowers and fruit in Spain for their own political reasons. These included exotic items, spray carnations and avocados – the latter being Israel's largest single export to Europe. Thus the accession of Spain was regarded with considerable apprehension by producers both inside and outside the EEC.

The Spanish certainly anticipated that membership of the Common Market would aid their exports of most varieties of fresh fruits and vegetables. However a forecast made in 1986, estimated that the production of citrus would only rise at a moderate rate over the ensuing five years.

However many within the community, which was scheduled to be completely integrated by 1992, feared the competition from Spanish expansion for 90% of its output was destined for the EEC. This was based on the belief that the limitations of the Spanish infra-structure and shortages of water for irrigation would soon be overcome – especially once EEC funds were made available. Different countries adopted their own individual views on these developments. Thus the French were not concerned with the growth of Spanish citrus but found their exports of asparagus and strawberries created a difficult situation in 1987.

They also worried over the future competition from Andalusian peaches and nectarines and over the increasing production of apples which they saw as a real threat to some of their own export markets. This was also a matter of some misgivings amongst British apple growers already under much pressure from other exporters. On the other hand although the enormous expansion of Spanish strawberry shipments created a major problem for France it was largely accepted by the trade in Britain as a useful means of extending their season:-

Exports of Spanish Strawberries (tons) 1984-91

1984	1985	1986	1987	1988	1989	1990	1991
33,451	50,452	71,910	103,356	114,941	112,152	112,140	121,930

Europe - Opportunities & Threats

From the foregoing it should be clear that membership of the Community provided many opportunities for national industries but also created additional competition in some products. Further problems for domestic producers were caused by the changing levels in the reference prices which were designed to regulate the quantities of imports during the European season. These adjustments were seen by many as distorting trade by affecting retail prices and limiting choice for the consumer. A high reference price may also have had the effect of encouraging the purchase of cheaper, domestically produced, substitutes while a low one may have been responsible for such poor results that the local growers could only survive with expensive support. The alternative season of the Southern Hemisphere ensured that their products were generally welcomed at certain times of the year but additional controls could be exercised by limiting their exports to within specific dates.

Arguments in respect of the beginnings and endings of these periods, which were critical to the prosperity of many traditional producers, were frequently supported by political pressure provided by their former trading partners. The use of the Green Pound designed to offset fluctuations in the relationship between national currencies was yet another potential bone of contention which further complicated the overall picture. It was, therefore, fortunate that a number of officially recognised bodies had evolved to help present the interests of their constituents to the European Commission These bodies included the European Consumers Association, the COPA-Cogeca (which represented the growers) and the European Federation (EUCOFEL) which bound together the trade associations which were responsible for the majority of the Community's marketing and distribution of fresh produce. In many respects EUCOFEL helped to hold the balance between the concerns of the consumer and those of the producers. Its then President, Jacques Onona, speaking in 1990 confirmed his support for the principles of free trade but recognised the need for a degree of intervention. In his view a working partnership was necessary to reconcile these frequently conflicting claims and controversial matters such as the maintenance of the "gentlemen's" agreement over Southern Hemisphere apples and the solving of the problems of the European banana market could only be achieved by ongoing discussion and mutual respect.

[9]

From Orchard to Market

12
Changing Patterns of Supply

The UK's entry into the EEC was to have a major impact on its fruit and vegetable production and import trades. Also of fundamental significance to both domestic output and overseas supplies were ongoing developments in transport and distribution facilities. As can be seen from the graph below the costs of both ocean and air freight fell quite sharply in the period from 1920 to 1990. As these declines were parallelled by reductions in the cost of land - especially road - transport the real cost of importing fresh fruit and vegetables was progressively lowered. In addition the charges for transatlantic and other long-distance phone calls and satellite communications also steadily fell after their introduction in the early post-war years. According to Mr A J Ellis, Chairman and Chief Executive of the Fyffes Group, these innovations were equally significant in promoting the growth of international trade for they encouraged confidence and enabled control to be more effectively exercised. [1]

The falling costs of transport and communications

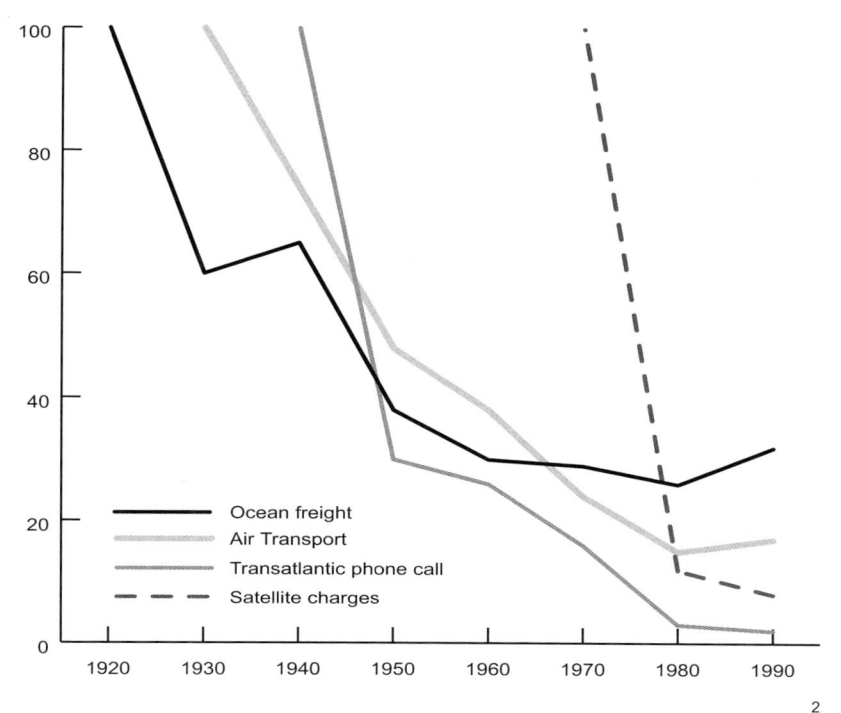

- Ocean freight
- Air Transport
- Transatlantic phone call
- Satellite charges

[2]

From Orchard to Market

The net effects of these technical improvements were not only that imports were cheapened but that their sources of supply were considerably widened. As a result the seasons of many items could be greatly extended and, as indicated in the following table, the import of almost all items rose substantially:-

Annual Imports of Fresh and Dried Fruits, 1976 - 1994
(000 Tonnes)

		1976	1980	1984	1990	1994
Fruit and Nuts	Total	1,559	1,796	1,898	2,389	2,559
	EEC Share	399	524	662	1,133	1,129
	Total (£m)	311	591	800	1,286	1,483
	EEC Share (£m)	084	176	288	624	675
Oranges, Mandarins and Clementines	Total	415	467	452	534	510
	EEC Share	8	26	45	263	201
Other citrus fruit inc. Lemons and Grapefruit	Total	148	159	128	144	140
	EEC Share	18	18	13	46	27
Bananas (inc. Plantains)	Total	312	322	309	470	613
	EEC Share	22	68	57	79	171
Apples: Fresh	Total	381	374	400	466	435
	EEC Share	256	260	254	273	249
Grapes	Total	53	169	196	241	256
	EEC Share	6	19	103	119	112

In general terms the impact of Britain joining the Economic Community meant that the importation of non-EU produce gradually fell as a share of the total. This was to be anticipated because of the ending of Imperial Preference in 1971 and its progressive replacement by the regulations and impositions of the Common Market. Thus while the EU supplied only 25.5% of the total fruit imports (by weight) in 1976 this proportion had risen to over 44% by 1994. Within these totals the shares of individual commodities varied substantially over time. However all except apple supplies were increasingly obtained from the EU.

Changing Patterns of Supply

European Community Shares in UK Fruit Imports

	1976	1994
Oranges:	1.9%	39.4%
Other Citrus:	12.1%	19.2%
Bananas:	7.0%	27.8%
Apples:	67.0%	57.2%
Grapes:	11.3%	43.7%
Edible Nuts:	10.0%	20.7%
Not Elsewhere Specified:	42.5%	67.4%
Total:	25.5%	44.0%

[4]

Although these statistics may be distorted by the expansion of the EU they provide a clear indiction that the sources of many of Britain's fruit imports were in the process of change. Thus in the case of oranges the struggle for dominance between Israel and Spain was settled in the latter's favour when it became a full member of the EU in 1986. To some extent Israel's concentration upon other products was also a factor in its decline as the UK's former principal supplier. However the growth of South African exports (aided by its different season) plus significant contributions from Morocco, Cyprus and Uruguay demonstrate that the range of sources for citrus fruit has become very much wider in recent years.

By 1976 Jamaican banana exports which had been responsible for 60% of the UK market ten years earlier had declined to only 25%. This fall continued so that in 1981 they supplied only 5.3% and although they were to subsequently recover they remained a minor player in a rapidly growing trade. The gap was largely filled by the development of Geest's imports from the Windward Islands and Fyffes' initiative in promoting supplies from both Belize and Suriname. Any balance that was required was provided by dollar fruit from Central America but this was only permitted under licence when the Banana Advisory Committee (established in 1973) agreed it was necessary. [5]

As Southern hemisphere suppliers were extending their seasons and shipping times reduced the EU lost some ground in the provision of apples to the UK. In the early 1970s the EU supplied approximately 67% of British imports with France being responsible for a large proportion of these shipments. At that time South Africa was becoming the biggest of the external suppliers as the once dominant Australian and New Zealand growers were providing declining - though still substantial - cargoes. Thereafter France continued to hold it's position as the

From Orchard to Market

leading EU exporter to the UK but the Southern Hemisphere producers were able to increase their share of the market so that by 1994 the EU was responsible for only 57% of what was a larger total of British imports. However it should be noted that this decline was part of a much larger problem. Over production of apples had led to low prices and by January 1993 European stocks had reached a record 3 million tonnes. As a result the European Commission had established a system of voluntary limitation which did something to restrict imports without providing the complete protection which many producers would have preferred. The net effect of this development was that imports into the EU (and thus the UK) continued at a high level and created huge problems for British top fruit growers:-

EC Imports of Southern Hemisphere Apples 1988-1992 (in tonnes)

	1988	1989	1990	1991
Chile	147,000	147,000	145,000	213,000
Argentina	79,000	69,000	80,000	86,000
South Africa	195,000	203,000	197,000	196,000
New Zealand	128,000	117,000	130,000	152,000
Australia	6,000	2,000	3,000	3,000
Brazil	600	4,300	6,000	4,000
Total	555,000	542,000	562,000	654,000
Total	92.29%	90.94%	87.40%	77.95%
Non-EC	602,000	596,000	643,000	839,000
Total Exports to Non-EC	190,000	161,000	153,000	144,000

Most other items, including grapes, followed the general pattern so that the EU contributed an increasing share of the British fruit market. The import of grapes grew five fold from 1976 to 1994 and this period marked its transition from what was still regarded as a luxury to what became an everyday purchase. Originally Italy was the largest of the internal growers but the accession of Spain and later, Greece, significantly changed this situation. Thus the proportion produced within the EU rose from 11 to 43% with South Africa and Cyprus (subsequently joined by Chile) providing most external cargoes.

The 'Seventies' and 'Eighties' were also to be characterized by the appearance of some new varieties and the growth of some previously small ones. The import

Changing Patterns of Supply

of these aptly named exotics expanded rapidly once cheap air transport become available and included avocados, carambola, (star fruit), durian, guavas, kiwi fruit, kumquats, lychees, mangos, mangosteens, passionfruit, paw paw (papaya), peppers and persimmons (sharon fruit). By 1985 the UK market was worth a total of £148m - a rise of 51% since 1981 - but it should be kept in mind that by then both avocados and kiwi fruit had already become well established and were increasingly regarded as mainstream products. [7]

The increasing demand for exotics in Britain led to a number of experiments using existing glasshouses in Guernsey and kiwi fruit was successfully grown. However as this coincided with the emergence of a world glut in this item - global production rose from 362,000 tonnes in 1987 to 884,000 tonnes in 1990 - it was not commercially viable and quantities remained low.

The importation of vegetables followed a similar pattern to that of fruit. Thus while in 1976 the EU share amounted to only 35% by 1994 this had risen to over 68% of a substantially larger total. The principal items varied by differing amounts but all with the exception of beans, peas and other leguminous vegetables, (which remained stable) showed a greater dependence upon produce grown within the EU.

European Community Share in UK Vegetable Imports

	1976	1994
Potatoes	44.7%	67.7%
Beans etc	4.4%	4.5%
Tomatoes	28.4%	55.7%
Other	36.5%	82.4%
Total	25.5%	44.0%

[8]

The sources for imported potatoes were extremely varied and in 1976 included the Netherlands, Egypt, the Canaries, Spain and Morocco. These countries remained important over the ensuing two decades with Belgium, France and Italy also contributing substantial quantities toward the end of this period. Imports of legumes were much more stable with the United States and Canada providing the majority of cargoes throughout this era. In the case of tomatoes the Canary Islands, the Netherlands and Spain supplied virtually all of Britain's requirements with Southern Ireland sending moderate quantities during the 'Seventies'. However it should be noted that the Channel Islands' output was classified as domestic production so do not form part of the import statistics.

From Orchard to Market

As will be seen from the above Table a significant proportion of imported vegetables were included in the broad classification of *Other: not elsewhere specified*. The origins of this produce lay in a wide range of countries in which the Netherlands, Spain and France were always prominent. The Canaries, Israel and Eire were also usually important while the Southern Hemisphere growers continued to make large contributions at particular times of the year.

**Annual Imports of Fresh, Frozen and Dried Vegetables,
1976 - 1994 (000 metric tonnes)**

		1976	1984	1990	1994
All vegetables, not elsewhere specified	Total EEC Share	1.364 .481	1.675 .793	1.726 1.080	1.924 1.318
Potatoes (not including sweet potatoes)	Total EEC Share	.630 .282	.383 .112	.371 .188	.375 .254
Beans, Peas, Lentils and other leguminous vegetables: dried, shelled and split	Total EEC Share	.158 .007	.175 .017	.184 .009	.176 .008
Tomatoes	Total EEC Share	.130 .037	.235 .097	.253 .162	.242 .135
Other vegetables (including onions, shallots, garlic and leeks)	Total EEC Share	.312 .114	.551 .306	.728 .584	.751 .619

Note: Does not include Channel Islands.

[9]

The growth and increasing diversity of fruit and vegetable imports inevitably had a significant impact on the domestic production of many items. These also benefitted from the improvements in transport which had done so much to reduce the cost of overseas production to the British consumer. However as the distances involved were so much smaller the proportionate effect was much less. The increasing share of imports provided by the EU countries were, of course, partly due to the support provided by the Common Agricultural Policy. This assistance was also available to UK producers but in spite of its aid the value of agriculture's contribution to the Gross Domestic Product (at constant 1990 prices) only rose from an average of £6,286m in 1984-86 to £6,550m in 1995. As a result the UK's overall degree of self sufficiency in food and feedstuffs rose

Changing Patterns of Supply

only slightly and remained on a plateau around 58% throughout the 'Eighties' and 'Nineties'.

The competition from imports whether from EU or non-EU sources inevitably created major problems for British fruit growers. These proved to be so difficult to overcome that, as the following table indicates, the quantity they marketed fell by almost 50% in the period from 1971 to 1996:-

Home Grown Fruit Marketed in the UK
('000 tons)

	1971	1976	1981	1986	1991	1996
Orchard Fruit						
Dessert Apples	271.4	210.1	162.2	147.9	148.3	105.4
Culinary Apples	174.6	134.7	94.7	134.0	157.1	118.3
Pears	58.2	46.9	37.9	45.3	36.0	35.8
Plums	34.4	28.6	12.4	25.8	21.5	19.7
Cherries	9.0	6.2	2.6	3.2	1.0	3.6
Total (inc. others)	594.6	484.5	309.8	356.2	363.9	282.8
Soft Fruit						
Strawberries	50.4	35.1	48.3	43.1	42.2	40.2
Raspberries	14.3	15.6	21.0	22.5	18.3	12.2
Blackcurrants	22.9	17.4	18.8	22.7	20.7	22.1
Gooseberries	10.5	7.0	}			
Red & White Currants	1.9	1.4	}10.8	10.5	7.4	5.6
Logan & Blackberries	2.4	2.8	}			
Total	102.4	79.3	98.9	98.8	88.6	80.1
Glasshouse Fruit	0.3	0.6	-	-	-	-
GRAND TOTAL	697.3	564.4	408.7	454.9	452.5	363.0

British producers of vegetables fared rather better than those in the fruit industry. This was partly due to the relatively high/weight - low/cost nature of much of their output. This advantage in transport costs provided a small degree of protection from overseas items and, as a result, the quantities they marketed remained largely stable for most of this era:-

From Orchard to Market

Vegetable Output Marketed in the UK (tonnes)
(Domestic Production)

	1971	1976	1981	1986	1991	1996
In the Open: (Field)						
Beetroot	114.7	84.7	89.4	81.4	86.7	71.6
Carrots	479.0	444.1	513.7	488.1	543.9	617.4
Parsnips	54.7	43.3	43.5	50.4	49.4	75.2
Turnips and swedes	121.3	121.0	117.2	120.3	156.3	123.4
Onions dry bulb	145.6	153.8	201.7	190.0	213.0	284.6
Onions green	21.2	26.9	25.3	28.0	22.8	28.4
Brussels sprouts	196.6	131.9	162.5	150.4	96.7	79.9
Cabbage	590.9	485.8	485.1	574.3	388.0	345.5
Cauliflower	284.9	216.6	313.9	337.6	311.6	238.2
Calabrese	-	-	-	15.0	35.0	64.7
Peas harvested dry	63.2	70.1	40.7	43.8	44.4	52.5
Beans, broad	50.5	31.2	15.2	12.8	20.0	9.4
Beans, runner and French	88.7	93.3	65.0	56.2	36.7	35.3
Peas, green for market	41.3	18.3	21.7	17.5	8.0	6.7
Peas, green for processing	191.3	169.3	260.8	218.9	223.3	216.8
Asparagus	0.7	0.6	0.5	1.0	1.5	1.4
Celery	57.6	54.5	41.6	59.3	48.7	37.8
Leeks	24.4	23.8	35.6	53.4	68.2	51.9
Lettuce	130.2	87.2	113.8	129.2	193.5	181.1
Rhubarb	45.5	31.8	37.2	23.3	27.5	21.1
Watercress	6.0	4.6	4.5	3.9	5.0	2.4
Others	113.0	107.3	-	132.7	473.5	421.7
Sub-Total	2821.3	2399.5	2586.9	2787.5	2709.1	2680.3
Protected Crops:						
Tomatoes	108.5	127.7	120.2	131.4	132.7	116.7
Cucumbers	38.7	51.9	50.6	75.7	103.9	85.6
Lettuce	21.7	30.1	36.7	49.8	46.7	26.4
Mushrooms	48.2	51.1	64.5	100.3	101.5	106.6
Celery, self-blanching	-	-	-	8.6	10.7	8.1
Sweet-Peppers	-	-	-	2.8	3.6	5.9
Others	7.4	9.7	-	6.0	7.5	5.2
Sub-Total	224.5	270.5	272.6	374.6	406.6	354.5
GRAND TOTAL	3045.8	2670.0	2859.5	3143.1	3115.7	3034.8

The decline in fruit production and the stagnation in vegetable output indicated above makes miserable reading. However the details supplied by the tables only show the quantities being marketed so do not provide a complete picture. This requires account to be taken of the growth of the UK population and of the rise

Changing Patterns of Supply

in demand encouraged by a number of campaigns to promote healthy eating. As the following table shows the British market had, in fact, expanded considerably over the period so the performance of the domestic industry is much worse than previously indicated. This is best seen by its declining market shares: in the case of fruit the British proportion has fallen from 32.3% of the total in 1971 to only 12.8% in 1996. Over the same period the home production of vegetables has dropped less steeply but has still been reduced from 83% to 73.5%:-

Supplies of Fruit and Vegetables in the UK
(000 tonnes)

	1971	1976	1981	1986	1991	1996
Vegetables						
Home Production Marketed	3,045	2,670	2,859	3,143	3,115	3,034
Plus: Imports	716	673	838	1,073	974	1,157
Minus: Exports	92	61	161	79	56	63
Total Supply	3,669	3,282	3,536	4,137	4,034	4,129
HPM as % of Total Supply	83.0	81.3	80.8	75.9	77.2	73.5
Fruit						
Home Production Marketed	697	564	408	454	452	363
Plus: Imports	1,486	1,501	1,572	1,847	2,192	2,552
Minus: Exports	23	41	45	59	85	80
Total Supply	2,159	2,024	1,936	2,243	2,560	2,835
HPM as % of Total Supply	32.3	27.8	21.1	20.2	17.7	12.8

The decline in the market-share of home-produced fruit and vegetables could potentially have been offset by an expansion of British exports and re-exports. However, as the table above indicates, while fruit sales abroad did increase at a modest rate those of vegetables actually fell. In any event the net impact was minute.

It should also be remembered that horticulture included a substantial non-edible aspect. This included a wide range of items such as bulbs, fruit trees, plants, ornamental bushes and cut-flowers. Although this activity made a useful and growing contribution to the value of the domestic industry it, too, was increasingly challenged by imports and the level of exports remained relatively small:-

From Orchard to Market

Non-Edible Horticultural Crops
(£m current prices)

	1971	1976	1981	1986	1991	1996
Total Value of Output Marketed in the UK	64	105	188	274	517	660
Imports from all sources except Channel Islands	14	26	80	194	332	446
Imports from Channel Islands	6	9	12	21	25	28
Total Imports	20	35	92	215	357	474
Exports from UK to all sources	0.7	3.7	6.7	17	23	39

13

Although the flower trade had existed for many centuries it was not until 1917 that it was organized on a formal basis. In that year the British Flower Industry Association came into being and helped to encourage the business by negotiating special rates with the railway companies. The industry was then particularly aided by the emergence of regular flights which connected the growers on the Continent and the Channel Islands with the principal markets in Britain. These included a special facility at Spitalfields which was opened in 1935 and the new Flower Market which was created when Covent Garden moved to Nine Elms. The trade was given further impetus by the development of Interflora and this progress continued through the work of the Flowers Publicity Council.

A further innovation which was to challenge the traditional domestic industry was the emergence of organic systems of production. A seminal article on this topic appeared in the Journal on the 2nd of July 1949. This had been written by Lady Eve Balfour the then Secretary of the Soil Association and while the Editor was at pains to distance himself from "unorthodox or even (some would say) heretical views" he was anxious that the fullest possible discussion should take place. Over the next few years this certainly took place with accusations of "crankery" on the one hand and extravagant claims for organic achievements on the other. By 1956 the Journal had published many accounts of successful, commercial ventures which had grown a number of different crops within Britain without the benefit of artificial fertilizers, insecticides or fungicides. However it was not yet convinced that these were anything more than flukes and called for a thorough, prolonged

Changing Patterns of Supply

and impartial investigation at the appropriate Research Centres. [14]
Although the research which was subsequently undertaken was not accepted as conclusive by either side there was a slow but steady rise in demand so that twenty years later the organic market for fruit and vegetables in Britain was valued at over £1million annually. By then it was anticipated that this was the beginning of a large expansion in interest due to the trend towards healthier eating and the desire to have a more balanced diet. At the same time the rising use of chemicals by mainstream producers was a matter of great concern to many customers. This in turn led many members of the public being prepared to pay a premium for organically-grown items and thus helped to encourage both consumption and imports. [15]

Israel was to be one of the first countries to see the potential for this new range of crops and exports of 886 tonnes during the 1985-86 period had increased to over 5,000 tonnes by the 1989-90 season. In Europe the progress of the organic movement was originally inhibited by the lack of a policy on common standards. This was rectified by the EC in April 1991 by which time the activity in different countries was as follows:-

Organic Production In Europe 1991

	Area (ha)	No. of Companies
Belgium	1,200	150
Denmark	15,500	520
France	60,000	4,000
Germany	54,295	2,685
UK	16,000	700
Ireland	3,700	150
Holland	7,600	440
Portugal	550	61
Spain	5,500	1,000

[16]

In 1990 the British market for all types of organically produced food amounted to £40m. By 1992, aided by inflation, this had risen to £120m and by 1997 was estimated to be approximately £173m. Of this latter total some 60% was in the form of fresh fruit and vegetables which were valued at £36m and £88m respectively.[17] At this time almost 80% of these organic fruit and vegetables needed to be imported but there were signs that this situation would gradually be reversed. Organic Food Farms, for example, claimed in 1997 that considerable expansion was taking place in Britain and that output would steadily increase in future years.[18] and this forecast was supported by the official statistics:-

From Orchard to Market

Organic Farming in the UK

	No. of Holdings	Total Hectares
April 1993	849	30,424
February 1994	n/a	30,745
April 1995	757	45,185
April 1996	848	48,185
April 1997	880	50,798
April 1998	1032	55,000
September 1998	1291	68,798

This process was greatly helped by the Organic Aid Scheme which was introduced in 1994 to give direct financial assistance to farmers converting to organic production.

The difficulties experienced by the domestic vegetable and, especially, fruit industries were further compounded by the emergence of a strong pound and high interest rates. On the other hand the increase in demand for many items provided a rising market for British producers to sell their output In the case of fresh vegetables consumption rose throughout the EC in the period between 1980 and 1995. However while this averaged only 5.5% within the Community that in the UK increased by 13.5%:-

Average Annual Per Capita Consumption of Fresh Vegetables (kgs)

	1980	1989	1995(est)	89-95 %
Belgium	153.97	174.9	217.38	+24.3
Denmark	126.7	141.47	162.66	+15.0
France	145.23	150.99	160.03	+ 6.0
Germany	124.21	116.25	116.42	+ 0.1
Greece	242.1	260.57	281.92	+ 8.2
Ireland	164.26	203.6	268.55	+31.9
Italy	134.79	135.69	141.82	+04.5
Netherlands	142.28	161.06	177.39	+10.1
Portugal	185.9	163.63	200.0	+22.2
Spain	286.45	253.2	230.08	- 9.2
UK	157.96	173.95	197.38	+13.5
EU	162.33	163.69	172.65	+05.5

Changing Patterns of Supply

It should, however, be noted that while the demand for some products expanded others tended to decline. An examination of these changes shows the winners and losers since 1960 with mushrooms making the greatest gains and Brussels sprouts the biggest losses:-

Household Consumption Trends for Vegetables (oz per person per week)

	1960	1970	1980	1986	% Change 1970-86
Potatoes	56.03	51.84	40.96	38.76	- 25
Mushrooms	*	0.36	0.55	0.89	+147
Miscellaneous	*	0.80	1.35	1.58	+ 98
Other green	0.27	0.22	0.31	0.36	+ 64
Cucumber	*	0.76	0.98	1.11	+ 46
Leafy Salads	1.31	1.21	1.42	1.66	+ 37
Carrots	2.32	3.00	3.65	4.04	+ 35
Onions/Leeks	*	3.00	3.31	3.48	+ 16
Cauliflowers	2.50	2.77	2.56	2.61	+ 6
Turnips/Swedes	2.39	1.12	1.38	1.12	0
Tomatoes	4.50	4.00	3.79	3.77	- 6
Other Roots	3.23	0.91	0.84	0.82	- 10
Cabbages	4.90	4.50	4.39	3.63	- 19
Beans	2.07	1.29	1.51	1.01	- 22
Peas	1.51	0.66	0.36	0.44	- 33
Brussels Sprouts	2.62	2.47	1.88	1.40	- 43

* Not available

A similar analysis of fruit consumption indicates that grapes made the largest progress with oranges the most substantial losses:-

From Orchard to Market

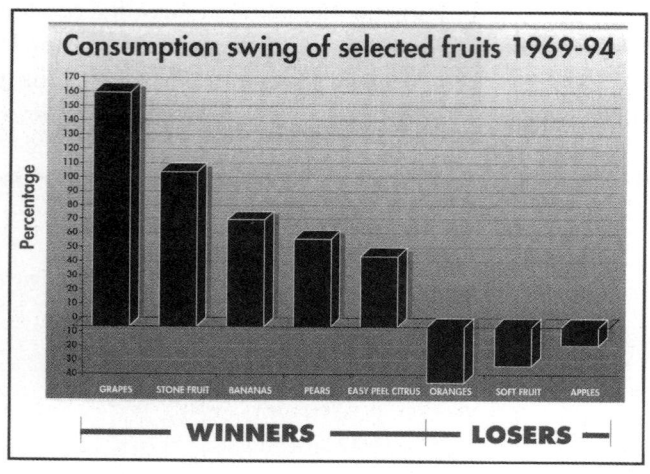

Consumption swing of selected fruits 1969-94

WINNERS: GRAPES, STONE FRUIT, BANANAS, PEARS, EASY PEEL CITRUS
LOSERS: ORANGES, SOFT FRUIT, APPLES

Throughout the period from 1973 to 1995 British agriculture was able to maintain the UK's degree of self-sufficiency in food at approximately 58%. Unfortunately its horticultural sector was less able to cope with the rising flood of fresh produce imports and the proportion of home grown fruits and vegetables continued to fall. Nevertheless the upward trend in consumption did provide a larger market and the more efficient domestic growers were able to cope with the reduced prices they received for their products:-

Total Volume of UK Fresh Fruit and Vegetable Market ('000 tonnes)

	1989	1990	1991	1992	1993
Fruit	2,632.1	2,525.6	2,612.4	2,728.7	2,664.5
Vegetables	3,002.0	2,897.0	2,868.0	2,686.7	2,801.1
Salads	1,107.0	1,082.0	1,116.4	1,143.2	967.9
Potatoes	6,332.0	6,178.0	6,084.0	6,325.0	6,584.0
Total	13,073.1	12,682.6	12,680.8	12,740.6	13,017.5

Total Value of UK Fresh Fruit and Vegetable Market (£m Retail Sale Price)

	1989	1990	1991	1992	1993
Fruit	2,274.5	2,437.2	2,518.0	2,623.3	2,455.9
Vegetables	1,144.7	1,267.9	1,666.3	1,423.5	1,296.3
Salads	998.3	1,092.1	1,049.0	1,070.0	860.7
Potatoes	950.1	913.3	1,043.7	935.8	826.9
Total	5,367.5	5,710.5	6,276.7	5,989.6	5,439.8

Changing Patterns of Supply

As the above statistics indicate the early 1990s saw a 2% increase in the volume of potatoes and vegetables while competitive pricing in the high street led to an 8% drop in the total value of the fresh produce market. In these circumstances all aspects of production, marketing and distribution were placed under ever-increasing pressure to become more cost-effective.

From Orchard to Market

13
Developing Efficiency in Distribution

While both domestic and overseas supplies were undergoing fundamental change influenced by the UK's membership of the EEC, significant developments were also taking place in transport and distribution. In spite of the growth of alternatives mainstream shipping continued to cater for a large proportion of most imports. However the technical innovations which had characterised the "Sixties" accelerated so that a wide-range of highly efficient options steadily emerged. Most of these involved inter-modal, unit load systems and these increasingly included provision for refrigeration or cooling. At first the use of pallets in standard or specially adapted vessels offered considerable savings on cargo – handling times and labour costs and on many routes these offered even greater economies when they were gradually integrated into, or superceeded by the use of containers.

Unfortunately it proved to be difficult and expensive to introduce the new technology into those ports which were members of the National Dock Labour Scheme. As these included London, Liverpool, Southampton, Bristol, Hull and Glasgow – the UK's principle entry points for imported produce – many smaller ports were able to take advantage of this situation until the Scheme was ended in 1989. For most of this period, therefore, the traditional centres tended to decline while many others were able to attract substantial investments and expand. This was essential during an era when rail was giving way to road and the evolution of roll-on/off services were to transform the entire transport system. Thus Barry and Newport in South Wales became important for fruit imports as did Great Yarmouth, Plymouth and Portsmouth. Dover, Felixstowe and Sheerness were to emerge as the fastest growing fruit ports although Southampton was later to regain its position as the biggest handler of fresh produce.

The new systems were at first mainly used for the long-distance carriage of deciduous fruit. Thus by 1970 the Australian trade had been largely containerised with specially designed cellular vessels providing a service from Freemantle, Sydney and Melbourne to London. While Tilbury was the only port of entry the containers were distributed via London East (Orsett), Liverpool and Glasgow with sub-feeder bases being sited at Leeds, Manchester and Birmingham. A similar service was planned by the four British lines which normally brought New Zealand fruit to the UK but, in the event, a contract was agreed with J. Lauritzen, the Danish operator, for it to carry two-thirds of the country's apples and pears. These cargoes were then handled within Britain by Saphir and Sons

From Orchard to Market

and processed by East Kent Packers Ltd. The balance of New Zealand fruit was to be shipped in a largely palletised form by conventional refrigerated tonnage but over the years specialised vessels have taken an even larger share of the trade.

The need for Cape fruit to be similarly palletised and containerised was recommended by Matthew Mack of M. and W. Mack Ltd. after his return from a tour of the major deciduous production areas of South Africa in 1970. For a variety of reasons as late as 1974 the problem of sending 15 million packages from the Cape to a number of European ports in a period of under five months had still not been resolved. Containerisation was not, in fact, to begin until the 1977/78 season and it then took several years before it was fully implemented. However by 1983 a very sophisticated system was in operation and this illustrated the major advantages which a cool-chain and containerisation could bring:-

> *"Previously most (Deciduous Fruit Board) fruit has been delivered by rail to Cape Town docks, entailing up to 700 rail trucks and a possible delay of three days. There, pre-cooling tunnels would reduce the temperatures before the fruit partially palletised, was loaded onto refrigerated vessels.*
>
> *This year, all the fruit in the Western Province, which accounts for by far the major exports, is palletised, pre-cooled in the production area, before being transported by lorry to the docks, a journey of only a few hours ensuring a maximum temperature increase in the produce of only two degrees. Furthermore some 35% is containerised, much of it at the packhouse, with plug-in refrigerated units maintaining a steady low temperature. At the docks, which no longer require the pre-cooling tunnels, an extensive refrigerated store has just been opened which acts as a holding area for produce, before trans-shipment. All this has been done with a considerable cost saving, since now only 50 lorries are required".*
>
> [1]

All of those countries whose produce required a long sea journey to the UK and other European markets found it helpful gradually to extend the scope of their palletisation and containerisation systems. This was true for Chile and the other South American producers and in turn, brought about a further significant change. While exports were small they could at first be catered for by the conventional vessels of the regular lines which served their ports. The growth in scale of these shipments encouraged the companies concerned to build or charter more specialised ships but, over time, these were found to be less competitive than the service offered by the Pools of refrigerated vessels which operated on a global basis. By 1990:-

Developing Efficiency in Distribution

"Six major groups dominate(d) the market. Cool Carriers, Seatrade, Lauritzen Reefers, Alpha Reefer Transport, Star Reefers and Universal Reefers and other Netherlands, British, German, Greek, Japanese and South African operators are also very important. All six together comprise a fleet of about 250 ships. There are also notable companies of less importance. They own refrigerated ships and charter them on the world market".

[2]

These Reefer Pools provide commercial management for groups of shipowners who continued to be responsible for the registration, financing, technical arrangements and crewing of their own vessels. The Pool administration is then usually responsible for marketing, contracting, scheduling, bunkering and cargo-handling. For these services one group, Cool Carriers - which in 1990 had a 20% share of the reefer market - charged 6.95% of a vessel's total net earnings.

[3]

The major products carried by the world's refrigerated tonnage at this time were as follows:-

Major seabourne reefer commodities (part of total transport demand)

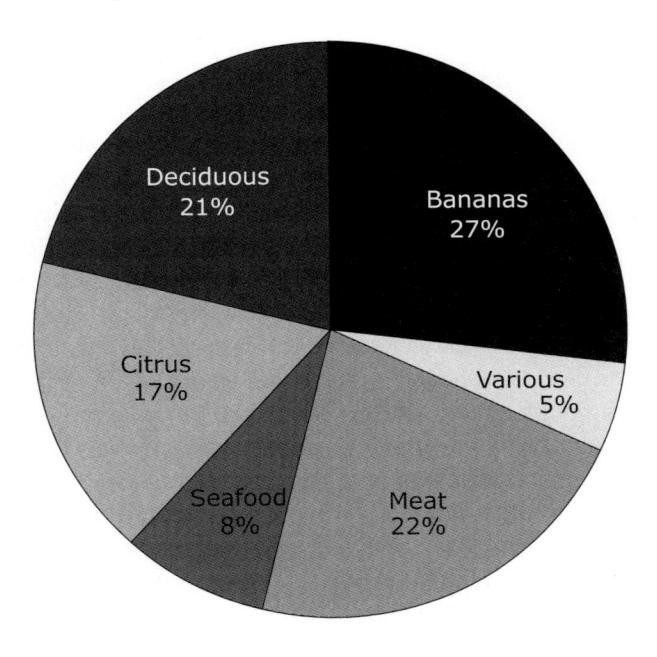

- Deciduous 21%
- Bananas 27%
- Citrus 17%
- Various 5%
- Seafood 8%
- Meat 22%

[4]

While the Reefer Pools carried a very substantial proportion of the long-distance deciduous trade their share of other fruits differed widely. In the case of the banana three American-owned multi-national companies were responsible for a significant percentage of its production and marketing. At first Standard Fruit, Del Monte and the United Fruit Company – later United Brands – depended upon their own vessels for the carriage of most of their cargoes. Thus the UFC developed what became known as the Great White Fleet which in 1908 either owned or chartered over 70 ships. UFC's British subsidiary Elders and Fyffes, also owned and operated nearly 100 vessels on behalf of the Group from 1902 to 1981.

United Brand's sale of the Fyffes Group to Fruit Importers of Ireland in 1985 coincided with Fyffes developing new sources of supply in Suriname and Belize. As a result four banana carriers were ordered and these maintained a regular service between Suriname and Portsmouth. [5]

The other banana importers which catered for the British market in 1990 were Jamaica Producers and Geest. At this time both employed a mixture of company owned or chartered vessels to bring their cargoes from Jamaica and the Windward Islands into Newport and Barry respectively. Pooling arrangements between these three firms meant that cargoes were frequently divided to ensure a regular flow of supplies to their distribution networks. In addition the arrival from Central and South America of Dollar fruit which was used to top-up the traditional sources of supply was mainly shipped by independent lines and landed at Sheerness. Some part-cargoes were also dropped off at Continental and Irish ports and then moved to the UK by road vehicles and cross-channel Ro-Ro services.

Throughout the "Seventies" and "Eighties" Israel and Spain continued to be Britain's major sources of citrus. Israel initially depended upon the ZimLine and other members of the Israel-UK Conference to carry its oranges and other fruit in individual boxes and cartons. By 1983 about 70% of these cargoes had been palletised and were being landed at Sheerness and Newport, with Newcastle and Liverpool being utilised later in the season. Gradually, however, both Cool Carriers of Sweden and Lauritzen Reefers of Denmark carried an increasing share of the Citrus Marketing Board of Israel's exports. By 1991 these had reached 80% and it was decided that the two shipping groups would establish a new firm to handle this growing traffic. Thus the Mediterranean Reefer Lines came into being and as they could call upon a combined fleet of over 120 refrigerated vessels, they were in a position to carry all of Israel's fruit exports if required.

Spanish citrus and other fruit shipments were more fragmental because of the size of the country and the diversity of its producing regions. Thus a number of ports were involved in addition to the competition provided by rail and, later, road transport. In spite of its distance from Valencia and Zaragossa by

Developing Efficiency in Distribution

1970 Bilbao had become the largest centre for the export of fruit and vegetables. Amongst the lines sailing from this port were MacAndrews who had been involved in the business for over 200 years and who ran regular services to both Southampton and Liverpool, as well as a weekly service between Valencia and Liverpool. Many other companies were also concerned with catering for fruit exports. These included the Spanish Contenemar and Golfo lines which were based in Bilbao and the Aznar and Fred Olsen firms which called on Northern Spain as part of their Canary Island and Madeira routes.

As can be seen from the following graph the demand for the carriage of the three most important categories of fruit grew steadily, with only minor fluctuations, throughout the "Eighties":-

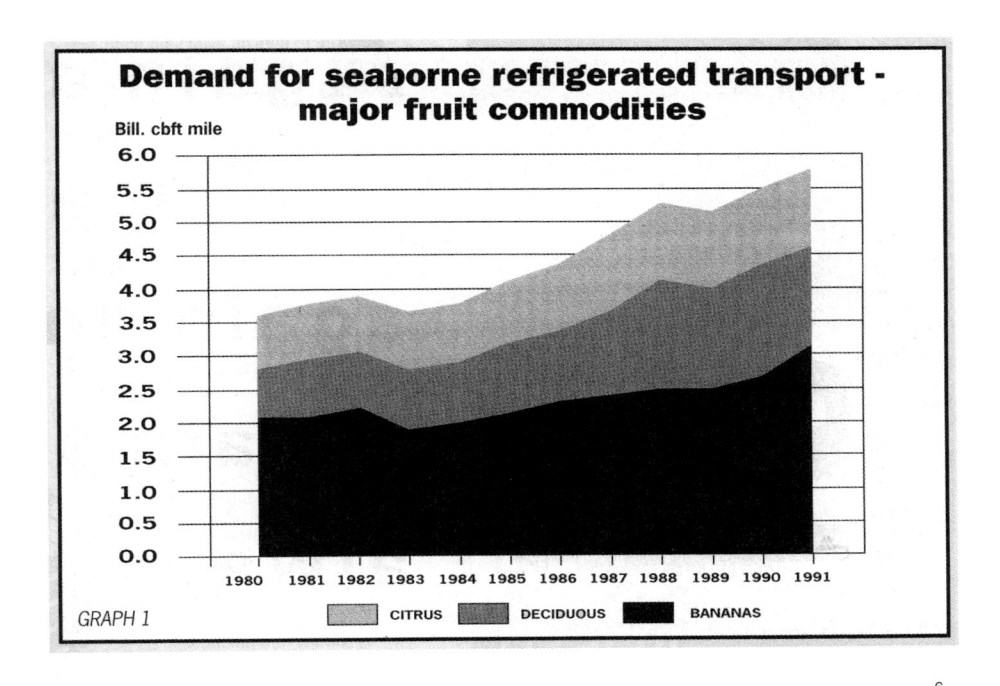

Demand for seaborne refrigerated transport - major fruit commodities

GRAPH 1 — CITRUS, DECIDUOUS, BANANAS (1980–1991, Bill. cbft mile)

This expansion in demand resulted in a gradual increase in the scale and performance of the average reefer. Thus in 1968 'Sazebediela' of 8,035 gross tonage had a cargo capacity of 11,773m^3 and an operating speed of 17 knots. By 1990 'Ditlev Lauritzen' of 14,406 gross tonage had a cargo capacity of 20.844m^3 and could carry 480 TEUs at 20.2 knots. This last vessel operated with a crew of only 7 or 9 men.

It should not be thought that this trend towards ever bigger vessels was iniversal.

From Orchard to Market

Many trades continued to require smaller ships either because of the need to enter small ports or due to the advisability of preventing extra-large supplies arriving at one time and saturating markets.

On the shorter-sea routes smaller types of vessels were employed . Many of these utilised roll-on/roll-off systems which enabled turn-around times in port to be kept to an absolute minimum. An example of this was the service introduced by Brittany Ferries between Roscoff and Plymouth in January 1973. The first ship on this route was m.v. 'Kerisnel' which took only six hours to complete the crossing and carried 45 vehicles and trailers. With the aid of her sister ship, m.v. 'Pen ar Bed' a daily sailing could be maintained and although planned with the cauliflower crop in mind it was soon extended to include a wide range of other vegetables and passengers. In 1976 Brittany Ferries started a seasonal, passenger service between St Malo and Portsmouth – in the following year this became a year-round route on which freight became increasingly important. Brittany Ferries acquired Truckline in 1985 and so took over their Cherbourg-Poole service and in 1986 they established a further ro-ro service between Caen and Portsmouh. Another major operator at this time was P & O Short Sea Shipping Ltd. This firm was responsible for much of the cargo which then moved between Great Britain and Northern Ireland. Amongst its many other activities were the twice weekly sailing's between Southampton and San Sebastian which were organised by its subsidiary, Southern Ferries, in 1975. Similar ro-ro sailing's were arranged by its sister Company, Normandy Ferries, from Southampton to Le Havre. Both of these routes were subsequently to cater for huge quantities of fruit which originated in Spain and Italy as well as in France.

Hull, on the East coast, had long been a terminus for many of the more distant fruit producers. Then in 1967 Link Line established a trailer-ferry service with Holland and this aspect of Hull's trade was greatly enlarged when the port became the terminal for North Sea Ferries. The Norfolk Line also helped to cater for the vast imports of fresh produce from The Netherlands. Originally an independent Dutch firm it was acquired by Unilever in 1975 and subsequently expanded rapidly so that in 1984 its three specialised vessels carried 70,000 trailers to and from its base in Great Yarmouth. Further down the coast the port of Felixstowe witnessed enormous growth since its re-construction began in 1951. As the nearest British harbour to Rotterdam it benefited from this Dutch connection and from being not involved with the Dock Labour Registration Scheme. As a result Felixstowe emerged as the UK's premier container port and handled both general cargo and produce from a wide range of countries as well as being particularly convenient for shipments from Holland. Its near neighbour, Harwich, was a major centre for train ferries which brought large amounts of fruit and vegetables from Italy and Spain, via Zeebrugge. (See Chapter 10). However, this trade suffered badly from

Developing Efficiency in Distribution

the competition of road vehicles and was ended in the early "Seventies".

The sale of Sheerness by the Admiralty to private owners in 1959 was to be followed by its emergence as an important fruit port. Early links with Holland by Westland Imports Ltd, (See Chapter 10) were followed by shipments from many other sources. Cargoes from Israel were significant from the "Sixties" and the opening of a new banana berth for Jamaica Producers in 1972 marked the beginning of a new era. Thus by 1981 fruit represented about a third of the port's throughput and included Israeli, Cuban, Outspan and Sunkist citrus; J P and Fyffes bananas; Chile and New Zealand deciduous items together with other Cape and Moroccan produce. Further investments, particularly in cold stores, helped Sheerness to continue to expand. This process was aided by an absence of industrial stoppages and by its proximity to Rotterdam which made it convenient for part cargoes to be landed by ships on route to Europort. Further progress continued throughout the "Eighties" and accelerated after the port was acquired by the Mersey Dock and Harbour Company in 1993.

As noted earlier Dover has been the terminal for train-ferry services which brought substantial quantities of fruit and vegetables from the Continent via Dunkirk. In 1959 this had consisted of 7,320 tons of French produce; 49,140 tons from Spain and 39,058 tons from Italy. This total of 95,518 tons was supplemented by direct shipments of fruit and vegetables from many sources including Israel, Cyprus and Spain. By 1965 this overall total had risen to 310,000 tons but the character of the trade was beginning to change. The Car Ferry Terminal, opened in 1953, was becoming more and more inadequate so was extended in 1970 and, thereafter, ro-ro services became increasingly important. This trend was further confirmed when the freight train-ferries ended their sailing's in 1977. Since then various types of vehicles and trailers –many utilising containers – have coped with the rising flood of imports. In addition the construction of many extra facilities, culminating in the completion of deepwater quays in 1990, enabled the largest of fruit carriers to visit the port. This investment by the Port of Dover authorities was complimented by George Hammond plc who handled the harbour's fresh produce imports. The increase in throughput was aided by the building of extensive coldstorage and by the convenient links with the motorway system. A further development involved part-cargoes. In the past a few vessels called at Dover to discharge some items for the UK before moving on to the continent. While this system continued with ever-larger vessels some unloaded completely and a portion of their cargoes taken on to their European destinations by utilising the port's ro-ro services.

All of these arrangements for the importation of fruit and vegetables and for their ongoing distribution within the UK were to be greatly influenced by the growth of air freight and the potential of the Channel Tunnel. The import of perishable items by air had already reached substantial proportions during the 1960's but these tended to be of products which either extended the season or were of an exotic character. In these cases their relative scarcity enabled premium prices to be changed but it was widely appreciated that the general public would only be prepared to pay a small extra increment for out-of-season items and greater freshness. Thus it was felt that further expansion could only take place if a number of difficulties could be satisfactorily solved. These included the streamlining of the loading and unloading of the aircraft and a reduction in the bureaucracy of custom clearance. If the times of these two operations could be reduced to manageable proportions it was thought that the potential of the new aircraft coming into service would ensure that the real cost to the consumer would be only marginally greater than consignments which were moved by other forms of transport. In this event the market would be sufficiently widened so that the year round availability of many products would be viable.

By the 1970's three types of air freight operation were being commonly employed. Space on scheduled passenger services was utilised whenever it was available and on some routes a fixed percentage was allocated on each flight. A number of airlines had by then introduced freight-only services between certain airports and these included some producing areas and their markets. In addition arrangements for air charters with independent operators or with the major lines provided another option for many exporters or their British importing agencies.

The improvements in other forms of transport meant that many European products did not need to use airfreight but this was a matter of commercial judgement and many items were airlifted when the market made this advantageous. Thus in 1973 Dutch winter lettuce and other produce was carried by British Air Ferries from Rotterdam to Southend on a daily basis. The plane usually employed was a Carvair which could carry 3,000 cartons – each contained 12 lettuces weighing approximately 6oz.

It was, inevitably, on the long-haul routes that the development of air-freighted fruit and vegetables was to be most marked. This can best be seen from the example of Egyptair which, also in 1973, was using its five passenger flights a week to bring artichokes, grapes, celery and mangoes from Cairo to Heathrow. The aircraft employed were Boeing "707s" and could only cater for a load of up to 8 tons even if no passengers were carried. At the same time Francis Nicholls had arranged to import 1,200 tons of Cyprus grapes over a three week period in July. This involved 44 flights at the rate of two per day with each plane carrying 4,800 wooden trays. Exotics from the Windwards, arranged by Geest and strawberries from New Zealand, organised by Griffin and Brand were typical

Developing Efficiency in Distribution

of the relatively small consignments which made up much of the cargoes carried by air until the mid-Seventies. Of greater significance for the future was the impact being made by the use of air charters which were gradually opening-up new markets for producers all over the world. This process was considerably aided by the employment of larger aircraft. Thus while the VC10 on passenger service carried about five tons on its longest flights and the freighter version could cope with about 15 tons the CL-44 swingtail freighter could load up to 26m tons. This enabled Transmeridian Air Cargo to move 27,000 kilos of kiwifruit from Auckland to Amsterdam utilising only a singe plane in 1974. Similar increases in capacity encouraged many producers, especially in Israel and South Africa, to expand their use of airfreight and this trend was given a high boost when the Boeing "747" –known as the Jumbo – came into service.

In the case of Israel Agrexco began to use a chartered Boeing 747 freighter during its 1976 season. This could carry a load of 100 tons to European destinations: this was later raised to 115 tons and, with a strengthened undercarriage, to 125 tons. This had the effect of reducing costs by 50% so that in 1977 it was estimated that the airfreight to Marseilles was in the region of US$ 250 per ton compared with US$ 150 for transport by sea to the same destination. The smallness of this margin when set against the advantages of rapid delivery encouraged the carriage of many perishable items which became viable for even the longest journeys when a premium could be charged.

Over the next decade more and more fresh produce was imported by air with air charters providing much of the additional capacity. Thus in 1989 most of the South African avocado crop of 7 million cartons was transported to its markets by air. This was in spite of a 90p difference in carton charge between the cost of air and sea freight because the trade was able to offset the additional price against the higher quality and freshness of the fruit. The relative cheapness of the airfreight on this route was largely due to the use of the 747.

The handling of these increasing substantial quantities of fresh fruit and vegetables by air required ever more sophisticated treatment. One aspect of this was the move from miscellaneous and assorted packages and trays to standardised pallets which could be readily moved by forklift trucks. A further refinement of this system was the development of wing pallets which helped to fill otherwise unusable spaces. The airlines also experimented with a number of different styles of container which were frequently shaped so as to fit the contours of the aircraft for which they were designed.

From Orchard to Market

An "igloo" refrigerated container specially designed for air transport

By 1978 AGREXCO alone was planning to move over 50,000 tons by air from Israel to Europe. Operations on this scale required massive investments at both the sending and receiving airports in order to provide the necessary facilities for efficient transit. Some of the fresh produce was packed by the growers and was timed to arrive just before loading was due. Others sent their consignment to an airfield depot where it could be packed and then held ready for the flight. These arrangements ensured that the aircraft would have a rapid turn-around and that its freight would come onboard in the peak condition. A similar system was evolved at the receiving airport. At Heathrow all cargo was being tracked and controlled from as early as 1969. This enabled customs clearance to be simplified and expedited so that containers and pallets were quickly directed to their destinations or to holding centres. The ever-rising quantities of fresh fruit and vegetables, which continued to increase throughout the "Eighties" lead to the further expansion of facilities at Heathrow. This was also the case at Gatwick, Manchester and many of the smaller airports, some of which developed special links with particular areas.

As quantities grew and the technical arrangements were streamlined the need for highly specialised forwarding agents who dealt only with air-freighted perishable items became ever more vital. While a number of the larger exporting concerns

Developing Efficiency in Distribution

made their own in-house arrangements many others came to rely in part or completely upon specialist firms. One such was Anglo-Overseas Perishable Services which had been established in 1925 as the Anglo-Overseas Transport Co Ltd, and had joined the P and O Group in 1950. By 1975 this firm had an office and cold chambers at Heathrow and were also represented at Gatwick, Stanstead and other provincial airports:-

> "Part of Anglo-Overseas' total service is that they pick up air cargoes as soon as they have been cleared by customs and bring them back to the new depot for sorting, labelling and cool storage as instructed, in preparation for delivery the same night to London and provincial markets". [8]

Typical of the many other perishable handling and distribution companies which then emerged was C and R International Produce which was formed in 1990. This was soon dealing with 35 to 40 arrivals per day via its extensive cold storage and loading facilities on the Dolphin Estate near Heathrow. Its links with Kensington Freight enabled it to offer its clients a daily transport service by motorway to all parts of Great Britain. Another company which offered similar facilities was M S Cargo Services Ltd. In 1991 this firm tended to specialise in the more unusual items including pineapples, carambola, papaya, garlic and exotic flowers but was prepared to cope with any perishable commodities via its extensive thermostatic fridge's, a ripening room and chill-blasting facilities. Amongst the major operators who found it convenient to develop their own air freight depots was Geest Tropical Produce. This was established in 1990 and was soon fully equipped with a cold store and the latest blast-chilling facilities at its depot at Colnbrook on the perimeter of Heathrow. This was not designed as a storage facility – it was intended that consignments would spend a maximum of 12 hours there before being moved on to its consumers. A further development came in 1994 when the London based clearing agent, Unifresh, was able to reduce the time it took airfreighted produce to reach its warehouse from five or six hours to only two. This was achieved by becoming the first perishables clearing agent to attain bonded warehouse status under a new Customs and Excise scheme:-

> "This new development called ERTS (which stands for enhanced remote transit shed) allows goods to be taken to a clearing agent's warehouse before Customs clearance is given. Twenty agents this week began operating the scheme – Unifresh is the only one among them to handle fresh fruit and vegetables". [9]

From Orchard to Market

Another firm which quickly adopted the ERTS arrangements was Perishable Transport. This had originally been based at Hither Green and Covent Garden but had moved to new premises close to Heathrow and Gatwick in 1970.

A similar ERTS systems was introduced at Manchester airport, later in 1994. The opening of a huge, new, cold storage unit within the perimeter fence by BOC Distribution Services was another major step forward in reducing the time which perishable items spent outside controlled conditions. Pressure for this change came from the multiples (especially Marks and Spencer with whom BOC had important links) for it was found that on average 30% of fresh fruit and vegetables were ruined by the time they reached the consumer. This was a new venture for the BOC Group which was mainly involved in the national distribution of chilled products with over 1,000 temperature controlled vehicles and 42 depots – a significant indication of this growing business.

The growth in air freight was challenged to some extent by the rise of controlled atmosphere container loads carried by sea which increased from 800 in 1988 to 12,000 in 1994. The factor which these two methods of importing fresh produce had in common was that both relied upon road transport for their distribution after their arrival in Britain. This was partly due to the extension of the motorway which had grown from the 800 miles of 1971 to nearly 2,000 miles in 1992 by which time it was a fully national system.

The rail network also continued to provide a comprehensive service even though its route mileage was reduced by 10% from the 11,000 miles of the late "Sixties". While by then 3,000 of the remaining miles had been electrified the railways steadily lost the traffic to road haulage. Part of the reason for this were a succession of industrial disputes and delays which were especially damaging for perishable items. In addition the ending of the freight train-ferry sailing's from Zeebrugge and Dunkirk to Harwich and Dover greatly reduced the amount of ongoing rail traffic. This cargo was then largely carried by roll-on/roll-off cross-channel ferries which enabled vehicles and trailers from the producing areas of the Continent to link up with the British motorway network.

The ro-ro ferries from other European ports added to this traffic and almost all of the deep-sea vessels came to employ road haulage to convey their cargoes on to their final destinations. The economies obtained by using the largest possible vehicles encouraged an increase in scale but this trend was seriously threatened in 1981. At that time the greater London Council proposed a ban on all lorries over 8 tons. This was later revised so that only weekend and night-working was to be restricted and even this possibility was ended in 1985. The result was that the move towards bigger units continued and by 1989 the 22-pallet trailer was

Developing Efficiency in Distribution

the norm – by 1994 24-pallet vehicles were becoming common and 26-pallet equipment was being ordered. Much of this transport was increasingly operated by specialist companies. Thus Geest developed a long-standing relationship with British Road Services and firms such as Christian Salvesen, Gilbert International and Wood Distribution evolved comprehensive networks which included depots as well as fleets of vehicles.

A number of other developments also emphasised the increasing convenience of road transport. In 1992 P and O Ferrymasters joined Nippress Forwarding and the Maersk Line subsidiary, Laros, in adding fresh produce groupage to its services from the Dutch auctions to the British market. Its trailers, whether loaded for a single or several owners, were delivered to the Hook of Holland ferry terminal before being carried unaccompanied across to Harwich, Ipswich or Hull. A new set of drivers then took the trailers on to their appropriate distribution centres. This proved to be highly efficient and according to the Company was due to the integration of its service:-

> "P and O Ferrymasters has its own ships, its own staff in each country, its own trucks, vehicles and trailers. That gives us excellent control from A to B. And that's why our business is still growing". [10]

A further innovation also came in 1994 when Henley Transport was authorized to operate a customs warehouse at Paddock Wood. This enabled their customers to pay their import duties when they took delivery rather than when their produce entered the country. In the same year Kanolty Distribution adopted yet another change which was being widely accepted within the industry. This allowed their drivers to purchase their vehicles and then operate as individual self-employed contractors under their logo.

The growth of road transport in facilitating the importation of fresh fruit and vegetables was parallelled by its use for internal transportation within the UK. Thus in addition to moving imports to the wholesale markets or increasingly, to the receiving depots of the Multiples road haulage became the almost universal method of distributing domestic production. These developments meant that throughout this period rail continued to decline in both relative and absolute terms when compared with road:-

From Orchard to Market

Goods Transport in Great Britain

	1974	1979	1984	1989	1994
Total tonne kilometres (thousand million)	141.1	172.8	173.2	222.8	220.8
Road	89.9	104.6	106.9	137.8	143.7
Rail (British Rail only)	21.7	19.9	12.7	17.3	13.3
Total (million tonnes)	1,817	1,825	1,674	2,206	2,051
Road	1,537	1,504	1,444	1,812	1,689
Rail (British Rail only)	176	169	79	146	97

(Note: The balance of the totals includes Coastal and Canal traffic and pipelines) [11]

However one way in which it was anticipated that railways would be helped to carry a larger proportion of goods - especially perishable items - was because of the construction of the Channel Tunnel. Although the British and French Governments had agreed in principle to this project much earlier it was not until May 1994 that Le Shuttle freight service began to operate. The first crossing was by invitation only and at a special price of £75 each way. Geoff Gilbert International had a lorry on the first Shuttle and was subsequently to use the service on a regular basis to bring back produce from the Dutch auctions. Towards the end of June some trucks which had arrived without reservation were allowed to use the Shuttle at the "normal" price of £310 single. G's Salads started to try the service in July 1994 and Hargreaves International of Spalding was another early user. Most in the fresh produce trade gave the system a cautious welcome believing that if it did nothing else it would encourage the ferries to become more efficient and helpful. However by October 1994 the Shuttle was already carrying 350 trucks a day or 12% of the Dover/Calais traffic. Further progress then led Euro Tunnel to claim that after 12 months operation it was moving 35% of the HGV market on the short-sea crossing and it aimed to secure 50% by the end of the year. By June 1995 it had already replaced P and O European Ferries and Stena Sealink as the leading operator between Dover/Folkstone and Calais.

The opening of Le Shuttle's freight service further enhanced the convenience and efficiency of road transport and soon proved to be a serious competitor to the cross-channel ferries. Its main advantage for fresh fruit and vegetables was with the producing areas of Holland, Belgium and Northern France which lay close to the terminal at Calais. For some of these items the extra cost could be justified by the time which could be saved. This was not the case when bringing consignments from Greece or Italy where the reduction of a journey by an hour or so was not significant. However the potential of the Tunnel to cater for these long-distance trades was one in which the railways could expect to play a major role.

Developing Efficiency in Distribution

In practice from as early as July 1994 over 100 cargo trains a month were running through the Tunnel. Some of these included the 720 wagons which had been specially built for use on this route by Allied Continental Intermodal which was 50% owned by Interfrigo and was already moving much fruit within Europe by rail. Daily departures between Milan, Avignon, Perpignan and the UK had begun that month and services connecting Barcelona and Valencia with the British market were planned. All were utilizing containers which could be quickly transferred from rail wagons to lorries so a door-to-door system was promised and was attracting much interest in the trade.

The major supermarket groups were particularly concerned with a direct link with Spain but were constrained by the initial lack of refrigerated wagons. Never the less a two day a week service began in April 1995 with Interfrigo running the Spanish end and, incidently, utilizing the citrus packhouses which still had railway loading bays remaining from the ferry routes which ended in the 1970s. By then the daily Milan service was running to capacity taking only 36 hours and it was expected that a second train would soon be added each day. On the other hand the Valencia to UK route was at first scheduled to take three days and this needed to be improved if a complete range of produce was to be moved by rail.

It was estimated that the introduction of through freight trains via the Chunnel would eventually lead to a three-fold increase in the goods carried by the British railway system. These developments coincided with the establishment of Railtrack in April 1994 which was to mark the beginning of the process of the privatization of British Rail. Railtrack, which was to be floated on the Stock Exchange two years later, was then vested with the ownership of all operational track and was given the task of managing the network and the reward of being able to charge for access to it !

By this date Railfreight International, the international freighting arm of British Rail had forged links with many Continental railway companies and was able to offer direct access via the Channel Tunnel to the pan-European network. Thus by the end of 1995 RfI was operating 160 trains a week. These fell into three main types: The International system was used to cater for the movement of containers and swop bodies (demountable lorry bodies) while Connectrail was using high capacity wagons to carry heavy or bulky commodities and Automotive which specialized on the long-haul carriage of finished cars and components between factories and distribution centres.

From Orchard to Market

Channel Tunnel rail freight services were officially launched on June 27, 1994

One of the British firms to utilize the Intermodal system was Andrew Weir Shipping. This employed temperature controlled units to bring sensitive products including lettuce and watermelons as well as clementines and onions from Spain. Another firm, Bell Express, a division of Bell Lines operated trains to Italy and, later, Spain from the earliest days. As they also owned a large fleet of 40ft pallet-wide refrigerated reefers which were compatible with shipping and road transport it could offer a comprehensive cool-chain service to the multiples which were its principal customers. This system was to be greatly aided when government legislation was introduced which permitted lorries of up to 44 tonnes gross weight to operate on UK roads providing they were moving to or from an intermodal railway head.

The creation of separate operating companies in 1996 marked the next stage in the break-up of British Rail and all of its bulk haulage activities, including Freightliners were subsequently to be offered for sale to the private sector. By then the arrangements for intermodal transport were well advanced and were playing increasingly important roles in providing Britain with a highly efficient method of importing and distributing its fresh fruit and vegetables.

14
New Challenges Facing the Trade

The impact of EEC membership on the trade proved to be less serious than many predicted. Of far greater significance were the effects of consolidation at producer and retail level, although more particularly the latter. During the last decades of the twentieth century this was but one of many pressures bearing on the industry. The traditional dominant role played by wholesale markets began to be eroded as the supermarket groups increasingly sourced their produce direct from producers using existing wholesaler/import firms operating from distribution centres to undertake sourcing, logistics and packaging.

Paddock Wood in Kent was one such site which had originally been developed as a convenient centre for the packing and distribution of produce grown in the orchard and market gardens of south east England. It was expanded in 1968 when it become the base for Simba Fruit International Ltd which had been established by J O Sims Ltd, the Beeson Group and Henry W Arnold Ltd to serve their customers in the south east counties. [1] The facilities were further enlarged in 1974 when it became Transfesa's alternative rail terminus to Hither Green. [2] At a later date it also become one of the largest depots for produce brought in by refrigerated lorries from many parts of Europe.

The opening of the Channel Tunnel was subsequently to aid the growth of consignments brought in via both road and rail transport, although the original concept of a rail-head from the Tunnel itself never materialised. In addition, many cargoes of overseas products including apples, bananas and citrus were increasingly handled. In the case of Florida grapefruit this was usually landed at Felixstowe and much was then moved to Paddock Wood. The bulk was broken-down at this time before being pre-packed or otherwise prepared for final dispatch to its customers. Fyffes were another major group which used the site as a principal depot for receiving both home-grown and overseas fruit and vegetables. These were then distributed to the multiples, to provincial wholesalers and to their own facilities throughout the UK. Fyffes also contributed some of these items to what became a growing, if small, export trade from Paddock Wood. This utilized the returning road and rail vehicles to back-load British produce and other goods to many parts of the Continent. The Mack Organisation was another company that chose the venue to develop a major distribution depot.

The development of major receiving and distribution depots at other convenient locations around the UK were in many respects at the expense of the traditional system. This can best be seen by an examination of the changing function of the London markets. To a large extent these had evolved to meet the demands of the capital which grew to include a population of 10 million - almost 20% of the UK total. However the emergence of a national rail network meant that a central market was both practical and necessary in order to establish price levels and to compensate for gluts and shortages. Thus while many important markets had grown-up in the provinces - especially at the ports - it was to London that the trade looked for a lead in almost all activities.

In 1956, for example, Covent Garden supplied the Greater London area with a third of its requirements and a similar volume was sent to other wholesalers throughout Britain. This business was roughly equal to the sales of all the other London markets combined and only Spitalfields offered a comparable service to the metropolis and the provinces. Part of the latter's throughput was due to the London Fruit Exchange which catered for over 500 provincial wholesalers at this time.[3] In 1973 the last remaining auctions in London, those held twice weekly at the London Fruit Exchange came to an end, and an institution which at one time provided supplies to 100 import and commission agents had lost its role.[4]

In spite of these trends and events the ever-increasing congestion in Central London led to a decision to move the Covent Garden market to a new site at Nine Elms. However many in the trade thought that it might prove to be a white elephant due to the continuing expansion of the multiples:-

> "All of this is of major significance to a market such as Covent Garden now in the throes of investing more than £30m in its new market at Nine Elms, Vauxhall. There can be no escaping the fact that the (retail) chains are using the traditional markets less and less. During the past six years Safeway, for instance, has moved from a greengrocery operation which was 100% market-based to one which by-passes markets almost completely."

> "As a portent of things to come one has only to stand in J. Sainsbury's Hoddesdon depot and watch truck-loads of produce arriving direct from Lincolnshire farms (much of it already pre-packed for the store), moved into Sainsbury vehicles to reach the shelves less than 24 hours after leaving the farm gate."

> "It is a similar story with imported produce, although it may first go to an outside packer before arriving at Hoddesdon. Sainsbury's greengrocery business has nearly trebled in the past five years, and there are plans to double it again in the next five. Hoddesdon alone probably already

New Challenges Facing the Trade

handles produce equal to a fifth of the volume that moves through Covent Garden". [5]

These dire predications were not sufficient to prevent Covent Garden's move and the new market at Nine Elms opened in 1974.

New Covent Garden under construction. This photo montage shows the fruit and vegetable market at the top (which is actually further to the right) with the flower market in the foreground

After ten years of operation it appeared that New Covent Garden Market was viable with turnover in fruit and vegetables increasing from £74,000 in 1973-4 to £216,418 ten years later. However these figures take no account of inflation.[6]

During the same period a breakdown of companies operating within the market indicate the fundamental changes which were taking place during this period:-

From Orchard to Market

Types of Company in New Covent Garden

	1974	1977	1979	1981	1984
Fruit and vegetable Wholesalers	107	99	102	93	85
Flower Wholesalers	98	87	85	73	71
Growers	32	35	32	24	21
Importers/Exporters	63	97	103	87	77
Pre-packers	-	2	4	4	4
Hotel/Catering Distributors	1	13	11	17	25
Retailers/Caterers	1	6	6	5	3

[7]

From the above it will be seen that there was a steady decline in the number of wholesaling firms utilizing the New Covent Garden market. To some extent this was due to a series of mergers and amalgamations which were themselves a sign of the pressure under which they were operating. The other significant change indicated above concerns the rise in the scale of the hotel and catering sector. In fact by 1988 the Catering Industry was responsible for supplying 15% of all food consumed in the UK. This included 1.6m tonnes of fresh produce although it required only 100,000 tonnes of fresh fruit.

Structure of the Catering Market in 1988
Number of Outlets and Value of Food Purchases

Sector	Number of Outlets	Food Purchases (£ Million)
Hotels	48,910	1,065
Restaurants	13,450	640
Pubs/Wine Bars	43,000	485
Cafes/Take Aways	31,165	585
Clubs/Leisure & Entertainment	59,730	200
Fast Food	1,500	185
Travel	300	90
Sub-Total : Profit Sector	198,105	3,250
Canteens	23,500	355
State Health	8,885	140
Private Health	2,300	10
Education/Public Services	34,950	405
Sub-Total : Cost Sector	69,635	910
TOTAL	267,740	4,160

New Challenges Facing the Trade

NB 1. The data above exclude:
   Pubs which do not serve meals (ie snacks, crisps, etc only)
   Farms, Nursery Schools
2. Values are expressed at Caterers' buying prices
3. Purchases include food and dried beverages but exclude alcohol and soft drinks.

[8]

While the growth of demand by the Catering sector helped to offset some of the business being lost to the supermarket chains it could not disguise the fundamental weakness of wholesale markets. The net effect of the continued expansion of the Multiples can be seen by subsequent events. Thus by 1991 most of the principal national groups of traders had withdrawn from New Covent Garden and this process was virtually completed when Fyffes also decided to stop working from this location. [9]

Share of fresh vegetable sales by type of outlet 1978-1990 (%)

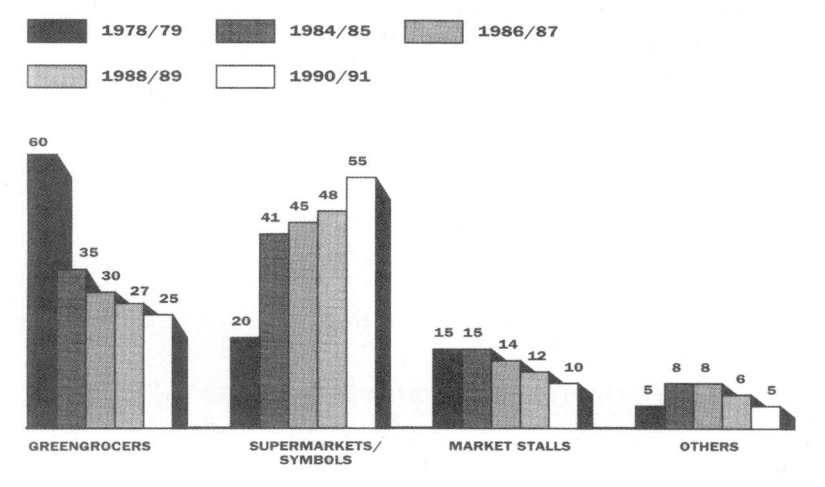

■ 1978/79 ■ 1984/85 ▨ 1986/87
▨ 1988/89 □ 1990/91

Outlet	1978/79	1984/85	1986/87	1988/89	1990/91
GREENGROCERS	60	35	30	27	25
SUPERMARKETS/SYMBOLS	20	41	45	48	55
MARKET STALLS	15	15	14	12	10
OTHERS	5	8	8	6	5

[10]

These trends continued so that by 1995 the Multiples enjoyed a 68.1% share of the fresh fruit and vegetable market and by 1996 this had risen further to 72.8% [11] The corollary to these developments was that the trade available to New Covent Garden and the other primary markets was progressively reduced. Fortunately the growth in the UK catering and processing sector also continued to expand and thus provided some relief to what had been the traditional wholesale system.

In addition to its impact on the primary and wholesale markets the development of super and hypermarkets was to transform the pattern of British food

From Orchard to Market

retailing. While some of the earlier establishments had paid little attention to fruit and vegetables these items very rapidly became an essential ingredient in the comprehensive stocks which it was found necessary to offer. In the highly competitive retail market which was emerging, a wide range of fresh produce was widely perceived as providing the most effective means of differentiating the various chains. This resulted in a more rapid growth of exotic imports and 'designer' species of fruits and vegetables.

The domination of the market which the Multiples achieved then had many significant consequences. Their great financial strength and buying power, together with the competitive situation which they had engendered, were large factors in enabling them to raise the quality of the products they handled. They were also leaders in the development of the concept of "Out of town, one stop, shopping" which has become the norm for many families. Furthermore their very scale made it easier to comply with ever more onerous hygiene regulations.

The rapid growth of the Multiples inevitably had a significant effect on other retailers. Thus in 1975 greengrocers and fruiterers were responsible for 42% of retail expenditure on fresh fruit and vegetables while market stalls accounted for a further 17% [12] Ten years later greengrocers and fruiterers were supplying only 32% of the total although market stalls were still providing 17% [13] These trends continued, with some fluctuations, so that by 1993 the greengrocer/fruiterer/market stalls sector was selling only 22.2% of vegetables and 39.5% of fruit.

Percentage Share of Produce by Retail Outlet (£ Sales)

	Potatoes		Cauliflowers		Lettuce		Capsicum	
	92	93	92	93	92	93	92	93
Multiples/Co-ops	50.7	58.9	39.6	45.7	58.4	63.7	69.3	72.2
Greengrocer/Fruiterer/Stalls	30.0	23.6	47.4	42.9	30.8	26.2	24.5	22.2
Independent Grocer	7.7	6.7	5.7	4.3	4.1	3.6	2.3	2.3
Farm Shops	3.3	3.3	2.7	2.3	1.4	1.2	0.9	0.9
Others	8.3	7.5	4.6	4.8	5.3	5.2	3.0	2.4

New Challenges Facing the Trade

Percentage Share of Produce by Retail Outlet (£ Sales)

	Apples 92	Apples 93	Bananas 92	Bananas 93	Oranges 92	Oranges 93
Multiples/Co-ops	59.8	64.8	54.4	61.4	44.8	51.3
Greengrocer/Fruiterer/Stalls	31.6	27.4	35.8	29.6	46.4	39.5
Independent Grocer	3.7	3.3	4.7	4.6	3.8	3.5
Farm Shops	1.8	1.4	1.4	1.1	1.5	1.3
Others	3.1	3.2	3.7	3.4	3.5	4.4

[14]

By 1996 the share of the combined greengrocer/fruiterer/market stall sales had fallen to 17.5%. [15]

Of course not all of this loss of market share was entirely due to the expansion of the Multiples. The emergence of Farm Shops and Pick Your Own schemes also had a small role to play. Indeed much of the retail trade were at first extremely antagonistic to these enterprises especially when they choose to sell additional brought-in produce from local wholesalers. This indignation was felt even more deeply when imported fruit such as oranges were sold under the Farm Fresh banner! [16] On the other hand it was claimed that these direct sales acted as a boost to consumption and was a useful way of informing the public as to when British produce was available. Thus, it was argued, many visitors would be encouraged to seek these items from their local retailers when they returned home. [17] By 1990 it was generally considered that PYO sales had reached a peak but it was still expected that Farm Shops would continue to expand as part of the general growth of countryside tourism. By then, however, though the effect would be small, this was seen as more of a challenge or alternative to the supermarkets than a threat to other retailers. [18]

The pressure under which the non-multiple sector found itself was a considerable incentive to the expansion of Cash and Carry methods of trading. These developed during the 1960s to cater for the many independent grocers who were beginning to experience severe competition from the growth of supermarket chains. By 1970 these centres were supplying a wide range of items and these increasingly included many fresh fruit and vegetable products. As a result many grocers and others not normally engaged in the fresh produce trade found it convenient to take advantage of this extra opportunity. Many specialist greengrocer and fruiterers

From Orchard to Market

also found it profitable to utilize their services. This was because the flexible nature of the system meant that supplies could be obtained throughout the day - up to 8.30 pm in some cases. Thus it was not necessary to visit a traditional wholesale market at an early hour and, as any omissions could be quickly repaired, stock-holding could be kept to very safe levels. [19]

Although Cash and Carry centres were only a different form of wholesaler they did not see their role as merely supplying retailers with one particular set of commodities. Any business was usually able to access whatever the outlet had available, though some attempted to keep food as a separate department. One such enterprise was MAKRO which by 1974 were operating six, self-service, depots in the UK. Supplies were arranged centrally but acquired from local growers were possible while overseas items were usually obtained from the major panellists. [20] Over time the acceptance of cheques from regular clients and the possibility of deliveries were to gradually change the character of the business. However Cash and Carry outlets were for a few years to remain a major boon to the retailer and a further blow to the remaining business of the traditional wholesale markets.

A large proportion of the fruit and vegetables supplied by the Cash and Carry wholesalers was in a pre-packed form. Although limited experiments had been made earlier it was not until 1955 that the formation of the Produce Pre-Packaging Development Association encouraged the industry to make serious progress. Thus while only 100,000 pre-packs were sold in Great Britain in 1954 this figure had risen to 70 million by 1956 and to 200 million by 1958. [21] These developments were then to be further enhanced by the simultaneous expansion of self-service retailing and by the growth in demand for convenience foods including both quick-frozen items and prepared vegetables. The trade in potatoes was one which had been largely transformed by the mid-"Sixties". By then much of this crop was being washed, graded, weighed and filled into polythene bags at the farm or at specialist - perhaps co-operative - packhouses before being delivered to a wholesaler or a multiple. Alongside this trade was one in "dirty" potatoes as many customers continued to wish to select their own produce and some thought that washing and packaging resulted in a deterioration in flavour and quality. Further developments meant that by 1973 most of the multiples included in a trade survey claimed that at least half of their fresh fruit and vegetables were being sold in prepackaged form.[22] However many also felt that it was wise to continue to provide a large proportion of loose produce so that their customers could still exercise a degree of self-selection.

The increasing demand for produce to be pre-packed led to ever more advanced machinery being installed by growers within Britain as well as overseas. Thus by the mid-"Seventies" a wide range of items including celery, cos lettuce, parsnips,

New Challenges Facing the Trade

corn-on-the-cob, rhubarb and apples together with carrots, sprouts and spring greens were all being successfully prepared and bagged ready for sale. [23] Simple types of prepared vegetables had been available for many years. These relied upon a process of dehydration which was only suitable for certain fruits and vegetables. The subsequent evolution of cooling techniques enabled other options to be considered and by the mid-"Eighties" mixed stir-fry vegetables, chopped salads, sliced onions and fruit salads were all being regularly supplied. [24] Further developments were typified by the activities of Messrs Hannan and Davy Ltd who in 1991 opened a new, state of the art, vegetable preparation complex. This included hightech machinery, all in stainless steel, which could dice, slice and shred the full spectrum of fresh produce ready for despatch daily, via cool chain delivery to wherever necessary. [25]

The ongoing growth in the demand for these items was considerably encouraged by steady improvements in the quality of the packaging. Wholesalers were particularly concerned with the protection which it supplied to the product but, like retailers, were also interested in it providing attractive displays. Of particular importance was the transparency of the wrapping for it was felt that the ability to see the contents was essential for sales to be maximized. While some items like onions and oranges were best sold in net bags many others relied upon their packaging to assist in regulating their temperature. By the late "Seventies" both controlled and modified atmosphere systems were in use and were ensuring that all types of produce were reaching the shelves in prime condition. [26] The later development of micro-perforated plastic films which were sufficiently permeable to permit the appropriate atmospheres to be more easily maintained was yet another significant advance. Sophisticated packages were sometimes criticized as being too lavish and extravagant and some commentators argued that coverings of all kinds should be reduced or even eliminated where possible. However, these arguments ignore the benefits which packaging can bring by protecting the product and thus reducing waste. These advantages, plus their convenience to the shopper meant that by 1986 approximately a third of all vegetables were sold in a packaged form.

Another product heavily dependent upon appropriate forms of packaging were quick frozen foods. Although these had been originally introduced before World War II it was not until 1949 that they were to make substantial progress. Apart from the increasing availability of food this year saw a rising number and variety of cabinets becoming available. In turn this encouraged more processors and importers to supply a wider range of quick-frozen items and this persuaded many more wholesalers to install low-temperature cold-rooms [27] Thus by 1952 many firms in Covent Garden had cold storage facilities.

From Orchard to Market

Fresh innovations which resulted in freeze-drying, the air-borne or blast freezing of peas and improvements in the production of quick-frozen chips led to a further expansion of the industry. Hence by 1968 it was estimated that the previous ten years had seen the production of quick-frozen vegetables grow from 23,000 to 97,000 tons - the latter representing 11% of all green vegetables and 24% of all frozen food sales in the UK. Of these vegetables 34% were green peas, 15% were green beans and 14% were Brussels sprouts. By then there were 175 firms engaged in packing, processing and importing frozen foods and Birds Eye, with a 62% share of the market, were by far the leading company. [28] However by this time most of the distribution was in the hands of specialist suppliers serving the expanding food manufacturing industry and thus removed from the wholesale market operations.

The growth in the market share of frozen-foods and the rise in the sale of all types of prepared items - including vegetables - were all part of a move towards what became known as convenience foods. While overall consumption continued to increase because of the larger population and a higher standard of living it was the ever rising numbers of working women and one-parent homes which made convenience foods so attractive. In some respects this could be seen as an alternative to the emergence of the many types of fast food outlets which have characterized the past twenty years or so!

It was this section of the community which found the development of self-service something of an advantage especially when competition between the Multiples obliged them to provide ever-longer opening hours. It was more difficult for many retail shops to adapt to self-service and extended hours of business and these factors undoubtedly hastened their demise in many cases. However they also encouraged the so-called convenience stores which, frequently under family ownership, often of ethnic origins, were prepared to open from "8 till late" or even for 24 hours. Many filling stations, especially those which operated throughout the night, also diversified into food on a small scale. While these mainly provided quick-frozen items small quantities of other products - including fresh fruit and vegetables - were frequently available at the busier centres.

The move towards out-of-town stores which had its beginning in the mid-"sixties" [29] was soon to gain pace and by the 1990s they were clearly the predominant form of retail food outlet. The reasons for this are not hard to discover. Membership of substantial, nation-wide, groups provide massive purchasing power and enabled full advantage to be taken of many other economies of scale. In addition it was only in establishments above a certain size that the full benefits of self-service could be allied to a sufficiently wide range of fresh and quick-frozen items. These, in turn, were only a part of the much larger weekly grocery shop which increasingly

New Challenges Facing the Trade

became the norm for many people. The convenience of the one-stop system was further enhanced by the provision of massive free car parking facilities to serve ever growing car owning families. This was critical to many customers at a time when many High Streets had become congested and were expensive to stop for any length of time.

The greater concentration of firms which characterized most parts of British industry in the post-war era were largely due to the economies which could be achieved by operating on a large scale. These considerations were equally valid for the retail food sector and resulted in two, separate, trends. In the first of these the actual number of supermarkets declined as the size of the outlet increased. Thus the move from smaller, city-centre, sites to out-of-town locations in the "Seventies" led to many of the multiples reducing the number of their units though not, of course, the total of their throughput:-

**Numbers of Supermarket Stores
Operated by the Principal Groups**

	1970	1979
Allied	2,500 +	1,030
Fine fare	1,087	683
International	1,149	793
Key Markets	350	112
Sainsbury	225	231
Tesco	790	510

30

The second trend was the amalgamation movement between the Multiples themselves. As the statistics below indicate both Sainsbury and Tesco grew steadily through the late 1980s with the former only staying ahead because of its association with Savacentre. The Argyle Group had become the 3rd largest chain by 1990-91 because of its acquisition of Safeway while Asda, which purchased 60 superstores from Gateway in 1989 has risen to fourth place. This sale then led to the latter losing some of its market share and to its fall to fifth position. The net effect of these changes was that the big five groups increased their proportion of the trade from 56% to 62% over this period while the next four largest grew from 10% to 11%:-

From Orchard to Market

Market Share of Grocers Sales
1986-1991 (%)

	1985/6	1986/7	1987/8	1988/9	1989/90	1990/1
Sainsbury	13.2	13.9	14.3	14.5	16.0*	16.7*
Tesco	13.6	13.5	14.3	14.9	15.3	16.2
Gateway	12.7	11.5	11.8	11.2	8.0	7.3
Argyll	5.7	9.9	10.9	11.0	11.0	11.3
Kwik Save	2.9	3.0	3.0	3.5	3.9	4.4
Waitrose	2.6	2.7	2.6	2.6	2.5	2.5
Iceland	0.4	0.5	0.6	1.8	1.9	1.9
(Bejam)	1.8	1.8	1.7	-	-	-
Morrisons	1.5	1.6	1.7	1.9	2.2	2.3
Other multiples	7.9	7.7	5.2	5.0	4.0	3.2
Co-operatives	12.4	12.1	11.7	11.3	11.0	10.7
Independents	14.8	14.6	14.4	14.0	13.7	13.0

* includes Savacentre

The ever increasing success of the larger Multiples led to considerable rivalry amongst the small chains as they sought to compete. One strategy adopted by some was to reduce costs by offering a more limited range of products and only basic facilities for their customers. This policy enabled these Discounters to cut their prices to very low levels and it was found that this simple type of service was attractive to a significant number of customers. The pioneers in this respect were Kwik Save, Lo-Cost and Normans but by 1992 these had been joined by Aldi, Netto and Shoprite. By then the French firm, Carrefour, had also opened its first discount outlet at Maidstone and this was soon to be followed by the American Warehouse Club Banner.

The consolidation of the retail food sector was parallelled by those engaged in importing and distributing fresh produce. Thus in 1986 the top five companies operating in the UK-Ireland market were already responsible for 40% of the total and it was anticipated that this proportion would inevitably rise:-

New Challenges Facing the Trade

The UK-Ireland Market

(Based on figures from the National Food Survey conducted on behalf of the UK Ministry of Agriculture, the UK-Ireland market for fresh produce is estimated to have been worth £2,446m in 1986).

	Turnover, fresh produce (£ million)	Market Share (per cent)
Geest	390	15.9
F I I Fyffes	200 (pro formo)	8.2
Glass Glover	120	4.2
Hunter Saphir	90	3.7
M & W Mack	80*	3.3
Total	880	36.0

[32]

* Industry estimate, company not listed.

Amongst the major losers in the British food market were the Co-operative Retail Societies. This inevitably had a knock-on effect on the Co-operative Wholesale Society which had traditionally supplied many of the retail outlets, including supermarkets, operated by its members. In 1976 its national office, situated near Manchester still co-ordinated the procurement, distribution and marketing of greengroceries which was then channelled through eight depots, five in England and three in Scotland. These were supplemented by strategically situated cold and dry bulk storage warehouses and by sub-contracted prepacking stations which serviced 90% of the UK's retail societies. [33]

The subsequent decline in market share then led to a desire to reform the structure of the organization. While it was thought to be impractical to merge all the retail societies into a single body negotiations were started to combine the Co-operative Wholesale Society (CWS) and the Co-operative Retail Services (CRS) as early as 1980. These were subsequently ended without agreement and the CRS continued to expand. Thus by 1991 it had become Britain's biggest co-operative retail body and was reported to be moving 150,000 cases of produce each week through its four fresh produce distribution centres. By then its outlets included 122 Leo's Superstores and supermarkets which ranged from 10,000 to 60,000 sq-feet, two branches of a new category of superstore branded Pioneer and 342 Stop and Shop convenience stores. [34] Further discussions between the CWS and the CRS took place in 1994-5 but it was still not possible to reach agreement. [35] Both then continued to operate very vigorously on an independent basis as did many separate retail societies. However this development meant that the co-operative movement as a whole remained vulnerable to the growing competition provided by the principal multiples.

The relative decline of co-operative retailing did nothing to inhibit the progress of co-operative grower associations and marketing schemes. One of the earliest was that established by Littleton and Badsey Growers in 1908 [36] and this was to be followed by many others. Amongst these was the AIM Group which was formed in 1970 by ten firms connected with the English top fruit trade. These included growers, co-operative packhouses, distributors as well as those involved with wholesaling. It was intended that this organization would collect and pool information for the benefit of the members who would, however, remain free to market their fruit in whatever way they chose. [37] Other associations went a great deal further in their co-operation and arranged for packing, distribution and marketing of a growers' output and provided many of their requirements which were acquired on a collective basis. What was to become the largest co-operative of its type was Home Grown Fruits (HGF) which was set up in 1960. By 1974 it was marketing its members' fruit through either a country-wide panel of wholesale salesmen or by its direct sales to major retail groups and selected secondary wholesalers. Another indication of its expanding scale was that by then it had 40 wholesalers acting as selling agents in 15 primary markets, 22 wholesalers in 17 secondary markets and 13 wholesalers in 13 country markets. [38] Operations of this size made it advantageous to seek a commercial company as a partner and arrangements were then made with the Glass Glover Group which for a while proved to be mutually beneficial. [39] This can best be seen from the fact that while HGF catered for 250 growers in 1976 this number had risen to 300 in 1985 by which date it was utilizing 75 packhouses. [40]

East Kent Packers Ltd (EKP) were another major top fruit co-operative which was established in the early "Sixties". Its rapid success encouraged it to also seek a commercial partner and in 1969 it began what proved to be a long standing association with Saphir, Sons and Company, Ltd. Further expansion saw its 52 grower members supplying 13% of the dessert crop and 20% of pears to the market in 1982. [41] The following decade proved to be difficult for all domestic fruit producers and both HGF and EKP found it convenient to work together in many promotional and advertising projects. After two particularly disappointing years this co-operation reached a logical conclusion when in 1994 the two co-operatives joined together to form the English Fruit Company (ENFRU). At the time it was stated that the new concern would control over 50% of the English apple and pear market as well as having substantial interests in both soft and stone fruits. [42]

New Challenges Facing the Trade

East Kent Packers's state of the art automated packhouse in 1969

Graded and sorted apples flow into the packing line

From Orchard to Market

Not all of HGF's members were solely concerned with fruit and its largest co-operative, Checkers Growers Ltd, was also interested in some types of vegetable. In addition many co-operatives were entirely or largely involved with vegetables but within this group there was some degree of specialization. Thus Anglian Produce dealt only with potatoes and LMO of Lincolnshire concentrated upon just potatoes and onions. There were also co-operatives such as Sidlesham Growers and Snaith Salad Growers which were mainly engaged in the production of items under glass while East Coast Salads' activities were split equally between glasshouse and field crop products. However more typical of many co-operatives was Grower Marketing Services which by 1988 was handling a wide range of vegetables including courgettes, dwarf beans, lettuce, Brussels sprouts, salad onions, spring greens, watercress, plums, tomatoes, soft fruit, apples and winter cauliflowers. [43] Another important co-operative which dealt with many products was East Lincolnshire Growers Ltd. This had been formed in 1964 and by 1991 was an important supplier of potatoes and brassicas to the domestic market and also contributed 50% of the UK's exports of onions. [44] In 1989 there were 636 of these co-operatives in existence and these had a membership of 270,000 farmers and growers. At this time the combined turnover of 462 marketing co-operatives amounted to £1,607m and 41 of the larger societies handled 62% of the business. [45]

There were, of course, many other forms of organization which provided collective benefits besides the co-operatives. The Apple and Pear Development Council had been a statutory body formed in 1966 to promote and improve the marketing of home grown fruit, later disallowed under EEC regulations. Also amongst these numerous types and diverse varieties were the British Independent Fruit Growers Association, the Farm Shop and Pick Your Own Association, The Mushroom Growers Association, and the British Flower Industry Association. In addition a number of national bodies had emerged early in the 20th Century which were designed to cater for sectional interests. These included the Retail Fruit Trade Federation, [46] and the National Federation of Fruit and Potato Trades, [47] These were joined later by the Produce Packaging & Marketing Association [48] and the Fruit Importers Association.

There was some limited degree of co-operation between these national bodies. This was usually concerned with aspects of publicity and presentation and these factors were a major consideration when, in 1976, it was decided to establish the Fresh Fruit and Vegetable Information Bureau. It was stated that its aims were internal promotions, the sponsorship of meetings, the provision of information and contact with the media. [49] A further link between the National Federation and the Fruit Importers Association came in 1987 when both joined EUCOFEL, the European union of the fruit and vegetable wholesale, import and export trades,

New Challenges Facing the Trade

and it was agreed that they would work closely together to represent UK interests [50] This example, allied to ever-stronger pressure from Brussels, led to demands for the industry to have a single body to speak for the trade. [51] Unfortunately it proved to be extremely difficult to reconcile the many conflicting interests which were involved and it was only after Sir John Harvey-Jones spoke at the Produce Packaging and Marketing Association's 1991 conference that the case for a single voice was finally accepted. [52] It was then expected that the National Federation, the PPMA and the FIA would recommend that their members should support the formation of a new Fresh Produce Consortium but in the event the Executive of the FIA was not prepared to do so. Consequently although the Consortium was overwhelmingly backed by the members of the PPMA and the National Federation only a limited number of those from the FIA give it their support. This inevitably meant that the new body was less inclusive than had been hoped but, even so, it was established on firm foundations and held its first convention at Harrogate in October 1993.

One of the main functions of the new organization was to represent the industry's viewpoint on many issues to the EU and to the UK's Parliament. The British Governments of the "Sixties" and "Seventies", under strong inflationary pressures, felt obliged to take a direct interest in the economy and the finances of the fruit and vegetable sector - like many others - was kept under severe scrutiny. Thus a number of factors including margins were closely examined in the Report on Prices, Profits and Costs in Food Distribution which was published by the National Board for Prices and Incomes in 1971. [53] This was to be followed by a number of other reports which were produced by the Price Commission later in the "Seventies". These also commented on the prices and margins earned by the handling of fruit and vegetables. These enquiries led to much discussion in the press as the trade struggled to justify its claims that while operating costs- especially wages, rents, rates and transport - were steadily rising there were no corresponding increases in the value of the commodities they sold. [54]
It was widely felt that these arguments would have received a much better response from both the Government and the public if the case had been made by a single body speaking for the entire industry. This was a situation which the new Fresh Produce Consortium intended to bring to an end.

The election of a Conservative Administration in 1979 marked the emergence of a less interventionist policy although a close watch remained on prices. One aspect of this was the critical view it took of the Potato Marketing Board. This was the last of the statutory bodies in the industry as the Tomato and Cucumber Marketing Board had been wound-up in 1964 also because of EC regulations. Thus what was increasingly regarded as an unnecessary function lost government support in 1993 and it was planned to dismantle it in 1997. It should be noted, however, that discussions in respect of a successor organization were still taking place in that year. [55]

On the other hand the Government did take a more positive approach in respect of the establishment of a national marketing organization to promote British food. As a result Food from Britain was set up in 1983. This had the twin objectives of securing a greater share of the home market for domestic producers and of encouraging the development of exports in priority areas. [56]

However while the domestic marketing boards lost favour those overseas bodies which catered for imported fresh fruit continued to play an important role in the structure of the UK trade. These were essentially produce boards which aimed at regulating the export of particular items on a national basis. A study of the system by Wye College published in 1971 provides a comprehensive guide to these Boards and to the primary market panellists which they supplied. [57] Although there were to be many subsequent changes the principle of restricting sales to a limited number of outlets has largely been maintained even though special arrangements had to be made to cope with the increasing power of the Multiples. While there is much to be argued for a controlled market this method of trading inevitably results in the Boards enjoying a considerable degree of authority over their panellists. While market forces also played a role it was this position of power which largely determined the relationship between the two groups. The most visible indication of this was the level of commission rates which successive reports suggested were the lowest in Europe. [58] The weakness in the bargaining power of the panellist being their vulnerability to loss of supplies and the certain knowledge that others were always waiting to step into their shoes! On the other hand it will be appreciated that the Boards and their panellists had a common interest in maintaining good relations and that, over time, a satisfactory modus vivendi was usually achieved.

The importation of bananas continued to be handled in a different way to other fruits and vegetables. For such a delicate item to be delivered over long distances to World markets at a price which makes it competitive with other fruits and substitutes requires a very extensive organization. This, in turn, demands substantial capital investment which can only be justified if a constant throughput can be guaranteed. As a wide geographic spread of producers helps to ensure continuity of supply by offsetting the dangers of blow-downs in particular areas this has helped a small number of trans-national corporations to dominate the trade. The big three in this regard have been United Brands (formerly the United Fruit Company), Del Monte and Dole, and they, or their subsidiaries, remain as the major players in the global market. However in recent years Fyffes, Geest and Jamaican Producers have emerged as the principal suppliers to the UK

New Challenges Facing the Trade

banana business even though strong links are retained with the international corporations.

The need to balance the interests of these firms with those of the consumer is seen by all concerned as critical to the future of the industry. In addition there is an ongoing conflict between those who wish to buy from the cheapest producer and those who wish to continue to support former colonial linkages. The complexity of this problem is such that it remains one of the last which the European Union has still to resolve. [59]

From Orchard to Market

THE WORSHIPFUL COMPANY OF FRUITERERS

In mediaeval times craftsmen and traders formed themselves into guilds in order to govern their trade, maintain quality, train apprentices and care for their members. In due course the Crown, recognizing their increasing power and importance, granted charters of incorporation. They adopted a common heirarchy headed by the Master or Warden, for one year, and took to wearing distinctive dress known as the Livery.

The Fruiterers Company, in existence before 1300 AD, is among the oldest, and though its political connection with the trade ceased in the early 19th Century it has continued to maintain its association with the fruit industry (see above page 5).

In 1882 it introduced an annual prize for an essay on profitable fruit growing, then in 1890 under the Mastership of past Lord Mayor Sir James Whitehead the company organised the first exhibition and conference for fruit growers in London's Guildhall. This attracted some 35,000 visitors to the 450 exhibitors over three days. "The primary object of the Exhibition was to interest the great landowners, the City Guilds, and others in fruit culture, and to induce them to come to the aid of the Fruiterers' Company in their efforts to educate farmers, cottagers and the public generally in this important subject" (Gould p 92)

Over the ensuing years the Company continued its support for English growers awarding scholarships, prizes and medals through its Fruit Culture Fund, and in 1918 organising a further conference in London in conjunction with the National Federation of Fruit Growers. The Company also published a number of books and guides to good fruit culture, and was involved in the formation of the Chamber of Horticulture in 1921. In the latter half of the Century the Fruiterers focussed their activities on extending support for education and research, developing strong links with the leading research centre at East Malling in Kent. The Company was also involved in securing the future of the National Fruit Collection at Brogdale, the site of the world's largest collection of apple and pear varieties. More recently the Fruiterers instigated an annual Food Lecture at Guildhall in collaboration with other Livery Companies associated with the the food industry.

15
A Century of Publishing

The enormous changes which took place in the 20th Century transformed the global fruit and vegetable industries impacting on all aspects of domestic production and marketing in Britain. One result was that the British consumer in 1995 enjoyed a much wider range of choice than his predecessor one hundred years earlier when the *Fruit Trades Journal* had started its weekly magazine. Furthermore, although the quality of fresh produce was greatly improved and the seasons substantially extended, the cost for most items was considerably reduced in real terms.

Unfortunately it is extremely difficult to compare the size of this 1995 market with that of its predecessor one hundred years earlier. This is because inflation and other factors have so altered the value of the currency that this cannot be used to provide anything like an accurate picture of the increase in scale which has taken place. It is equally hard to calculate the actual rise in volume which has occurred over the period due to the changes in the units of account which have been employed. Thus although the move from bunches, bushels and cwt to tons and then to tonnes can be estimated the new totals are far from precise. In addition it is certain that the earlier statistics, especially in respect of domestic production and consumption, were much less complete than those of today. Nevertheless it is quite clear that the past century has witnessed a huge growth in both the value and volume of the British market for fresh fruit and vegetables.

This increase has been due to two separate factors. The first saw the UK population rise from 38.2 million in 1901 to nearly 56.5 million in 1991.[1] The second was the increase in consumption per head which rose significantly for all items except potatoes. Thus potatoes amounted to 208 lbs per head, other vegetables 60 lbs per head and fruit 61 lbs per head. These details should be compared with those for 1995 which showed potatoes down to 92 lbs per head while other vegetables and fruit rose to 79 and 77 lbs per head respectively.[2]

From Orchard to Market

Total Volume of UK Fresh Fruit & Vegetables 1995 ('000 tonnes)

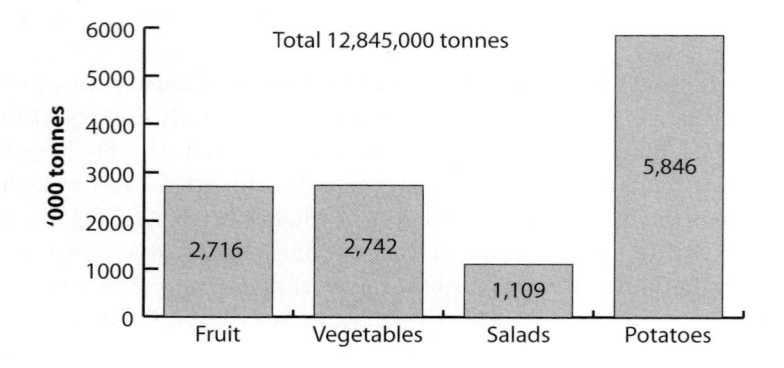

Total 12,845,000 tonnes

Fruit	Vegetables	Salads	Potatoes
2,716	2,742	1,109	5,846

Total Value of UK Fresh Fruit & Vegetables 1995 (£m RSP)

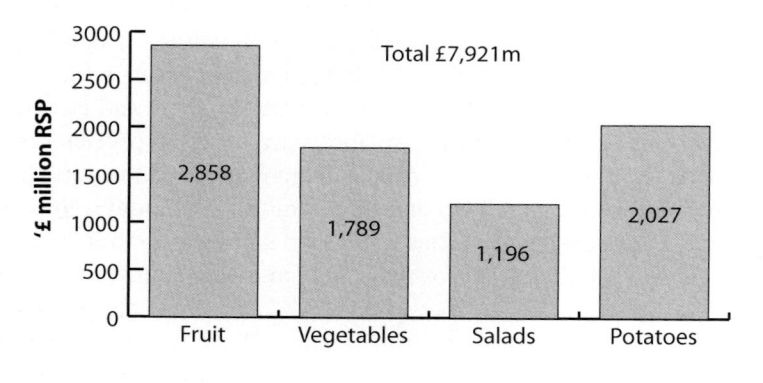

Total £7,921m

Fruit	Vegetables	Salads	Potatoes
2,858	1,789	1,196	2,027

There has, of course, also been an enormous expansion in the range of fresh produce which has become available to the British consumer. In many respects this has been due to improvements in quality, variety and seasonality rather than in entirely new products. Thus, as indicated in the tables on pages 50 and 51 above, by 1895 all of the temperate fruits together with potatoes and onions were already being imported in large quantities. In addition substantial cargoes of tropical items including oranges, lemons, raisons and dried fruits were already arriving at British ports while a number of luxury products - the exotics of their day - such as bananas, coconuts, grapes, melons and pineapples were all establishing small niches in the market. Apart from the range of products available the major differences were that the equivalent of

A Century of Publishing

approximately 100,000 tonnes of apples were imported in 1900, compared with 717, 000 tonnes in 1985, and 500,000 bunches of bananas were landed in 1895 - less than 10,000 tonnes - whereas over 633,000 tonnes arrived in 1995. Details of the principal imports in 1995 are provided below:-

Volume and Value of Fresh Fruit Imports 1995

	Volume '000 tonnes	Value £m RSP
Apples	716.7	617.9
Avocados	12.6	23.2
Bananas	633.5	566.4
Grapes	117.1	250.2
Kiwifruit	21.2	33.3
Melons	165.3	127.9
Oranges	327.0	207.7
Peaches, Nectarines	59.4	110.0
Pears	130.5	143.7
Pineapples	20.9	19.0
Plums	52.3	51.1
Soft Citrus	167.0	180.5
Strawberries	66.7	149.3

Volume and Value of Fresh Vegetable Imports 1995

	Volume '000 tonnes	Value £m RSP
Asparagus	4.3	17.7
Carrots	625.7	203.83
Cauliflower, Calabrese	370.0	246.16
Mushrooms	156.7	400.0
Onions	523.4	220.1
Potatoes	5,846.0	2,079.0

From Orchard to Market

Volume and Value of Fresh Salad Imports 1995

	Volume '000 tonnes	Value £m RSP
Capsicum	52.3	120.4
Celery	83.1	46.8
Cucumbers	129.6	170.2
Lettuce	365.4	315.2
Tomatoes	389.8	423.13

6

A number of other influences stimulated or restricted the demand for fresh fruit and vegetables. These included the availability of substitutes which in 1895 were mainly provided by canned or dried products. These systems of preservation was only satisfactory for a limited number of items and their range and quality was regarded as much inferior to the fresh commodity. The 20th Century saw considerable improvements in both of these methods but it was the development of quick-freezing techniques which transformed the situation and provided a viable alternative to the natural product. A steady rise in the standard of living for the majority of the population enabled a growing number to opt for these convenience foods and latterly some also chose to buy the more expensive but environmentally friendly organically produced items. Many more were also receptive to the introduction of exotic crops. The latter tendency was considerably aided by the presence of a larger ethnic group within the community and by the ability of numerous consumers to travel abroad. On the other hand the continued existence of poverty amongst some sections of the population ensured the ready sale of some basic fruits and vegetables as they remained the cheapest ingredients of many meals.

The expansion in the demand for fresh or preserved fruit and vegetables could not of course be met from increased domestic production. As noted above, see page 34, from c1870 onwards many overseas producers had been able to under-cut local producers and the retention of a Free Trade policy meant that agricultural interest had to be sacrificed in favour of that of industry. This policy attracted much criticism which intensified after 1900 when the trade statistics became more detailed. However in spite of this opposition it was only during the two world wars that the policy was fully reversed although the move to Imperial Preferences in 1932 meant that Empire as distinct from Foreign producers were given more favoured access to the UK market. The subsequent adoption of GATT in 1947 and Britain's joining of the EEC also weakened the Government's ability to protect the industry and the decline in the home-grown share in the domestic market was to continue until the end of this period:-

A Century of Publishing

Shares by Home-Grown and Imported Produce 1995 by volume

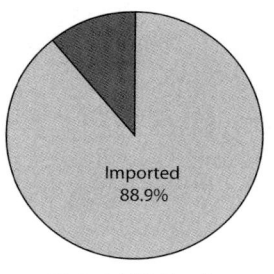

Total UK Fruit
2.7m tonnes
(Imported 88.9%)

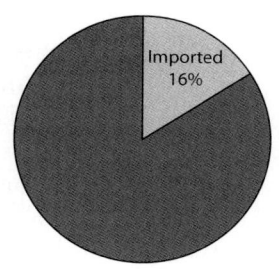

Total UK Vegetables
9.7m tonnes
(Imported 16%)

[7]

The expansion of imports was encouraged by the growth of the British market and made possible by the developments in transport which by 1895 had already brought most of the world in effective reach of the UK consumer. Thus the subsequent improvements in the 20th Century were largely refinements of an existing system based on steam driven ships and railways. (See above, pages 24-25). However although larger and faster vessels employing turbines or diesel engines and the electrification of the rail network undoubtedly increased efficiency these innovations were greatly enhanced by other technical advances. These included the introduction of cargo-carrying aircraft, of particular importance for perishable products, and the emergence of mechanical road transport which helped to revolutionize internal distribution. At a later stage the opening of the Channel Tunnel provided a further option for both rail and road traffic while all forms of carriage were enabled to reach their full potential with the aid of two additional developments.

The first of these was the move from single items to various types of unit load. This involved the consolidation of cargoes so that they could be carried on pallets or, later, in containers which had the advantage of reducing the turn-round times for both ships and aircraft as well as marking a change from labour to capital-intensive systems. Within these developments were a number of other innovations particularly concerning packaging and the introduction of the cardboard carton the advent of which with its reduced weight and bulk and non-returnability transformed the carriage of all fruits and vegetables. It also had a significant effect on the supply of bananas which had previously been shipped on their stems.[8]

The second key factor vital for the import of a comprehensive range of fruit and

From Orchard to Market

vegetables was the progress made to the cooling methods available in 1895. By that date chilled and frozen meat had been successfully landed in Britain for some years but Australian apples and pears were the only substantial, long-distance, fruit trades. The few bananas then being imported were shipped from the Canary Islands with only the draft created by the ship's movement helping to restrict the ripening process. The much longer voyage from Jamaica required artificial cooling and the machinery adopted in 1901 set a pattern which was followed for the next fifty years. This cool-air system was at first employed in ships which catered for a single, homogeneous cargo but by 1960 it had become modified so that a number of different products could be accommodated at the temperature they required. Other technical innovations made possible the establishment of a cool-chain so that many products were pre-cooled at their point of origin and then transported and stored at their optimum temperature until their arrival on the shelves of their retail outlets.

For these improvements to be fully implemented another form of communications also needed to be developed. In 1895 information was mainly transferred by the excellent postal and telegraphic services which covered the entire country. The telephone was also available within the major towns and cities but the trunk network was incomplete and not yet in general use. This was also the case for the international cable system which had the added disadvantage of being expensive and unreliable. Over the Century these methods of communication were extended in numerous ways with the growth of the telephone network being the key factor. Not only did it become practical and cheap to talk to individuals throughout the world but its offshoot, facsimile, and - with the aid of the computer - electronic mail and the internet made instant contact a simple matter of routine. With this revolution in communications came the additional benefit of a more efficient market in fresh produce brought about by greater transparency of costs and availability.

The transformation of the distribution system inevitably impacted on importers and wholesalers who were concentrated in the established wholesale markets. As both the retail and catering sectors consolidated the emphasis shifted from a supply led industry to one dominated by the increasingly powerful large buyers. One obvious consequence has been the decline of the traditional wholesale market system and its replacement by a series of direct links between growers and importers, and retail chains and processors.

The Century also saw continuous improvements in species and varieties which emerged from the specialist fruit and vegetable research stations around the world. In the UK, East Malling had long led the way in the development of top fruit and latterly soft fruit, but similar research in Europe, Israel the US and

A Century of Publishing

the Southern Hemisphere produced many succesful new types. Research also played a major role in improving growing techniques as well as reducing the need for chemical inputs in the form of pesticides and fungicides. Most fruits and vegetables received some kind of treatment and their application proved beneficial to growers and consumers alike. As a result the post-war era saw impressive increases in the yield and quality of many crops. On the other hand the growth of environmental awareness and food safety issues resulted in growing consumer resistance to 'artificial' applications which resulted in political action to legislate and restrict their use. [9] These concerns, aided by the knowledge that many pests were adept at evolving resistance to man made chemicals, encouraged a move toward forms of biological control of production. Thus by the "Eighties" most glasshouse production was achieved with the assistance of integrated (chemical and biological) methods of pest and disease management. [10]

Throughout the hundred years since 1895 the *Fresh Produce Journal* (under various titles) endeavoured each week to describe, monitor, analyze and criticize the many activities which form the British fruit and vegetable industry and its overseas suppliers.

For most of this time the business has been in the hands of one family, Harvey Hope-Mason having purchased it from Briggs and Company as the Journal of Greengrocery, Fruit and Flowers in 1907. His subsequent twenty-eight years as Editor marked its rise to become the voice of the trade and essential reading for all involved with the growing, importing, distribution and marketing of flowers, fruit and vegetables. Gordon, Harvey's only son, succeeded his father in 1939 but due to his extended war service did not to take control of Lockwood Press, the publishing company of the *'Journal'* until after 1945, guiding its fortunes through the difficult days of the early post-war era. These were to be particularly onerous because of the ongoing problems caused by government restrictions and, especially, by the continuing shortage of newsprint. He enjoyed the support of successive editors, first Montague Keen and then William Shapley, who used the name Bill Sandford, and who received the OBE for services to the fruit industry, one of the first journalists to be so honored. In conjunction with them Gordon helped develop new initiatives confirming the central role which the weekly was occupying in the fresh produce business. Amongst these were the introduction of foreign tours which took members of the trade to overseas producing areas - these trade visits being among the first of any sort organised after the war.

On his retirement in 1979, Gordon handed control of the business to his eldest son, David who had already spent sixteen years with Lockwood Press having previously worked for five years in an advertising agency. In 1973 in conjunction with Günter Schweinsberg, publisher of the German fruit trade weekly *'Fruchthandel'*, he

From Orchard to Market

had launched a new international monthly magazine *'Eurofruit'* under a sister company to Lockwood Press. This was followed by the development of a European trade conference, the biennial Eurofruit Congress which has since provided a regular and popular meeting place for the international industry. The monthly was then
augmented by a weekly news service by facsimile, and in 1995 the business launched *'Asiafruit'* a bi-monthly magazine for the Asian market.

With the increasing sophistication of the UK fruit business demand for specialist services offered new opportunities for Lockwood Press. First came a marketing company promoting public and trade relations - 'Fresh Marketing Services' and this was followed by a recruitment agency - 'Fresh Appointments'. The Company also launched a monthly magazine for the flower industry, *'Flower Trades Journal'*, later to be sold to its editor, Margarette Worsfold. All these activities in which David was strongly supported by his editor David Shapley, son of Bill Shapley, enhanced Lockwood Press in their time.

In 1988 the Journal became the first weekly magazine to pioneer computer desktop publishing in the UK, resulting in greatly improved efficiency in the business. Then in 1989, just ten years after his father had been made Master of the Fruiterers' Company, David also attained this position. One lasting result of his year in office was the formation of the Fruiterers Awards Council and he was also active in measures to secure the rescue of Brogdale Orchards, the National Fruit Collection in Kent.

With an increasing need to consolidate the several UK trade representative organisations, the wholesale and retail federations, the fruit importers and the packers organisation, and when merger discussions between them broke down, David, with wide industry support, formed a steering committee. This lead in 1993 to the formation of the Fresh Produce Consortium, with him elected as its first President.

In October 1995 the *Fresh Produce Journal* had completed its first century of publication. For almost all of this long period the weekly has been nurtured and guided by the Hope-Mason family with the fourth generation, David's son Justin taking over in 2000 on David's retirement. With his background in computing and internet development and supported by a strong team, the magazine looks set to continue its succesful role as the voice of the UK fresh produce industry.

A Century of Publishing

FRESH PRODUCE JOURNAL

1895-1995
A century of publishing for the industry

6 October 1995

Journal clocks up first century

On October 5, 1895 a new magazine, *The Journal of Greengrocery Fruit and Flowers* was launched. "With the whole world becoming England's kitchen garden, traders must keep themselves fully aware of the ever-changing state of their markets," said the first editorial.

It soon became the weekly bible of the industry with regular market reports and shipping details, and in 1907, after changing its name to *The Fruit, Flower and Vegetable Trades Journal*, the publication was bought by Harvey Hope-Mason, grandfather of the present executive chairman, David.

The *Journal* is celebrating its centenary in a number of ways, and last week held a lunch in the Innholders Livery Hall in the City of London, for around 70 people in the industry. David Hope-Mason underlined the *Journal's* commitment to the industry and used the opportunity to announce the forthcoming launch of a news service for the busy executive. There will be a full report on this event in next week's issue.

Lockwood Press, publisher of The *Journal*, has commissioned a full history of the British fruit and vegetable trade to commemorate the occasion, a shortened version of which is included with this issue, for our subscribers. The finished book, by Professor Peter Davies, of the University of Liverpool, will be published next year.

FPC accomplishes first mission, now for action

By Lynda Seaton

The Fresh Produce Consortium's Action '95 campaign to raise an initial £500,000 for the ongoing promotion of fresh fruit and vegetables was given the green light this week. The breakthrough on achieving this milestone came through a £40,000 last ditch contribution from the British Retail Consortium.

"It is particularly encouraging to have gained such considerable cross-sector support," FPC president Christopher Mack stressed. "Now that we have reached our target, people will see we mean business and we hope to gain wider support from former doubters. First year pledges of £500,000, plus the £250,000 in the launch fund, means that we already have a meaningful budget."

Keith Sadler, chairman of the produce committee of the BRC added: "Major supermarkets have been very supportive of this initiative and our contribution was made because it is an opportunity which is valuable for all. I hope this will get those who have been sitting on the fence to respond positively.

"This is a one-off contribution, but it addresses the hard work done by all in every sector of the fresh produce industry. Had Action '95 not got off the ground I doubt whether the industry would have been able or willing to resurrect any other generic promotion beyond sectional interests."

This view was echoed by Action '95 chairman Mark Swanwick. "All of our attention over the past few weeks has centred on achieving the threshold. But we shouldn't lose sight of the fact that this is only the beginning, our fund raising continues. Then, it will be

(continued on page 3)

The Journal celebrates its centenary with a host of the biggest names in the fresh produce industry. A specially produced commemorative book - Fresh Every Week - is included in this issue.

Trader to serve the community

Covent Garden trader Hernan Cortes, of West London, was sentenced to 200 hours of Community Service on charges brought by the Inland Revenue at Knightsbridge Crown Court, on Friday. He was also ordered to pay £32,500

(continued on page 4)

GEEST

ENGLISH VILLAGE SALADS
ACHIEVING EXCELLENCE
IN SPANISH PRODUCE

Tel: 01757 617161
Fax: 01757 614119

ACHIEVING EXCELLENCE
—*Together*—

INSIDE French apple flood 3 • Banana takeover bid 4 • CIMO criticises entry price 5 • New plant vitality for Vitacress 6 • Spain makes salad investment 10 • Ingles fleet on the move 22 • Xmas countdown 31

Front page of the Centenary issue of the Journal in October 1995. The title had changed from 'Fruit Trades Journal' in March 1989.

From Orchard to Market

Postscript

by David Shapley

As the industry moved into the new millenium the most obvious visible sign that things were changing was the demise of the Ministry of Agriculture, Fisheries and Food to be replaced by the Department for the Environment, Food and Rural Affairs (DEFRA) in 2001. Horticulture both national and in terms of imports has always tended to be outside the main political stream of events and this has remained so with some notable exceptions. The long running 'banana wars' continued to be the most headline grabbing issue effecting the industry. The European Union seemed likely to lose out in its row with the United States over the privileged access it grants to imports from former colonies in the Carribean and Africa. Under the influence of powerful producer organisations in Latin American countries the US seemed successful in persuading the World Trade Organisation that EU tariffs should be reduced.

The EU continues to exert its influence with the most significant development being the impact of enlargement with new countries from Eastern Europe now embraced. The extensive horticultural production in Poland in particular has caused concerns to producers across Europe fearing greater competition. On the other hand the market is now that much greater. One of the few benefits to flow from Brussels was the formal recognition of Producer Organisations which, providing certain criteria were fulfilled, allowed the provision of grant aid for marketing assistance and research and development.

In 1995 the total volume of fresh fruit and vegetables consumed in the UK had been 6.8m tonnes, with a market value of £3.4bn. By 2003 the market had grown in volume terms by an average of 1% per year to 7.2m tonnes, and an average of 2.4% in value to £4.2bn. Meanwhile imports increased correspondingly and in 2003 accounted for 92% of fruit consumed and 38% of vegetables. A recent report by Mintel estimates that sales of fresh fruit have accelerated since 2002 and are likely to expand by a further four per cent in 2005. Fresh vegetable sales rose by 13% between 2000 and 2004 and are also estimated to rise by another four per cent in 2005.

Meanwhile the increasing power of the multiples continued to cause concern to suppliers resulting in a review of the multiple Code of Practice in 2003 by the Office of Fair Trade. It was sparked by what producers claimed were unreasonable practices which included everything from sudden requests for promotional payments to cancelling contracts without consultation. Despite

From Orchard to Market

a further review in 2005 an uneasy peace exists for although the OFT found little evidence of malpractice, the industry continues to press for independent auditing. One concern is that any complaints about major customers would have a detrimental effect on the future relationship between suppliers and multiples By 2003 the multiples claimed 85% of the retail market in fruit and vegetables - greengrocers just 4%.

The call by supermarkets for more information from both producers and distributors to use their expertise to create strategies, to keep ahead in the battle for the High Street had never been fiercer. Production, sourcing, distribution and selling was always a 24 hour business but new pressures were created by retail chains opening seven days a week, and often 24 hours a day.

Meanwhile the various constituent parts which make up what had always loosely been defined as "the trade" continued to become more and more integrated in order to survive. Category suppliers became far more than sales desks. The new breed of youthful managers responsible for a specific or similar range of products year round were often university trained, and no longer male dominated. Their range of skills included long term development embracing promotion, packaging design, and keeping a close watch on in-store consumer response to their product. It has been argued that these 'managers' minimised the supermarket buyers' role itself. At the very least it gave more substance to the once much used term "partnership", though it has been argued that such loyalty actually reduced the freedom to trade more widely.

In terms of UK production the period saw a further decline from 398,000 tonnes in 1995 to 243,000 tonnes in 2003. Almost all of this 39% reduction is attributable to the decline of apple growing in the UK. However many English growers forged international links with compatible suppliers they once regarded as competitors. This was particularly evident in both salad and vegetable production, where several English farming groups moved on from simple contract growing outside the UK season, to investing in farms and nurseries, at first in Spain and Portugal and more recently in Africa and Eastern Europe. In retrospect the benefits of this expansion now seem obvious. Growers operating in different climates and with different seasons can share skills as well being able to more easily plug gaps in supplies. Overseas costs may often be more economic and have led to more packing and grading ready for the supermarket shelf at source. But the need to check quality and label price in the UK, and to provide short term storage for importers or facilities for growers remained.

There were few signs that multiples would invest in actual production, but their technologists still played a pivotal role in the selection of new varieties, often with

Postscript

an eye to eventual exclusivity. This had always been seen as making a powerful point of difference in wooing the consumer.

The arrival of plant breeders' rights leading to trade marked varieties became a new phenomenon, and to some extent also allowed growers to retain some level of autonomy. Greater control of rootstock only planted in the most suitable areas by licensed nurserymen led to "Apple Clubs" being formed across national borders, of which Pink Lady, Cameo and Jazz were outstanding examples. These clubs comprised growers' groups often locked into licensed distributors packing and selling to strict common quality standards, as well as controlling output so allowing fruit to maintain a premium.

This period was also remarkable for other influences which reshaped fruit and vegetable marketing. Public concern for the environment accelerated the restriction of pesticides which had begun in the '90's. A number of voluntary disciplinary schemes emerged such as the UK LEAF programme, while most British growers joined the Assured Produce scheme - itself part of the wider international EurepGAP code of practice. But while an increasing section of the industry recognised the significance of such self control it was not without its critics mainly in the third world, who argued that costs were too high, despite such disciplines becoming virtually obligatory when dealing with the large retailers.
Third world growers nevertheless won public support through the Fair Trade Foundation which established its own brand on a range of food including fruit and vegetables. The premium price enjoyed by such products allows an improved return to improve social conditions.

Greater public interest in a healthy lifestyle also gave a boost to organic produce. The sector had passed from the hands of the committed often small scale pathfinders, to full scale agricultural production, which spread across deciduous and tropical fruit, salads, vegetable and root crops.

In the face of increasing obesity in the population, political pressure grew for the encouragement of a more healthy national diet. Ensuing government funding encouraged the resurrection of the 5-a-Day campaign begun on a voluntary basis by the Fresh Fruit and Vegetable Information Bureau over 20 years previously. Simultaneously a new concept pioneered by Bangor University and supported by the Fresh Produce Consortium and other trade organisations tested the effect of free fruit for children in primary schools, and the principal became part of a national drive.

And what of the wholesale markets which had seen their traditional customers, the independent greengrocers eroded to a point where it was estimated that by

From Orchard to Market

2000 there were less than 8,000 left - a fifth of the number in the sixties ?

Inevitably the number of wholesalers shrank through consolidation, retirement and closure through lack of business. The commercial importance of being appointed to the "panel " which provided many with a franchise to sell for a specific marketing organisation or group of growers dwindled, simply because per 80 percent of fresh produce was now sold direct to the multiples.

It was all a far cry from when wholesalers under the umbrella of 'marketing' were invited on expense paid week long trips aboard to meet growers. Time is money, and visits now mainly by supermarket buyers funded by their category suppliers were measured in hours. Trade association conferences which lasted for long weekends still played their part, but confined to a single day with the trade press taking a leading role as organisers.

Meanwhile, despite the lack of traditional customers the markets still survive on sites where they were rehoused through then generous government grants in the sixties, many tenants sustaining their presence by supplying the food service industry - loosely defined as everything from local restaurants and hotels to the large scale catering companies. In the main however they still concentrate on providing bulk raw material leaving preparation to the specialists. To this extent they perhaps surprisingly outlived the recommendations of the University of Strathclyde's report in the nineties which saw regional consolidation as one way to exist in an eroding trade sector.

The wind of change however has not stopped blowing, perhaps no more so than in the London markets themselves. Government became determined to divest itself of the ownership of New Covent Garden at Vauxhall. The Covent Garden Market Authority meanwhile attempted to turn the site into the "Larder of London" by attracting other food wholesalers, but this was thwarted by the Corporation of London because of ancient charters protecting the role of Smithfield meat market.

Strategies have also changed on the promotional front with shrinking margins causing belt tightening all round. The days of collective industry wide voluntary efforts at publicity had passed notably for the banana industry which had come together at the time that EU Commission rules began dismantling the protected Caribbean industry for one with freer access for Central and South America. The Banana Group which included all major growers /exporters and ripeners played a real part by boosting UK consumption - low by European standards - from 300,000 tonnes to 700,000 tonnes. But all good things come to an end and the banana campaign, like the Fresh Fruit and Vegetable Information Bureau,

Postscript

has now taken its place in the history books. What funding there was now in the main went directly to the multiples, who were quick to encourage the fruit and vegetable sector to follow the grocery trade with demand for contribution to the cost of point-of-sale, in-store tastings, and support of their own consumer magazines.

Once famous names such as Jaffa, Outspan, Cape, New Zealand apples and Carmel hastened by the dissolution of the marketing boards have become less prominent, as far as the public are concerned, as private retail brands have become more dominant. They still exist at trade level, as do other generic identities like Washington Reds and Florida Pink grapefruit. Nearer home images for French apples, stone fruit and some other crops were still created by Sopexa, the national agency, although these never achieved the prominence of the famous Le Crunch campaigns of the seventies. Similarly Foods from Spain continued to take the initiative for a range of crops covering cherries, grapes, melons and salads mainly at trade level. Its citrus industry continued to make an appearance on TV benefiting from a EU funded scheme. The concept of single variety industries supporting each other for the common good still appeared from time to time, as for example South African avocado growers working with other suppliers to build a global approach to avocado sales.

Meanwhile British horticulture saw new levels of investment, among the most significant being the berry fruit industry funding generically supported strawberry and raspberry campaigns as the industry benefited from a consumer boom. Asparagus growers, too, were quick to identify the added value of their seasonality and stimulated demand and initiated a substantial planting programme which was estimated to increase the crop by 25 percent in the near future. Tomato growers continued to wage their campaign to highlight taste, and the long established mushroom industry put out a strong general message which had been unabated since the sixties. English Apples and Pears, a scion of the Apple and Pear Development Council spread the word for dessert fruit not just based on Cox, but including Gala - now the second most significant variety, and Cameo, Braeburn and most recently Jazz widened its remit. Bramley, the UK's unique cooking apple soldiered on with some success despite the trend towards convenience, and not to be beaten despite the arrival of other speciality new potatoes such as Charlotte, the unique Jersey Royal celebrated its 125th anniversary in 2005 appearing on the screen and in the national media.

Produce presentation itself had also undergone a transformation. The recycled Dutch tray, or the Jaffa orange bruce box once used to send field vegetables to wholesale market, alongside returnable bushel boxes was only a memory. Much produce was still retailed loose, but prepacks are hygienic, easy to handle and a blessing when it comes to stock control. Check weighed they also carried increasing amounts of information demanded by the shopper. Packaging had become increasingly sophisticated with film tailored to the respiratory rates of the contents. Moulded trays which cushion the fruit, and netting in different colours which present even crops like onions in the most attractive light became common place.

The identity of growers was once a closely guarded secret by the multiples, but increasingly their names and locations appeared on the labels. Some retailers even included details of web sites where customers could dial up to get a virtual case history on what they are buying. This also allowed multiples to differentiate and add value. Varieties were flagged up as being exclusive and "new seasons" trumpeted loudly. Children became a target with small portions attractively packed as an alternative to confectionery, and instant edibility became a further means of adding value.

Packs were publicised as ripe or ready-to-eat, initially with avocados and pears and later stone fruit. Prepared vegetables appeared both raw and ready to microwave and steam, and prepared fruit salads, blurring further the boundaries of what constitutes fresh produce.

So what changes can be foreseen ahead?

At retail level certainly the battle will become even fiercer with winners and losers, although the government may still be inclined to blunt competition. The number of superstores appear to have reached saturation point, with retailers turning their attention to soaking up smaller convenience outlets and in so doing re-establishing themselves on the high street where they first began. The next step is forecast to be the resurgence and identification of regional food which will become possible as distribution chains grow more sophisticated. However whether this will ever compete with the growing numbers of farmers' markets which have struck a chord in the human psyche remains to be seen.

The convenience factor along with health will continue to be major drivers in the market and likely to increasingly impact on the business as a whole.

Distributors already facing shrinking margins can be expected to cut deeper into costs. Fears have already been sounded by the Fresh Produce Consortium that the UK could loose its position as a market for top quality and ultimately follow the same route as Germany with its discounters. For the grower horticultural technology will provide an even faster response time so that new varieties will appear and disappear with exclusivity being commonplace. Against this

Postscript

background conventional overproduced varieties such as of apples, citrus and stone fruit will continue to struggle unless a unique sales proposition (USP) can be found. Sourcing and sales will encompass untapped potential across Eastern Europe and China.

To paraphrase a famous observation: It may not be the beginning of the end, but it is certainly the end of the beginning.

From Orchard to Market

Notes

Chapter 1 - The Historical Background

1. Encyclopedia Britannica, 11th Ed. Vol. XVI, 945 and 965
2. Encyclopedia Britannica, 11th Ed. Vol. IX, 418
3. A.W. GOULD, History of the Worshipful Company of Fruiterers of the City of London, 1912, xiii
4. HANDBOOK: The Worshipful Company of Fruiterers, 1992, 3
5. GOULD, xiv
6. GOULD, xvi (1789)
7. GOULD, xvi-xvii
8. GOULD, xix
9. PETER MATHIAS, The First Industrial Nation, Second Edition, Methuen, London, 1987, 26
10. T. BUISHAND, H.P. HOUWINE and K. JANSEN, The Complete Book of Vegetables, Admiral Books, Leicester, 1986, 130
11. *Ibid.*, 130
12. *Ibid.*, 7
13. RALPH DAVIS, The Rise of the English Shipping Industry, 1972, 184
14. Encyclopedia Britannica, 11th Ed. Vol xx, 148-9
15. S. TOLKOWSKY, Hesperides-History of the Culture and Use of Citrus Fruits, London, 1938
16. Fruit Trades' Journal, Mar 11, 1967
17. Statistics quoted in PETER MATHIAS, op.cit., 224 and 226
18. MITCHELL AND DEAN, 1962, 94-5

Chapter 2 - The effect of the industrial economy

1. MATHIAS, 59
2. J.C. DRUMMOND and A. WILBRAHAM, The Englishman's Food, Jonathan Cape, London, 1958, 183
3. GOULD, 53
4. JOHN BURNETT, Plenty and Want : A Social History of Diet in England from 1815 to the Present Day, Nelson, London, 1966
5. BURNETT, 1
6. C. 398, VIII, 377
7. J. WALKER and C.W.MUNN British Economic and Social History, 1700-1977, MacDonald and Evans, Plymouth, 1979, p.77.
8. WALKER and MUNN, 139
9. MATHIAS, 257
10. R.S.BEST, The Day of the Sailing 'Fruiterer', Sea Breezes, May, 1972.
11. C.KONINCKX, (ed), Quinquennial International Congress for Maritime History, I.C.M.H. Brussels, 1990

Notes

12. See WILLIAMS, 523-6
13. L.ISSERLIS, Tramp Shipping, Cargo and Freights, Journal of the Royal Statistical Society, Vol 101, 1938, Part 1, table 8, 122.
14. M.G. MULHALL, Dictionary of Statistics, 4th edn. (1898), 130

Chapter 3 - Developing International Trade

1. MATHIAS, 229
2. Statistical Abstract of the U.K., H.M.S.O., 13th and 17th editions
3. Statistical Abstract of the U.K., H.M.S.O.
4. WILLIAMS, 525 and 528
5. P.N. DAVIES, Fyffes and the Banana, Athlone, London, 1990
6. BASIL GREENHILL, The Merchant Schooners, Conway Maritime Press, London, 1988
7. Fyffes, op.cit. 48
8. Foreign Office Misc., 246 : Report on the Social and Economic Conditions of the Canary Islands, London, 1892, p. 35
9. R.A. PETERS, Refrigerated Shipping, Wakefield lecture presented at the University of Southampton, February, 1982
10. The Fruit-Grower, Fruiterer, Florist and Market Gardener, 3 January 1901
11. MATHIAS, 317
12. DRUMMOND, 323
13. Encyclopedia Britannica, 10th Edition, Vol. 28, p. 528
14. *Ibid.*, p. 529
15. *Ibid*
16. JOHN BURNETT, Plenty and Want, Nelson, London, 1966
17. C.4073, Vol. 39
18. THE WORSHIPFUL COMPANY OF FRUITERERS, HANDBOOK, P. 19
19. Encyclopedia Britannica, 10th Edition, Vol. 28, p. 532

Chapter 4 - Dawn of a New Era

1. F.F.V.T.J., 5 Jan 1935, 2
2. Based on Statistical Abstract of the United Kingdom, (HMSO) for the relevant years.
3. Based on Annual Statements of the Trade of the United Kingdom, for the relevant years
4. G.F.M.G., December 25, 1895
5. F.F.V.T.J., July11, 1908
6. Based on Annual Statement of the Trade of the United Kingdom for the relevant years
7. Based on Annual Statement of the Trade of the United Kingdom for the relevant years
8. Based on statistics quoted in VINCENT ABAD, Historia de la Naranja (Comité de la Gestión de la Exportación de Frutos Citros), p.59.
9. Based on Annual Statement of the Trade of the United Kingdom for the relevant years
10. Fyffes, op.cit. 99-101

Notes

11. Based on Annual Statement of the Trade of the United Kingdom for the relevant years
12. F.F. & V.T.J., 27 August 1910, p. 172
13. Based on Annual Statement of the Trade of the United Kingdom for the relevant years
14. Based on Annual Statements of the Trade of the United Kingdom
15. Based on Annual Statements of the Trade of the United Kingdom
16. Encyclopedia Britannica, 11th Ed., Vol. XI, 1911, Cambridge, 266-7

Chapter 5 - The Impact of War

1. Based on LORD ERNLE, English Farming: Past & Present. 6th ed. London. Frank Cass, 1961, pp 395-397
2. Encyclopedia Britannica, 12th Ed., 1922, Vol. 31-32, p. 20
3. Based on details provided in DEWEY, Appendix A, p. 244
4. G.P. JONES and A.G. POOL, 'A Hundred Years of Economic Development', 1959, Chapter 16
5. DEWEY, p. 227
6. F.F.V.T.J., 12 Jan. 1918
7. ERNLE, p. 397
8. Based on Annual Statement of the Trade of the U.K., (H.M.S.O.) for the relevant years.
9. Based on Annual Statement of the Trade of the U.K., (H.M.S.O.) for the relevant years.
10. F.F.V.T.J., 8 Aug. 1914
11. F.F.V.T.J., 28 Sep. 1918
12. F.F.V.T.J., 5 Oct. 1918
13. F.F.V.T.J., 9 Jan. 1915
14. F.F.V.T.J., 4 Aug. 1917
15. F.F.V.T.J., 15 Aug. 1914
16. F.F.V.T.J., 22 Aug. 1914
17. F.F.V.T.J., 28 Sep. 1918
18. F.F.V.T.J., 21 Aug. 1915
19. F.F.V.T.J., 21 July, 1917
20. F.F.V.T.J., 22 June, 1918
21. F.F.V.T.J., 27 July, 1918
22. F.F.V.T.J., 22 Dec. 1917
23. F.F.V.T.J., 16 Nov. 1918

Chapter 6 - Problems of the 'Twenties'

1. Based on Annual Statement of the Trade of the U.K. (H.M.S.O.) for the relevant years.
2. Encyclopaedia Britannica, 12th ed., Vol. 29-30, p.76
3. P.E. DEWEY, 239
4. F.F.V.T.J., 11 Dec 1915
5. S. POLLARD, The Development of the British Economy, (2nd Ed.), 188

Notes

6. Based on Annual Statement of the Trade of the U.K. (H.M.S.O.) for the relevant years.
7. Based on Agricultural Statistics, M.A.F., 1931, Vol. LXVI, Part I, pp. 66-67
8. F.F.V.T.J., 30 December 1922
9. WALKER, 331
10. F.F.V.T.J., 27 May 1922
11. F.F.V.T.J., 17 April 1909
12. F.F.V.T.J., 9 May 1925
13. Encyclopaedia Britannica, 5032, 14th Ed., 1936, I, 400
14. Encyclopaedia Britannica, 5032, 14th Ed., 1936, 9, 881
15. F.F.V.T.J., 25 February 1922
16. Fyffes, op. cit., p. 261

Chapter 7 - Depression and Recovery

1. Based on Annual Statement of the Trade of the U.K. (H.M.S.O.) for the relevant years.
2. M.A.F., Agricultural Statistics, LXVI,I,6
3. M.A.F., Agricultural Statistics, LXVI,II,93 and LXVI,II,99
4. M.A.F., Agricultural Statistics, LXVI,II,91.
5. S. POLLARD, 197
6. Source: C.L. MOWAT, Britain Between the Wars, 1918-1940, Methuen, 1964, 437
7. Based on Annual Statement of the trade of the UK, (H.M.S.O.)
8. J. YUDKIN and J.C. McKENZIE, Changing Food Habits, Macgibbon and Kee, 1964, p.26
9. S. POLLARD, The Development of the British Economy, 2nd Edition, 1968,139-40
10. F.F.V.T.J., 4 May 1935.
11. S. POLLARD, 138
12. LORD ERNLE, English Farming: Past and Present, Frank Cass, 6th Ed., 441
13. F.F.V.T.J., 18 Feb, 1939
14. F.F.V.T.J., 22 July, 1939

Chapter 8 - The Shadow of War

1. F.F.V.T.J., 7 May 1938
2. F.F.V.T.J., 7 May 1938
3. Based on Annual Statement of the Trade of the U.K., (H.M.S.O.) for the relevant years
4. Fyffes, op. cit., 167-8
5. Based on Annual Statement of the trade of the U.K., (H.M.S.O.) for the relevant years
6. Based on Agricultural Statistics, 1939-44, United Kingdom, Part I, (M.A.F.F., H.M.S.O., 1947, p8)
7. Based on Agricultural Statistics, 1939-40 to 1945-46,UK, Part II (M.A.F.F., H.M.S.O., 1949, p.41)
8. Based on Agricultural Statistics, 1939-44, UK, Part I (M.A.F.F., H.M.S.O., 1947, pp. 44-5).
9. J BURNETT, 259

Notes

10. Based on S. POLLARD, 317
11. F.F.V.T.J., 19 April 1941
12. F.F.V.T.J., 28 November 1942
13. F.F.V.T.J., 3 March 1945
14. J. BURNETT, 261

Chapter 9 - Peace and Recovery

1. S. POLLARD, 354
2. Based on Annual Statements of the Trade of the U.K., (H.M.S.O.), for the relevant years.
3. Based on Annual Statements of the Trade of the U.K., (H.M.S.O.), for the relevant years
4. F.F.V.T.J., 8 May 1948
5. Based on Annual Statements of the Trade of the U.K., (H.M.S.O.), for the relevant years.
6. Based on S. POLLARD, p. 385
7. Based on Agricultural Statistics, M.A.F., (H.M.S.O.), U.K., Part I, 1953, Tables 28 and 29.
8. Based on Agricultural Statistics, M.A.F., (H.M.S.O.), U.K., Part II, 1953, Table 20
9. F.F.V.T.J., 15 March 1947
10. F.F.V.T.J., 17 February 1945
11. F.F.V.T.J., 7th February 1948
12. F.F.V.T.J., 10 September 1949
13. F.T.J., 30 December 1950
14. See T.R. GOURVISH, British Railways, 1948-73, C.U.P., 1986, Ch.1
15. F.F.V.T.J., 2 October 1948
16. F.T.J., 24 December 1949.

Chapter 10 - Fruits of Freedom

1. F.T.J., 8 October 1971, p.60
2. F.T.J., 7 November 1959, p.39
3. F.T.J., 11 May 1957
4. Based on S. POLLARD, (4th Edition), p.251
5. Based on Annual Statements of the Trade of the U.K. (H.M.S.O.) for the relevant years.
6. Fyffes, op.cit. pp. 184-187
7. Based on Annual Statements of the Trade of the U.K. (H.M.S.O.) for the relevant years.
8. Source: Agricultural Statistics, U.K., M.A.F., H.M.S.O., London, for the relevant years
9. The British Economy, Key Statistics, 1900-1966, Table C, London and Cambridge Economic Service
10. Source: Agricultural Statistics, U.K., M.A.F., H.M.S.O., London, for the relevant years
11. Source: Agricultural Statistics, U.K., M.A.F., H.M.S.O., London, for the relevant years
12. Source: S. POLLARD, The Development of the British Economy, (4th Ed.), 1990, p.277.

Notes

13. Source: National Income and Expenditure Blue Books, Central Statistical Office, H.M.S.O., Table 18, p.19, 1962 and Table 22, pp.22-27, 1972.
14. R.L. SMYTH, The Distribution of Fruit and Vegetables, Gerald Duckworth, London, 1959).
15. Sources: Census of Distribution, 1950 (domestic producers and total retail outlets - text and footnotes). See also R.L. SMYTH, op.cit., p.20

Chapter 11 - Europe - Opportunities & Threats

1. S. POLLARD, 4th Ed., 318 and 429
2. F.T.J., 8 July 1961, 9
3. F.T.J., 17 February 1962, 20
4. F.T.J., 6 October 1972, 35
5. F.T.J., 6 January 1978, 3
6. F.T.J,. 5 June 1981, 15
7. F.T.J., 1980, 28
8. F.P.J., 28 February 1992, 12
9. F.P.J., 27 April 1990, 12

Chapter 12 - Changing Patterns of Supply

1. Author's interview with Mr Ellis in 1991
2. Reproduced from the 'Royal Society of Arts Journal', vol CXLVI, No 5485, 214,1998, p.55
3. Based on Overseas Trade Statistics of the UK, London, HMSO, (and Business Monitor, M A 20)
4. Author's calculations from the Overseas Trade Statistics of the UK
5. Fyffes op.cit. 207-8
6. Extract from Eurofruit, March 1993, p.33. Source: Eurostat
7. See F.T.J., 17 July 1987, 22
8. Author's calculations from the Overseas Trade Statistics of the UK
9. Based on Overseas Trade Statistics of the UK, London, HMSO, (and Business Monitor, M A 20 for the relevant years)
10. Based on Horticultural Statistics for the UK, (Calendar years), (MAFF, for the relevant years).
11. Based on Basic Horticultural Statistics for the UK, (Calendar Years), (MAFF, for the relevant years)
12. Based on Agriculture in the United Kingdom for 1991 and 1996 details and author's calculations from Basic Horticultural Statistics for the UK, for the remaining years. MAFF, HMSO, London, relevant years for both sources.
13. Based on Horticultural Statistics for the UK, for the relevant years
14. See F.F.V.T.J., 7 January 1956, 1
15. See F.T.J., 13 June 1986, 21
16. Source: Onkologie Landbau 1991. (See F.P.J., 11 March 1992, 14).

Notes

17. See Fresh Produce Desk Book, 1998, 6
18. See F.P.J., 10 October 1997, 17
19. Source: (Figures supplied to the author by the MAFF Organic Unit in October 1998)
20. Source: F.P.J., 5 February 1993, 4.
21. Source: National Food Survey. Extract from F.P.J., 29 September 1989, 17.
22. Extract from F.P.J., 9 February 1996, 10.
23. Source: FFVIB/MAFF estimates. F.P.J., 18 November 1994, 6.

Chapter 13 - Developing Efficiency in Distribution

1. F.T.J., 25 March 1983, 28
2. ROBERT GARDINER, (Ed), Consultant Editor:A.D. COUPER, Conway's History of the Ship. The Shipping Revolution:Conventional General Cargo Liners and Refrigerated Ships, (Conway, London,1992) 38.
3. The Shipping Revolution, op.cit., 38
4. F.T.J., 14 June 1991, 17
5. Fyffes, op.cit. 221
6. F.T.J., 14 June 1991, 15
7. The Shipping Revolution, op. cit.,41
8. F.T.J., 28 February 1975, 16
9. F.P.J., 22 April 1994, 13
10. F.P.J., 22 April 1994, 31
11. Based on Whitakers Almanack for the relevant years

Chapter 14 - New Challenges Facing the Trade

1. See F.T.J., 29 June 1968, 10
2. See F.T.J., 1 November 1974, 4
3. F.T.J., 12 May 1956, 41
4. See F.T.J., 3 September 1982, Supplement, 17
5. Source: F.T.J., 19 June 1971, 10
6. F.T.J., 15 November 1974
7. Source: F.T.J., 23 November 1994, Supplement, ii.
8. Source: Marketpower report: Catering Scenarios. Extract from F.T.J., 8 April 1988, 12.
9. See F.P.J., 1 February 1991, 3
10. Extract from F.P.J., 29 September 1989, 20
11. Fresh Produce Desk Book, 1998, 1
12. F.T.J., 23 April 1976, 22
13. F.T.J., 22 April 1988, 20
14. Source: AGB Superpanel. Extract from F.P.J., 18 November 1994,6
15. Fresh Produce Deskbook 1998, 1
16. F.T.J., 21 December 1973, 14

Notes

17. F.T.J., 14 May 1982, 3
18. F.T.J., 19 January 1990
19. F.T.J., 2 May 1970, 47
20. F.T.J., 12 July 1974, 29
21. F.T.J., 27 December 1958, 11
22. F.T.J., 27 April 1973, 40
23. F.T.J., 27 September 1974, 27
24. F.T.J., 17 August 1984, 20
25. F.P.J., 6 March 1992, 14
26. F.T.J., Special Feature on Packaging 1978, 5
27. see F.F.V.T.J., 2 July 1949, 1
28. F.T.J., 18 May 1968, 77
29. F.T.J., 7 October 1967, 4
30. Source: F.T.J., Retail Report, 1980, 7
31. Source: F.P.J., 27 March 1992, 10
32. Extract from F.T.J., 18 September 1987, 2
33. See F.T.J., 23 April 1976, 7
34. See F.P.J., 19 July 1991, 40
35. See F.P.J., 26 May 1995, 1
36. F.T.J., 24 May 1985, 40
37. F.T.J., 5 September 1970, 29
38. F.T.J., 8 November 1974, 37
39. F.T.J., 26 September 1976, 35
40. F.T.J., 18 October 1985, v
41. F.T.J., 1 October 1982, 16
42. F.P.J., 8 July 1994, 1
43. F.T.J., 29 July 1988, iii
44. F.P.J., 8 November 1991, 18
45. F.P.J., 13 July 1990, 3
46. F.T.J., 28 May 1955, 44
47. F.T.J., 17 February 1962, 14
48. F.T.J., 26 November 1955, 1
49. F.T.J., 31 December 1976, 7
50. F.T.J., 20 February 1987, 2
51. F.T.J., 30 September 1988, 1
52. F.P.J., 3 May 1991, 3
53. F.T.J., 24 April 1971, 8
54. F.T.J., 21 January 1977, 6 and 6 March 1977, 38
55. F.P.J., 7 February 1997
56. F.T.J., 29 July 1983, 2
57. F.T.J.. 3 April 1971, 10
58. F.T.J., 3 July 1971, 8: 15 March 1974, 2 and 19 April 1985, 34

59. F.P.J., 5 April 1996

Chapter 15 - A Century of Publishing

1. WHITAKER'S Almanack, 1994, 118
2. See Fresh Produce Desk Book, 1998, 6
3. Fresh Produce Desk Book, 1998, 1
4. Source: DTI Customs and Excise/FFVIB/Banana Group.
5. Source: DTI Customs and Excise/FFVIB/British Potato Council/Mushroom Bureau.
6. Source: DTI Customs and Excise/FFVIB. Fresh Produce Desk Book, 1998, 4-5
7. Fresh Produce Desk Book, 1998, 4
8. Fyffes, op.cit. pp. 192-3
9. F.P.J., 6 October 1989, 12
10. F.P.J., 17 March 1989, 17

BIBLIOGRAPHY

All sources of information used in this study are cited in the above notes - a separate bibliography is not therefore considered necessary.

Index

Africa 35, 36, 38
African Steamship Company 36
Agricultural Organisation Society 102-4, 126
Agrexco 247-8
Agricultural Research Council 127
Algeria 201
Almeria 39
American Fruit Importers Ltd 192
Anglian Produce Ltd 270
Anglo-Overseas Transport Ltd 249
apples 2, 6, 10, 11, 18, 21, 25, 27, 32-3, 38, 39, 58, 60, 62, 69, 73, 75, 76-8, 83-4, 87, 93, 97, 100-1, 113, 118, 123, 124, 143, v146, 150, 154-5, 162, 164, 179, 182, 189, 198, 216-7, 220, 225, 255
Apple & Pear Development Council 270
apricot 13, 65, 143, 177-8,
Argentina 15, 38, 163, 199
Arnold, Henry W 255
artichokes 246
Asda 265
Asiafruit 282
asparagus 18, 143, 151, 177, 191, 192, 220,
Associated Containers Transportation 189
Australia 15, 38, 55, 60, 62-4, 75, 100, 118, 131, 143, 163, 189, 199, 209, 225, 239
Australian Apple & Pear Export Council 125
Australian Apple & Pear Board 207
Australasia 51, 57,
avocadoes 220, 227, 247
Avonmouth 163
Azores 12, 18, 26, 27, 32 3, 35, 40, 59, 64, 65,
Aznar Line 187, 243

bananas 35 - 40, 52, 55, 58, 62, 69, 73, 75, 84, 99, 118-9, 123, 146, 162, 164, 165, 179, 196-9, 216, 225, 242, 245, 255, 279, 280
Batchelor's Peas 135
BC Tree Fruits Ltd 192
BEA 177, 189
beans 2, 11, 18, 32, 71, 113, 151, 227
Beeson Group 255
beetroot 151
Belfast Market 132
Belgium 40, 60, 62, 163, 227
Belize 225
bilberries 2, 87
Birmingham 23, 132, 239
blackberries 2, 124
BOC Distribution Services 250
BOAC 177, 189, 190, 192
Board of Agriculture 42
Bonny & Co 191
Borough Market 132
Boston 178
Bradford Market 132
Brazil 40, 51, 118-9, 162-3, 199, 200
Brentford Market 132, 192
Briggs & Co 47
Bristol 8, 132, 207, 239
British Airways 177
British Air Ferries 246
British Flower Industry Association 190, 232, 270
British Fruit Packing Co 104
British Rail 188, 193-7, 253
British Road Services 176, 251
British Transport Commission 176
British United Air Ferries 178
Brittany Ferries
broccoli 151, 154, 200
Brogdale 10

Brussel sprouts   151, 154, 235
Burma   11

cabbage   2, 11, 18, 71, 154, 200
California   57, 99, 100, 130, 192
Cameroons   162, 199
Campbell, Malcolm   210
canals   23 - 25
Canada   32, 39, 51, 55, 61, 64, 94, 100, 118, 120, 163, 192, 199, 227
Canadian Horticultural Council   125
Canary Islands   35 - 37, 40, 52, 56, 57, 65, 73, 75, 118-120, 162, 166, 186, 191, 199, 201, 227, 243, 280
Cape   39, 62, 240, 245
carrots   6, 9, 11, 18, 40, 143, 151, 154, 200
cauliflowers   18, 151, 154, 217, 244
celery   18, 151, 246
Chamber of Horticulture   105, 107, 126
Channel Islands   58, 62, 65, 73, 120, 143, 166, 189, 201, 216, 227, 232
Checkers Growers Ltd   270
cherries   2, 6, 7, 10, 18, 21, 52, 65, 85, 87, 113, 124, 143, 177, 192
Chile   166, 201, 226, 240, 245
China   11
Citrus Marketing Board of Israel   207, 242
Citrus Marketing Board of Palestine   125
coconuts   40
Colombia   62, 75, 118
Commercial Grower   47
Common Agricultural Policy   213, 228
Cool Carriers   241-2
co-operatives   102-3, 106, 267-8
COPA-Cogeca   221
cos-lettuce   18
Costa Rica   118
Covent Garden   12, 13, 37, 38, 40, 44, 50, 54, 80, 84, 86, 89, 99, 103, 132, 156, 190, 211, 232, 256-8
Craze, William   106
Cuba   245

cucumbers   143, 173, 200
currants   11, 52, 85, 87, 113
custard apples   52
Cyprus   163, 200-1, 218, 225-6, 245

dates   11, 52, 79, 89, 101, 181
damsons   52
Deciduous Fruit Board   (see South African Deciduous Fruit Board)
Del Monte   242, 272
Denmark   102, 163
Dole   272
Dowd, Thomas   56
Dover   100, 130, 178, 207, 239, 245
dried fruits   11, 12
Drake, Sir Francis   10
'Drummond Castle'   39
Dublin   132
Dundee   41

East Kent Packers   240, 268
East Lincolnshire Growers Ltd
East Malling   105, 126
European Economic Community   212-3, 216, 224
Edinburgh Market   132
Egypt   32, 40, 65, 73, 119, 132, 155, 166, 201, 227, 246
Elders & Fyffes   37, 55, 56, 61, 75, 119, 124, 130, 146, 156, 162, 196, 199, 223, 225, 242, 245, 255, 272
Elder Dempster & Co   36, 55, 56
Ellis, A.J   223
endive   18, 143
ENFRU   268
EUCOFEL   221-2
Eurofruit   282

Farmers Magazine   44
Faversham   10
Felixstowe   207, 239, 244, 255
figs   2, 11, 52, 86

Flanders   9, 11
Florida   57, 192, 255
flowers   66, 88, 91, 131, 151, 190, 220, 231
Flowers Publicity Council   232
Flower Trades Journal   282
Flying Transport Ltd   98
Food Controller   70-72, 76, 79, 137
Food from Britain   272
France   15, 17, 20, 21, 25, 60, 62, 64, 65, 73, 75, 87, 89, 91, 104, 118, 143, 178, 191, 193, 199, 201, 220, 225, 227, 245
Fred Olsen Line   178, 187
Fresh Fruit & Vegetable Information Bureau   270
Fresh Produce Consortium   271, 282
Fresh Produce Journal   281-2
Fruchthandel   281
Fruiterers   (see Worshipful Company of Fruiterers)
Fruit Flower & Vegetable Trades Journal   48, 76, 78, 89, 108, 135, 140, 170, 173
Fruit Trades Journal   44, 212, 275
Fruiterer & Greengrocer   44
Fruit Grower, Market Gardener & Glasshouse Nurseryman   47
Fruit Importers Association   270
Fruit Importers of Ireland   242
Fyffe, Edward Wathen   37
Fyffes   (see Elders & Fyffes)

Gardeners Chronicle   44
garlic   7
General Agreement on Tariffs & Trade   159, 204, 214, 278
Geest Industries Ltd   199, 225, 242, 246, 251, 272
Germany   21, 25, 64, 65, 87, 143
Gerrards   210
Glasgow   130, 132, 163, 195-6, 207, 239

Glass Glover Group   268
Gilbert International   251-2
Gold Coast   162, 199
gooseberries   2, 18, 52, 85, 113, 124
grapes   2, 33, 39, 58, 62, 63, 73, 79, 86, 89, 100, 143, 164, 177, 181, 191, 198, 217, 226, 235, 246
grapefruit   123, 164, 182, 255
Greece   32, 52, 218, 226
Greengrocer, Fruiterer & Market Gardener   47
Greenwich Market   132
Griffin & Brand   247
Grower Marketing Services Ltd   270
guilds   4, 5
guavas   227

Hall, J & E   55, 56
Hammond, George plc   245
Hannan & Davy Ltd   263
Harwich   51, 100, 188, 244
Henley Transport Ltd   251
herbs   2
Hither Green   101, 194, 255
Holland   9, 40, 60, 65, 73, 75, 87, 119, 131, 163, 166, 188, 191, 201, 227, 244
Holland America Line   99
Home Grown Fruits   268
Honduras   118
Hope-Mason, David   281-2
Hope-Mason, Gordon   135, 140, 170, 281
Hope-Mason, Harvey   48, 78, 135, 281
Hope-Mason, Justin   282
Horticulture Act   202
Horticultural Times   44
Hull   24, 50, 51, 132, 207, 239, 244
Hungary   194, 201

Imperial Airways   131
Imperial Fruit Show   108-9
India   11, 33, 94
Industrial Revolution   15

Interflora 232
Interfrigo 176, 193-4
International Airfreight Ltd 131
Ireland 56, 120
Israel 191, 199, 216, 218, 220, 225, 242, 245, 247-8
Italy 33, 38, 59, 64, 143, 163, 166, 177, 188, 194, 199, 201, 226-7, 244

Jackson, George 56
Jamaica 40, 55, 56, 61, 75, 118-9, 162, 199, 225, 242, 280
Jamaica Fruit Importing Co. 55
Jamaica Producers 199, 242, 245, 272
Japan 94
Jeffs, W.A 135, 140
Jones, Sir Alfred 36, 37, 55, 61
Journal of Greengrocery, Fruit and Flowers 45, 47

Keen, Montagu 281
Kent 18, 22, 52
Kenya 191
King, Tom 56
kiwifruit 227
KLM 189
kumquats 227

Las Palmas 36, 37
Lauritzen, J 239, 241-2
Leeds 24, 132, 239
leeks 2, 18, 173
lemons 11, 12, 18, 26, 32, 33, 40, 58, 64, 89, 99, 153-5, 181
lettuce 2, 11, 101, 143, 151, 191, 200
Lewis, C.H 142
limes 18, 26
Lisbon 39
Liverpool 23, 24, 29, 34, 36, 37, 39, 50-52, 56, 98, 131, 132, 187, 191, 207, 239, 242-3
Livery Companies 5, 12

LMO 270
London 1 - 13, 15, 18, 19, 21, 22, 27, 28, 34, 35, 37, 39, 43, 50, 51, 52, 56, 98-9, 130-2, 163, 192, 194 ,207, 239, 256
Long Ashton 105, 126
loquats 52
Los Angeles 99
lychees 52, 227
Lyons 101

Mack, M&W. Ltd 240, 255
MacAndrews 178, 243
Madeira 35, 52
Makro 262
Malaga 39, 40
Malta 197, 201
Manchester 23, 24, 239
mangoes 227, 246
mangolds 71
Market Record 44
Marks & Spencer 170, 250
marrows 2
McCann, Charles 56
Mediterranean 18, 26
melons 13, 83, 86, 164, 198
Ministry of Agriculture 93, 105, 108, 113, 138 ,140, 174,
Ministry of Food 143, 152, 154, 164-5, 172, 174
Monro, George 32, 40
Morocco 166, 200-1, 220, 225, 227, 245
mushrooms 177, 235
Mushroom Growers Association 270

National Farmers Union 93, 104, 126
National Federation of Fruit & Potato Trades 49, 106-7, 126, 152, 170, 270
National Freight Corporation 196
National Fruit Growers Federation 105-7, 126

National Vegetable Marketing Co.   154
nectarines   83, 86, 220
Nell Gwyn   11
Netherlands   (see Holland)
Newhaven   51, 207
New York   100
New Zealand   100, 118, 130, 143, 162, 199, 225, 240, 245, 247
New Zealand Apple & Pear Board   207
New Zealand Export Control Board   125
Nicholls, Francis   246
Nine Elms   13, 211, 232, 256
Norfolk Line   244
North America   15, 31, 33, 57, 64, 75, 87, 143, 201, 209
Nurseryman & Seedsman   44
nuts   2, 6, 101, 146, 164, 181, 198

Olsen, Fred   243
Onona, Jacques   221
onions   2, 11, 18, 25, 32, 33, 40, 69, 73, 89, 93, 119, 121, 143, 151, 153, 155, 166, 181, 192, 200-1
oranges   7, 11, 12, 18, 26, 32, 33, 40, 58, 59, 62, 69, 73, 76, 85, 86, 89, 97, 99, 118-9, 143, 146, 151, 153-5, 163, 164, 182, 193, 198-9, 225, 235, 242
Ottawa Agreement   115, 118-120, 123, 162
Outspan   see South African Citrus exchange Ltd

Paddock Wood   251, 255
P & O Ferrymasters   251
Palestine   57, 59, 100, 119, 163
Panama Canal   99
papaya   227
Paris   99, 131
parsnips   11, 18, 151
Parsons, S.J   191
peaches   39, 65, 83, 86, 100-1, 123, 143, 164, 178, 181, 191-2, 217, 220
pears   2, 6, 10, 11, 18, 21, 25, 38, 52, 58, 64, 69, 76, 83, 87, 93, 96, 100, 113, 123-4, 143, 146, 150, 162-4, 189, 198, 216-7
peas   2, 11, 32, 33, 38, 113, 132, 143, 151, 227
pepper   227
Perishables Transport Ltd   250
Perpignan   101
pineapples   35, 40, 164, 177, 191
plums   18, 33, 52, 58, 64, 83, 87, 113, 123. 143, 178, 192
Poland   143, 201
pomegranates   40
Portsmouth   178, 207, 239, 242
Portugal   18, 26, 33, 35, 40, 51, 59, 60, 62, 75, 218
potatoes   6, 10, 11, 32, 40, 65, 69-72, 79, 93, 97, 101, 113, 119, 121, 123, 143, 145, 151, 154, 160, 166, 173-4, 179, 200-1, 217, 227
Potato Marketing Board   123 ,173, 209, 271
Poupart, John   40
Poupart, T.J   40
prickly pears   52
Produce Packaging & Marketing Association   262, 270
publicity   107-8, 125-6
pumpkins   2

radish   18, 192
Raleigh, Sir Walter   10
raspberries   85, 113
Retail Fruit Trade Federation   49, 106-7, 126, 140-1. 170, 270
Rothamstead   126
Royal Horticultural Society   44
rhubarb   18, 151, 173
Rochford, Joseph   40
Romania   194
Runciman Report   211
Russia   15, 87

Safeway 265
Safmarine 186
Sainsbury, J 132, 210, 256, 265
Salvesen, Christian 251
Sam Cook 210
Sandford, Bill see Shapley, William
Saphir & Sons 239, 268
Scammel Lorries Ltd 195
Schweinsberg, Günter 281
Sea-Land Services Inc 188
Shapley, David 282
Shapley, William 281
Sheerness 178, 239, 242, 245
Shoreham 178
Sicily 11, 12, 18, 64, 155
Silver City Airways 177, 189
Smedley, S.W 134
Soil Association 232
Sims, J.O 255
South Africa 39, 51, 57, 59, 64, 65, 104, 118-9, 163, 186, 191-2, 199, 201, 218, 225, 225-6, 247
South African Citrus Exchange Ltd 125, 131, 207
South African Co-operative Deciduous Exchange Ltd 125
South African Deciduous Fruit Board 207, 240
South America 57
Spain 11, 18, 26, 32, 33, 35, 40, 51, 52, 59, 64, 65, 73, 86, 87, 100, 101, 119, 143, 163, 166, 176-7, 187, 190, 193, 199, 201, 216, 218, 220, 225-7, 242, 245, 253
Southampton 131, 196, 207, 239, 243
Spitalfields 12, 132, 232, 256
Standard Fruit 242
Stockley, Arthur 61
Stratford Market 132
strawberries 18, 52, 85, 86, 99, 113, 143, 177, 190, 192, 220, 247
Sunkist 245

Suriname 225, 242
swedes 71, 151
Switzerland 163

Tenerife 36
Tesco 210, 265
tomatoes 10, 11, 32, 36, 37, 40, 65, 69, 73, 84, 93, 100, 119-121, 143, 151, 154, 166, 177, 191, 200, 215, 217
Tomato & Cucumber Marketing Board 209, 215, 271
Trafume Line 187
Transfesa 176, 193, 255
Tunisia 191
Turkey 11, 52, 59
turnips 9, 11, 17, 18, 113

Union Castle Line 130
United States 38, 39, 41, 51, 55, 59, 61, 64, 65, 94, 100, 105, 118, 120, 144, 163, 199, 200, 227
United Fruit Company 61, 118, 242, 272
Uruguay 225

Vale of Evesham 41

Waterworth Brothers 132, 210
Weir Shipping, Andrew 254
West Indies 35, 40, 51, 59, 65
Westland Imports Ltd 187, 245
Williams, L & H 56
Windward Islands 162, 225, 242, 246
Whitehead, Sir James 43
Wilkinson, Charles & Co 99
Wood Distribution 251
Worshipful Company of Fruiterers 4, 6, 7, 8, 10, 12, 18, 21, 42, 43, 105, 282
Worsfold, Margarette 282
Wye College 105, 127, 272

Yeoward Brothers 187
Zeebrugge 100